W9-AQZ-994

DATE DUE

DEMCO 128-5046

REFERENCE

Heroes and Pioneers

MACMILLAN
PROFILES

Heroes and Pioneers

MACMILLAN LIBRARY REFERENCE USA
New York

Copyright © 1998 by Simon & Schuster, Inc. Introductory material © 1998 by Simon & Schuster, Inc.

Produced and designed by Miller Williams Design Associates, Lake Villa, IL

Macmillan Library Reference USA
1633 Broadway
New York, New York 10019

Manufactured in the United States of America

Printing number
1 2 3 4 5 6 7 8 9 10

Library of Congress Cataloging-in-Publication Data

Heroes and pioneers / [editor Judy Culligan].
        p.   cm. — (Macmillan profiles ; 3)
    Includes index.
    Summary: Alphabetical articles profile men and women who have been leaders in many fields, including Arthur Ashe, Amelia Earhart, Andrew Jackson, Helen Keller, Nelson Mandela, and Rigoberta Menchu Tum, among many others.
    ISBN 0-02-865059-X (alk. paper)
    1. Heroes—Biography—Juvenile literature. 2. Biography—Juvenile literature. [1. Heroes. 2. Biography.] I. Culligan, Judy. II. Series.
CT107.H47 1998
920.02—dc21
[B]   98–38909
                                                                CIP
                                                                 AC

Front cover clockwise from top: Norman Schwarzkopf (Department of Defense/U.S. Army); Mae Jemison (NASA/Corbis); Mother Teresa (Gavin Wickham; Eye Ubiquitous/Corbis); Abraham Lincoln (Corbis/Bettmann)
Cover design by Berrian Design

This paper meets the requirements of ANSI/NISO A39.48-1992 (Permanence of Paper)

Contents

Macmillan Profiles: *Heroes and Pioneers* is a unique reference featuring over 125 profiles of notable heroes and pioneers from the antiquity to the present. Macmillan Library Reference recognizes the need for reliable, accurate, and accessible biographies of notable figures in world and American history. The Macmillan Profiles series can help meet that need by providing new collections of biographies that were carefully selected from distinguished Macmillan sources. Macmillan Library Reference has published a wide array of award-winning reference materials for libraries across the world. It is likely that several of the encyclopedias on the shelves in this library were published by Macmillan Reference or Charles Scribner's Sons. All biographies in Macmillan Profiles have been recast and tailored for a younger audience by a team of experienced writers and editors. In some cases, new biographies were commissioned to supplement entries from original sources.

The goal of this volume is to present an inspiring introduction to the life and times of heroic and pioneering figures in American and world history. We understand that everyone has their own idea of what constitutes a "hero," and do not claim that this volume offers an exhaustive account of heroism throughout history. Moreover, we recognize the inherent contradiction of placing wartime leaders such Douglas MacArthur and Simón Bolívar alongside advocates of nonviolence such as Mahatma Gandhi and the Dalai Lama. But we believe heroism takes different forms in different places and settings. Ultimately, everyone must find their own heroes, and we hope this volume will provide readers with an inspiring place to start the search.

The article list for *Heroes and Pioneers* was based on the following criteria: relevance to the curriculum, importance to history, and representation of as broad a cultural range as possible. Within that criteria, we selected figures from the following categories: (1) America's founding fathers, (2) American and foreign national heroes, (3) wartime heroes, (4) reformers, humanitarians, and civil rights activists, (5) crime fighters, (6) peace activists, (7) explorers and astronauts, and (8) pioneers. The result is a balanced, curriculum-related work that brings these historical figures to life.

FEATURES

To add visual appeal and enhance the usefulness of this volume, the page format was designed to include the following helpful features:

- **Time Lines:** Found throughout the text in the margins, time lines provide a quick reference source for dates and important accomplishments in the life and times of these heroes and pioneers.

- **Notable Quotations:** Found throughout the text in the margins, these thought-provoking quotations are drawn from interviews, speeches, and writings of the person covered in the article. Such quotations give readers a special insight into the distinctive personalities of these great men and women.

- **Pull Quotes:** Found throughout the text in the margin, pull quotes highlight essential facts.

- **Definitions and Glossary:** Brief definitions of important terms in the main text can be found in the margin. A glossary at the end of the book provides students with an even broader list of definitions.

- **Sidebars:** Appearing in shaded boxes throughout the volume, these provocative asides relate to and amplify topics.

- **Suggested Reading:** An extensive list of books and articles about the heroes and pioneers covered in the volume will help students who want to do further research.

- **Index:** A thorough index provides thousands of additional points of entry into the work.

ACKNOWLEDGMENTS

We thank our colleagues who publish the *Merriam Webster's Collegiate® Dictionary*. Definitions used in the margins and many of the glossary terms come from the *Distinguished Webster's Collegiate® Dictionary*, Tenth Edition, 1996.

The biographies herein were written by leading authorities at work the fields of American, European, and world history. *Heroes and Pioneers* contains over 80 photographs. Acknowledgments of sources for the illustrations can be found on page 361.

This work would not have been possible without the hard work and creativity of our staff. We offer our sincere thanks to all who helped create this marvelous work.

Macmillan Library Reference

Abegg, Elisabeth

1882–1957 ● RESCUER OF JEWS
DURING WORLD WAR II

Raised in Strasbourg (Alsace) when it was part of Imperial Germany, Elisabeth Abegg became involved in activities for the Quakers when she moved to Berlin. A history teacher at the Luisen girls' school, she was dismissed in 1933 by the Nazi school director for her pronounced anti-Nazi views.

In 1942, at the age of sixty and while looking after her bedridden mother and sick elder sister, Abegg began using her home in the Tempelhof district as a temporary shelter and assembly point for many Jews. She created a rescue network made up of friends from the Quaker movement, pastors, and former students, and over a period of almost three years helped dozens of Jews escape deprivation and deportation. Her activities included sheltering Jews either in her own home (in a building that also housed several Nazi party members) or in temporarily empty adjoining apartments in her care. Abegg found safe and permanent refuges both in Berlin and in more distant locations such as Alsace and East Prussia; she sent provisions to enable those who escaped to survive and provided them with false identities. She helped still others to escape across the Swiss border, selling her jewelry and other valuables in order to finance this work. She also tutored Jewish children at her home to compensate for their not being able to attend school. Bringing false identification papers, money, and provisions, she visited her charges in various locations.

In a booklet dedicated to her on her seventy-fifth birthday in 1957, entitled "And a Light Shone in the Darkness," her former charges offered profuse praise of Elisabeth Abegg's dedication, care, and humanity. ◆

1933 Abegg is fired from her teaching job for her anti-Nazi views.

1942 Abegg sets up rescue network and offers her home as shelter for Jews.

1957 Survivors dedicate "And a Light Shone in the Darkness" to Abegg.

Adams, John

1735–1826 ● PRESIDENT OF
THE UNITED STATES

"The judicial power ought to be distinct from both the legislative and executive, and independent upon both, that so it may be a check upon both, as both should be checks upon that."

John Adams, 1776

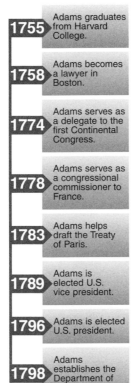

1755 Adams graduates from Harvard College.

1758 Adams becomes a lawyer in Boston.

1774 Adams serves as a delegate to the first Continental Congress.

1778 Adams serves as a congressional commissioner to France.

1783 Adams helps draft the Treaty of Paris.

1789 Adams is elected U.S. vice president.

1796 Adams is elected U.S. president.

1798 Adams establishes the Department of the Navy.

Born in Braintree (now Quincy), Massachusetts, John Adams could say even in those very early days that he was a fourth generation American. After attending Harvard College and receiving his bachelor's degree in 1755, he became a schoolmaster in Worcester, Massachusetts, where he lived in the home of a prominent Worcester lawyer, James Putnam, who inspired him to study law. After three years, he was admitted to the Boston bar in 1758.

His law practice led him to action on behalf of the Revolution. As a lawyer he argued against the Stamp Act before the royal governor, pointing out that it was truly taxation without representation since the colonists were not represented in the British parliament that passed this law. Although he was strongly opposed to the Stamp Act, he disapproved of the so-called Stamp Act riots. First and foremost he was an advocate, to the point of defending British soldiers who fired on civilians in the Boston Massacre. He grew closer to the revolutionary cause by appearing in important cases connected to it, such as the smuggling charges against John Hancock, a prominent colonist.

In 1774 he was one of the Massachusetts delegates to the first Continental Congress and in the second Continental Congress became one of the leaders of the Revolution. He was appointed to a committee charged with drafting the Declaration of Independence. Adams's greatest contribution to the Declaration of Independence, of which he was a signatory, was to serve as the driving force that supported and defended it through Congress.

Between 1778 and 1788 Adams primarily served his country as a diplomat. In 1778 he was a congressional commissioner to France and in 1780–1782 served in the Netherlands, securing its recognition of the United States as an independent country. He negotiated a treaty of amity and commerce with the Netherlands as well as, most important in those days, a loan. In 1783 he was one of the negotiators who drafted the Treaty of Paris, which officially brought the American

Revolution to an end. From 1785 to 1788 he served as the first U.S. ambassador to England.

In 1788 Adams returned home and the following year was elected the first vice president of the United States, an office to which he was reelected in 1792. This was followed by his election as president in 1796.

During his presidency John Adams's notable achievements included the establishment of the Department of the Navy in 1798, the signing of the Alien and **Sedition** Acts, and, in 1800, the signing of a treaty with France that averted war. In 1800 he was defeated by Thomas Jefferson for the presidency. Both he and Jefferson died on the same day—the fiftieth anniversary of the signing of the Declaration of Independence—the year after Adams's son John Quincy Adams was elected president of the United States. ◆

sedition: speech or action causing rebellion against the government.

Alcock, Sir John William

1892–1919 ● PIONEER AVIATOR

Born in Manchester, England, the eldest son of a horse dealer, Alcock's interests centered on the new century's means of transportation. He began work as an apprentice at the Empress Motor Works but his interest in motor cars soon gave way to an enthusiasm for flying. He began learning in Brooklands in 1910 and, as mechanic to French pilot Maurice Ducrocq, acquired skills that were to make him into one of the country's foremost pilots. He gained his flyer's license in 1912 and worked as a racing pilot before World War I.

In 1914 Alcock was commissioned into the Royal Naval Air Service. For several years he served as a flying instructor in Kent and then was sent on active service on the Turkish war front. He gained a reputation as a highly competent and brave pilot with a warm and generous nature that easily won admirers. He received a gallantry award after emerging triumphant from a **dogfight** with three enemy sea planes. Returning from a bombing raid on Constantinople, he was forced by Turkish antiaircraft fire to ditch his plane in the sea. Alcock and the other two members of the crew were not spotted by British ships. When their Handley Page bomber started to sink they swam ashore but were captured, and Alcock spent more than a year as a prisoner.

In 1919 Captain Alcock became a test pilot for Vickers Aircraft Company, eager to win the £10,000 prize offered by the *Daily Mail* newspaper for the first nonstop flight across the Atlantic. On June 14 Alcock took off from Saint John's in Newfoundland in a Vickers Vimy bomber, with Lieutenant Arthur Brown as navigator. It was a flight dogged by disaster and as severe a test for Alcock's skills as could be imagined. In succession the radio failed and then the exhaust pipe fell off causing poisonous fumes to invade the cockpit. Alcock and Brown wore specially heated suits against the cold and these also failed them. Then, as if this had not been disastrous enough, they encountered a snowstorm and the engines kept clogging with ice. Showing great daring, Brown climbed out onto the wings in a strong wind, and bent down and chipped away the ice. He had to repeat this feat five times. It was a moment of great relief as well as achievement when they touched down in Clifden in the west of Ireland, sixteen hours and twenty minutes and almost two thousand miles after takeoff.

The secretary of state for war, Winston Churchill, presented the *Daily Mail* prize and spoke in flowery terms of "that terrible waste of desolate water . . . in almost ceaseless storms and shrouded with an unbroken canopy of mist. Across this waste, through this obscurity, went two human beings, hurtling through the air, piercing cloud and darkness." Churchill went on to depict the implications for uniting the English-speaking world and crowned his speech by announcing the award of Knight Commander of the British Empire to both Alcock and Brown. Alcock did not live to enjoy his fame long. A few months later, flying an amphibian airplane to Paris, he ran into a severe storm and died after a crash-landing. ◆

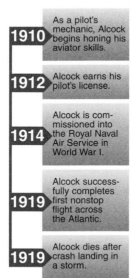

1910 As a pilot's mechanic, Alcock begins honing his aviator skills.

1912 Alcock earns his pilot's license.

1914 Alcock is commissioned into the Royal Naval Air Service in World War I.

1919 Alcock successfully completes first nonstop flight across the Atlantic.

1919 Alcock dies after crash landing in a storm.

Ali, Muhammad

1942–PRESENT ● BOXER

"I know I got it made while the masses of black people are catching hell, but as long as they ain't free, I ain't free."
Mohammed Ali, in an interview, 1975

Muhammad Ali was born Cassius Marcellus Clay Jr. in Louisville, Kentucky. He began boxing at the age of twelve under the tutelage of Joe Martin, a Louisville policeman. Having little interest in school and little affinity for intellectual endeavors, young Clay devoted himself whole-heartedly to boxing. He showed great promise early on and soon developed into one of the most impressive amateurs in the country. He became the National Amateur Athletic Union (AAU) champion in 1959 and in 1960, and also won a gold medal in the light-heavyweight division at the 1960 Olympics in Rome. As a result of his boyish good looks and his outgoing personality—his poetry recitations, his good-natured bragging, and his undeniable abilities—Clay because famous after the Olympics. Shortly after returning from Rome, he turned professional and was managed by a consortium of white Louisville businessmen. Carefully nurtured by veteran trainer Angelo Dundee, he accumulated a string of victories against relatively mediocre opponents and achieved a national following with his constant patter, his poetry, and his boyish antics. At 6'3" and a fighting weight of around 200 pounds, he astonished sportswriters with his blazing hand and foot speed, his unorthodox style of keeping his hands low, and his ability to avoid punches by moving his

Ali astonished sportswriters with his blazing hand and foot speed.

head back. No heavyweight in history possessed Clay's grace or speed.

On February 25, 1964, Clay fought as the underdog for the heavyweight title against Sonny Liston. Liston, an ex-convict, was thought by many to be virtually invincible because of his devastating one-round victories against former champion Floyd Patterson. An air of both the theater of the absurd and of ominousness surrounded the bout in Miami. Publicly, Clay taunted and comically berated Liston. He called him "the Bear," harassed him at his home, and almost turned the weigh-in ceremony into a shambles as he seemingly tried to attack Liston and appeared on the verge of being utterly out of control. Privately, however, Clay was seen with Malcolm X and members of the Nation of Islam (NOI). Rumors started that he had joined the militant, mysterious sect. Soon after, it was discovered that he had been secretly visiting NOI mosques for nearly three years and that he had indeed become a friend of Malcolm X, who sat ringside at the Liston fight.

Clay beat Liston fairly easily in seven rounds, shocking the world by becoming heavyweight champion. Immediately after the fight, he announced that he was a member of the NOI and that his name was no longer Cassius Clay but Muhammad Ali. The response from the white press, white America, and the boxing establishment generally was swift and intensely hostile. The NOI was seen, largely through the rhetoric of Malcolm X, its most stylish spokesman, as an anti-white hate group. (When Malcolm X broke with the NOI, shortly after the Liston fight, Ali remained loyal to Elijah Muhammad and ended his friendship with Malcolm X.) Following his public conversion to Islam, Ali was publicly pilloried. Most publications and sports journalists refused to call him by his new name. Former champion Floyd Patterson nearly went on a personal and national crusade against the NOI in his fight against Ali on November 22, 1965, but Patterson later became one of the few fighters to defend Ali publicly during his years of exile. Indeed, not since the reign of Jack Johnson was the white public and a segment of the black population so enraged by the opinions and life of a black athlete.

After winning his rematch with Liston in Lewiston, Maine, on May 25, 1965, in a bizarre fight that ended with

1960 Clay wins a gold medal in the 1960s Olympics in Rome.

1964 Clay becomes heavyweight champion by defeating Sonny Liston.

1964 Clay announces he is now Muhammad Ali.

1967 Ali is convicted of violating the Selective Service Act.

1971 Ali is hospitalized after a brutal fight with Joe Frazier.

1974 Ali beats George Foreman to regain the heavyweight title.

1987 Ali is elected to the Boxing Hall of Fame.

Liston apparently being knocked out in the first round, Ali spent most of the next year fighting abroad, primarily because of his unpopularity in this country. Among his most important matches during this period were a fifteen-round decision over George Chuvalo in Toronto, a sixth-round knockout of Henry Cooper in London, and a fifteen-round decision over Ernest Terrell in Houston. While Ali was abroad American officials changed his draft status from 1-Y (unfit for Army services because of his low score on Army intelligence tests) to 1-A (qualified for induction). Many saw this change as a direct response to the negative public opinion concerning Ali's political views and the mounting war in Vietnam. Ali refused to serve in the Army on the grounds that it was a violation of his religious beliefs. (Elijah Muhammad, leader of the NOI, had served time in prison during World War 11 for refusing to serve in the armed services.) In 1967, Ali was convicted in federal court of violation of the Selective Service Act, sentenced to five years in prison, and immediately stripped of both his boxing title and his boxing license. For the next three and one-half years, Ali, free on bond while appealing his case (which he eventually won on appeal to the U.S. Supreme Court), was prohibited from boxing. Still, Ali had inspired black athletes to become more militant and more politically committed. Medal winning track stars John Carlos and Tommie Smith gave a clenched-fist salute during the playing of the National Anthem at the Olympic Games in Mexico City in 1968, and Harry Edwards became one of the more outspoken leaders of a new cadre of young black athletes who saw Ali as a hero.

By 1970, with public opinion decidedly against the Vietnam War, and a growing black influence in several southern state governments, All was given a license to fight in Georgia. He returned to the ring on October 26 to knock out Jerry Quarry in the third round. Although he was still a brilliant fighter, the nearly four year layoff had diminished some of Ali's abilities. He took far more punishment in the ring during the years of his return than he had taken before. This was to have dire consequences for him as he grew older.

In the early 1970s Ali fought several of his most memorable matches. On March 8, 1971, he faced the undefeated Philadelphian Joe Frazier in New York City. Frazier had become champion during Ali's exile. The fifteen-round fight,

"I believe I was born to help my people be free."
Mohammed Ali, in an interview, 1969

which Frazier won in a close decision, was so fierce that both boxers were hospitalized after it. Many have speculated that this fight initiated Ali's neurological deterioration. In July of that year Ali won the North American Boxing Federation (NABF) heavyweight title by knocking out Jimmy Ellis in twelve rounds. His next major boxing challenge came in March 1973, when Ken Norton captured the NABF title from Ali in a twelve-round decision. Ali regained the title six months later with a twelve-round decision over Norton. In January of the following year, All and Frazier staged their first rematch. This nontitle bout at Madison Square Garden ended with Ali victorious after twelve hard-fought rounds. Ali finally regained the World Heavyweight title in Kinshasa, Zaire, on October 30, 1974, when he knocked out a seemingly indestructible George Foreman in eight rounds. To counter Foreman's awesome punching power, Ali used what he called his "rope-a-dope" strategy, by which he leaned back against the ropes and covered his head, allowing Foreman to punch himself out. The next year, Ali and Frazier faced off one last time in what Ali dubbed "The Thrilla in Manila." Both boxers received tremendous punishment during this bludgeoning ordeal. Ali prevailed, however, when Frazier's trainer refused to let the boxer come out for the fifteenth round.

lionized: to treat as an object of importance.

During the 1970s Ali was **lionized**. No longer seen as a race demon, he virtually became a national icon. He appeared in movies—including the film *The Greatest* (1977), based on his autobiography of the same name (1975). Like Jackie Robinson and Joe Louis before him, Ali played himself in the film—he also appeared in television programs and in commercials. He was one of the most photographed and interviewed men in the world. Indeed, Ali even beat Superman in the ring in a special issue of the comic devoted to him. Part of Ali's newfound popularity was a result of a shift in attitude by the white public and white sportswriters, but part of it was also a reflection of Ali's tempered approach to politics. Ali became a great deal less **doctrinaire** in the political aspects of his Islamic beliefs and he eventually embraced Wallace D. Muhammad's more ecumenical form of Islam when the NOI factionalized after the death of Elijah Muhammad in 1975. Finally, as befitting a major celebrity, Ali had one of the largest entourages of any sports personality in history, resembling that of a head of state.

doctrinaire: impractical; stubbornly theoretical.

On February 15, 1978, Ali again lost the title. His opponent this time was Leon Spinks, an ex-Marine and native of a north St. Louis housing project. Spinks fought in only eight professional bouts before he met Ali. Ali, however, became the first heavyweight in history to regain the title for a third time when he defeated Spinks on September 15 of the same year.

In 1979, Ali was aged and weary; his legs were shot, his reflexes had slowed, and his appetite for competition was waning as a result of the good life that he was enjoying. Ali retired from the ring at that time, only to do what so many other great champions have so unwisely done, namely, return to battle. His return to the ring included a savage ten-round beating on October 2, 1980, at the hands of Larry Holmes, a former sparring partner who had become champion after Ali's retirement. His next fight was a ten-round decision lost to Trevor Berbick on December 11 of the following year. After the Berbick fight, Ali retired for good. His professional record stands at 56 wins, 37 of which were by knockout, and 5 losses. He was elected to the Boxing Hall of Fame in 1987.

During Ali's later years, his speech became noticeably more slurred, and after his retirement he became more aged: moving slowly, speaking with such a thick tongue that he was almost incomprehensible, and suffering from attacks of palsy. There is some question as to whether he has Parkinson's disease or a Parkinson's-like deterioration of the neurological system. Many believe that the deterioration of his neurological system is directly connected to the punishment he took in the ring. By the early 1990s, although his mind was still sound, Ali gave the appearance of being a good deal older and more infirm than he actually was. He found it difficult to write or talk, and often walked slowly. Despite this, he is living a full life, travels constantly, and seems to be at peace with himself.

His personal life has been turbulent. He has been married four times and has had several children as well as numerous affairs, especially during his heyday as a fighter. His oldest daughter, Maryum, is a rap artist, following in her father's footsteps as a poet. Ali made a poetry recording for Columbia Records in 1963 called *The Greatest*—Maryum has recorded a popular rap dedicated to her father.

It would be difficult to overestimate Ali's impact on boxing and on the United States as both a cultural and political

Ali became the first heavyweight in history to regain the title for a third time when he defeated Spinks in 1978.

figure. He became one of the most recognized men in the world, an enduring, if not always appropriate, stylistic influence on young boxers, and a man who showed the world that it was possible for a black to speak his mind publicly and live to tell the tale. ◆

Allen, Ethan

1738–1789 ● VERMONT REVOLUTIONARY LEADER

Revolutionary War hero Ethan Allen was born on February 12, 1738, in Litchfield, Connecticut. Control over the region that is now Vermont was disputed between New York and New Hampshire in the 1770s. Ethan Allen settled there about 1769, and as leader of the local "Green Mountain Boys" insisted on separate treatment for Vermont under British rule. He was considered so dangerous that in 1771 the British governor of New York offered a reward for his capture.

When the Revolutionary War began, the Connecticut legislature authorized Allen to capture Fort Ticonderoga. He led his men victoriously into the sleeping fort on May 10, 1775. The capture of Ticonderoga gave the American army its first heavy guns, and those guns eventually were used to drive the British out of Boston.

In September 1775, Allen became a British prisoner after failure of an attack on Montreal. His captivity lasted two years, when he returned to command the Vermont militia. Late in 1778, Allen demanded that Vermont be recognized by Congress as a state. When Congress would not do so, Allen returned to the Green Mountains and began a guerrilla war against New York settlers. Later, he corresponded with British commanders in Canada, who apparently promised to recognize Vermont as a separate colony.

Colonel Allen did not continue on active military duty beyond the year 1778. He turned his attention to local affairs and to his farm, on which he lived the rest of his life. ◆

1775 ▶ Allen captures Fort Ticonderoga.

1775 ▶ The British take Allen prisoner.

1778 ▶ Allen begins fighting New York settlers in Vermont.

Anthony, Susan Brownell

1820–1906 ● Reformer & Women's Rights Activist

Born in Adams, Massachusetts, Susan B. Anthony was raised in a progressive household in which her father respected his daughters' intelligence and gave them a good education. As one of eight children, Anthony saw her quiet, worn-out mother as a symbol of married life and it made her eager to improve the condition of married women in the United States.

Growing up in a Quaker household, Anthony heard women speaking freely and participating equally in church affairs. She was sent to a boarding school in Philadelphia, and received an education superior to that usual for girls at that time.

In 1838 Anthony experienced discrimination firsthand after a brush with what she considered unfair property laws in Rochester, New York. Rochester was considered a center of reform and many abolitionist and temperance workers became friends of the family; Anthony became known for her honesty, sense of humor, and sympathetic view of people. While working as a schoolteacher in nearby Canajoharie Academy she joined the local chapter of the Daughters of Temperance, soon becoming an officer of the organization.

Anthony became bored with teaching and returned home to Rochester, where she directed her father's farm for two years and became increasingly involved in reform circles. In 1852 she organized the first women's state temperance society in the United States, and soon became active in the antislavery movement.

After attending several reformers' conventions at which women were not allowed to participate fully, Anthony heeded the advice of her friend Elizabeth Cady Stanton and began to work full-time for the women's rights movement, becoming secretary of the National Woman's Rights Convention. As she toured the country with Stanton, she was the main organizing force behind the tours, though Stanton gave the

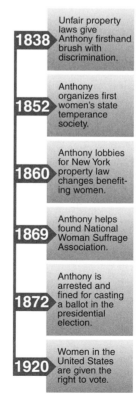

1838 Unfair property laws give Anthony firsthand brush with discrimination.

1852 Anthony organizes first women's state temperance society.

1860 Anthony lobbies for New York property law changes benefiting women.

1869 Anthony helps found National Woman Suffrage Association.

1872 Anthony is arrested and fined for casting a ballot in the presidential election.

1920 Women in the United States are given the right to vote.

> *"It was we, the people; not we, the white male citizens; nor yet we, the male citizens; but we, the whole people, who formed the Union."*
> Susan B. Anthony, 1873

speeches. In March 1860, she and Stanton were successful in lobbying to change a New York state property law to give women the right to keep their own earnings, enter into contracts, or use their earnings as they saw fit. Widows now had the same property rights as widowers.

Anthony soon turned her attention to suffrage for women, helping to found the National Woman Suffrage Association in 1869, which she served as the vice president at large until 1892, when she became the president. From 1868 to 1870, she was the proprietor of a weekly newspaper, *The Revolution*, whose motto was "The true republic—men, their rights and nothing more; women, their rights and nothing less." With Stanton, Anthony helped to bring previously taboo subjects, such as divorce, into public debate.

In 1872 Anthony cast a ballot in the presidential election, as she felt she was entitled to do according to the 14th amendment of the Constitution. She was arrested and fined $100 but never paid the fine. As the debate over women's suffrage heated up, Anthony continued fighting for her cause. "Abraham Lincoln said, 'No man is good enough to govern another man without his consent.' Now I say to you, 'No man is good enough to govern any woman without her consent,' " she said in 1895. Her pioneering led to women's suffrage in the United States in 1920.

The Susan B. Anthony Dollar

In 1971, the U. S. government began issuing the Eisenhower dollar, the first dollar coin issued in the United States since the 1930s. Americans resisted using the Eisenhower dollar, however, because it was too large and heavy. As a result, in the mid-1970s the government decided to issue a smaller dollar coin, hoping that it would circulate more widely. The new coin, which was a little larger than a quarter, bore a picture of Susan B. Anthony on one side, making Anthony the first real woman to be pictured on a United States coin in general circulation. President Carter approved the new Susan B. Anthony dollar in 1978, 750 million of them were minted, and the coin was issued for circulation in 1979. The new dollar coin was a notorious failure with Americans, however. People complained that the new dollar was so similar to a quarter in color, size, and weight that they often confused the two coins. In 1981, the government ended production of the Susan B. Anthony dollar. The coin almost disappeared from circulation until 1993, when the United States Post Office began using Susan B. Anthony dollars for change in its stamp vending machines.

She organized the International Council of Women, and, along with Stanton, Matilda Joslyn Gage, and Ida Husted Harper, published a four-volume history of their cause, called *The History of Women's Suffrage* (1902). In the last years of her life, though she suffered from a serious heart condition, she continued to work for women's rights, attending her last convention two months before her death at the age of eighty-six. Anthony's last public words were said at her eighty-sixth birthday celebration: "Failure is impossible." ◆

Aquino, Corazon Cojuangco

1933–PRESENT ● PRESIDENT OF THE PHILIPPINES

> *"I challenged the dictator; he made fun of me and called me the housewife with no experience. I told him yes, it is true I have no experience with lying, cheating, stealing and killing."*
>
> Corazon Aquino, 1997

Corazon Cojuangco Aquino was president of the Philippines from February 1986 to 1992. She was born in the province of Tarlac and completed her freshman year of high school in Manila. In 1946 she and her family moved to the United States, and she completed her high-school studies at the Notre Dame Convent in New York. She graduated from Mount Saint Vincent College in New York in 1953 and married Benigno "Ninoy" Aquino, then a young journalist and law student in Manila, the following

1972 Benigno Aquino is imprisoned by Phillipine President Ferdinand Marcos.

1983 Benigno Aquino is assassinated.

1986 Corazon Aquino is elected President of the Philippines.

1987 A new constitution is enacted in the Philippines.

1992 Aquino declines to run for reelection.

coup: violent overthrow of the government.

year. Until 1972, Corazon Aquino was a homemaker raising five children while her husband rose from mayor to governor and finally senator.

Cory Aquino's political involvement began when her husband was imprisoned by his political archrival, President Ferdinand Marcos, in 1972. During the eight years he spent in prison, she served as his liaison with the political opposition to Marcos. In 1980, when Marcos released Ninoy Aquino from prison in order that he might undergo heart surgery in the United States, the family moved to Newton, Massachusetts.

After her husband's assassination upon his return from exile in August of 1983, Cory Aquino came back to the Philippines. When Marcos announced presidential elections in November 1985, support for Corazon Aquino as the opposition candidate grew vigorously. Amid intense political negotiations that threatened to split the opposition wide apart, Aquino ran for president, choosing political rival Salvador Laurel as her running mate.

Seeing Aquino as the embodiment of her husband's dream to restore democracy to the country and as a person of impeccable integrity, Filipinos supported her campaign with an enthusiasm never before witnessed in their country's political history. With only two months of campaigning, she claimed victory on February 9, 1986, on the basis of favorable election returns and called on Marcos to concede defeat. The four-day "people power" revolution began on February 22 as Filipinos poured into the streets to support Marcos defectors Defense Minister Juan Enrile and General Fidel Ramos and ultimately brought Aquino to power. Aquino and Marcos were both sworn in as president on 25 February, but that same evening, Marcos left Malacanang Palace for the United States, and Corazon Aquino became the seventh president of the Philippine Republic.

Aquino survived several **coup** attempts during her first year as president. After February 2, 1987 her government operated under a newly enacted constitution that gave her a six-year term as president. President Aquino faced many crises, including a growing armed insurgency movement and the need for formidable economic reform measures. Her broadly based political support was separate from any close association with a particular party. A widely held belief among Filipinos was that Cory Aquino was brought to power by the occurrence of a miracle, and her popular following is likely to endure. The Philippines experienced economic growth during Aquino's presidency, although some critics charged her administration with corruption and mismanagement. She did not run for reelection in 1992, and her secretary of defense, Fidel Ramos, was elected president. ◆

Arias Sánchez, Oscar

1941–PRESENT ● PEACE ACTIVIST & PRESIDENT OF COSTA RICA

Oscar Arias Sánchez was president of Costa Rica (1986–1990) and winner of the Nobel Peace Prize in 1987 for designing a plan for peace in Central America. Arias Sánchez's father was an early follower of José Figueres Ferrer and an active member of the National Liberation Party (PLN). His mother's family is part of the Costa Rican coffee elite that emerged during the nineteenth-century coffee boom. Arias Sánchez came to international prominence shortly after his inauguration in 1986 when he took bold initiatives to propel Central America into a peace process. His proposals for peace and stability in the region led to an agreement, signed in 1987, between Honduras, Guatemala, Nicaragua, El Salvador, and Costa Rica.

The Arias plan, or Esquipulas II, established the framework for the pacification and democratization of Central America. It provided for the restoration of civil liberties, for amnesty for political prisoners, for free elections, and for genuine dialogue between governments and opposition forces. The plan contributed to the process that brought peace and free elections to Nicaragua and new hope for the eventual demilitarization of the region.

"Democracy must uphold principles such as fair political representation, free elections, equal rights, individual freedoms, accountability, tolerance, and peaceful resolution of conflicts. More importantly, the protection of human rights lies at the heart of democracy for it ensures the right of every citizen to live without fear and to live in peace."

Oscar Arias Sánchez, 1997

Even though Arias came to the international scene at a relatively young age, he had served a long apprenticeship in the highly competitive arena of Costa Rican party politics and in the rigorous intellectual environment of the University of Costa Rica (UCR). He received his law and economics degrees from the UCR, was awarded a master of arts degree in political science and economics from the London School of Economics (1967), and earned a doctor of philosophy degree from the University of Essex, England (1974). He joined the faculty of UCR in 1969 and served as a member of the ad hoc Commission of the National University (1972–1975). He was a director of the Costa Rican Technological Institute from 1974 to 1977.

Arias began his political career in the PLN and held high elected and appointed positions in the national government and in the party. He served as secretary to the president (1970–1972) during the last José Figueres Ferrer administration. From 1972 to 1977, he held a cabinet-level position as minister of national planning and economic policy. While serving as a member of the National Assembly (1978–1982), he also held other leadership positions. He was secretary of international affairs (1975–1979) and he was elected secretary general in 1979 on a reformist platform that brought a new generation of leaders to the fore. Arias ascended to the presidency chiefly by serving in positions of party leadership and in the administration of President Luis Alberto Monge Álvarez. He won the PLN primary and then defeated Rafael Angel Calderón Fournier in the general election.

Arias has received many awards and honorary degrees from universities in Europe, Central America, and the United States. Since his presidency he has lectured widely on the related questions of world peace and the environment, donating the proceeds from the lectures to the Arias Foundation, which was established to support research on these issues. He has also continued to be active in politics. ◆

1972 Arias becomes minister of national planning and economic policy.

1975 Arias becomes secretary of international affairs.

1986 Arias becomes president of Costa Rica.

1987 Arias is awarded the Nobel Peace Prize.

Armstrong, Neil Alden

1930–PRESENT ● ASTRONAUT

> *"Houston, Tranquillity Base here. The Eagle has landed."*
> Neil Armstrong, on reaching the moon, 1969

Neil Armstrong will always be remembered as the first man to walk on the moon. At 9:56 P.M., Houston time, Sunday, July 20, 1969, he stepped off the footpad of the lunar module Eagle, saying, "That's one small step for a man, one giant leap for mankind."

With every one of his early steps a theory about the lunar surface evaporated. The worry that an astronaut would sink in a deep coating of dust? Armstrong reported that his boots sank "maybe an eighth of an inch." Would an astronaut trying to walk in the unwieldy space suit and backpack simply fall over? "There seems to be no difficulty," he said. "It's even perhaps easier than the simulations at **one-sixth G**."

As millions watched on television, Armstrong dug a small "contingency" sample of lunar soil, in case the moon walk had to be cut short. Then, joined by Buzz Aldrin, he began to set up scientific experiments and searched for more comprehensive rock samples. He and Aldrin also set up an American flag and took a phone call from President Richard Nixon. They also read the words printed on a plaque mounted on the descent stage of the Eagle, which would remain forever on the Sea of Tranquility: "Here men from the planet Earth first set foot upon the Moon, July 1969 AD. We came in peace for all mankind."

one-sixth G: a measurement of Earth's gravity.

Just over two and a half hours later Armstrong, Aldrin, and the precious box containing the first moon rocks were safely back inside the Eagle. At 12:55 P.M. the next day the Eagle lifted off from the moon to rejoin the orbiting Columbia and its pilot, Michael Collins.

Apollo 11 ended with a successful splashdown in the Pacific and recovery by the carrier USS *Hornet*. Armstrong, Collins, and Aldrin faced three weeks of quarantine, and months of public appearances.

Armstrong had commanded one previous spaceflight, Gemini 8 in March 1966. Gemini 8 accomplished the first docking between two spacecraft when it linked up with an unmanned Agena 6.5 hours after liftoff. It also became the first American spaceflight to be aborted. A thruster on the Gemini began to fire uncontrollably, sending the combined Gemini-Agena vehicle into a spin. Suspecting at first that the Agena was causing the problem, Armstrong and pilot David Scott separated from the unmanned craft, which only made matters worse. Forced to use reentry thrusters to stabilize the Gemini, Armstrong and Scott then had to return to earth. They splashed down 600 miles south of Yokosuka, Japan, and waited in the floating spacecraft for 45 minutes until divers could reach them from a C-54 rescue plane. It wasn't until three hours after splashdown that the weary, seasick astronauts were safe aboard the destroyer *Leonard F. Mason*. They had completed fewer than eleven hours of a planned three-day mission.

Armstrong was born August 5, 1930, at a farm six miles outside Wapakoneta, Ohio. His father was an auditor for the state of Ohio so the family moved every year, though Neil graduated from high school in Wapakoneta. He built model airplanes and got his student pilot's license on his sixteenth birthday.

Armstrong wanted to go to college and study aeronautical engineering, but couldn't afford it without some sort of aid. He applied for a U.S. Navy scholarship, got it and enrolled at Purdue University in 1947. A year and a half later the Navy called him to active duty. He entered flight school at Pensacola, Florida, and became a fighter pilot. Before he could return to Purdue, however, the Korean War broke out. Armstrong was assigned to Fighter Squadron 51 and served in Korea until the spring of 1952. He described his combat expe-

1955 Armstrong receives a BS in aeronautical engineering from Purdue University.

1960 Armstrong is assigned to the X-20 program.

1965 Armstrong serves as backup commander for Gemini 5.

1966 Armstrong commands the Gemini 8 space flight.

1969 Armstrong becomes the first person to walk on the moon.

1971 Armstrong becomes Professor of Engineering at the University of Cincinnati.

rience as "bridge breaking, train stopping, tank shooting and that sort of thing." In September 1951 he had to bail out of his F9F-2 jet when a wire stretched across a Korean valley tore the wing off his plane.

Out of the Navy, he returned to Purdue in the fall of 1952 and graduated with a B.S. in aeronautical engineering in January 1955. He would later receive an M.S. from the University of Southern California in 1970.

Armstrong went to work for the National Advisory Committee on Aeronautics (NACA), the forerunner of NASA, at its Lewis Flight Propulsion Laboratory in Cleveland. He soon transferred to the NACA station at Edwards AFB, California, where he became an aeronautical research pilot. Among other vehicles, he flew the X-5, F-102A, F5D-1 Skylancer (making simulated X-20 Dyna-Soar launchings and landings in these two), the Paresev, and the X-15 rocket plane.

He was one of the first pilots assigned to the X-20 program in the summer of 1960. At the same time he was involved in the X-15 program, making six flights in the rocket plane between December 1960 and July 1962, ultimately reaching an altitude of 207,000 feet.

Considered a shoo-in for the second group of NASA astronauts selected in 1962, Armstrong was one of the first two civilians chosen for the manned space program. He underwent

Sally Ride

Physicist Sally Kristen Ride became the first American woman space traveler on June 27, 1983. Ride was born on May 26, 1951, in Los Angeles, California. She attended Stanford University, where she earned a BA in English and a BS in physics in 1973. She earned her Ph.D. in physics from Stanford in 1978. Ride was a teaching assistant and researcher in laser physics at Stanford when selected by NASA for astronaut training in January 1978. Five years later, she became one of five astronauts launched aboard the Space Shuttle Challenger. During the six-day flight Ride served as flight engineer, took part in the deployment of two communications satellites, and in the deployment and retrieval of the German-built Shuttle Pallet Satellite. Ride made a second shuttle trip to space in 1984. During this mission, Ride became the first American woman to walk in space. Ride logged a total of 337 hours in space. She resigned from NASA in 1987 to join Stanford University as an arms control scholar. Ride became head of the Space Science Institute at the University of California at San Diego in 1989.

survival training, then became involved in Gemini development. One of his jobs, beginning in 1964, was to supervise the work of the fourteen new astronauts, including Aldrin and Collins. Armstrong was assigned as backup commander for Gemini 5, the third manned Gemini mission, in early 1965. He served as capcom for Gemini 5 and for Gemini 9 as well, and also served as backup commander for Gemini 11.

Following Apollo 11 Armstrong served at NASA Headquarters in Washington, D.C., as deputy associate administrator for aeronautics, and became known as an advocate of research into computer control of high performance aircraft.

He resigned from NASA in August 1971 to become professor of engineering at the University of Cincinnati. He remained there through 1979, joining the Cardwell International Corporation of Lebanon, Ohio, as chairman of the board. In 1984 he became chairman of the board of CTA, Inc., in Lebanon.

An intensely private person, Armstrong refrained from making public appearances for many years. However, in early 1984 he accepted an appointment to the National Commission on Space, a presidential panel whose members included, in addition to Armstrong, astronaut Kathryn Sullivan, former test pilot Chuck Yeager, and former NASA administrator Thomas Paine. The NCOS was to develop goals for a national space program extending into the twenty-first century. Before its report could be delivered, however, the Shuttle Challenger exploded during launch on January 28, 1986. Armstrong was immediately named vice-chairman of the committee investigating the disaster.

He also served as host for the television series *First Flights* on the Arts & Entertainment Network (1991). ◆

Ashe, Arthur Robert, Jr.

1943–1993 ● TENNIS PLAYER & POLITICAL ACTIVIST

> *"Some folks call tennis a rich people's sport or a white person's game. I guess I started too early, because I just thought it was something fun to do."*
>
> Arthur Ashe, 1992

Born in Richmond, Virginia, Arthur Ashe traced his lineage back ten generations on his father's side to a woman who in 1735 was brought from West Africa to Yorktown, Virginia, by the slave ship *Doddington*. Ashe's mother, Mattie Cunningham, also of Richmond, taught him to read by the time he was four. She died when Arthur was six, one year after giving birth to her second son and last child, Johnnie.

Ashe, who was frail in his youth, was forbidden by his father, a police officer in Richmond's Department of Recreation and Parks, to play football on the segregated Brookfield playground adjacent to the Ashes' home. Instead, young Ashe took to playing tennis on the four hard courts of the playground. By the time he was ten, Ashe had attracted the keen eye of Dr. Walter Johnson, a Lynchburg, Virginia, physician and tennis enthusiast who had previously discovered and coached Althea Gibson, the first black woman to win Wimbledon.

Ashe's father and Dr. Johnson were both stern disciplinarians who insisted that Ashe cultivate self-discipline, good manners, forbearance, and self-effacing **stoicism**. These qualities would characterize Ashe throughout his entire life and, even in the midst of the most turbulent social conditions, would define him as a man of reason, conscience, integrity,

stoicism: indifference to pleasure or pain.

and moral authority. His cool disposition enabled him not only to survive, but to distinguish himself in an overwhelmingly white tennis environment.

In 1960, Ashe was awarded a tennis scholarship to UCLA, where he earned All-American status. Two years after Ashe graduated with a business degree, he became the first black man to win one of the preeminent Grand Slam titles, accomplishing that as an amateur and U. S. Army representative at the U.S. Open of 1968. Numerous titles would follow, highlighted by Ashe's place on three victorious Davis Cup squads and the addition of two more Grand Slam titles, one at the Australian Open in 1970, and the other, his *pièce de résistance*, at Wimbledon in 1975.

Throughout those years, Ashe devoured considerable time and energy to civil rights issues. In 1973, after three years of trying, he secured an invitation to play in the all-white South African Open. Although his participation was controversial, it personified Ashe's lifelong belief in constructive engagement— an attitude that he abandoned only on one noteworthy occasion in 1976, when he joined in the call for an international embargo of all sporting contact with South Africa.

In 1979, at age thirty-six, Ashe suffered a myocardial infarction, which forced him to have bypass surgery and retire from tennis. Nevertheless, over the ensuing years he served as the U.S. Davis Cup captain (1981–1985), he worked as a journalist and television commentator, and he served or helped create various foundations, ranging from the American Heart Association to the United Negro College Fund to his own Safe Passage Foundation.

Eighteen months after undergoing a second heart operation in 1983, Ashe learned that he had contracted the AIDS virus through blood transfusions. He immediately set to work on his definitive three-volume history of black athletes in America, *A Hard Road to Glory* (1988). Forced by the national newspaper *USA Today* to reveal that he was suffering from AIDS in April 1992, Ashe worked as an activist for the defeat of AIDS until he died of the disease in February 1993. ◆

1959 Ashe receives a tennis scholarship to UCLA.

1968 Ashe wins the U.S. Open.

1975 Ashe wins Wimbledon.

1979 Ashe retires from tennis for health reasons.

1988 Ashe publishes *A Hard Road to Glory*.

1992 Ashe reveals he is suffering from AIDS.

1993 Ashe dies from AIDS.

Asoka

REIGNED CA. 273–232 BCE ● EMPEROR
OF INDIA & RELIGIOUS REFORMER

Asoka was one of the hundred sons of Bindusura and the grandson of Chandragupta, the first Mauryan emperor of northern India. Asoka was serving as viceroy of Ujjain in Malwa at his father's death. Bindusura's death prompted a bloody war of succession; Asoka was the only son to survive. Some historians choose to point to contemporary records in which Asoka shows his concern for his brothers and sisters as discrediting the legend. There was, however, an unexplained four-year gap between his father's death and his own coronation.

Asoka was appalled by the carnage of war.

Little information is available on the early years of Asoka's forty-year reign. Some thirteen years after his accession Asoka attacked Kalinga near the Bay of Bengal in an attempt to expand his realm. Despite his military victory Asoka was appalled by the carnage of war. There were 100,000 casualties and 150,000 prisoners were taken; millions more may have died from famine and disease. The sight prompted a radical transformation in Asoka. Whereas he had previously enjoyed the life of a royal prince, the memory of Kalinga inspired him to adopt the philosophy of *ahimsa*, or noninjury of living things. Asoka abandoned the hunt and became a vegetarian. He provided for his subjects by planting trees, digging wells, and building hospitals and began exporting medicinal herbs to many of the neighboring states.

Asoka adopted the *dharma*, Buddhist laws encouraging respect for one's parents and teachers, charity, honesty, moderation, and tolerance of all people. He exhorted his officials to treat his subjects as if they were his own children. Although Asoka's empire was the largest that the dynasty would know, he abandoned military conquests, preferring to send missionaries abroad in a program he referred to as "conquest through faith." (He did not, however, disband the army, nor did he abolish capital punishment.) Asoka's missionaries reached as far as Greece in Europe, Egypt in Africa, and Burma and Ceylon in Asia.

In his own realm Asoka established a group of educators,

the *dharma-mahamatras*, who roamed the country preaching the teachings of the Buddha. He is said to have built 8,400 temples, some of which can still be seen. Perhaps his greatest achievement was carving the teachings of the *dharma* on countless cave walls and pillars throughout the kingdom. These records provide historians with a thorough understanding of Asoka's reign. They are highly ornate monuments, polished by a technique that has yet to be reproduced, written in both Pali and local languages. The writings designate Asoka as *Devanampiya* ("Beloved of God") and *Piyadashi* ("One concerned about the welfare of his subjects").

polygamous: having more than one spouse at one time.

Little is known about Asoka's personal life. He was apparently **polygamous** but only one wife, Kalivaki, is known. Two of his children, a son, Mahendra and a daughter, Sanghamitra, may have been missionaries in Ceylon. Asoka was not succeeded by his oldest son, Tivara; however, two grandsons, Dasaratha and Samprati, divided the empire after Asoka's death. They were unable to consolidate their power and within fifty years the Mauryan empire had crumbled.

Some scholars are skeptical as to whether Asoka actually embraced Buddhism. Although he adhered to the *dharma*, there is no record of other important Buddhist principles, such as the Four Noble Truths and the Eightfold Way, being promoted during his reign, while the principles of *dharma* and *ahimsa* are common to Buddhists, Jains, and Hindus. These scholars claim that Asoka was actually the founder of a new universal faith combining the pacifist principles common to all Indian religions. Some legends contradict this claim, telling that Asoka spent his final years attempting to prevent schisms developing in Buddhism.

Aung San Suu Kyi

1945–PRESENT ● HUMAN
RIGHTS ACTIVIST

"It is not enough merely to call for freedom, democracy, and human rights. There has to be a united determination to persevere in the struggle, to make sacrifices in the name of enduring truths, to resist the corrupting influences of desire, ill will, ignorance, and fear."
Aung San Suu Kyi, "Freedom from Fear," 1991

Aung San Suu Kyi is a Burmese human rights activist and the head of Burma's popular opposition party, the National League for Democracy (NLD). She won the 1991 Nobel Peace Prize for her nonviolent struggle to bring democracy to Burma. In 1989, she was placed under house arrest by the country's military regime and was detained through much of the 1990s.

Aung San Suu Kyi was born on June 19, 1945, in Rangoon (also spelled Yangon), the capital of Burma, which is now called Myanmar. Her mother, Khin Kyi, became a prominent Burmese diplomat, and her father, Aung San, was a nationalist leader who helped bring about Burma's independence in 1948 after more than 50 years of British colonial rule and three years of Japanese occupation during World War II. He was chosen to become the first prime minister of independent Burma in 1947, but was assassinated on July 19, 1947, when Suu Kyi was two. Aung San Suu Kyi eventually came to emulate her father in his struggle against oppression, but only after living much of her life abroad.

As a child Aung San Suu Kyi attended schools in Burma until 1960. That year she moved to India with her mother, who became Burma's ambassador to India. Aung San Suu Kyi led a privileged existence in India and attended good schools there. While in India she became familiar with the teachings of Mohandas K. Gandhi, the Indian spiritual and political leader known for his use of nonviolent civil disobedience against British colonial rule.

In 1964, Aung San Suu Kyi began studies at St. Hugh's College at Oxford University in England, where she majored in politics, philosophy, and economics. Her friends remembered her as a devout Buddhist who was always eager to learn. She received her B.A. in 1967. Following graduation Aung San Suu Kyi worked in England as a teacher and research assistant and later in New York City at the United Nations.

While at Oxford, Aung San Suu Kyi met Michael Aris, a scholar of Tibetan culture. The couple married in 1972, and Suu Kyi followed her husband to the kingdom of Bhutan, where he worked as a tutor for the royal family. In Bhutan she held a job in the Foreign Ministry as a research officer on United Nations issues. In 1973 the couple returned to England, where Suu Kyi gave birth to two sons, Alexander and Kim. Aung San Sue Kyi lived comfortably as a mother and homemaker while her husband worked as a scholar at Oxford. During this period, her interest in her father intensified, and she began to research his life. Through her research, Aung San Suu Kyi found that she shared many attitudes with the father she had never known, and like Aung San she developed a sense of duty toward serving Burma in its time of need.

In 1985 Aung San Suu Kyi traveled to Japan to continue scholarly work on her father at the University of Kyoto in Japan, bringing her youngest son, Kim, with her. She then spent a year in Simla in northern India with her husband and sons. In 1987, she enrolled in a doctorate program in Burmese literature at the School of Oriental and African Studies at London University. Her studies were interrupted in April 1988, when she returned to Burma to care for her dying mother.

At the time of her arrival in Burma, the country was seething with hostility toward the socialist government. After years of political repression, limited civil freedoms, and continued economic decline, people took to the streets in revolt. In mid-1988 student demonstrations calling for an end to the country's one-party rule led to violent clashes with riot police and hundreds of demonstrators were killed. The protests spread and tens of thousands of people took to the streets.

1947 Aung San Suu Kyi's father, the Burmese Prime Minister, is assassinated.

1988 Aung San Suu Kyi helps found the National League for Democracy (NLD).

1989 The Burmese government places Aung San Suu Kyi under house arrest.

1990 The NLD wins about 80 percent of the seats in parliamentary elections.

1991 Aung San Suu Kyi is awarded the Nobel Prize for Peace.

1995 Aung San Suu Kyi is released from house arrest.

1996 The Burmese government steps up pressure against the NLD.

The army responded to demonstrations by firing into the crowds, killing thousands.

Unable to remain a silent bystander while the Burmese government massacred unarmed citizens, Aung San Suu Kyi joined in the protest movement. She made her first major public appearance before 500,000 people at the Shwe Dagon Pagoda in Rangoon on August 26, marking the beginning of her nonviolent struggle for democracy and human rights. In September the army overthrew the government and replaced it with the State Law and Order Restoration Council (SLORC), which scheduled elections for 1990. At the same time, however, the military cracked down on civil rights. It immediately banned political demonstrations and political gatherings of more than four people. Once again, thousands of people took to the streets in protest, and soldiers fired upon them, killing hundreds.

In September 1988 Aung San Suu Kyi helped found the National League for Democracy (NLD), the leading opposition party. She campaigned all around the country for the NLD and spoke openly against the military in command. On July 20, 1989, the government placed Aung San Suu Kyi under house arrest. In January the following year she was denied the right to have visits from family members and in July all written communication with her was severed. In the May 1990 elections the NLD won about 80 percent of the seats in parliament, but the government refused to step down. Many NLD candidates were subsequently arrested.

Aung San Suu Kyi spent her time under house arrest meditating and reading literature and works on politics, philosophy, and Buddhism. On several occasions the government offered to let her go free on the condition that she leave Burma, but Aung San Suu Kyi refused to go unless the country was returned to a civilian government and political prisoners were released. She also rejected all suggestions to move to an armed struggle, believing that such a move would perpetuate a cycle of violence. In 1991 Aung San Suu Kyi was awarded the Nobel Peace Prize for her nonviolent struggle for democracy and human rights. Her son Alexander traveled to Oslo, Norway, to accept the award on her behalf.

In 1995 the government suddenly released Aung San Suu Kyi from house arrest, but she remained in Burma to continue her work for democracy. From her front gate she gave

"It is not power that corrupts but fear. Fear of losing power corrupts those who wield it and fear of the scourge of power corrupts those who are subject to it."

Aung San Suu Kyi, "Freedom from Fear," 1991

Aung San

Aung San (1915–1947), father of Aung San Suu Kyi, was the leader of the Burmese independence movement during and after World War II. Aung San was at the center of Burma's nationalist politics from 1936, the year he led a national student strike. In 1940, seeking aid against the British from the Chinese Communist Party, he went to Amoy, where he met Japanese agents who offered to train and arm a Burmese nationalist force. Accepting their offer, Aung San returned to Rangoon and gathered twenty-nine others as the nucleus of an anti-British Independence Army in Bangkok. Under Aung San's command, the army entered Burma with the invading Japanese in January 1942. Aung San became minister of defense and commander of the re-formed Burma Defense Army in August 1942, but he grew disillusioned with the Japanese. He took a leading role in the underground Anti-Fascist Organization in cooperation with the Communist and People's Revolution movements and publicly turned his troops against the Japanese on March 27, 1945. He then became a leading figure in the Anti-Fascist People's Freedom League (AFPFL), which was trying to regain Burma's independence from Britain. After signing the Kandy Agreement, which incorporated his forces into the British Burma Army, Aung San resigned from the military and became president of the AFPFL. Aung San was able to supplant the Communist leaders of the league, thanks to his popularity and their mistakes, and to dominate the organization. In 1946 he became, in effect, prime minister of Burma in the Governor's Executive Council, and in January 1947 he traveled to England where he negotiated the Aung San-Attlee Agreement, which guaranteed Burma's independence in one year. His assassination by a political rival made him a martyr, and Aung San is now Burma's major national hero.

weekly speeches on democracy, human rights, and ethnic tolerance to thousands who gathered there to listen. Her words were heard around the world and a number of nations began to withhold economic aid to Burma because of SLORC's human rights violations. In late 1996 and early 1997 repression against Aung San Suu Kyi and other members of the NLD mounted. The government banned the gatherings at her house, arrested hundreds of NLD party members, prevented journalists and diplomats from speaking with her, and put her under house arrest once more. Despite her isolation from the world, Aung San Suu Kyi has remained a potent symbol of the nonviolent struggle for democracy and human rights. ◆

Barrios de Chamorro, Violeta

1929–PRESENT ● PRESIDENT OF NICARAGUA

Elected president as the representative of the fourteen-party National Opposition Union (Unión Nacional Opositora—UNO) coalition, Violeta Barrios de Chamorro seemed an unlikely candidate. She was born in the southern Nicaraguan province of Rivas to wealthy, landowning parents and attended Catholic schools. In 1950 she married Pedro Joaquín Chamorro Cardenal, a leader of the middle-class opposition to the dictatorship of the Somoza family. Nonetheless, her political participation during the decades of the 1950s, 1960s, and 1970s was confined to that of supportive wife and mother.

In January 1978 Chamorro Cardenal was assassinated, probably by a member of the Somoza family. The assassination set off a wave of strikes and mass insurrection that helped carry the Sandinista Liberation Front (Frente Sandinista de la Liberación Nacional—FSLN) into power. Doña Violeta, as she is called, was named a member of the five-person ruling junta. She resigned from that body less than a year later.

For the remainder of the 1980s, her political participation was confined to criticizing the FSLN and supporting the Contra war from her position as owner of the daily newspaper *La Prensa*, which she inherited from her late husband. Other members of her family took more prominent roles in politics.

Barrios de Chamorro reentered formal politics when she ran for president in 1990. Running on the promises to end the

> *"This is the dawn of a new republic . . . born not of screams and bullets, but of the deepest silence of the Nicaraguan soul—the conscience."*
>
> Violeta Barrios de Chamorro, 1990

Contra war and repair the economy, she portrayed herself as the traditional mother who would reconcile the Nicaraguan family just as she had reconciled her own politically torn family. She won the election with 55 percent of the vote.

Since Barrios de Chamorro's election, the civil war has ended, for the most part. Massive devaluations and cuts in real wages (now among the lowest in the hemisphere) have eliminated hyperinflation. Her relative independence from the United States, whose support was essential in putting her into power, has come as something of a surprise to both her supporters and detractors. Her administration has often chosen to govern in coalition with moderates in the FSLN rather than with the far-right members of the UNO. This choice has hastened the disintegration of the inherently unstable fourteen-party UNO coalition. ◆

1950 ▶ Violeta marries Pedro Joaquín Chamorro Cardenal.

1978 ▶ Chamorro Cardenal is assassinated.

1990 ▶ Barrios de Chamorro becomes president of Nicaragua.

Biko, Steve

1946–1977 ● SOUTH AFRICAN CIVIL RIGHTS LEADER

"Powerlessness breeds a race of beggars who smile at the enemy and swear at him in the sanctity of their toilets; who shout 'Baas' willingly during the day and call the White man a dog in their buses as they go home."

Stephen Biko,
1978

Steve Biko was born in Kingwilliamstown, in eastern Cape Province, South Africa. After graduating from Marianhill in Natal, he attended the University of Natal, where he studied medicine from 1966 to 1972.

Throughout the late 1960s and early 1970s, Biko was the chief proponent of black consciousness, a movement influenced by black liberation movements in the United States. The movement was based on two main principles. First, as Biko wrote in "White Racism and Black Consciousness," the institutional divisions between Blacks and Whites in South Africa were so great that Blacks could not rely on Whites, not even reform-minded liberal Whites, to end apartheid: "Total identification with an oppressed group in a system that forces one group to enjoy privilege and to live on the sweat of another, is impossible." Second, Biko insisted that Blacks must form separate political structures and change the way they understood their own identities. This included awareness of and renewed pride in black culture, religion, and ethical systems.

To this end, Biko helped establish several all-black associations, such as the South African Students Organisation (1969) and the Black People's Convention (1972), a coalition of black organizations. In 1973, as a result of his political activities, the government restricted Biko's movements and forbade him to speak or write publicly. Thereafter he was repeatedly detained by the police. In August 1977, police arrested him for violating his travel ban and held him without trial. In early September, soon after being tortured by the police, he died of a brain hemorrhage. Biko's death became a rallying cry for opponents of apartheid, and he has been commemorated around the world in popular music, drama, and cinema. ◆

> *"The most potent weapon in the hands of the oppressor is the mind of the oppressed."*
> Stephen Biko, 1971

Bolívar, Simón

1783–1830 ● SOUTH AMERICAN POLITICAL & MILITARY LEADER

> *"The distinguishing characteristic of small republics is stability; the character of large republics is mutability."*
> Simón Bolívar, 1815

Born in Caracas to a wealthy landed family with slave-worked cacao plantations, Simón Bolívar received little formal education, although his private tutor, Simón Rodríguez, helped instill in him an admiration for the thinkers of the European Enlightenment. Bolívar traveled to Europe in 1799, and in Madrid in 1802 he married María Teresa Rodríguez de Toro, the daughter of a Caracas-born aristocrat. Upon her death soon after they returned to Venezuela, he made a second trip to Europe, during which he vowed to work for the liberation of Spanish America.

When the Napoleonic invasion of Spain triggered the crisis of the Spanish monarchy in 1808–1810, Bolívar played a minor role in the various attempts to set up a governing **junta** in Caracas. However, once a junta was created, in April 1810, he became an active participant in the revolutionary movement. After heading a diplomatic mission sent to London, he pressed for an outright declaration of independence, which was issued on July 5, 1811.

Having served as a colonial militia officer, though without formal military training, Bolívar was eventually given military command of the key coastal fortress of Puerto Cabello, whose loss in July 1812 served to hasten (though it hardly caused) the collapse of Venezuela's First Republic. When the Venezuelan dictator Francisco de Miranda accepted the inevitable and signed a capitulation to the **royalists**, Bolívar was one of those who angrily arrested him and by preventing his escape in effect turned Miranda over to the Spanish. Bolívar himself soon escaped to Curaçao and from there to Cartagena in New Granada, where he issued the Cartagena Manifesto (the first of his major political documents) and sought assistance for a new attempt to liberate Venezuela. With help from the United Provinces of New Granada, he invaded his homeland in 1813, and in less than three months swept into Caracas. This *campaña admirable* (admirable campaign), as it has been called, first earned Bolívar the title of "Liberator" and made him the acknowledged political as well as military leader of Venezuela.

Bolívar chose not to restore the federal constitution adopted in 1811 by the First Republic, believing that federalism was a dangerously weak form of government. The Second Republic that he then created, a frank military dictatorship, was no more successful than its predecessor, for it was soon being worn down by the assault of royalist guerrilla bands. Appealing to the Venezuelan masses to reject an independence movement whose principal figures (like Bolívar) were drawn from the creole elite, the royalists found a favorable

junta: a political or military group holding power after a revolution.

royalist: a supporter of a king or queen.

response especially among the rough cowboy population (*llaneros*) of the Orinoco plains. Before the end of 1814, Bolívar was again a fugitive in New Granada.

Despite his distaste for federalism, Bolívar repaid the New Granadan federalists grouped in the United Provinces for the aid they had given him by helping them subdue Bogotá, whose leaders favored a strong central authority. But he had little desire to take part in this or other **internecine** conflicts of the New Granadan patriots, especially when the defeat of Napoleon in Europe and restoration of Ferdinand VII to his throne now permitted Spain to redouble its efforts to suppress colonial rebellion. In mid-1815 Bolívar left New Granada, shortly before the arrival of the Spanish expeditionary force that would reconquer most of it for the king. Bolívar went first to Jamaica, where in his "Jamaica Letter" he offered a keen analysis of the present and future state of Spanish America. He next moved to Haiti, where he obtained help from the Haitian government for a new attempt to liberate Venezuela—and for a second attempt when the first ended in failure. By the end of 1816, he had regained a foothold and made contact with revolutionary bands still active in northeastern Venezuela.

internecine: deadly; mutually destructive.

In July 1817, Bolívar's forces seized Angostura (today Ciudad Bolívar), on the lower Orinoco River. The port of Angostura gave Bolívar a link to the outside world, while the Orinoco River system facilitated contact with pockets of patriot resistance in other parts of the Orinoco Basin, including the Apure region, where José Antonio Páez had won increasing numbers of llaneros over to the patriot cause. When Páez accepted Bolívar's leadership, the Liberator gained a critically important ally. As a llanero himself, Páez helped to give the independence struggle a more popular image. So did Bolívar's declaration (issued soon after his return to Venezuela in 1816) making abolition of slavery one of the patriot war aims. The mostly llanero cavalry of Bolívar and Páez could not dislodge the veteran Spanish troops occupying Andean Venezuela, but neither could the royalists make much headway on the Orinoco plains.

Bolívar sought to institutionalize the revolutionary movement by calling elections for a congress, which assembled at Angostura. in February 1819 and ratified his leadership. Yet Bolívar's long-term objectives were not limited to Venezuela.

In May 1819 he embarked on the campaign that took him westward across the llanos and over the Andes to central New Granada, where on 7 August he won the decisive battle of Boyacá. The victory opened the way to Bogotá, occupied three days later, and gave Bolívar control of an area with important reserves of recruits and supplies. It also gave him a victorious momentum that he never entirely lost.

Bolívar placed the New Granadan officer Francisco de Paula Santander in charge of the recently liberated provinces and then returned to Angostura, where, at his urging, in December 1819, the congress proclaimed the union of Venezuela, New Granada, and Quito (Ecuador) a single Republic of Colombia (usually referred to as Gran Colombia). The following year Bolívar turned his attention to the part of Venezuela still under royalist control. Military operations were suspended temporarily by an armistice of November 1820, but the victory at Carabobo, in June 1821, brought the war in Venezuela to a close except for royalist coastal enclaves that held out for another two years.

Meanwhile Gran Colombia was given a constitution by the Congress of Cúcuta, meeting in 1821 on the border between Venezuela and New Granada. The document was not entirely to Bolívar's liking, but he agreed to serve under it when the Congress named him first constitutional president, with Santander as vice president. Since Bolívar intended to continue leading the military struggle against Spain, Santander became acting chief executive in the Colombian capital of Bogotá, charged with organizing the home front and mobilizing resources.

After a local uprising in Guayaquil threw off royalist control of that port city, Bolívar sent his trusted lieutenant Antonio José de Sucre to Ecuador with a Colombian auxiliary force. While Bolívar fought his way through southern New Granada, Sucre penetrated the Ecuadoran highlands. After Sucre defeated the royalists at the battle of Pichincha (May 1822), on the outskirts of Quito, Bolívar entered Quito as well. Continuing to Guayaquil, he obtained its semivoluntary incorporation into Gran Colombia just before he met there with the Argentine liberator José de San Martín. The exact substance of their discussions was never revealed, but it would seem that one thing they disagreed on was how to complete the liberation of Peru, where San Martín controlled the coastal cities but not

1802 His uncle's arrest in Spain cements Bolívar's life-long contempt for monarchy.

1807 Bolívar returns to Venezuela just as rebellion against the Spanish grows.

1813 Bolívar takes over as commander of newly liberated Venezuela.

1814 Spanish royalist forces defeat patriots, triggering five years of war.

1819 Victorious Bolívar establishes Republic of Columbia.

the highlands. Soon afterward, San Martín abandoned Peru, and Bolívar accepted a call to take his place.

Once he reached Peru, in September 1823, Bolívar found Peruvian collaboration to be somewhat fickle, but by mid-1824 he was ready for his last great campaign. On 6 August he scored an important victory at Junín, in the central Peruvian Andes, and on 9 December, in the battle of Ayacucho, his army (commanded by Sucre) obtained the surrender of the main royalist army. In the following weeks Sucre mopped up remnants of royalist resistance in Upper Peru (modern Bolivia).

A few days before Ayacucho, Bolívar, from Lima, issued a call to the Spanish American nations to meet at Panama and create a permanent alliance. He did not have a Pan-American gathering in mind, for he failed to invite the United States, Brazil, and Haiti—even while hoping that Great Britain would send an observer. The United States and Brazil were invited by the administration of Vice President Santander in Bogotá, though in the end they did not take part; and neither did the Panama Congress of 1826 produce the hoped-for league of Spanish American states. Bolívar's design for the congress, however, revealed his ambivalence toward the United States, whose institutions he admired in principle but considered unsuited to Latin American conditions and whose growing power he foresaw as a long-term threat. His interest in having British representation clearly reflected both his belief that British friendship was essential for the security and economic development of the new republics as well as his deep admiration for Great Britain and its system of constitutional monarchy.

Bolívar soon followed Sucre to Upper Peru, where he assumed provisional direction of the newly independent nation that was to name itself Bolivia in his honor. Bolívar did not stay there long, but when the Bolivians invited him to draft their first constitution, he gladly accepted. The proposal that he later submitted (in May 1826) had some progressive features, yet its centerpiece—a president serving for life with power to name his successor—aroused wide criticism as a disguised form of monarchy. Bolívar was gratified that both Bolivia and Peru adopted, at least briefly, the main lines of his scheme. However, his hope that Gran Colombia, too, would adopt some form of it was never realized.

Bolívar's design for Congress revealed his ambivalence toward the United States, whose growing power he foresaw a threat.

Bolívar is revered today as the one person who made the greatest contribution to Spanish American independence.

Bolívar's interest in reforming Colombian institutions was heightened by the rebellion of Páez in April 1826 against the government of Santander, The Liberator returned home before the end of the year, settled Páez's rebellion with a sweeping pardon, and added his support to demands for an immediate reform of the constitution. These actions led to a conflict with Santander, who became a leader of the opposition to Bolívar at the constitutional reform convention that met at Ocaña from April to June 1828. When the sessions ended in deadlock, Bolívar's supporters called on him to assume dictatorial powers to "save the republic," and he agreed to do so.

As dictator, Bolívar rolled back many of the liberal reforms previously enacted in Gran Colombia, including a reduction in the number of monasteries and abolition of Indian tribute. He did not necessarily oppose the reforms in question; he merely decided they were premature. And he did not touch the free-birth law that Gran Colombia had adopted for gradual elimination of slavery.

Bolívar's dictatorship was bitterly opposed by the adherents of Santander, some of whom joined in the abortive September 1828 attempt to assassinate Bolívar. After that, political repression became harsher, and Santander was sent into exile, but scattered uprisings still broke out. Also, serious disaffection arose in Venezuela, which was ideologically the most liberal part of the country as well as generally resentful of being ruled from Bogotá. The last straw was an intrigue by Bolívar's cabinet to recruit a European prince to succeed him as constitutional monarch when the Liberator died or retired. Páez again rose in rebellion in late 1829, and this time Venezuela became a separate nation.

Another convention that met in Bogotá in January 1830 did produce a new constitution, but it could not stem dissolution of the union. Ailing and disheartened, Bolívar stepped down from the presidency in March 1830 and set off for self-imposed exile. He died at Santa Marta before he could board ship, though not before Ecuador seceded from the union and newly autonomous Venezuela prohibited its most famous son from setting foot on its soil.

Though at the end it seemed to Bolívar that his work had been in vain, he is revered today as the one person who made the greatest contribution to Spanish American independence. His contribution was not just military but also political, in the articulation of patriot objectives and the establishment of new states. Moreover, he has been claimed as a precursor by every ideological current, from the revolutionary Left (which admires him for his opposition to slavery and distrust of the United States) to the extreme Right (which approves his authoritarian tendencies): there is something about Bolívar to appeal to every taste and every age. ◆

Boone, Daniel

1734–1820 ● TRAILBLAZER & FRONTERSMAN

"Felicity, the companion of content, is rather found in our own breasts than in the enjoyment of external things; and I firmly believe it requires but a little philosophy to make a man happy in whatever state he is."
Daniel Boone, 1784

With a lust for the wilderness and an adventurous spirit, Daniel Boone epitomizes the American frontiersman. In 1775, he spearheaded the opening of the Wilderness Road leading to Kentucky and there established Boonesborough, the principal Euro-American settlement in the region; in 1799, pushing farther west, he led settlers into what is now Missouri.

Born in Berks County, Pennsylvania, Boone began exploring the backwoods surrounding his home as a young man. At the age of sixteen, he moved with his family to the

Yadkin Valley of North Carolina. Four years later, he volunteered as a wagoner during the French and Indian War. During that service, Boone heard stories from his companion John Findley (or Finley) of abundant game and virgin lands in Kentucky. Boone put his zeal for exploration on hold and returned to the Yadkin Valley to marry Rebecca Bryan on August 14, 1756. Over the next twelve or thirteen years, he concerned himself with providing for his growing family.

In 1768, Findley asked Boone to head an expedition through a gap in the Cumberland Mountains and locate an Indian trail known as the Warrior's Path leading into Kentucky. On May 1, 1769, Boone, Findley, and four others began their journey. Almost without incident the group arrived in Kentucky, which Boone found to be everything he had expected. Soon the explorers had a bounteous load of furs and skins for trade; twice, however, a band of Shawnee Indians stole Boone's skins and supplies. After two years in Kentucky, he returned to his family deeper in debt than when he departed.

In 1773, Boone decided to explore Kentucky again and establish a settlement there. He recruited relatives and neighbors to join his venture. Following an attack by Indians, who killed some of the group including Boone's eldest son, James, the settlers returned home.

Richard Henderson, a lawyer and land speculator, spurred Boone's next attempt at settling Kentucky. Henderson had formed the Transylvania Company and planned to cash in on the West's abundant land after establishing a new American colony in Kentucky. Under Henderson's supervision, Boone negotiated the purchase of a huge tract of land from the Cherokee Indians in 1775 and soon thereafter began cutting a trail from Virginia to Kentucky. The resulting path, known as the Wilderness Road, led settlers to the banks of the Kentucky River where Boone established Fort Boonesborough.

Indian assaults continually plagued Boonesborough. One of the attacks resulted in the capture of Boone's daughter, Jamima, and her two friends. During Boone's surprise attack against the Indian captors, he retrieved the girls unharmed but was himself seized later by Chief Blackfish's Shawnee tribe. In order to free himself, Boone skillfully found favor with the Indian chief, and the tribe adopted him. He soon learned of Blackfish's plan to attack Boonesborough, howev-

1756 Boone marries Rebecca Bryan.

1769 Boone leads an expedition through the Cumberland Mountains into Kentucky.

1773 Boone's son James is killed by Indians.

1775 Boone negotiates a purchase of land from the Cherokee Indians.

1799 The Spanish government issues Boone 850 acres of land in Missouri.

1803 Boone's claim to the land is invalidated following the Louisiana Purchase.

er, and after more than four months of acting as a loyal Shawnee brave, Boone escaped to warn the settlers. Shortly after his return to Fort Boonesborough, the Indians attacked; Boone and the settlers repelled the onslaught. On other occasions, however, the Indians had greater success.

Despite those troubles, settlers continued to pour into Kentucky. Boone became heavily involved in selling portions of his land, yet problems with overlapping claims and his failure to secure proper legal titles led to numerous lawsuits. When he began to feel the crunch of too many people in Kentucky, he led a group of settlers into Missouri, in 1799, where the Spanish government issued him 850 acres of land. Following the Louisiana Purchase in 1803, however, his land transferred from Spanish to American hands and his claim was invalidated. In 1814, the U.S. Congress reissued his original 850 acres as a reward for his effort in opening the West, but Boone's deep indebtedness forced him to sell the land. Despite his unfortunate financial circumstances, Boone continued to hunt, trap, and enjoy the wilderness, which he had been so instrumental in exploring and opening for America's westward push. ◆

Booth, William

1829–1912 ● FOUNDER OF THE SALVATION ARMY

Willliam Booth was born on 10 April 1829 in Nottingham, England, the only son of the four surviving children of Samuel and Mary Moss Booth. The elder Booth, an unsuccessful building contractor, and his wife were no more than conventionally religious, but William, intelligent, ambitious, zealous, and introspective, was earnest about Christianity from an early age. He was converted at the age of fifteen and two years later gave himself entirely to the service of God as the result of the preaching of James Caughey, a visiting American Methodist **revivalist**.

revivalist: an evangelist preacher.

From the age of thirteen until he was twenty-two Booth worked as a pawnbroker's assistant, first in Nottingham and, after 1849, in London. His zeal and compassion for the poor among whom he passed his youth drove him to preach in the streets and, in 1852, to become a licensed Methodist minister. Although Booth had been forced by his father's financial ruin to withdraw from a good grammar school at age thirteen, he read avidly, sought instruction from older ministers, and developed an effective style in speech and writing. In 1855 he married Catherine Mumford, a woman of original and independent intelligence and great moral courage, who had a strong influence on him. They had eight children.

In 1861 Booth began to travel as an independent and successful evangelist, sometimes appearing with Catherine, who publicly advocated an equal role for women in the pulpit. In 1865 the couple established a permanent preaching mission among the poor in the East End of London, in a place where Booth had conducted an especially effective series of meetings. This new endeavor, which soon included small-scale charitable activities for the poor, was known for several years as the Christian Mission. In 1878 the mission was renamed the Salvation Army.

The military structure suggested by the new name appealed to the Booths and to the co-workers they had attracted to their work. Booth remained an orthodox Methodist in doctrine, preaching the necessity of repentance and the promise of holiness—a voluntary submission to God that opened to the believer a life of love for God and for humankind. A premillennialist as well, he was convinced that the fastest way to complete the work of soul winning that would herald the return of Christ was to establish flying squads of enthusiasts who would spread out over the country at his command. The General, as Booth was called, saw evangelism as warfare against Satan over the souls of men; the militant tone of scripture and hymn were not figurative to Booth and his officers, but literal reality. The **autocracy** of military command was well suited to Booth's decisive and uncompromising personality; and it appealed both to his close associates, who were devoted to him and who sought his counsel on every matter, and to his more distant followers, the "soldiers" recently saved from sin, most of them uneducated, new to religion, and eager to fit themselves into the great scheme.

autocracy: a form of government in which one person holds all authority.

William and Catherine were convinced from the beginning of their work in London that it was their destiny to carry the gospel to those untouched by existing religious efforts; to them this meant the urban poor. Their sympathy for these people led them to supplement their evangelism by immediate and practical relief. They launched campaigns to awaken the public to the worst aspects of the life of the poor, such as child prostitution and dangerous and ill-paid piecework in neighborhood match factories. Soup kitchens, men's hostels, and "rescue homes" for converted prostitutes and unwed mothers became essential parts of the Army's program.

In 1890 William Booth published *In Darkest England and the Way Out*, which contained a full-fledged program to uplift and regenerate the "submerged tenth" of urban society. The heart of the scheme was a sequence of "city colonies" (urban missions for the unemployed), "land colonies" (where rest would be combined with retraining in agricultural skills), and "overseas colonies" (assisted emigration to America or one of Britain's colonies). The book also explained existing programs like the rescue homes and promised many new schemes in addition to the colonies: the "poor man's lawyer," the "poor man's bank," clinics, industrial schools for poor children, missing-persons inquiries, a "matrimonial bureau," and a poor-man's seaside resort, "Whitechapel-by-the-Sea." The *Darkest England* scheme, which was widely endorsed, represents an important turning point in public support for the Army.

Booth would not have claimed to be a saint in any conventional sense, and there are certainly controversial aspects to his life and work. Always overworked and chronically unwell, he often had strained relationships with his close associates, especially after the death of Catherine in 1890. Many of his statements about the Army overlooked the fact that much of its program was not original. He offered no criticism of the basic social and political structure that surrounded him, and his confidence in the desirability of transferring the urban unemployed to the more healthful and "natural" environment of the country was romantic and impractical. Yet the fact remains that Booth combined old and new techniques of evangelism and social relief in an immensely effective and appealing program. He displayed great flexibility in adapting measures to the needs of the moment, altering or

1852 Booth becomes a licensed Methodist minister.

1861 Booth begins traveling as an evangelist.

1865 Booth and his wife establish a mission in London.

1878 Booth's mission is renamed the Salvation Army.

1890 Booth publishes *In Darkest England and the Way Out*.

1912 Booth delivers his last public sermon.

eliminating any program, however dear to him, if it had ceased to function. He abandoned anything in the way of theology (like sacraments) or social theory (like the then still popular distinction between the "worthy" and "unworthy" poor that might confuse his followers or dampen their zeal for soul winning and good works.

Guileless and unsentimental, Booth showed a rare and genuine single-mindedness in the cause of evangelism. His last public message, delivered three months before his death on August 20, 1912, is still cherished by the Army that is his most fitting memorial. The concluding words of the message were these: "While there yet remains one dark soul without the light of God, I'll fight—I'll fight to the very end!" ◆

Bradley, Omar Nelson

1893–1981 ● AMERICAN GENERAL

"In war there is no second prize for the runner-up."

Omar Bradley, 1948

Born in Clark, Missouri, Omar Bradley overcame the disadvantages of a modest family background to enter the United States military academy at West Point. Upon graduation in 1915 he was commissioned a second lieutenant in the artillery corps but saw no action in World War I. Nonetheless he rose to the rank of major.

Between the world wars Bradley pursued a career as an instructor of mathematics and military science and tactics at several institutions, among them West Point. As commander of the Fort Benning Infantry School, in Georgia, he impressed General George C. Marshall with his capabilities and innovative approach. Marshall's patronage enabled Bradley to rise through the ranks.

In 1938, Bradley was appointed to the general staff in Washington, D. C., and therefore did not see active duty in World War II until 1943. As commander of the U.S. Army Second Corps under General Dwight D. Eisenhower, Bradley led his troops in the final stages of the campaign to drive the Germans out of North Africa. He then served as deputy commander to General George Patton in the invasion of Sicily.

Bradley's grasp of frontline combat and his well proven talents as an officer and tactician prompted Eisenhower, to give him a key role in planning D-Day. In June 1944 Bradley led the U.S. First Army across the English Channel to storm the Normandy beaches.

Having succeeded in securing a bridgehead on the continent, Bradley was placed in command of all U.S. forces (1,300,000 men) in northwestern Europe. It was the largest contingent of troops ever under the control of one American officer. The relationships he cultivated with soldiers in the field helped him understand the mentality of men such as "the rifleman who trudges into battle knowing that statistics are stacked against his survival." General Patton did not favor Bradley's cautious attitude in advancing his troops.

Breaking out from the Normandy salient, Bradley's army swept across France toward Paris, only to be met by a surprise German counteroffensive. Conflict arose in turn with General Eisenhower who wanted to put some of Bradley's army under the command of British general Bernard Montgomery. These confrontations climaxed during the Battle of the Bulge, during which, although threatening resignation, Bradley held his own and led his forces across the Rhine into Germany. There his troops made the first Allied contact with advance units of the Red Army.

Shortly before the war ended in March 1945 Bradley's contribution to the Allies was recognized with his promotion to full general. After the war he carried out important work as

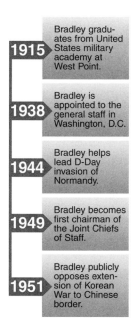

1915 Bradley graduates from United States military academy at West Point.

1938 Bradley is appointed to the general staff in Washington, D.C.

1944 Bradley helps lead D-Day invasion of Normandy.

1949 Bradley becomes first chairman of the Joint Chiefs of Staff.

1951 Bradley publicly opposes extension of Korean War to Chinese border.

administrator of veterans' affairs. In 1949 he became the first chairman of the Joint Chiefs of Staff—the highest position attainable in the U.S. defense establishment. In 1951 he opposed General Douglas MacArthur's extension of the Korean War to the Chinese border, saying that this was "the wrong war, at the wrong place, at the wrong time, and with the wrong enemy." That same year Bradley's wartime memoirs, *A Soldier's Story*, were published; they contained harsh criticism of his colleagues, particularly General Montgomery. After retirement from the army in 1953, Bradley turned to business. ◆

Braille, Louis

1809–1852 ● DEVELOPER OF READING AND WRITING SYSTEMS FOR THE BLIND

Louis Braille was the son of a harness maker from Coupvray, France. When he was only three years old, while playing in his father's shop, an awl slipped off the table and struck him in the left eye. Within weeks the ensuing infection left Braille completely blind.

Since few opportunities then existed for the blind, Braille's father insisted that his son pursue a standard education in the village school. With his phenomenal memory, Braille surpassed his sighted classmates and was awarded a scholarship to the prestigious National Institute for Blind Children. There, too, he excelled at his academic studies and took up piano and the organ. At the institute's library, a collection of only three titles, each consisting of twenty volumes with large, **embossed** letters, Braille taught himself to read by running his fingers over the words. In just a few years, Braille was teaching the younger students the academic and musical skills he had mastered.

Braille's stay at the institute coincided with the visit of Charles Barbier, an artillery captain who had developed a system of night reading for soldiers. The advantages of Barbier's

embossed: a pattern that stands out from the surface.

alphabet, a series of raised dots and dashes, was apparent to Braille, and he immediately began to modify it. He abandoned the dashes and placed all the dots in a rectangular grid measuring two by six dots. This new system, first published in 1829 and revised in 1837, included all the letters of the French alphabet (W was added later), punctuation, mathematical symbols, and even musical notation.

Although "Braille" was soon adopted by the institute, its author was better known as a musician and a minor composer. Not long after the death of the institute's director, "Braille" was abandoned in favor of the earlier, more tedious, embossed letters. Braille, now suffering from tuberculosis, was quietly forgotten, only to be rediscovered accidentally. A talented blind musician, a former student of Braille, was asked to play in one of the fashionable salons of Paris. After a moving performance, the girl unassumingly explained that all the credit must go to her teacher, who had developed the system by which she had learned and who was now dying. News of the forgotten system created a stir in the audience, and national recognition was soon forthcoming. The National Institute for Blind Children reintroduced its use in 1854, two years after Braille's death. In 1952 he was reburied in the Pantheon in Paris. ◆

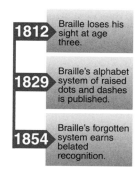

1812 ▸ Braille loses his sight at age three.

1829 ▸ Braille's alphabet system of raised dots and dashes is published.

1854 ▸ Braille's forgotten system earns belated recognition.

Bruce, Robert

1274–1329 ● SCOTTISH KING & NATIONAL HERO

Robert Bruce bore the same name as his grandfather, a claimant to the Scottish throne after the death of Margaret Maid of Norway in 1290. Edward I of England supported the rival claim of John Baliol in return for recognition of English **suzerainty**. Baliol, however, had no intention of paying fealty to Edward. In 1295 he signed the Auld Alliance with France in a bid to assert Scottish independence. Edward responded by devastating the country and

suzerainty: a government with control over a dependent state.

capturing its royal symbols, among them the Stone of Destiny, believed to have been Jacob's pillow, upon which Scottish kings were crowned. With Baliol exiled to Normandy the revolt was resumed by William Wallace and supported by the native Scottish aristocracy led by Robert Bruce and John Comyn. Edward's military prowess and personal rivalry among the Scottish nobles doomed the revolt. After a crushing defeat at Falkirk in 1298, Wallace fled to France, leaving Bruce and Comyn in command of the disheartened forces. Rivalry among the two resulted in Comyn nearly killing Bruce in a brawl in 1299. At the same time, Bruce shared the Anglo-Norman descent of the English nobility and possessed extensive estates as far south as London. His defection to Edward in 1302, therefore, came as no surprise. In fact, Bruce believed that it was not yet time for Scotland to rise in revolt.

For four years, Bruce feigned fealty to England. By 1306, believing that the disastrous defeats of the past were forgotten, he approached several rebel leaders to probe their readiness to resume hostilities. At a church in Dumfries he described his plans to Comyn, but the animosity between them still lingered. Threatened with betrayal, Bruce killed Comyn. Bruce now faced opposition from both Edward's and Comyn's supporters. Although the country was as yet ill-prepared for war, Bruce fled to Scone and, with the support of the local clergy, declared himself king (Robert I).

When news of the revolt reached Edward, he swore never to rest until Bruce had been punished. Bruce and his supporters were hounded incessantly; once captured, they were treated callously. A brother was hanged and a sister was suspended in a cage from the walls of Berwick Castle. Only at the last minute was Bruce's twelve-year-old daughter spared a similar fate. Bruce himself only narrowly eluded capture. The Scottish MacDougal family still possesses a brooch supposedly ripped off Bruce's shoulder in battle. The fugitive king was in despair when, hiding in a cave, he watched a spider spinning its web. Swinging from a slender strand, it narrowly missed the cave's wall several times before finally succeeding in attaching the thread. The spider's perseverance was said to have inspired Bruce to continue the struggle.

His fortune turned upon the death of Edward I in 1307. The new king, Edward II, lacked his father's military acumen, while under Wallace, Bruce had mastered the necessary guer-

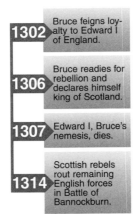

1302 Bruce feigns loyalty to Edward I of England.

1306 Bruce readies for rebellion and declares himself king of Scotland.

1307 Edward I, Bruce's nemesis, dies.

1314 Scottish rebels rout remaining English forces in Battle of Bannockburn.

rilla tactics for fighting larger forces. Major assaults were often conducted at night. Bruce's men, disguised by dark cloaks, would creep up to the walls of English castles, scale them, and force an entry. Even some of his opponents began supporting Bruce covertly. A secret entrance to Edinburgh Castle was revealed by an aristocrat who used it to visit his mistress in town.

By 1314 only the countryside surrounding Stirling remained in English hands. Bruce's brother Edward, in command of the besieged local castle, agreed to surrender to the English if he was not relieved within a year. British chroniclers claim that one hundred thousand English troops surrounded the castle. Twenty thousand is more likely, and no less a significant adversary to Bruce's six thousand men. Edward, however, disregarded the local topography, vital for Bruce's guerrilla tactics. The road to Stirling ran through a forest, below which was a boggy field traversed by several sluggish streams known as burns. By one such stream lay the village of Bannock. In the first day of the Battle of Bannockburn, Bruce repelled Edward twice. Scottish troops attacked the English horses; their enormous corpses prevented English mobility in the bog. On the second day Edward mistakenly placed his archers behind his soldiers, ultimately denying them the protection of a hail of arrows. While the Scottish decimated the imposing English forces, Edward fled so hastily that his contemporaries claim he could not even "make water." Scotland was now completely independent.

Although Bruce had the support of the Scottish clergy, the pope still supported English suzerainty even after Edward himself disclaimed his rights to Scotland in 1323. Bruce pleaded for papal recognition in the Declaration of Arbroath (1320), but it was not received until 1328. Shortly after, Robert Bruce died, possibly of leprosy. ◆

Bruce's men, disguised by dark cloaks, would creep up to the walls of English castles, scale them, and force an entry.

Byrd, Richard Evelyn

1888–1957 ● EXPLORER & AVIATOR

> *"To think men toiled for years over this ice, a few hard-won miles a day; and we travel luxuriously a hundred miles an hour. How motors have changed the burdens of man!"*
>
> Richard Evelyn Byrd

Richard Evelyn Byrd was born in Winchester, Virginia, and at age fourteen he wrote in his diary that he would someday explore the North Pole. A year later he was excited to learn that the Wright brothers had flown an airplane. From that day forward Byrd kept the themes of exploration and aviation intertwined with his life's goals.

Byrd graduated from the U.S. Naval Academy in 1912 and went on to become an aviator. He spent World War I teaching flying and also invented several aviation instruments. After the war he was as signed to the MacMillan Arctic Expedition in Greenland. On May 26, 1926, Byrd and his aviator friend Floyd Bennett made what is believed to be the first flight over the North Pole. On that day he wrote in his log, before arriving at the North Pole: "To think men toiled for years over this ice, a few hard-won miles a day; and we travel luxuriously a hundred miles an hour. How motors have changed the burdens of man!" Both aviators received the Congressional Medal of Honor for their historic flight. In 1927, accompanied by a third man, they flew nonstop from New York to Paris.

The fame achieved by these two exploits at the time enabled Byrd to raise $800,000 to fund an expedition to the

Antarctic. Major funding came from wealthy philanthropists, including John D. Rockefeller Jr. and Edsel Ford. Contributions were accepted from the general public as well, including $4.35 from Byrd's eight-year-old son, who had worked all summer to raise the money. The 1928 expedition included forty-two men, four airplanes, powerful radio transmitters, a motor tractor, ninety-five Greenland huskies, and a correspondent from the *New York Times*. Four ships transported the 665 tons of cargo needed for the expedition.

Byrd constructed a base village on the Ross Ice Shelf, known as Little America. From Little America they explored as much surface area as practical and set up an advance base. On November 28, 1929, Byrd and three companions flew the expedition's Ford Tri-motor from the advance base over the 10,500-foot Hump of Liv's Glacier on the way to the South Pole. The next day they became the first to fly over the South Pole. To honor his friend Floyd Bennett, who had died in 1928, Byrd named the airplane in his memory and dropped an American flag weighted with a rock from Floyd Bennett's grave on the South Pole. Byrd flew a circular course around the pole and experienced the rapid crossing of all twenty-four-hour time zones as they converged on the pole. He also noted some confusion in that every direction was northward and the positions of east and west had reversed.

Byrd named a newly discovered mountain range Edsel Ford Range and a large plateau Rockefeller Plateau, in recognition of his chief funders. A large tract of land was named Marie Byrd land in honor of his wife's support for him. For his heroic efforts Byrd was promoted to the rank of rear admiral.

Funding for his second Antarctic expedition was far more difficult, as the stock market crash of 1929 had affected the generosity of his patrons. He raised only $150,000 in cash for the 1934 expedition. Considerable equipment and supplies were donated by industrialists in return for being allowed to advertise that the Byrd expedition was using their products. During this expedition he and two others traveled south of Little America to establish a small base from which to monitor winter weather, but due to the loss en route of a large tractor, only enough supplies to support two men arrived at the station. Byrd believed that three men could spend an Antarctic winter in isolation but that two would only get on

1926 Byrd and his friend make the first flight over the North Pole.

1928 Byrd organizes first expedition to the Antarctic.

1929 Byrd becomes the first to fly over the South Pole.

1934 Byrd begins his perilous stay alone through an Antarctic winter.

Roald Amundsen

Roald Amundsen, a Norwegian explorer, was the first person to reach the South Pole. His original goal was to become the first person to reach the North Pole; he was shattered when Robert Peary beat him there. After some consideration however, Amundsen simply changed his plans and decided to head for the South Pole. In January 1911, Amundsen and his team set up a base camp 480 miles away from the Pole. Because the harsh Antarctic winter was approaching, Amundsen was forced to delay any attempt to reach the Pole for at least eight months. During the long winter, the explorers reviewed their supplies and discovered ways to lighten their load. As summer neared, the men were anxious to begin their journey. On October 20, 1911, Amundsen and four companions set out for the Pole. Four sledges pulled by 52 dogs carried provisions for four months. Keeping to a strict routine, they traveled for five hours and covered about twenty miles each day. Two hours were spent digging a snow cavern, and the remainder of the time resting. Nearing the Pole, steep slopes blocked their passage. Since no route was found around the towering mountain range, Amundsen decided to climb it. Upon reaching the top, most of the dogs were so weakened by exhaustion that they had to be shot. On December 14, 1911, Admundsen and his team reached the South Pole, where they planted a Norwegian flag. Amundsen reached his base camp safely on January 25. In 1928, while searching for a lost Italian ship in the Arctic, Amundsen's plane disappeared and was never found.

each other's nerves. He therefore decided to stay by himself, and wrote the book *Alone* to describe his experiences.

After three months at the station Byrd almost died from carbon monoxide fumes from a faulty burner, as the fresh-air ventilators had become blocked with snow, but he recognized the problem and took corrective measures. Additionally, gas fumes from his radio's generator were making him ill. Although he did not disclose the fact that his health was failing, fellow expedition members at Little America sensed his condition from his radio contacts. A rescue team arrived and stayed two months nursing him back to health before returning to home base.

Byrd took part in two more Antarctic expeditions in 1946–1947 and 1955–1956 and flew over the South Pole during each of these expeditions. ◆

Carter, Jimmy

1924–PRESENT ● U.S. PRESIDENT
& HUMANITARIUM

"No poor, rural, weak, or black person should ever again have to bear the additional burden of being deprived of the opportunity for an education, a job, or simple justice."

Jimmy Carter, 1971

James Earl Carter Jr. was born on October 1, 1924, in Plains, Georgia. His father, Earl, was a successful local businessman who operated a brokerage business in peanuts; his mother, Lillian Gordon, was a registered nurse. Bright, disciplined, and self-directed, Jimmy graduated from high school in 1941 near the top of his class. In 1946, he graduated from the United States Naval Academy and married Rosalynn Smith. He spent the next seven years in the Navy, most of the time working for Captain Hyman Rickover on the *Seawolf*, a **prototype** of the nuclear submarine.

prototype: first or original model.

In 1953 Carter resigned from the Navy and returned to Plains, where he turned his father's faltering peanut business around and became a successful businessman and community leader. In 1962, he ran successfully for the Georgia Senate and quickly established a reputation as a moderate progressive supporting "good government" measures and educational reform. In 1966 he gave up his seat to run unsuccessfully for governor.

In 1970, he made a second bid for governor, this time winning by appealing to segregationist and white supremacist elements in the state. After assuming office, however, he established a reputation as a racial moderate and a reform leader.

By the end of his second year in office, Carter had established a solid record of achievement; in 1971 *Time* featured him
on its cover as representative of a new, progressive leadership in
the South. The next year, Carter decided to prepare for a run for
the presidency, despite the fact that he was virtually unknown
outside Georgia. After a tough campaign, Carter defeated Republican incumbent Gerald Ford by a narrow margin, and
become the thirty-ninth president of the United States.

After his inauguration, polls showed that the American
people trusted Carter. People hoped that because he was a
Washington outsider, he would bring a new way a doing business to government. However, most of Carter's domestic initiatives were hampered by his failure to build close ties with
congressional leaders. Early in his presidency, he angered
Congress when he fulfilled a campaign promise to cut the
worst examples of wasteful govenment spending by eliminating funds for construction projects in seventeen states.
Senators and representatives from these states were furious at
this attack on their pet projects. Carter's decision to pardon

Habitat for Humanity International

Habitat for Humanity International is a nonprofit, ecumenical Christian housing ministry
dedicated to the elimination of substandard housing and homelessness worldwide.
Founded in 1976 by Millard and Linda Fuller, Habitat is now one of the top twenty house
builders in the United States, and the largest among nonprofits. Through volunteer labor
and tax-deductible contributions of money and materials, Habitat builds and rehabilitates
houses with the help of partner families, who then are able to purchase these homes
through no-interest loans. Habitat has built more than 65,000 houses around the world,
with more than 1,300 affiliates located throughout the United States and more than 250
international affiliates located in 59 other countries. Since 1984, former President Jimmy
Carter and his wife, Rosalynn, have been involved with Habitat for Humanity International
as leaders of the Jimmy Carter Work Project (JCWP). Through the Work Project, the
Carters lead teams of volunteers for one week each year helping to build or renovate
houses across the United States and internationally. In addition, the Carters work with the
organization to help raise funds, publicize its works, and recruit other volunteers.

Vietnam War draft evaders further exacerbated tensions between the White House and Congress. Meanwhile, the United States economy, which had shown signs of recovery during the first half of 1977 started to turn downward. The rate of economic growth declined, and unemployment and inflation began to rise.

Carter's efforts in international relations were somewhat more successful. He won a major victory in March 1978, when the Senate ratified the Panama Canal treaties, ceding the canal to Panama at the end of 1999, but giving the United States the right to use military force if necessary to keep the waterways open. In September 1978, Carter recorded the most important foreign policy achievement of his administration when Egyptian president Anwar Sadat and Israeli prime minister Menachem Begin signed the Camp David Accords, promising an end to thirty years of hostilities between Israel and Egypt.

Developments in Iran and Afghanistan at the end of 1979 dominated the last year of Carter's presidency. In November 1979, radicals in Iran invaded the U.S. embassy in Tehran, captured sixty American employees, and held most as hostages. The Carter administration was unable to secure the release of the hostages and a United States military rescue attempt in April 1980 failed due to miscalculation and mishap. During this period Carter was also faced with an invasion of Afghanistan by the Soviet Union. He responded to the Soviet invasion with a trade embargo and a boycott of the 1980 Olympics Games in Moscow.

Carter was challenged for the 1980 Democratic presidential nomination by Senator Edward Kennedy of Massachusetts, who was supported by discontented liberals. Carter won the Democratic nomination, yet the Iranian hostage crisis, together with the slumping economy, damaged Carter's bid for reelection. He was defeated decisively by the former governor of California, Ronald Reagan.

Although Carter's four years as president were largely viewed as unsuccessful, his public stature has grown significantly in the years since he left office.

Immediately following Reagan's inauguration on January 20, Carter, Rosalynn, and their daughter, Amy, returned to Plains. The next day, at President Reagan's invitation, Carter flew to Germany to welcome back to freedom the Iranian hostages. It was an exhilarating moment for Carter, but it was

1946 Carter graduates from West Point Military Academy.

1970 Carter is elected governor of Georgia.

1973 Habitat for Humanity is established.

1976 Carter is elected president of the United States.

1980 Carter looses his bid for reelection to Ronald Reagan.

1986 Carter establishes the Carter Center.

1990 Carter is awarded the Liberty Medal.

Carter has traveled throughout the world, promoting improved agricultural methods and better health care in the most poverty-stricken countries.

followed by a difficult period of transition from president to private citizen. Carter had not recovered from the shock of his defeat, and he was faced with serious financial problems. His principal financial asset, his peanut warehouse business, which had been in a blind trust while he was president, was broke, and he was deeply in debt. After a few months, however, the Carters settled into a new routine. They sold the warehouse business, and both Carters signed lucrative book contracts, thereby ensuring their financial security.

During the first half of the 1980s, the former president all but vanished from the national political scene. Carter spent most of his time writing his memoirs, teaching at Emory University, and raising funds for the Jimmy Carter Library, Museum, and Presidential Center in Atlanta.

Determined that the Carter complex be more than a monument to his presidency, the former president has made the Center a locus of research and social and political activism, with programs on such diverse problems as human rights, preventive health care, the world environment, and conflict resolution in the Middle East, Latin America, and Africa. To further its work, he has traveled throughout the world, promoting improved agricultural methods and better health care in the world's most poverty-stricken countries, especially in Africa. In addition, he has been increasingly active in Habitat for Humanity, a charitable organization started in 1973 to provide housing for the poor.

Since the mid 1980s, Carter has also been publicly and politically more visible. Beginning around 1985, he began to speak out more frequently on national issues and to criticize the Reagan administration's policies and programs, such as its SDI and its policy of "constructive engagement" with South Africa. He has also played an increasinaly important role as an elder statesman, attempting to mediate the long-running war in Ethiopia between that country's Marxist government and Eritrean rebels (1989) and monitoring elections in Panama (1989) and in Nicaragua (1990).

But the Middle East remained the region of most concern to Carter. As he watched the promise of the Camp David accords of 1978 go largely unfulfilled, he became publicly critical of Israel for its refusal to stop building settlements on the West Bank and to grant Palestinians greater autonomy. He was also a proponent of an international peace conference to mediate the Arab-Israeli dispute and spoke out strongly aginst military intervention in the Persian Gulf following Iraq's invasion of Kuwait in 1990.

As Carter has become publicly more active, the media have paid more attention to his activities as a private citizen, and he has gained a degree of popularity and stature with the American people that would have been hard to imagine when he left office in 1981. In May 1990, he was awarded the Liberty Medal and a $100,000 prize for his involvement in "issues of liberty around the world." Commentators frequently refer to him as a model of a successful former president, and his reputation as one of the nation's best ex-presidents continues to grow. ◆

Chávez, César

1927–1993 ● LABOR ACTIVIST

> "When a man or woman, young, or old, takes a place on the picket line for even a day or two, he will never be the same again. He has confirmed his own humanity. Through non-violence, he has confirmed the humanity of others."
>
> César Chávez

César Estrada Chávez was a Mexican-American labor activist. He is known for his years of tireless work to improve the lives of migrant farm workers through nonviolent action. In the mid-1900s he led one of the most successful agricultural boycotts in American history. Chávez

"When the man who feeds the world by toiling in the fields is himself deprived of the basic rights of feeding, sheltering, and caring for his own family, the whole community of man is sick."

César Chávez

1952 Chávez joins the Community Service Organization.

1962 Chávez forms the National Farm Workers Association.

1965 NFWA merges with the Agricultural Workers Organizing Committee; strike begins.

1966 United Farm Workers Organizing Committee is established.

1970 Strike ends when grape growers sign a contract with the union.

founded what is now the United Farm Workers of America (UFW), the first successful union of agricultural workers in the United States.

At the time Chávez founded his union in the 1960s farm workers in California earned an average of $1.50 per hour and had no benefits or rights to challenge abuses by employers. Unionization eventually helped bring about wage increases, medical benefits, pensions, and other benefits to farm workers.

Chávez was born on March 31, 1927, near Yuma, Arizona to Juana and Librado Chávez. He lived on the family's 160-acre farm in Arizona until he was 10, when the family lost the farm due to the effects of the Depression. His family then moved to California to become migrant farm workers. They lived in poverty and resided in tents or shacks in various migrant labor camps. César attended dozens of different schools during his youth because his family was always on the move. He finally graduated from eighth grade at the age of fifteen, when he quit school to work full-time in the fields and help support his family. At the age of seventeen, Chávez joined the U.S. Navy and served two years during World War II. He then returned to migrant work and married Helen Fabela in 1948. They had eight children.

Chávez first became involved in organizing workers in 1952, when he joined the Community Service Organization (CSO). He spent the next ten years helping to register Mexican American voters and aiding them on immigration, welfare, and other issues. He quit the CSO in 1962 after the organization refused to support his proposal of a union movement for farm workers. He then formed the National Farm Workers Association (NFWA).

To build membership for his union, Chávez spent several months in the fields and towns of California, convincing workers to join the union. Building membership and getting dues from a migratory population was difficult, but by 1965, the association had 1,700 members. By that time he had also succeeded in persuading two crop growers to raise worker wages. In 1965, NFWA joined forces with the Agricultural Workers Organizing Committee (AWOC), part of the AFL-CIO, and embarked on one of the longest and most successful strikes in labor history. The strike was against California grape growers and it stemmed from protests over wage inequities.

In 1966, the two unions merged and formed the United Farm Workers Organizing Committee (UFWOC). After the merger, California's wine grape growers agreed to accept the UFWOC as the collective bargaining agent for the grape pickers. However, the table grape growers refused to negotiate with the UFWOC. Chávez reacted to their opposition by organizing a nationwide boycott against all California table grapes. The boycott was a tremendous success. An estimated 17 million Americans stopped buying grapes because of it. Finally, after losing millions of dollars, the growers agreed to sign a contract with the union in 1970 and the strike came to an end.

Over the years Chávez continued his efforts to organize farm laborers and obtain union contracts for them, and he remained committed to obtaining results through nonviolent means. He often urged consumers to boycott farm products produced by nonunion workers and sometimes used fasting as a nonviolent means of protest. In one instance after some Mexican-American strikers became tired with a drawn-out strike and threatened to use force against crop growers, Chávez went on a hunger strike, vowing not to eat until union members pledged themselves to nonviolence once more. Twenty-five days later, when he felt he had gotten his message across the ranks, he ended his fast.

Chávez was known for his gentle manner, his sincerity, and his religious devotion, and he won the admiration of many respected civil rights advocates of his time. Chávez died in his sleep on April 23, 1993, while on union business in Arizona. ◆

Chávez often urged consumers to boycott farm products produced by nonunion workers.

Churchill, Sir Winston Leonard Spencer

1874–1965 ● BRITISH STATESMAN

"History will be kind to me for I intend to write it."

Sir Winston Churchill

Winston Churchill was born in Blenheim Palace, Oxfordshire, the eldest son of Lord Randolph Churchill and his American wife, Jennie. His father was a leading Conservative politician who became chancellor of the exchequer but his career ended in ruin after he continually attacked his own government's policies. Churchill had a boundless admiration for his father, taking pride in his achievements, suffering with his political eclipse and, in 1906, writing his biography. The closeness he felt to his mother was not diminished by her hectic schedule of entertaining, leaving little time for her children. When a brother, Jack, was born in 1880, Churchill was delighted and they became inseparable friends. They loved playing with toy soldiers, arraying vast armies of tin against each other.

Churchill's early schooling did not proceed smoothly. He was accepted at the famous public school of Harrow despite poor results in the examinations, as the headmaster recognized his potential. In subjects he enjoyed, like English and history, he excelled, but in those he saw no use for, such as Latin, he made no effort and failed. Having already decided that he wanted to emulate his father and enter politics, he was confident he would succeed; the army offered a means of achieving the fame that would be a springboard to the House of Commons.

The first obstacle was failure in examinations for Sandhurst officer training college. After several attempts, he finally passed. He took well to the arduous training and boisterous social life of the cadets and graduated with an honorable place in his class. Family connections secured a posting as a lieutenant in the prestigious cavalry regiment, the Fourth Hussars. He was eager to see action and get a chance to make his name, but there were no opportunities while his regiment remained in England. He utilized his father's contacts and received permission from the government to travel to Cuba to observe the insurrection against Spanish rule. His reports from the front were published in the *Daily Graphic* and his writing met with acclaim.

Over the next few years Churchill saw action on the northwest frontier of India, in the Sudan, and South Africa. Everywhere he showed himself a capable officer and displayed great heroism, taking part in fierce hand to hand fighting in the Sudan and in South Africa, and making a daring escape from captivity in a Boer prisoner of war camp. His accounts of his experiences were eagerly bought in article and book form.

In 1900 he was elected as Conservative member of Parliament for Oldham on his second attempt. His concern for the plight of the poor and his advocacy of free trade distanced him ideologically from the Conservatives and in 1904 he joined the Liberal party. It was a timely move, for in 1905 the liberals came to power and he attained his first ministerial appointment as undersecretary of state at the Colonial Office. He discharged his duties well and was acclaimed for his role in the negotiations to secure a lasting settlement in South Africa. He served in several different capacities in the Liberal governments of 1905–1916 and played a prominent role in the development of its forward-looking welfare program. As home secretary he aroused the wrath of those campaigning to extend the vote to women and was attacked at Bristol railway station by an angry **suffragette** wielding a horsewhip; she almost pushed him over onto the track.

During his time at the admiralty he encouraged the formation of a fleet air arm and was commended on the readiness of the naval reserve when war began in 1914. In 1915 his enthusiasm for the assault on the Turkish garrison controlling

> *"Never give in, never give in, never, never, never, never—in nothing, great or small, large or petty—never give in except to convictions of honor and good sense."*
> Churchill, 1941

suffragette: a female activist who supports voting rights for women.

the entrance to the Black Sea (the Gallipoli Campaign) proved a major setback when the attack failed with heavy loss of life. He resigned from the government and went to serve with the army in France. Once more he showed no fear of the enemy's bullets, never ducking and mocking officers who did, telling them that by the time they ducked the bullet was well behind them. He did a wonderful job of restoring the morale of his battle-weary company. Though a strict disciplinarian, he had no taste for giving out punishments and took a keen interest in doing what he could to improve the men's rations and rid the ranks of lice.

In 1908 he had married the beautiful Clementine Hozier, with whom he enjoyed over fifty years of loyal companionship. Financial factors were the cause of numerous differences, with Churchill continually living beyond his means and then writing to cover rapidly accumulating debts. He had expensive tastes in cars, food and drink, and cigars, to list just some of his better known indulgences.

The establishment of a coalition government in 1916 brought Churchill back in the cabinet at the ministery of munitions. He took a dedicated interest in every detail of the ministry's work and again showed a visionary instinct, recognizing the importance of the tank and turning cavalry regiments into tank regiments.

From 1918 until 1929 Churchill held various ministries in several governments. As colonial secretary (1921–1922), he created the **emirate** of Transjordan and negotiated the Irish treaty of 1921. Disillusioned with Liberal support for the 1924 socialist government, he returned to the Conservative party and served as chancellor of the **exchequer** for five years. He brought to the office his now well-honed administrative skills, combined with a popular touch exemplified by his broadcasting on the BBC radio, explaining government financial policies in simple, lucid terms.

The Conservative defeat of 1929 led to ten years away from the center of power. He had more time to devote to painting and writing, producing a life of his illustrious ancestor, the Duke of Marlborough and the story of his own early life, among other works. He remained active in the House of Commons, becoming almost a lone voice warning of the growing power of Nazi Germany and calling for rearmament as a deterrent. He fiercely opposed the accepted policy of

emirate: region governed by an Arab or Turkish leader called an emir.

exchequer: department of finance and revenue in the British government.

appeasement, attacking the 1938 Munich accord as a capitulation, a temporary peace at Czechoslovakia's expense. It was "a total and unmitigated defeat . . . All is over. Silent, mournful, abandoned Czechoslovakia recedes into the darkness."

So strong was the desire for peace at any price that Churchill was excluded from government office out of fear of offending the Germans. When war came in 1939 and his warnings proved correct, he was invited back into the cabinet as first lord of the admiralty. In May 1940 Prime Minister Neville Chamberlain was forced from office at a dangerous moment, as Adolf Hitler was advancing through western Europe, and Churchill replaced him, a symbol of the aggressive bulldog spirit the nation felt the crisis demanded. Posters from 1940 showed him in a bulldog guise, fiercely standing guard over the map of Britain. The role he played in building up the nation's morale was crucial. His defiant V-for-victory sign and his speeches in Parliament and over the radio were rallying cries that brought out the very best spirit in his nation. The tone was set on his opening address as prime minister: "I have nothing to offer you but blood, toil, tears and sweat . . . You ask what is our policy? I will say: It is to wage war, by sea, land and air, with all our might and all the strength God can give us: to wage war against a monstrous tyranny, never surpassed in the dark, lamentable catalogue of human crime . . . What is our aim? I can answer in one word: Victory—victory at all costs. . . ."

Shortly after Churchill came to power, all Britons had to leave Europe via Denmark and Great Britain was subjected to bombardment by the German air force as Hitler prepared to invade. Thanks to the British air force the invasion never came, but for two years Britain stood alone against Nazi-occupied Europe and Churchill was the symbol and voice, as well as the power, behind fortress Britain.

In addition to offering inspiring words, he also visited bomb-damaged cities and military installations. These "walk abouts" were emotionally charged, both for Churchill and the ordinary citizens he met. He took a characteristic interest in the fine planning of every detail of wartime operations and worked a taxing schedule that many men half his age could not have endured. The warm personal relationship he established with U.S. president F. D. Roosevelt facilitated close cooperation between the two countries before the United

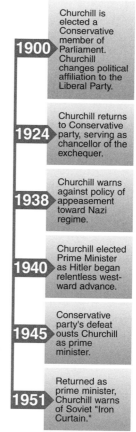

1900 Churchill is elected a Conservative member of Parliament. Churchill changes political affiliation to the Liberal Party.

1924 Churchill returns to Conservative party, serving as chancellor of the exchequer.

1938 Churchill warns against policy of appeasement toward Nazi regime.

1940 Churchill elected Prime Minister as Hitler began relentless westward advance.

1945 Conservative party's defeat ousts Churchill as prime minister.

1951 Returned as prime minister, Churchill warns of Soviet "Iron Curtain."

Churchill
warned of the
Soviet threat,
coining the
phrase "Iron
Curtain" to
describe
communist-
controlled east-
ern Europe.

States entered the war. Despite his long record of opposition to communism, Churchill did not hesitate in throwing his full support behind Soviet dictator Joseph Stalin when the USSR was invaded in 1941. On several occasions Churchill met with Roosevelt and Stalin to plan the course of the war and the face of the postwar world.

When victory came, everyone expected Churchill to be returned to power with a landslide victory at the 1945 election but his party suffered a severe defeat. This outcome was not so much a lack of gratitude for his skills as wartime leader but an expression of the desire to make a fresh start and not return to the depression of prewar years with which his party was associated. He remained in Parliament as leader of the opposition, returning as prime minister in 1951. In these post-war years he warned of the Soviet threat, coining the phrase "Iron Curtain" to describe communist-controlled eastern Europe and seeing the hydrogen bomb as a deterrent to aggression. He also wrote multivolume histories of World War II and of the English-speaking peoples, for which he was awarded a Nobel Prize in Literature. In 1955 he retired from the office of prime minister and devoted his time to painting; Churchill remained a member of Parliament even during his last, physically debilitated, years. ◆

Cid, El (Rodrigo Díaz de Vivar)

CA. 1043–1099 ● SPANISH MILITARY LEADER

El Cid lived in a Spain fragmented into Moorish and Christian kingdoms that subordinated religious differences to political and military expediency. In El Cid's Spain Christians fought Christians, Moors fought Moors, Christians and Moors fought each other, and both Christians and Moors were frequently allies in wars against their coreligionists.

Born into the minor nobility of the Christian kingdom of Castile, El Cid (Arabic for "the noble") resented the great nobles' power and wealth even though it was through his mother's connections with them that he was brought to the royal court, where he befriended the heir to the throne, Sancho II. He gained a reputation for military prowess at a young age; he was only twenty-two when Sancho became king and made him commander of the royal troops. El Cid helped Sancho fight against the Moorish kingdom of Saragossa and negotiate its status as a Castilian tributary. He also helped defeat Sancho's brother Alfonso in war, enabling the king to annex Alfonso's kingdom León. When Sancho died in 1072 and Alfonso inherited Castile's throne, El Cid found his position at court awkward and his influence declined considerably. Nonetheless he was allowed to remain there and even married Alfonso's niece. However his relationship with the great nobles eventually made his precarious position at court untenable. He deeply resented the nobles' influence over Alfonso and his own dismissal as commander of the royal troops. The nobles, in turn, were offended by his frequently humiliating them in public.

El Cid was finally exiled in 1081 for leading an unauthorized military expedition against one of Alfonso's Moorish allies and retaining part of the tribute collected from another. He was welcomed by the Muslim king of Saragossa, whom he served loyally for eight years, fighting both Moors and Christians and extending its borders at the expense of the Christian kingdom of Aragon.

When Alfonso was defeated by the Almoravid Moors from North Africa in their 1086 invasion; which threatened all of Christian Spain, he summoned El Cid back from exile. However, instead of fighting with Alfonso against the Almoravids, El Cid turned his attention to the rich Muslim kingdom of Valencia, making it first his tributary (1089) and then, after the death of its ruler and a year's siege, his own kingdom. He governed Valencia's Christian and Muslim citizens with ability, justice, an iron will, and an understanding of Islamic laws and customs. Valencia became a bulwark against Almoravid incursions, and, besieged by Jimema, continued to defend itself for three years after El Cid's death. Although Alfonso came to its aid, he was hard-pressed by Almoravid invaders elsewhere and, unable to spare the

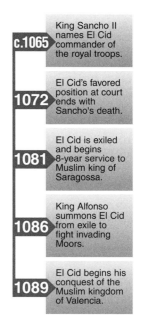

c.1065 King Sancho II names El Cid commander of the royal troops.

1072 El Cid's favored position at court ends with Sancho's death.

1081 El Cid is exiled and begins 8-year service to Muslim king of Saragossa.

1086 King Alfonso summons El Cid from exile to fight invading Moors.

1089 El Cid begins his conquest of the Muslim kingdom of Valencia.

troops to continue Valencia's defense, ordered it evacuated and burnt.

The legendary El Cid of hundreds of histories and poems—the idealistic, religiously motivated, indefatigible fighter for Christianity against Islam, which bears so little resemblance to the real El Cid—grew out of the *Poema del Cid*, a romanticized version of El Cid's life (with the less edifying parts falsified or omitted) written sixty years after his death. ◆

Clark, William

1770–1838 ● EXPLORER

Clark's long western adventure took him from Virginia and Kentucky to the Great Plains and the Pacific Northwest.

William Clark is inevitably associated with the epic journey he made to the Pacific in the company of Meriwether Lewis and the Corps of Discovery from 1804 to 1806. But Clark's life was much more than the events of one journey. His long western adventure took him from Virginia and Kentucky to the northern Great Plains and the Pacific Northwest.

Born on the eastern edge of the Allegheny Mountains in Virginia's Caroline County, Clark grew up in a world shaped by the values of order, authority, honor, and ambition. The struggles of the American Revolution were the common talk of the family and the region. Five Clark family sons served in the Revolution. Two of them—Jonathan and George Rogers—gained special distinction for courage and dedication to the Revolutionary cause. George Rogers Clark's daring drive into British-occupied Illinois captured Eastern attention and did much to aim the Clark family westward. At the close of the Revolution in 1784, the Clarks moved to Kentucky, and it was there that young William expanded his own knowledge of frontier ways.

The years after the American Revolution were marked by steadily increasing violence between Euro-American settlers and native people. Indians saw the greater Ohio Valley invaded by land-hungry squatters; white Americans saw that country as their rightful prize for winning the war against England. Coming of age in a culture that celebrated the military professions, William Clark soon found his place in the company of soldiers. First as a member of a local militia detachment and later as an infantry officer in the army led by General Anthony Wayne, Clark earned distinction for leadership and courage under fire. To his obvious military skills, Clark added abilities as a diplomat.

While military service shaped Clark's entire public life, the obligations he owed to family were perhaps even more influential. By the mid-1790s, George Rogers Clark's descent into debt and alcohol seriously endangered family landholdings in Kentucky and Indiana. Duty to family pulled William Clark away from the army, and he resigned his captain's commission in 1796. For the next eight years, he struggled to preserve and then expand the family estate. By the first years of the nineteenth century, he was a man rich in land and slaves—the real measure of Virginia culture transplanted to the Ohio country.

Like so many other Virginians, Clark valued sociability. While his close friends were few, he had a wide circle of acquaintances. In that circle was fellow Virginian and brother officer Meriwether Lewis. Both had served in the Ohio campaigns, and Clark had been for a brief time Lewis's commanding officer. They had never been close friends, but they had stayed in touch after Clark left the army. In June 1803, while Thomas Jefferson was busy completing instructions for the proposed expedition to the Pacific, Lewis wrote Clark to invite him to join the Corps of Discovery as a coleader. While there would be considerable official confusion about Clark's military rank on the journey, Lewis and Jefferson always viewed him as part of a joint command.

On their way up the Missouri, across the mountains, and down the Columbia to the sea, Lewis and Clark worked out a predictable pattern of duties and responsibilities. First and foremost, Clark was the expedition's cartographer. By training and temperament, Clark had the uncanny ability to comprehend complex land forms, rivers, and mountains and then reduce the three-dimensional world to the paper and ink of a two-dimensional map. He also proved to be an able negotiator in councils with native leaders. Because Clark's daily journal entries have survived and most of Lewis's have not, modern readers see and understand the journey through his eyes.

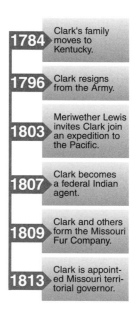

1784 Clark's family moves to Kentucky.

1796 Clark resigns from the Army.

1803 Meriwether Lewis invites Clark join an expedition to the Pacific.

1807 Clark becomes a federal Indian agent.

1809 Clark and others form the Missouri Fur Company.

1813 Clark is appointed Missouri territorial governor.

Clark never romanticized his two-and-a-half-year voyage to the Pacific. He saw the trip as just one more part of his long tour of duty as a soldier. The rest of his life (from 1806 until his death in 1838) was a continuation of that Virginia military code of conduct. In 1807, Clark assumed duties in St. Louis as federal Indian agent for the Western tribes. Clark believed, as did Jefferson, that commerce, especially the fur trade, was the key to establishing peaceful relations between native nations and the young United States. Clark was especially concerned that heavy-handed American traders and scheming Canadian merchants would incite violence in the West. To stop such trouble, Clark supported strict federal regulation of the fur business. But while Clark urged such regulation, he saw no reason to avoid personal participation in the lucrative fur trade. In 1809, he joined other prominent St. Louis citizens in forming the Missouri Fur Company. Led by Manuel Lisa, the company engaged in some of the earliest American fur ventures up the Missouri and into present-day Montana.

Clark's greatest test as an Indian agent came in the War of 1812 and its aftermath. In the West, the war came a full year before the beginning of its Atlantic phase. William Henry Harrison's attack on Tecumseh's camp at Tippecanoe Creek in 1811 was the signal for a wider war between Indians and Americans. While many Americans urged war, some thoughtful Western officials knew that area defenses were thin and poorly organized. As chief Indian agent, Clark did what he could to gather reliable information and strengthen alliances with friendly bands and tribes. Clark's military responsibilities increased when he was appointed Missouri territorial governor in June 1813. Many in the territory urged him to attack British posts on the upper Mississippi, especially Prairie du Chien, a key British establishment. In the spring of 1814, Clark organized a massive assault force of gunboats and infantry for the Prairie du Chien campaign. The British post fell easily, prompting Clark to withdraw most of his force back to St. Louis. A large British and Indian army returned to Prairie du Chien in July 1814 and successfully reclaimed the post. As Clark discovered to his dismay, the Prairie du Chien fiasco had consequences long after the official end of the War of 1812.

In July 1815, Clark moved to repair the damage done to Indian relations caused by the war in general and the Prairie

Clark never romanticized his two-and-a-half year voyage to the Pacific.

du Chien disaster in particular. At a series of treaty councils held at Portage des Sioux, Clark concluded agreements with more than a dozen tribes. The treaties all followed a common pattern. Each reasserted American sovereignty, emphasized friendly commerce between American traders and Indians, and made arrangements for handling problems of law and criminal justice. The treaties also offered the blessings of American civilization—schools, churches, plow agriculture, and private ownership of land. Clark was convinced that such institutional arrangements would preserve peace between Euro-Americans and Native Americans. If Clark's trust in rational negotiation and formalized institutions was misplaced, his commitment to peace was genuine. Indians who came to talk with him in St. Louis affectionately called him "the red-head chief."

William Clark's last years were marked by a steady decline in his diplomatic and political leadership. When Missouri became a state in 1819, Clark ran for governor and was soundly defeated. In Black Hawk's War crisis, he proved to be an ineffective negotiator. As a patron for artists and explorers heading west, he had greater success. Artists such as George Catlin and Karl (or Carl) Bodmer and explorers and travelers such as Wilson Price Hunt, Prince Maximilian of Wied-Neuwied, and Washington Irving all stopped to consult with the man one adventurer called "the patriarch of the West." ◆

If Clark's trust in rational negotiations and formalized institutions was misplaced, his commitment to peace was genuine.

Clovis (Chlodwig)

CA. 466–511 ● KING OF THE FRANKS

At the death of his father, Childeric I, Clovis inherited the realm of the Salian Franks, which extended over part of present-day Belgium, with its capital at Tournai. He united the Frankish tribes under his rule and in 486 attacked Syagrius, the last representative of Roman rule

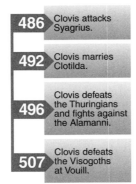

486 Clovis attacks Syagrius.

492 Clovis marries Clotilda.

496 Clovis defeats the Thuringians and fights against the Alamanni.

507 Clovis defeats the Visigoths at Vouill.

assimilation: to become similar; to absorb into the population.

in western Europe, who had established his rule at Soissons and governed northern Gaul. The defeat of Syagrius and the conquest of Soissons enabled Clovis to annex the territory between the North Sea and the River Loire. He founded the Frankish kingdom, establishing his capital at Paris. Continuing his wars eastward, he absorbed the Ripuarian Franks on the Rhine into his realm and began expanding toward Germany. His quarrel with the Burgundians, who threatened his southern boundaries, ended in 492 with his marriage to Clotilda, niece of the Burgundian king Gundobald. Brought up as a Catholic, Clotilda sought to persuade her husband to convert to Christianity.

Clovis allied himself with Theodoric the Great, king of the Ostrogoths, who had conquered Italy; Clovis gave Theodoric his sister as wife. This system of alliances allowed Clovis to extend his rule in Germany, where he defeated the Thuringians and fought against the Alamanni in 496 in a struggle so difficult that his victory was attributed to a divine miracle. Clovis's prayer to the God of Clotilda and his promise to convert to the Christian faith in the case of victory is testimony to the great battle. The victory enabled him to annex the Alamanni realm to his kingdom. His subsequent conversion was the result of a combined effort of persuasion by Clotilda and Remigius, the bishop of Rheims, whom Clotilda had brought to the court. Clovis was the first Germanic king to convert to Catholicism; the other rulers were Arians. He thus won the loyalty and support of the Gallo-Roman population, which was Christian. Moreover, religious unity allowed the emergence of peaceful relations between the conquerors and the conquered and created the conditions for their mutual **assimilation**, leading to the founding of France and the birth of the French people.

Clovis's achievements climaxed with the war against the Visigoths, who ruled southwestern Gaul. In 507 he defeated them at Vouill and undertook the conquest of Aquitaine and Toulouse, the capital of the Visigoths. The Visigoths were defeated in spite of the support of Theodoric.

Clovis is credited with the establishment of the Salic Law, the compilation of the legal traditions of the Salian Franks. In addition to his military and political achievements, he proved his organizational skills by enforcing rigorous discipline in his army, controlling the distribution of booty and rewarding the army chiefs. He also confiscated public lands and gave them as estates to his followers (the *leudes*), who became the new nobility of his kingdom. He did not, however, **expropriate** private property and was thus able to integrate the Gallo-Roman aristocracy into the ruling class of the kingdom, although they remained subordinate to the Franks.

expropriate: to take from the owner for public use.

After Clovis's death, Clotilda retired to the abbey of Saint Martin of Tours, where she was famed for her piety and good deeds. She later became the subject of many legends. ◆

Columbus, Christopher

1451–1506 ● ITALIAN EXPLORER

"I believe that this land which your highnesses have commanded me to discover is very great, and that there are many other lands in the south of which there have never been reports."

Christopher Columbus, describing his third voyage, 1500

Christopher Columbus was born in Genoa, Italy, the eldest son of Domenico Columbo, a weaver. Columbus himself was reticent about his birthplace and nationality, maintaining a discreet silence on the subject of his origins so that they would not impede his ambitions for wealth and position.

He went to sea at fourteen, trading in his father's wool. When he was twenty-five his ship was destroyed by pirates and he landed in Lisbon. Since 1453, the Portuguese had been seeking a new route to the Orient, as the traditional route had been closed by the Turks when they captured Constantinople. Expeditions to find a new route had been sent out from Lisbon, and Portuguese sailors had made discoveries in the Atlantic Ocean and along the west coast of Africa. These discoveries fascinated Columbus and were recorded by him and his brother Bartholomeo in the latter's map shop in Lisbon.

Columbus broadened his knowledge of geography by undertaking voyages. He sailed to Iceland and then gained sailing experience in the south Atlantic. His life long fascination with gold began with a voyage to Portugal's African gold fields, and he envisioned a new westward route to Asia.

The view of the ancient Greek geographer Ptolemy— that ships would run out of supplies long before reaching Asia—remained popular. In contrast, Columbus believed that the Eurasian landmass was much wider than Ptolemy had believed and formulated a plan to reach Asia by sailing west across a narrow Atlantic Ocean. He presented it to the king of Portugal, but was turned down.

Columbus next turned to Spain. He soon won over the devout Catholic queen Isabella by emphasizing the number of souls to be converted to Christianity and sharing his vision of recapturing Jerusalem with an army funded by Asian gold. A special commission was set up to study Columbus's proposals. Well aware that many members of the commission were better educated, Columbus tried to hide his ignorance, answering their questions briefly. However, after four years the commission decided against him. It took the euphoria following the fall of Granada in 1492 for King Ferdinand and Isabella to agree to Columbus's plan.

At that point Columbus stated his exorbitant price for leading the expedition: knighthood, hereditary appointment as admiral, the title of viceroy and governor over any lands he discovered, and a 10 percent commission on any commerce with those lands. Ferdinand and Isabella were persuaded to accept these terms (set forth in the Capitulations of Santa Fe) because they were to be fulfilled only if Columbus were successful. The port of Palos was ordered to provide Columbus with two ships or face charges of smuggling and possibly piracy. Martin Alonso Pinzón, a highly respected Palos shipowner, provided the third ship and half the cost of the voyage.

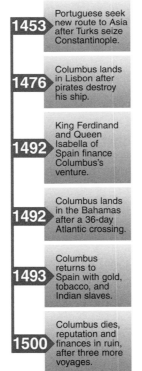

1453 Portuguese seek new route to Asia after Turks seize Constantinople.

1476 Columbus lands in Lisbon after pirates destroy his ship.

1492 King Ferdinand and Queen Isabella of Spain finance Columbus's venture.

1492 Columbus lands in the Bahamas after a 36-day Atlantic crossing.

1493 Columbus returns to Spain with gold, tobacco, and Indian slaves.

1500 Columbus dies, reputation and finances in ruin, after three more voyages.

On August 3, 1492, Columbus left Palos with three ships, the *Pinta*, the *Niña*, and the *Santa Maria*. He had the ships loaded with trinkets to trade for gold and took on a crew member who could speak both Hebrew and Arabic. After a stop at the Canary Islands for repairs, they set sail west across the Atlantic, carried by the trade winds.

The crossing took thirty-six days. Nervous and doubtful, the crew agreed to continue only if Columbus swore to turn back after seven hundred leagues. Columbus agreed but sailed on, deliberately misinforming them about the distance covered each day. On October 12, 1492, they landed on the island of Guanahani in the Bahamas, taking possession of it in the name of Ferdinand and Isabella; Columbus named the island San Salvador. They sailed on, searching for Japan but finding the Bahamas, Cuba, and Hispaniola. Columbus raised crosses everywhere he went, watching out for material wealth. The Indians they met were peaceful and had some gold, which they traded for Columbus's trinkets, but misled him as to the origin of the gold, directing him to yet another island; he set off in search of an island he never found. The *Santa Maria* foundered and he had to leave thirty-eight men in Hispaniola with provisions for a year—and orders to continue searching for gold.

In 1493 Columbus returned to Spain with gold, tobacco, and Indian slaves. Ferdinand and Isabella showered him with honors. Admired, feted, and rich, Columbus's career reached its peak between his first and second voyages. Ferdinand, a pragmatic man, saw some financial merit in Columbus's idea of capturing and selling Indians as slaves; Isabella, however, insisted that the Indians be made subjects of the Castilian crown and should not, therefore, be enslaved. She persistently ordered Columbus not to bring slaves back with him, but he persistently continued to do so.

His second voyage (1493–1496) theoretically combined colonization, exploration, and missionary activities, but in actuality everything was subordinated to the search for gold. The crew he had left behind in Hispaniola had all been killed; Columbus concerned himself with the gold he believed they might have hidden away. He founded a city named Isabella, whose colonists were mostly sick or busy prospecting for gold. With only two friars, missionary activities were of necessity limited, and were made more difficult by the Spaniards' way

"When I reached Cuba, I followed its north coast westwards, and found it so extensive that I thought this must be the mainland, the province of Cathay."

Christopher Columbus, 1493

Colombus
remained
convinced that
his discoveries
were part of
Asia and at
times wavered
between clarity
and madness.

of forcibly taking Indian possessions and women. Columbus did succeed in discovering the Lesser Antilles, Puerto Rico, and Jamaica before returning to Spain. In Hispaniola he was accused of being an incompetent, capricious governor, zealously guarding his power and prerogatives, unable to cope with local needs, and taking off on voyages of discovery when faced with administrative problems. Complaints were laid against him, partly inspired by spiteful jealousy of an outsider's rapid rise. The crown continued to stand behind Columbus, but its faith in him was shaken.

Columbus's third voyage (1498–1500) reached Hispaniola only to find his brother (who governed the island in his absence) confronted with a mutiny that Columbus solved by mollifying the mutineers before sailing off to discover Trinidad and the coast of Venezuela. Ferdinand and Isabella could no longer ignore the unflattering reports about Columbus and in 1499 appointed Francisco de Bobadilla as governor and chief magistrate of Hispaniola. Columbus refused to acknowledge Bobadilla, who thereupon had Columbus and his brother arrested, put in chains, and sent back to Spain. Insulted, Columbus, the "Admiral of the Ocean Sea," refused offers during the voyage to remove his chains. Shocked at the chains, Ferdinand and Isabella ordered his immediate release and sent him money to come to court. However, their sympathy did not change their opinion regarding his ability to govern.

Frustrated in his dreams of greatness and gold and by reports of new discoveries being made, Columbus turned down offers of compensation and pleaded to be allowed to lead another expedition. The crown agreed, provided that he did not return to Hispaniola. Columbus then sailed straight to Hispaniola where a fleet of twenty-one ships was preparing to set sail, and warned them of an approaching hurricane. His warning was contemptuously ignored and the fleet set off for Spain, to be destroyed by the hurricane.

On that fourth voyage (1502–1504), Columbus apparently found some gold along the Central American mainland, but it was in an inaccessible location. He remained convinced that his discoveries were part of Asia and at times wavered between clarity and madness. Finally the ships' hulls rotted and Columbus was shipwrecked for nearly a year in Jamaica before being rescued and returned to Spain.

Sick, Columbus spent the last two years of his life attempting to restore his governorship and disputing the amount of money owed him under the Capitulations by which he relinquished his claim to the governorship of the West Indies. His descendants continued the fight over his legacy in Spanish courts for generations. ◆

Crazy Horse (Sioux)

CA. 1840–1877 ● LAKOTA CHIEF & WARRIOR

The Oglala Lakota war chief Crazy Horse was born near Bear Butte, South Dakota. He defeated two of the army's best-known officers during the Great Sioux War of 1876. His father, also known as Crazy Horse, was a noted Oglala warrior and medicine man. His mother, Rattle Blanket Woman, was a Minneconjou Lakota.

"One does not sell the land people walk on."
Crazy Horse, 1875

By 1861, the young man had earned his adult name, Crazy Horse. He was a skilled warrior and leader who earned the admiration of his own people and of his foes. During the Oglala leader Red Cloud's war against white incursions on Lakota lands in Wyoming and Montana in the mid-1860s, Crazy Horse led warriors in the Fetterman fight at Fort Phil Kearny in 1866, the Hayfield fight in 1867, and the Wagon Box fight in 1867.

Crazy Horse earned a considerable following among non-treaty Lakotas, who increasingly looked to him as a chief. In 1868, Lakota Sioux gathered in northeastern Wyoming where, one witness recalled, the "old men or leaders" selected four young warriors, including Crazy Horse, as "head warriors [or "shirtwearers"] of their people." The leaders told the four that they "represented in their commands and acts the entire power of the nation." Crazy Horse was a "shirtwearer" until his participation in a violent controversy in 1870. A Lakota woman left her husband for Crazy Horse, and the husband shot Crazy Horse in the face with a pistol. His formal position as a "shirtwearer" then ended.

By 1875, government officials and army officers acknowledged Crazy Horse as one of the conspicuous leaders of Lakota resistance. The issue before the Lakotas was the Black Hills of South Dakota and Lakota hunting grounds in the Yellowstone River basin, which were allocated to the Lakotas in an 1868 treaty. The government now desired the Black Hills because, in 1874, gold was discovered there. By 1875, Lakota leaders were furious about the increasing numbers of prospectors and miners in the Black Hills.

In December 1875, the government ordered the Lakotas and Cheyennes in the Yellowstone River and Powder River region to move to reservations in Nebraska or on the Missouri River within six weeks or face military action. The nontreaty Lakotas had no intention of moving their families and villages to the reservations during the harsh winter weather.

In March 1876, an army attack on a Northern Cheyenne village persuaded Crazy Horse and other Lakota and Northern Cheyenne chiefs to fight the army. Crazy Horse and Sitting Bull, a Hunkpapa Lakota, emerged as two of the great leaders of the Lakota Cheyenne alliance.

Crazy Horse was central to two of the most significant battles of the Sioux War of 1876. On June 17, he led approximately fifteen hundred warriors against Brigadier General George Crook's thirteen-hundred-man military column. In the ensuing Battle of the Rosebud, Crazy Horse coordinated his warriors' attack and, in a strategic victory, stopped Crook's advance. Eight days later, Lieutenant Colonel George Armstrong Custer and units of the Seventh Cavalry attacked the Lakotas and Northern Cheyennes in the Battle of Little Bighorn. Crazy Horse played an important role in the counterattack, which annihilated Custer and his immediate command.

The army continued to strike the Lakotas and Cheyennes in the Yellowstone River country during the winter of 1876 to 1877. Crazy Horse realized that further fighting was useless, and he and his followers surrendered at Camp Robinson in Nebraska on May 7, 1877.

Government officials and army officers were eager to meet the warrior who had so adroitly fought them. Because of the

1866 Crazy Horse leads warriors in the Fetterman fight at Fort Phil Kearny.

1868 The Lakota Sioux choose Crazy Horse as one of their head warriors.

1876 Crazy Horse annihilates Custer in the Battle of Little Big Horn.

1877 Crazy Horse is killed during an attempt by army officers to arrest him.

Ben Nighthorse Campbell

When Ben Nighthorse Campbell was elected to the U.S. Senate in 1992, he became the first person of American Indian ancestry to hold a United States Senate seat since 1929. Campbell was born on April 13, 1933, in Auburn, California. His mother was a Portuguese immigrant and his father was a Northern Cheyenne Indian. In 1951, Campbell dropped out of high school to join the U.S. Air Force. While in the Air Force, Campbell earned his General Equivalency Degree (GED). He received a bachelor's degree in physical education and fine arts from San Jose State University in 1957. After college, Campbell earned his living as a rancher, a horse trainer, and a jewelry designer. He was elected to the Colorado State Legislature in 1982. From 1987 to 1992 he represented Colorado in the U. S. House of Representatives. A leader in public lands and natural resources policy, Senator Campbell was instrumental in the passage of landmark legislation to settle Indian water rights, and he sponsored and led the fight for legislation to protect Colorado's wilderness lands. In 1991, Campbell helped pass legislation to change the name of the Custer Battlefield Monument in Montana to the Little Bighorn Battlefield Monument, so that American Indians who died there would not be forgotten. Senator Campbell also initiated and passed legislation to establish the National Museum of the American Indians within the Smithsonian Institution.

attention to Crazy Horse, jealous Oglala and Sicangu chiefs spread rumors about him. Inexperienced junior army officers believed the gossip and reported it to their superiors. By September 1877, the rumors induced army officers to arrest Crazy Horse. On September 5, during an attempt to incarcerate Crazy Horse at Camp Robinson, a soldier mortally bayoneted him, and he died a few hours later. ◆

Crockett, David (Davey)

1786–1836 ● FRONTIERSMAN, CONGRESSMAN, & FOLK HERO

> *"I am at liberty to vote as my conscience and judgment dictates to be right, without the yoke of any party on me, or the driver at my heels, with his whip in hand, commanding me to ge-wo-haw, just at his pleasure."*
>
> David Crockett, 1834

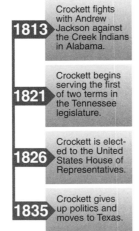

1813 Crockett fights with Andrew Jackson against the Creek Indians in Alabama.

1821 Crockett begins serving the first of two terms in the Tennessee legislature.

1826 Crockett is elected to the United States House of Representatives.

1835 Crockett gives up politics and moves to Texas.

David (Davey) Crockett was born near present-day Rogersville in East Tennessee. He was raised in the backwoods of the Appalachian Mountains and received a limited education. As a young man, he joined the Tennessee militia and fought with Andrew Jackson against the Creek Indians in Alabama from 1813 to 1814. After military service, he lived in Jefferson, Lincoln, Franklin, Lawrence, Carroll, and Gibson counties in Tennessee. After serving as a justice of the peace, he was elected to the Tennessee legislature in 1821 and served for two terms. In 1826, he was elected to the U.S. House of Representatives as a Democrat.

Although he was an early supporter of the Jacksonian Democratic party, he later broke ties with Andrew Jackson. Crockett demonstrated a rare comprehension of and appreciation for governmental affairs and cared little for party views on issues. He voted instead on his own convictions. Unable to overcome President Jackson's immense political power, Crockett failed to win reelection in 1830, but two years later, he was returned to Congress on the Whig ticket.

Giving up politics after his defeat in 1835, Crockett moved to Texas. When he arrived at the Alamo, he was offered, but declined, command of the old mission. Although

The Alamo

Authorized by the viceroy of Mexico in 1716, the Mission San Antonio de Valero was established in San Antonio, Texas, by the Franciscan Fray Antonio de Olivares. The mission was a four-acre walled complex that included priests' headquarters, Indian quarters, a granary, storehouses, and workshops. After epidemics depopulated the San Antonio missions in 1778, the San Antonio de Valero was converted to a parish church in 1793. Ignored by the church in the early 19th century, the structure became barracks for a company of Spanish cavalry, which used the mission from about 1801 to 1812 and gave it the name by which it became known: the Alamo. Spanish for "cottonwood," the name referred to a cottonwood tree on a ranch near the town of San Jose y Santiago del Alamo de Parras (now called Viesca) where the cavalry company was organized. The Mexican army occupied the Alamo from 1821 to 1835, when it fell into the hands of rebellious Texans at the outbreak of their war for independence from Mexico.

Mexican General Martin Perfecto Cos used the Alamo as his headquarters before the fall of San Antonio on December 1835, and he had built up the structure as a fortification. In the face of the advance of the Mexican army into Texas, a group of Texas troops led by Colonel William Travis took control of the Alamo on February 23, 1836. Travis had approximately 183 men and at least eighteen pieces of artillery to defend the fort against an estimated 4,000 Mexican soldiers. Among the defenders were Davey Crockett and Jim Bowie. On the morning of March 6, the Mexican army advanced to retake the Alamo. The defenders of the Alamo, all of whom were killed, became martyrs to the Texas cause. "Remember the Alamo" became the battle cry of the Texas army in its final victory over the Mexicans at San Jacinto in 1836.

tradition holds that Crockett was killed within the walls of the Alamo, modern research has revealed that he may have been captured by the Mexican army and executed with several other defenders.

Even during his lifetime, Crockett established himself as a folk hero. Magazines and books of the period carried outlandish tales of his battles with wild beasts and human enemies. His death at the Alamo enlarged his bigger-than-life image. During the 1950s, several fanciful Hollywood movies about his exploits were released and starred Fess Parker. Coonskin caps, toy rifles, lunch boxes, and songs abounded during the revival and brought Crockett and his times once again to the forefront of the American imagination. ◆

"If I could rest anywhere it would be in Arkansas, where the men are of the real half-horse, half alligator breed such as grows nowhere else on the face of the earth."

Davey Crockett, 1834

Dalai Lama

1935–PRESENT ● TIBETAN RELIGIOUS
LEADER AND PEACE ACTIVIST

> *"I always believe that it is much better to have a variety of religions, a variety of philosophies, rather than one single religion or philosophy. This is necessary because of the different mental dispositions of each human being.*
>
> Dalai Lama

The Dalai Lama is the religious and political leader of the Tibetan people. He is a renowned Buddhist scholar and a man of peace who is widely respected for his humanity, his compassion, and his qualities of leadership. Since 1959 he has led a campaign to end China's domination of Tibet through nonviolent means, and for this effort he won the 1989 Nobel Peace Prize.

On July 6, 1935, the Dalai Lama was born to a humble farming family in the small village of Taktser in northeastern Tibet. He was named Lhamo Thondup. In 1938, a delegation of monks recognized him as the reincarnated Dalai Lama, who is the leader of the Yellow Hat order, the chief Buddhist sect of Tibet. The monks then brought him to Lhasa to raise him according to the monastic tradition. He began his monastic education at the age of six and completed his Doctorate of Buddhist Philosophy when he was twenty-five.

In 1950 Communist Chinese troops poured over the Tibetan border with the intention of "liberating" Tibet from imperialist rule. The Chinese invasion frightened the Tibetan people and they turned to their spiritual leader for guidance. In response to their appeals for political leadership, the Dalai Lama was made head of the state of Tibet at the age of fifteen, three years short of the typical ascension to political power.

In order to avoid a confrontation with the advancing army, the Tibetan government sent a delegation to the Chinese capital of Peking to negotiate with the Communist authorities and make it clear that Tibet did not require liberation. The result of the negotiations was a document called the Seventeen Point Agreement, which provided that the Tibetan people would become a part of the People's Republic of China and that the Chinese would assume control of foreign affairs and military responsibilities in Tibet. In return the Tibetans would be assured religious and political freedom. The young Dalai Lama was alarmed by the terms of the agreement that surrendered the sovereignty of Tibet to the Chinese government, and he felt it must have been coerced out of the delegates. But rather than face the massive Chinese army with force, which seemed futile and was also against his Buddhist nature, the Dalai Lama decided to maintain further negotiations with the Chinese.

1938 He was recognized as the reincarnated Dalai Lama by a group of monks.

1950 Chinese Communist troops poured into Tibet to "liberate" it from imperialist rule.

1954 The Dalai Lama travels to China to meet with Communist authorities.

1959 The Dalai Lama fled to India to escape threats to his life.

1989 The Dalai Lama is awarded the Nobel Peace Prize.

In 1954 the Dalai Lama traveled to China, where he met with Mao Zedong, China's ruler, and Zhou Enlai, the premier of China. He found the Chinese leaders cordial but oblivious to the importance of Buddhism to himself and the Tibetan people. While traveling, he eagerly learned about the Chinese advances made in industry and science. He felt that Tibet was in dire need of reform in certain areas—including education, communications, the judicial system—and he was open-minded to the Chinese approaches in these areas.

Through the mid-1950s tension between the Chinese authorities and Tibetans increased and resistance to Communist authority was met with beatings and executions. In early 1959 thousands gathered on the streets of Lhasa in protest of Chinese rule and out of concern for what they perceived as a threat to the life of the Dalai Lama. In a show of authority, the Chinese sent armed troops to crush the demonstration. At the urging of his family and ministers, who were convinced that the loss of his life would mean the end of Tibetan life, the Dalai Lama fled with an entourage across the Himalaya to seek political assistance for his country in India.

Several hours after his departure, the Chinese began an attack on the Tibetan demonstrators. The crackdown continued into 1960, and by 1961 more than 80,000 Tibetans had been killed.

Once in India, the Dalai Lama was granted political asylum. In 1960 he established a government-in-exile in Dharamsala in northern India with military protection from the Indian government. From Dharamsala he devoted himself to supporting the increasing numbers of Tibetans refugees seeking exile in India and to preserving Tibetan culture against adverse odds. He also worked tirelessly on building international support for Tibetan autonomy. Throughout these campaigns he continued to conduct his life as a monk, meditating four hours a day and spending several hours more daily studying and writing on Buddhist texts.

In the meantime China continued to increase its control over Tibet and repress Tibetan culture. It placed restrictions on religious practice and the economy and installed Chinese as local government administrators and teachers. It began agricultural reforms that required peasants to sell a fixed amount of grain to the government and forced them to grow wheat rather than barley, their traditional crop. Aggressive farming methods also rapidly eroded the thin layer of topsoil on the Tibetan plains, and led to crop failure and years of famine. Communications and road systems were built, but China remained in control of the local media and travel for Tibetans was restricted in the early years. During the Cultural Revolution of the 1960s, formal religion was banned, and Chinese soldiers looted and destroyed all but about 10 of Tibet's 6,000 monasteries. Many thousands of Tibetans were killed and many others were thrown in prison to face starvation. Though the Chinese government began to relax some restrictions on the Tibetan economy, religious practice, and culture in the 1980s, restrictions were renewed after a riot in Lhasa against the slow pace of reform and the continued discrimination in Tibet.

In an effort to aid his people the Dalai Lama traveled around the world to talk about the disregard for human rights in Tibet and the destruction of the indigenous culture there. He met political, religious, and human rights leaders around the world, and formed large groups in support of his cause. And despite criticisms from some exiled Tibetans for his insis-

> *"True peace with oneself and with the world around us can only be achieved through the development of mental peace."*
> Dalai Lama

tence on nonviolence, the Dalai Lama has continued to advocate peaceful solutions to the Tibetan problem based upon tolerance and mutual respect with the Chinese people.

For his leadership in the pursuit of freedom and peace and for his distinguished writings in Buddhist philosophy the Dalai Lama has received numerous honors around the world. In 1989 he won the Nobel Peace Prize for his consistent opposition to the use of violence in his struggle for human rights in Tibet.

The Dalai Lama describes himself as a simple monk who spends at least four hours daily in meditation and much of the rest of his day tending Tibetan affairs of state and studying Buddhist texts. In the 1990s he began to speak out on the need for better understanding and respect among the different faiths of the world. ◆

de Klerk, Frederik Willem

1936–PRESENT ● PRESIDENT OF SOUTH AFRICA

"We are political opponents. We disagree strongly on key issues and we will soon fight a strenuous election campaign against one another. But we will do so, I believe, in the frame of mind and within the framework of peace that has already been established."

de Klerk, 1993

Frederik Willem de Klerk was born in Johannesburg on March 18, 1936. His father, Jan de Klerk, had been a cabinet minister and president of the Senate. De Klerk graduated B.A. and L.L.B. (cum laude) from Potchefstroom University for Christian Higher Education in 1958. He was an attorney at Vereeniging (1961–1972), where he was active in the National Party (NP). He was elected member of Parliament for Vereeniging in the by-election of 1972, and was returned, unopposed, in the general election of 1974. From April 1978 de Klerk held cabinet portfolios that included Posts and Telecommunications; Mining, Environmental Planning, and Energy; Home Affairs; and National Education. He became head of the NP in February 1989 and was elected president of South Africa in September 1989, serving until April 1994. De Klerk was corecipient, with Nelson Mandela, of the Nobel Peace Prize in 1993.

Prior to becoming president in 1989, de Klerk was some-thing of an unknown quantity. Over the years, he underwent a gradual political conversion from an overcautious approach to politics to fearless entrepreneurship, from ultraconser-vatism to outspoken enlightenment (*verligthied*), from ideo-logical correctness to open, critical pragmatism and realism. He came of age, politically, in an era in which he felt himself neither shackled to the baggage of the past nor historically bound to continue what became outdated policies. De Klerk brought a different style of government: he sought advice from civilians rather than the military, which for South Africa at the time was a sea change. Faced by issues that went to the heart of the status quo, issues that would change the face of South Africa, he embarked on the most radical period of political reform the nation had experienced.

No other NP leader had broken so fundamentally with party orthodoxy. De Klerk permitted peaceful mass demon-strations by extraparliamentary groups; in October 1989, he released eight long-term prisoners belonging to the African National Congress (ANC); on February 2, 1990, he started negotiations on South Africa's future with the ANC, the Pan-Africanist Congress, the South African Communist Party, and allied organizations. On February 11, 1990, de Klerk released Nelson Mandela from prison; subsequently, he initiated several meetings between the government and the ANC on the transitional process that led to the Groote Schuur Minute (May 1990) and the Pretoria Minute (August 1990). He also headed the government delegation to the Convention for a Democratic South Africa (December 1991–December 1993). In May 1994 he became second executive deputy president in the government of national unity, from which he resigned in June 1996 to reposition the NP (which he still led) for the next election in 1999.

Within a relatively short time span, the South African state self-consciously dismantled apartheid, thereby effecting socioeconomic reconstruction and reconciliation, and devis-ing a new political order in which race has no role in deter-mining life chances of citizens. De Klerk realized from the start that these actions would reform himself and the NP out of exclusive political power; he pursued this course knowing-ly and from a position of relative strength. ◆

1972 De Klerk is elect-ed a member of South Africa's Parliament.

1989 De Klerk becomes head of the National Party and president.

1990 De Klerk releases Nelson Mandela from prison.

1991 De Klerk heads the government delegation to the Convention for a Democratic South Africa.

1993 De Klerk and Mandela are awarded the Nobel Peace Prize.

1994 De Klerk becomes second executive deputy president.

Decatur, Stephen

1779–1820 ● U.S. NAVY HERO

Commodore Stephen Decatur was a daredevil naval officer who won his reputation and greatest victories in the Mediterranean fighting against the Barbary states. Decatur was born on January 5, 1779, in Bladensburg, Maryland. He entered the Navy as a midshipman under Commodore John Barry, and served in a variety of posts until he was assigned to the force attempting to punish the ruler and people of Tripoli for piracy against United States vessels.

The U.S. frigate *Philadelphia* was captured by the enemy when she ran aground near Tripoli. The Tripolitan Navy intended to use the big American ship against the American fleet. Decatur led a boarding force that sailed into the harbor, surprised the crew of Tripolitans aboard the *Philadelphia*, and destroyed her by fire. This took place on February 16, 1804, and made Decatur a hero in the United States.

During the War of 1812, he served with some distinction as commander of the U.S. frigates *United States* and *President*. He once more returned to glory in the Mediterranean in 1815 when he headed a squadron that set out to punish Algiers for attempted piracy. In this campaign he captured the Algerian flagship and dictated peace terms to the Algerian government. He filled a number of other posts, including a post on the Board of Naval Commissioners. While there, he refused to return Captain James Barron (who had commanded the *Chesapeake* in 1807) to active duty. Barron challenged Decatur to a duel in which he killed him. Decatur is remembered not only for his naval career, but for his famous toast: my country, right or wrong!" ◆

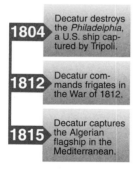

1804 Decatur destroys the *Philadelphia*, a U.S. ship captured by Tripoli.

1812 Decatur commands frigates in the War of 1812.

1815 Decatur captures the Algerian flagship in the Mediterranean.

Dewey, John

1859–1952 ● AMERICAN EDUCATOR

John Dewey was an American educator renowned for his educational philosophy of "instrumentalism," emphasizing "learning by doing" rather than by memorization of material. Dewey was born on a farm in Burlington, Vermont, and initially studied at the University of Vermont, receiving his bachelor's degree in 1879. For the next three years he taught school in Vermont and in Pennsylvania. From 1882 he did graduate work at Johns Hopkins University, receiving his Ph.D. in 1884. He became an assistant professor of philosophy at the University of Michigan and in 1890 he was appointed chairman of the philosophy department until 1894, when he assumed the chairmanship of the department of philosophy, psychology, and pedagogy at the University of Chicago, which he held until 1904.

In 1902 he published *The Child and the Curriculum*, presenting his philosophy of education. He believed that the educational process must begin with and build upon the interests of the child, opportunity must be provided in the classroom experience for the interplay of the child's thinking and doing, for which purpose the school should be organized as a miniature community, and the teacher should be a guide and coworker with the child rather than a mere taskmaster.

From 1904 until his retirement in 1930 he taught as professor of philosophy and education at Columbia University in New York City and remained an emeritus professor there until 1951. In 1919 and again in 1931 he was a lecturer in philosophy and education at the University of Peking in China. In the course of his extensive career, he even found time to serve on national organizations. He was president of the American Psychological Association and later president of the American Philosophical Association. In 1915 he was a founder and first president of the American Association of University Professors and helped organize the American Civil Liberties Union in 1920. The latter activity was related to his philosophy of legal realism, which is based on the belief that inasmuch as the judge plays such an active role in the making of the law, he should be aware of the inevitable social conse-

"Modern life means democracy, democracy means freeing intelligence for independent effectiveness—the emancipation of mind as an individual organ to do its own work."
John Dewey, 1903

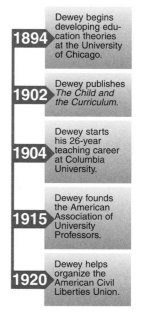

1894 Dewey begins developing education theories at the University of Chicago.

1902 Dewey publishes *The Child and the Curriculum*.

1904 Dewey starts his 26-year teaching career at Columbia University.

1915 Dewey founds the American Association of University Professors.

1920 Dewey helps organize the American Civil Liberties Union.

quence of the decisions he makes. This was in keeping with Dewey's feeling that the true function of philosophy was to solve human problems.

His extensive publications included *The School and Society* (1899), *How We Think* (1909), *The Influence of Darwin on Pllilosophy and Other Essays in Contemporary Thought* (1910), *Essays in Experimental Logic* (1916), *Human Nature and Conduct* (1922), his classic work *Experience and Nature* (1925), *The Quest for Certainty* (1929), *Philosophy and Civiilzation* (1931), *Art as Experience* (1934), *Experience and Education* (1938), *Freedom and Culture* (1939), and *Problems of Men* (1946).

As a philosopher he favored the pragmatism of William James, from which his theory of "instrumentalism" was derived. Dewey favored progressive education and did much to foster its development through the years. His views were adopted by the progressive movement in education, stressing that education should be student centered rather than subject-centered, that is, education through doing. ◆

Dix, Dorothea Lynde

1802–1887 ● SOCIAL REFORMER

D orothea Dix overcame the difficulties of an unhappy home life and severe personal illness to become a major influence in improving the conditions of some of society's weakest people, the inmates of insane asylums

Dix was born on April 4, 1802, in Hampden, Maine. As a ten-year-old she left her parents' home and moved in with grandparents who cared for her in Boston. She was an unusually energetic girl, who began to work as a schoolteacher in Worcester, Massachusetts, at the age of fourteen. She became a member of the first Unitarian congregation, under the guidance of Rev. William Ellery Channing in Boston, and taught Channing's children in a school she herself established in the Dix family mansion in that city. Her health broke while she

Dorothea Lynde Dix.

was in her thirties, and she had to give up her school and become a virtual invalid for the rest of her life.

She was never an inactive person, however. She took up the task of teaching Sunday School for the inmates of a Massachusetts jail in 1841. There she discovered that insane inmates were housed and treated like brutes, with no heat and no care. Dorothea Dix exposed these conditions and led the demand that they be changed. She then spent two years collecting information about conditions in poorhouses, asylums, and jails in Massachusetts. She turned her information over to influential friends who pushed reform laws through the State legislature.

Her first success in Massachusetts was followed by success in Rhode Island, New York, New Jersey, Pennsylvania, and

1802 Dix is born in Hampden, Maine.

1818 Dix begins teaching school in Worcester, Maine.

1841 Dix teaches Sunday school in a Massachusetts jail.

Canada. She conducted each campaign in the same manner: she carefully collected information, planned the needed changes, and then recruited important local leaders to act as spokesmen for reforming the conditions of prisons or insane asylums. She was responsible for the creation of state asylums in eleven states, and she influenced similar reforms in England and on the continent of Europe. Dorothea Dix did not appear in public herself, make long and impressive speeches, or write extensively. Yet, she became the most influential person in the drive to improve the treatment of the mentally ill people of the United States. ◆

Douglass, Frederick

1818–1895 ● ABOLITIONIST, JOURNALIST, & SOCIAL REFORMER

"No man can put a chain about the ankle of his fellow man without at last finding the other end fastened about his own neck."
Frederick Douglass, 1883

Born Frederick Augustus Washington Bailey to Harriet Bailey, a slave, and an unacknowledged father (perhaps his master, Aaron Anthony) in Tuckahoe, Maryland, Frederick Douglass—he assumed this name in 1838 when he escaped north to freedom—soon became the most famous African-American of the nineteenth century. Separated from his family while young, he was a personal slave to several whites during his formative years. Consequently, he early learned self-reliance and began honing the arts of survival. At the same time, he found a sense of belonging through his relationships with various families and individuals, white and black, who liked and encouraged the bright and precocious youth. Ultimately, the lure of freedom and equality proved irresistible and propelled him on an extraordinary journey of both individual achievement and service to his people and his nation.

Taken in 1826 to Baltimore—where, as an urban slave, he could expand his horizons greatly—he taught himself how to read and write with the witting and unwitting assistance of many around him. Similarly, this more open urban environment, with its large and expanding free African-American population, further whetted his desire to learn as much as possible about freedom, including runaway slaves and the abolitionist movement.

Around the age of thirteen, he converted to Christianity, but over time he became increasingly disillusioned with a religious establishment that compromised with and supported evil and injustice, especially slavery and racial prejudice and discrimination. Also around that age, he purchased his first book, *The Columbian Orator*, which deepened not only his understanding of liberty and equality but also the enormous power of rhetoric, as well as literacy. Indeed, throughout his life he firmly believed in the power of the written and spoken word to capture and to change reality.

As a rapidly maturing eighteen-year-old, developing spiritually and intellectually as well as physically, he revealed an intensifying longing to be free that led him to plan an unsuccessful runaway scheme with several fellow slaves. Several months previously he fought Covey, the "Negro breaker"— one versed in subduing unruly slaves—another sign of the depth of that longing. He later portrayed his triumph over Covey as a turning point in his struggle to become a free man. With the aid of Anna Murray, a free African-American woman in Baltimore with whom he had fallen in love, he escaped to freedom. They moved to New Bedford, Massachusetts (1838); Lynn, Massachusetts (1841); Rochester, New York (1847); and Washington, D. C. (1872).

In the North, Douglass found it very hard to make a living as a **caulker** because of racial discrimination and often

> **Douglass's fierce commitment to egalitarianism, freedom, and justice led him to embrace the women's rights movement.**

caulker: one who seal seams in ships and buildings.

had to resort to menial jobs. Anna worked hard as well, creating a comfortable domestic niche for a family that eventually included five children: Rosetta, Lewis Henry, Frederick Jr., Charles Remond, and Annie. Frederick's speeches within the local black communities brought him to the attention of the mostly white abolitionists allied with William Lloyd Garrison, and in 1841 they asked him to join them as a lecturer. An increasingly powerful lecturer and draw for the Garrisonian Massachusetts Anti-Slavery Society, Douglass learned a great deal from his work with such people as Garrison and Wendell Phillips. Most important, he adopted their pacifism and moral suasionist approach to ending slavery and was deeply influenced by their interrelated perfectionism and social reformism. As a good Garrisonian, he argued for disunion and rejected the political approach to ending slavery as a compromise with a proslavery Constitution.

Douglass also began to come into his own as an activist and a thinker. Drawing upon his experiences as a slave, he lambasted slavery and its notorious effects, most notably antiblack prejudice and discrimination in both North and South. As the living embodiment of a small measure of success in the enormous struggle against slavery, he spoke eloquently with uncommon authority. In 1845, his *Narrative of the Life of Frederick Douglass, an American Slave* was published and its huge success, followed by a successful speaking tour of Great Britain, heightened his celebrity immeasurably. Ever conscious of his public persona and his historical image, he carefully crafted both. *My Bondage and My Freedom* (1855) and *Life and Times of Frederick Douglass* (1881; revised 1892), fuller autobiographies, were likewise crucial in this regard.

His stirring narrative and equally stirring oratory derived much of their power and authenticity from Douglass's deep-seated engagement with the plethora of issues confronting blacks north and south, free and slave. His strong involvement in the national Negro convention movement, as well as with various state and local black conferences, furthered his impact and by 1850 made him the principal spokesman for his race. His fierce commitment to egalitarianism, freedom, and justice similarly led him to embrace the women's-rights movement, notably women's suffrage, and to become one of the most important male feminists of the nine-

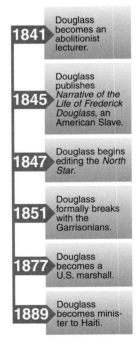

1841 Douglass becomes an abolitionist lecturer.

1845 Douglass publishes *Narrative of the Life of Frederick Douglass,* an American Slave.

1847 Douglass begins editing the *North Star.*

1851 Douglass formally breaks with the Garrisonians.

1877 Douglass becomes a U.S. marshall.

1889 Douglass becomes minister to Haiti.

teenth century. He attended the first Women's Rights Convention, in Seneca Falls, New York, in 1848; on the day of his death, February 20, 1895, he had earlier attended a meeting of the National Council of Women.

Shortly after his return from Great Britain in 1847, Douglass embarked upon a distinguished career in journalism. He edited the *North Star* (1847–1851), *Frederick Douglass' Paper* (1851–1860), *Douglass' Monthly* (1859–1863), and, for a time, the *New National Era* (1870–1874). Complementing the other aspects of his varied public voice and extending its reach and influence, Douglass's work as a journalist furthered his use of the printed word as a tool for agitation and change. Stressing self-reliance, hard work, perseverance, education, and morality, Douglass exemplified the embrace by many African Americans of middle-class values and the American success ethic. Likewise, invoking America's revolutionary tradition, he emphasized the imperative of full black liberation within the confines of the American nation. After 1851, when he formally broke with the Garrisonians and accepted political action against slavery as viable and necessary, he became more politically engaged. By the outbreak of the Civil War, he supported the Republican Party.

The tumultuous events of the 1850s convinced Douglass, like untold numbers of his compatriots, that war was unavoidable, the Union cause just, and slave emancipation inevitable. He urged his audience, most notably President Abraham Lincoln, to further ennoble the Union cause by accepting black troops into the Union army and treating them fairly. He exhorted his people to support fully the Union cause and to struggle ceaselessly to ensure that Union victory would mean emancipation and the necessary conditions for black progress. His often arduous efforts to recruit black Union troops, who braved strong white hostility and mistreatment, showed him grappling intensely with the central and complex issue of African-American identity. African Americans, he cogently argued, honored their group as well as national heritage and mission through vigorous support of an abolitionist Union cause.

Douglass emerged from the war even more widely known and respected. He continued to urge his nation to deal justly and fairly with his people, even after the nation **reneged** on its insufficient and shortlived efforts to do so during

"You have seen how a man was made a slave; you shall see how a slave was made a man."
Frederick Douglass, *Narrative of the Life of Frederick Douglass*, 1845

renege: to fail to fulfill a promise.

When Douglass married his white secretary in 1884, they endured much criticism from many blacks and whites.

Reconstruction. While many blacks questioned his continuing allegiance to the Republican party, Douglass valiantly albeit unsuccessfully-endeavored to help the party rediscover its humanistic and moral moorings. Appointed to serve as the United States marshal for the District of Columbia (1877–1881), recorder of deeds for the District of Columbia (1881–1886), and chargé d'affaires for Santo Domingo and minister to Haiti (1889–1891), he remained a stalwart Republican.

Over the years, Douglass's status as a comfortable middle-class elder statesman tended on occasion to blind him to the harsh conditions confronting rural, impoverished, and migrant blacks. Still, as in his fiery condemnation of the alarming growth in the number of lynchings of black men in the 1880s and 1890s (often upon the false accusation of an attack on a white woman), it was clear that his commitment to justice never wavered. Likewise, while many women's-rights advocates criticized him for supporting the Fifteenth Amendment, which failed to enfranchise women as it enfranchised black men, Douglass contended that the greater urgency of the black male need for the vote and its greater likelihood of passage made support imperative. After its passage, he continued his efforts on behalf of women's rights and sought to heal the rift within the movement.

When Douglass married Helen Pitts, his white secretary, in January 1884, a year and a half after the death of his first wife, they endured much criticism from many blacks and whites, including close family members. Nonetheless, Douglass, the quintessential humanist, steadfastly articulated his commitment to a composite American nationality, transcending race, as an integral component of his vision of a democratic and egalitarian country. When others criticized him for a lack of race spirit, Douglass, refusing to be imprisoned within a racialist universe, claimed ultimate allegiance to the human race.

Yet he also fully understood and vividly personified his people's struggle from slavery to freedom, from obscurity and poverty to recognition and respectability. His enduring legacy to his people and all Americans is best captured in his lifelong and profound dedication to the imperative of agitation and concerted action: "If there is no struggle," he declared, "there is no progress." ◆

Douwes, Arnold

1906–? ● RESCUER OF JEWS DURING WWII

The son of a pastor in the Dutch Reformed church, Arnold Douwes joined the Dutch underground and devoted himself to the rescue of Jewish adults and children. At first, he worked under the guidance of Johannes Post (an important underground figure who aided Jews), who was shot by the Germans. Douwes enlarged the scope of his mentor's rescue operations. Jewish families who had received notification to report for deportation to the Westerbork camp were referred to him by the Dutch underground. He concentrated his activities in the vicinity of the town of Nieuwlande, in the northeastern province of Drenthe. There, almost every household sheltered a Jewish person. Douwes looked after all the needs of these Jews, helping to supply them with food and other necessities, false identification papers, and financial support (through the underground). Together with Max Leons (nicknamed "Nico"), a Jew who posed as a Protestant colleague and friend of Douwes, he scoured the countryside and enlisted several hundred Dutch families in their mutual rescue activities.

Douwes personally met the children in Amsterdam, or at the train station upon their arrival in the Drenthe district. When the Germans staged raids in the vicinity, Douwes went for nocturnal rides on his bicycle, moving Jews—under the very noses of the Germans—to safer locations.

An operation of this magnitude could not go undetected for long, and Douwes was wanted by the authorities. To avoid arrest, he changed his appearance, growing a mustache and wearing a hat and eyeglasses. in spite of these precautions, he was apprehended in January 1945 and imprisoned in Assen, where he awaited his execution. The underground, however, succeeded in freeing him before that could take place. After the war, Douwes lived for a time in South Africa and then moved to Israel in 1956.

Arnold Douwes was responsible for saving the lives of hundreds of Jews, including some one hundred children. In 1965 he was recognized as a "Righteous Among the Nations" by Yad Vashem. More than two hundred residents of the Nieuwlande area were later awarded the title as well. ◆

> To avoid arrest, Douwes changed his appearance, growing a mustache and wearing a hat and eyeglasses.

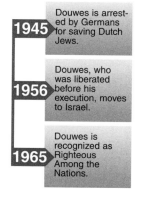

1945 Douwes is arrested by Germans for saving Dutch Jews.

1956 Douwes, who was liberated before his execution, moves to Israel.

1965 Douwes is recognized as Righteous Among the Nations.

Drew, Charles Richard

1904–1950 ● PIONEERING SURGEON

Born and raised in Washington, D.C., Charles Richard Drew graduated from Dunbar High School in 1922. In 1926 he received a B.A. from Amherst College. A first-rate basketball player, on graduation Drew was given an award as best athlete of the college. Between 1926 and 1928, he taught biology and chemistry at Morgan College (now Morgan State University) in Baltimore, where he also served as football coach and as director of athletics.

In 1928, Drew began medical studies at McGill University Medical School in Montreal, Canada. He excelled in medical science courses, won the annual prize in neuroanatomy, was elected to Alpha Phi Omega, the medical honorary scholastic fraternity, and received a prize for the top score in a medical exam competition. In 1933, Drew earned an M.D. and a master in surgery degree. He spent the next two years as an intern and as a resident in medicine at Royal Victoria and Montreal General Hospitals.

As a McGill medical student, Drew was introduced to research on the chemical composition of blood and blood groups by John Beattie, a British medical researcher. A major problem then facing medical science was that quantities of whole, fresh blood large enough to match blood group types between blood donor and blood receiver were not readily

1935 Drew begins teaching at Howard University's School of Medicine.

1940 Drew receives his doctorate from Columbia University.

1940 Drew becomes director of Red Cross Blood Bank Program.

1944 Drew receives the NAACP's Spingarn Medal.

available. Drew was bothered by the deaths of seriously ill or injured patients due to blood loss. Learning more about blood and how to preserve it over long periods of time became a research interest that Drew carried with him as he left Montreal to assume a teaching position at Howard University's College of Medicine in 1935.

In 1938, Drew received a research fellowship from the Rockefeller Foundation for study at Columbia Presbyterian Hospital in New York City. He and John Scudder undertook research that led to the finding that it was blood plasma (the liquid portion of the blood, devoid of blood cells) rather than whole blood that needed to be preserved for transfusions. Drew established an experimental blood bank at Columbia Presbyterian Hospital. In 1940 Drew was awarded a doctorate at Columbia University with a thesis on "Banked Blood."

Returning to Howard University in 1940, Drew devoted himself to training its medical students in surgery. His teaching was abruptly interrupted, however, by a call for blood plasma needed by wounded soldiers on the battlefields of Europe during World War II. The Blood Transfusion Association in New York City asked Drew to return to help. He was given leave from his instructional duties at Howard University to accept an assignment in the fall of 1940 as Medical Director of the Blood for Britain Program, to supply blood for the British Red Cross. Under Drew's guidance, dried plasma was flown across the Atlantic Ocean to England. Once England had established its own banks, a larger blood program for U.S. military forces was developed. The American Red Cross and the Blood Transfusion Association jointly conducted this program and Drew became its medical director.

In 1941 the military established a system of refusing blood donations from nonwhites to be used by whites. Blood donated by blacks was stored separately and given only to blacks. As director of the Red Cross Blood Bank Program, Drew took a strong stand against the racial separation of banked blood. As a result, he was asked to resign his directorship position. He did, and returned once again to teaching surgery at Howard University, where he became professor and head of the department of surgery and surgeon-in-chief at Freedmen's Hospital.

On March 31, 1950, after working a long day that included performing several operations, Drew agreed to drive with other colleagues to a medical conference in Tuskegee,

> **Drew took a strong stand against the racial separation of banked blood.**

Alabama. He dozed at the wheel, and the car went off the road near Burlington, North Carolina, and overturned. Though stories abound that his medical emergency was ignored because of his race, he received prompt medical attention. He died on April 1, 1950 from injuries resulting from the accident.

Drew gained much recognition during his lifetime: He was named Diplomate of Surgery by the American Board of Surgery in 1941; was a recipient of the Spingarn Medal from the NAACP (1944); was granted honorary Doctor of Science degrees from Virginia State College (1945) and Amherst College (1947); and was elected as a Fellow of the International College of Surgery (1946). ◆

Du Bois, William Edward Burghardt

1869–1963 ● Civil rights activist

"The problem of the twentieth century is the problem of the color line."
W. E. B. Du Bois, 1900

W. E. B. Du Bois was born in Great Barrington, Massachusetts. His mother, Mary Burghardt Du Bois, belonged to a tiny community of African Americans who had been settled in the area since before the Revolution; his father, Alfred Du Bois, was a visitor to the region who deserted the family in his son's infancy. In the predominantly white local schools and Congregational church, Du Bois absorbed ideas and values that left him "quite thoroughly New England."

From 1885 to 1888 he attended Fisk University in Nashville, where he first encountered the harsher forms of racism. After earning a B.A. (1888) at Fisk, he attended Harvard University, where he took another B.A. (1890) and a doctorate in history (1895). Among his teachers were the psychologist William James, the philosophers Josiah Royce and George Santayana, and the historian A. B. Hart. Between 1892 and 1894 he studied history and sociology at the University of Berlin. His dissertation, *The Suppression of the African Slave-Trade to the United States*, was published in 1896 as the first volume of the Harvard Historical Studies.

Between 1894 and 1896, Du Bois taught at Wilberforce University, Ohio, where he met and married Nina Gomer, a student, in 1896. The couple had two children, Burghardt and Yolande. In 1896, he accepted a position at the University of Pennsylvania to gather data for a commissioned study of blacks in Philadelphia. This work resulted in *The Philadelphia Negro* (1899), an acclaimed early example of empirical sociology. In 1897, he joined the faculty at Atlanta University and took over the annual Atlanta University Conference for the Study of the Negro Problems. From 1897 to 1914 he edited an annual study of one aspect or another of black life, such as education or the church.

Appalled by the conditions facing blacks nationally, Du Bois sought ways other than scholarship to effect change. The death of his young son from dysentery in 1899 also deeply affected him, as did the widely publicized lynching of a black man, Sam Hose, in Georgia the same year. In 1900, in London, he boldly asserted that "the problem of the Twentieth Century is the problem of the color line." He repeated this statement in *The Souls of Black Folk* (1903), mainly a collection of essays on African-American history, sociology, religion, and music, in which Du Bois wrote of an essential black double consciousness: the existence of twin souls ("an American, a Negro") warring in each black body. The book also attacked Booker T. Washington, the most powerful black American of the age, for advising blacks to surrender the right to vote and to a liberal education in return for

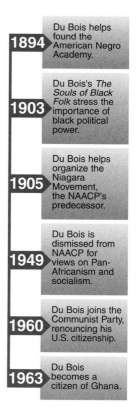

1894 Du Bois helps found the American Negro Academy.

1903 Du Bois's *The Souls of Black Folk* stress the importance of black political power.

1905 Du Bois helps organize the Niagara Movement, the NAACP's predecessor.

1949 Du Bois is dismissed from NAACP for views on Pan-Africanism and socialism.

1960 Du Bois joins the Communist Party, renouncing his U.S. citizenship.

1963 Du Bois becomes a citizen of Ghana.

white friendship and support. Du Bois was established as probably the premier intellectual in black America, and Washington's main rival.

His growing radicalism also led him to organize the Niagara Movement, a group of blacks who met in 1905 and 1906 to agitate for "manhood rights" for African Americans. He founded two journals, *Moon* (1905–1906) and *Horizon* (1907–1910). In 1909 he published *John Brown*, a sympathetic biography of the white abolitionist martyr. Then, in 1910, he resigned his professorship to join the new National Association for the Advancement of Colored People (NAACP) in New York, which had been formed in response to growing concern about the treatment of blacks. As its director of research, Du Bois founded a monthly magazine, *The Crisis*. In 1911 he published his first novel, *The Quest of the Silver Fleece*, a study of the cotton industry seen through the fate of a young black couple struggling for a life of dignity and meaning.

The Crisis became a powerful forum for Du Bois's views on race and politics. Meanwhile, his developing interest in Africa led him to write *The Negro* (1915), a study offering his-

The NAACP

The National Association for the Advancement of Colored People (NAACP) is the oldest and largest civil rights organization in the United States. Founded in 1909, it seeks to end discrimination against blacks and other minorities through nonviolent means. The NAACP backs affirmative action as a path to racial equality and supports racial integration rather than separatism. Through legal action and legislative lobbying, the NAACP has historically played a crucial role in the outlawing of segregation, job discrimination, and bias in the rental and sale of housing. It has also helped secure the vote for blacks. Today, the NAACP has more than 500,000 members in over 2,200 chapters and hundreds of youth councils. Headquartered in Baltimore, its president and chief executive officer is former U.S. representative Kweisi Mfume, and its chairman of the board is Julian Bond, former Georgia state representative and a professor of government. The NAACP's many activities include voter education and registration campaigns, efforts to end school segregation, youth-oriented programs that discourage black students from dropping out and reward them for academic excellence, attempts to secure fair treatment of black accomplishments in textbooks, and antihunger drives. Since 1910 the organization has published a magazine, *The Crisis*.

torical and demographic information on peoples of African descent around the world. Hoping to affect colonialism in Africa after World War I, he also organized Pan-African Congresses in Europe in 1919, 1921, and 1923, and in New York in 1927. However, he clashed with the most popular black leader of the era, Marcus Garvey of the Universal Negro Improvement Association. Du Bois regarded Garvey's "back to Africa" scheme as ill-considered, and Garvey as impractical and disorganized.

Du Bois's second prose collection, *Darkwater: Voices from Within the Veil* (1920), did not repeat the success of *The Souls of Black Folk* but captured his increased militancy. In the 1920s, *The Crisis* played a major role in the Harlem Renaissance by publishing early work by Langston Hughes, Countee Cullen, and other writers. Eventually, Du Bois found some writers politically irresponsible; his essay "Criteria of Negro Art" (1926) insisted that all art is essentially propaganda. He pressed this point with a novel, *Dark Princess* (1928), about a plot by the darker races to overthrow European colonialism. In 1926 he visited the Soviet Union, then nine years old. Favorably impressed by what he saw, he boldly declared himself "a **Bolshevik**."

The Great Depression increased his interest in socialism but also cut the circulation of *The Crisis* and weakened Du Bois's position with the leadership of the NAACP, with which he had fought from the beginning. In 1934, he resigned as editor and returned to teach at Atlanta University. His interest in Marxism, which had started with his student days in Berlin, dominated his next book, *Black Reconstruction in America* (1934), a massive and controversial revaluation of the role of the freedmen in the South after the Civil War. In 1936, Du Bois commenced a weekly column of opinion in various black newspapers, starting with the *Pittsburgh Courier*. He emphasized his continuing concern for Africa with *Black Folk: Then and Now* (1939), an expanded and updated revision of *The Negro*.

In 1940, Du Bois published his first full-length autobiography, *Dusk of Dawn: An Autobiography of a Concept of Race*, in which he examined modern racial theory against the major events and intellectual currents in his lifetime. In 1944, his life took another dramatic turn when he was suddenly retired by Atlanta University after growing tension between himself

"Herein lies the tragedy of the age: not that men are poor—all men know something of poverty; not that men are wicked—who is good? Not that men are ignorant—what is truth? Nay, but that men know so little of men."
W.E.B. Du Bois, *The Souls of Black Folk*, 1903

Bolshevik: a member of the Communist party.

and certain administrators. When the NAACP rehired him that year, he returned to New York as director of special research. In 1945 he was honored at the Fifth Pan-African Congress in Manchester, England, and published a bristling **polemic**, *Color and Democracy: Colonies and Peace*. A year later, he produced a controversial pamphlet, "An Appeal to the World," submitted by the NAACP on behalf of black Americans to the United Nations Commission on Civil Rights. In 1947 came his *The World and Africa*, an examination of Africa's future following World War II.

polemic: an argument.

By this time Du Bois had moved to the left, well beyond the interests of the NAACP, which generally supported the Democratic party. In 1948, when he endorsed the Progressive party and its presidential candidate, Henry Wallace, he was fired. He then joined Paul Robeson, who was by this time firmly identified with radical socialism, at the Council on African Affairs, which had been officially declared a **"subversive"** organization. In 1950, Du Bois ran unsuccessfully for the U.S. Senate from New York on the American Labor party ticket. Also that year, in another in move applauded by communists, he accepted the chairmanship of the Peace Information Center, which circulated the Stockholm Peace Appeal against nuclear weapons.

subversive: seeking to undermine or overthrow existing institutions.

Early in 1951, Du Bois and four colleagues from the Peace Information Center were indicted on the charge of violating the law that required agents of a foreign power to register. On bail and awaiting trial, he married Shirley Lola Graham, a fellow socialist and writer (his first wife had died in 1950). At the trial in November 1951, the Judge heard testimony, then unexpectedly granted a motion by the defense for a directed acquittal. Du Bois was undeterred by his ordeal. In 1953, he recited the Twenty-third Psalm at the grave of Julius and Ethel Rosenberg, executed as spies for the Soviet Union. For such involvements, he found himself **ostracized** by some black leaders and organizations. "The colored children," he wrote, "ceased to hear my name."

ostracized: to be shut out from of a group.

Returning to fiction, he composed a trilogy, *The Black Flame*, about the life and times of a black educator seen against the backdrop of generations of black and white lives and national and international events (the trilogy comprised *The Ordeal of Mansart*, 1957; *Mansart Builds a School*, 1959; and *World of Color*, 1961). After the government lifted its ban on his foreign travel in 1958, Du Bois visited various countries, including the Soviet Union and China. In Moscow on May 1, 1959, he received the Lenin Peace Prize.

In 1960 Du Bois visited Ghana for the inauguration of Kwame Nkrumah as its first president. He then accepted an invitation from Nkrumah to return to Ghana and start work on an *Encyclopedia Africana*, a project in which he had long been interested. In October 1961, after applying (successfully) for membership in the Communist Party, he left the United States. He began work on the project in Ghana, but illness the following year caused him to go for treatment to Romania. Afterward, he visited Peking and Moscow. In February 1963, he renounced his American citizenship and officially became a citizen of Ghana. He died in Accra, Ghana, and was buried there. ◆

Dunant, Jean-Henri

1828–1910 ● SWISS PACIFIST & FOUNDER OF THE RED CROSS

Jean-Henri Dunant was born in Geneva to a wealthy family and for a time worked in banking. A deeply religious man committed to the biblical precept "Love thy neighbor," he was an energetic supporter of the Young Men's Christian Association, for which he lectured and wrote about slavery in Muslim lands and the United States. During one such lecture tour in Italy in 1859, he visited the site of the Battle of Solferino and stared aghast at the carnage. Tens of thousands of casualties lay strewn before him, lacking even the most basic medical attention, heightening the inadequacy of his own feeble attempts to relieve their suffering. To the soldiers, he was the "gentleman in white," an anonymous stretcher-bearer and nurse who waded through blood and mire to save them; to himself, he was incapable of

"Would it not be possible, in time of peace and quiet, to form relief societies for the purpose of having care given to the wounded in wartime by zealous, devoted, and thoroughly qualified volunteers?"

Jean-Henri Dunant,
A Souvenir of Solferino, 1862

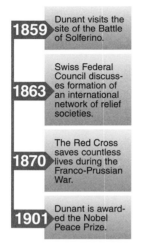

1859 Dunant visits the site of the Battle of Solferino.

1863 Swiss Federal Council discusses formation of an international network of relief societies.

1870 The Red Cross saves countless lives during the Franco-Prussian War.

1901 Dunant is awarded the Nobel Peace Prize.

fulfilling the most basic Christian charity to which he was bound.

Immediately after his return home, he wrote *A Souvenir of Solferino*, describing his haunting recollection of the aftermath of war and advocating the establishment of an international network of voluntary relief societies to tend to the sick and injured. Dunant's ideas were discussed throughout Europe and in 1863, the Swiss Federal Council called an international conference to find ways for their implementation. Sixteen states sent representatives to discuss Dunant's *Nine Articles*, calling "for the amelioration of the condition of the wounded in armies in the field." Twelve countries ratified the articles the following year in an international congress held in Geneva. The congress was known as the Red Cross and in recognition of Switzerland's contribution to the gathering, they adopted an inverse Swiss flag as its symbol.

For several years, Dunant was the prime mover behind the Red Cross. The organization grew rapidly, particularly in the wake of the Franco-Prussian War (1870–1871), where it was responsible for saving countless lives. Dunant, however, had neglected his personal affairs and found himself bankrupt. He

Clara Barton

Affectionately dubbed the "angel of the battlefield," Clara Barton transformed devotion to voluntary service into a national bastion of effective disaster relief—the American Red Cross. Barton overcame bouts of severe exhaustion to nurse soldiers on the battlefield and lobby tirelessly for their humane treatment. Born Christmas Day 1821, Barton began teaching at age 17. A supporter of women's suffrage, Barton left the school she founded when the board hired a man rather than allow a woman to run it. During the Civil War, she spearheaded the collection of medical supplies and delivered them to the front, becoming superintendent of Union nurses. During travels in Europe to rest, she learned about the Geneva Treaty, advocating humane treatment for soldiers and prisoners of war, and about the International Red Cross. Not permitted to work with the agency because of her sex, she volunteered as an independent relief worker during the Franco-Prussian War. Once home, she launched successful crusades for U.S. ratification of the Geneva Treaty and for the creation of the American Red Cross in 1881. Under Barton's 23-year tenure, the Red Cross expanded its peacetime role, providing aid during national disasters. Barton died in 1912, her life's mission immortalized in her own words: "You must never think of anything except the need and how to meet it."

retired to the resort town of Heiden where he continued writing pamphlets calling for international disarmament, a world court to arbitrate in international conflicts, and the establishment of a Jewish homeland. But none was as poignant as *A Souvenir of Solferino*, and Dunant soon faded into obscurity. He was rediscovered in 1895 by a journalist who was shocked to find Switzerland's leading humanitarian unacknowledged and impoverished.

Dunant was nominated for the first Nobel Peace Prize, awarded in 1901, despite claims by many, including Alfred Nobel's private secretary, that if indeed he did deserve the prize it should be for medicine since the Red Cross accepted war as a fact and only worked to **ameliorate** its effects. After lengthy debates, it was decided that Dunant should share the prize with French pacifist Frederic Passy. Although poor and sick, Dunant refused to spend the prize money and left it to charity.

ameliorate: to make better.

Later on, grants enabled him to live out the remainder of his life comfortably as an outspoken advocate of humanitarian ideals and international unity. By the time of his death, forty countries had ratified his *Nine Articles* of the Red Cross. It was only after his death, however, that many of his other ideas—an international ban on slavery, a world court, and a council of nations—were adopted. ◆

Earhart, Amelia Mary

1897–1937 ● AVIATION PIONEER

"Courage is the price that life exacts for granting peace."

Amelia Earhart

Amelia Earhart was one of the first American women to become a flier, and she won an international reputation for her skills and daring in the air. Earhart was born on July 24, 1897, in Atchison, Kansas. She had a varied experience as a girl and young woman, for her family moved frequently during the years she was growing up. When she graduated from Hyde Park High School, Chicago, it was the sixth high school she had attended in as many cities. In 1920 she made her first flight in an air plane. From then on she worked at a variety of jobs, but looked on aviation as her career.

In June 1928, Amelia Earhart became the first woman passenger on a transatlantic flight; she rode with two male aviators in a seaplane that crossed the Atlantic. Four years later, she piloted a single-engine plane on a solo transatlantic hop that set a speed record for that time (1932). Further speed and endurance records followed, including transcontinental flights across the United States, and a long overwater flight

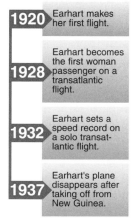

1920 Earhart makes her first flight.

1928 Earhart becomes the first woman passenger on a transatlantic flight.

1932 Earhart sets a speed record on a solo transatlantic flight.

1937 Earhart's plane disappears after taking off from New Guinea.

from Hawaii to the mainland. Her career ended in June 1937, when she was on the last leg of a round-the-world flight. She took off, with a navigator, from New Guinea and was never seen again. She was assumed to have crashed her plane near Micronesia. Amelia Earhart was an outspoken advocate of equality for women in all fields of endeavor. ◆

Eastman, Charles Alexander (Ohiyesa)

1858–1939 ● NATIVE AMERICAN CIVIL RIGHTS ACTIVIST

"It is simple truth that the Indian did not, so long as his native philosophy held sway over his mind, either envy or desire to imitate the splendid achievements of the white man."
Charles Alexander Eastman,
The Soul of the Indian, 1911

Charles Alexander Eastman, whose Indian name was Ohiyesa, was recognized in 1900 as the most educated Indian living in the United States. He devoted his career to helping Indian people through his writings, lectures, and criticism of federal Indian policies.

Born near Redwood Falls, Minnesota, Ohiyesa was raised in the traditional ways of a Santee Sioux hunter and warrior. At the age of fifteen, he reluctantly abandoned that life and agreed to his recently Christianized father's request that he attend a white school. Over the next seventeen years, Eastman attended a number of schools. He earned a B.S.

degree from Dartmouth in 1887 and a medical degree from Boston University School of Medicine in 1890.

Eastman held several government appointments. As government physician at the Pine Ridge Reservation in South Dakota from 1890 to 1893, he witnessed the Wounded Knee tragedy in 1890. He later held positions at the Carlisle Indian School in Pennsylvania in 1899 and the Crow Creek Reservation in South Dakota from 1900 to 1903. From 1903 to 1909, he was head of the revision of the Sioux allotment rolls. Then from 1923 to 1925, he was Indian inspector of reservations.

His nongovernment employment included a brief medical practice in St. Paul, Minnesota, in 1893, Indian secretary of the International Committee of the YMCA from 1894 to 1898, and a representative of a Santee Sioux claims case in Washington, D.C., for a number of years.

Eastman was a prolific writer. With the aid of his non-Indian wife, Elaine Goodale Eastman, he published numerous books and articles. Two of his books were autobiographies: *Indian Boyhood* (1902) and *From the Deep Woods to Civilization* (1916). Others, such as *The Soul of the Indian* (1911) and *The Indian Today* (1915), dealt with Indian-white relations and Indian culture and society. He even wrote a guidebook entitled *Indian Scout Talks* (1914) for Boy Scouts and Camp Fire Girls. He presented lectures throughout the United States and in England.

As an Indian reformer, Eastman helped organize and later served as president of the Society of American Indians, a pan-Indian organization established in 1911. He lobbied for Indian citizenship, condemned deplorable reservation conditions, and opposed the use of peyote by Indians. In 1933, he received the first Indian Council Fire's annual award in recognition of his work to help Indian and non-Indian people understand each other.

Eastman supported an acculturation policy in which Indians selected which non-Indian ways to adopt instead of an assimilation policy that often forced Indians to abandon their culture. He believed Indians could remain Indians and still operate successfully in the dominant culture. ◆

1887 Eastman receives a BA degree from Dartmouth.

1890 Eastman receives a medical degree from Boston University.

1894 Eastman becomes Indian secretary of the International Committee of the YMCA.

1911 The Society of American Indians is established.

1923 Eastman becomes Indian inspector of reservations.

1933 Eastman receives the first Indian Council Fire's award.

Eisenhower, Dwight David (Ike)

1890–1969 ● AMERICAN GENERAL & PRESIDENT OF THE UNITED STATES

"Humility must always be the portion of any man who receives acclaim earned in the blood of his followers and the sacrifices of his friends."

Dwight D. Eisenhower, 1945

Eisenhower was not well read and was never considered an intellect, but he had a sharp, orderly, analytical mind.

Dwight David Eisenhower was born in Denison, Texas, in 1890. His family moved the following year to Abilene, Kansas. Eisenhower's father, David, never earned more than $100 per month, but he and his wife, Ida, raised six boys, each of whom achieved success as adults. The Eisenhowers grew almost all of their own food and earned additional cash by selling the surplus. All of the boys worked to earn their own spending money.

Although Eisenhower was only an average student, he was an outstanding athlete in grade school and high school. After graduating from Abilene High School in 1909, he worked in the local creamery, and part of his salary went to help an older brother through college. He took a competitive examination for the U.S. Naval Academy because of the possibility of a free education and the opportunity to play football. After passing the examination, he found he was too old to attend Annapolis, and instead he entered West Point Military Academy in 1911. Here too Eisenhower proved an excellent athlete and during his second year played halfback on the army football team. Sportswriters praised his All-American capabilities, but a twisted knee cut his football career short.

Eisenhower graduated from West Point in 1915 and was sent to Fort Sam Houston in San Antonio, Texas, as a second lieutenant. Two weeks after reporting for duty, he met his future wife, Mamie Geneva Doud, who came from a wealthy Denver family. They were married in 1916 in Denver, Colorado.

Eisenhower was not particularly well read and was never considered an intellect, but he had a sharp, orderly, analytical mind, with the ability to look at a problem, see what alternatives were available, and decide wisely. In 1917 he was promoted to captain just after the United States entered World War I; although he wanted to lead men in battle in France, he was stationed at Camp Colt, a tank training center in Gettysburg, Pennsylvania, where he spent the entire war. Nevertheless, he was awarded the Distinguished Service Medal for his services as an outstanding instructor and trainer. He was promoted to major in 1920 and the following year graduated from the Tank Training School at Camp Meade, Maryland.

In 1922 Eisenhower was transferred to the Panama Canal Zone as the executive officer for the Twentieth Infantry Brigade. There he met General Fox Connor, who spoke to the young officer at length about military history and international problems. Certain that there would be another world war and that George C. Marshall (then colonel) would command the American forces, Connor suggested that Eisenhower seek an assignment under Marshall.

In 1925 Eisenhower was sent to the Command and General Staff School in Leavenworth, Kansas, finishing first in a class of 275. In 1928 he graduated from the Army War College, gaining the reputation of an outstanding staff officer. From 1929 to 1933 he served as the assistant secretary of war, and in 1933 he was made assistant to the chief of staff (General Douglas MacArthur), in which capacity he spent the next four years in the Philippines.

In December 1941 General Marshall, now army chief of staff, brought Eisenhower to Washington and put him in charge of the war plans division for the Far East. He was promoted to major general in March 1942, serving as head of the operations division, and in June of the same year, Marshall put Eisenhower in charge of the U.S. forces in the European Theater of Operations (ETO).

On November 8, 1942, with Eisenhower in command, British and American forces successfully landed near

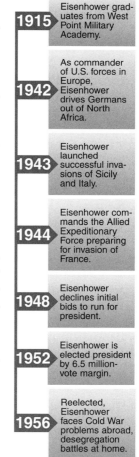

1915 Eisenhower graduates from West Point Military Academy.

1942 As commander of U.S. forces in Europe, Eisenhower drives Germans out of North Africa.

1943 Eisenhower launched successful invasions of Sicily and Italy.

1944 Eisenhower commands the Allied Expeditionary Force preparing for invasion of France.

1948 Eisenhower declines initial bids to run for president.

1952 Eisenhower is elected president by 6.5 million-vote margin.

1956 Reelected, Eisenhower faces Cold War problems abroad, desegregation battles at home.

> *"I call upon all who love freedom to stand with us now. Together we shall achieve victory."*
>
> Dwight D. Eisenhower, broadcast on D-Day, 1944

Casablanca, Oran, and Algiers and drove the Germans out of North Africa. In July 1943 Eisenhower, now a four-star general, launched the invasion of Sicily and the subsequent invasion of Italy. In December, the combined chiefs of staff sent him to London to take command of the forces gathered for the invasion of France. When he took over Supreme Headquarters, Allied Expeditionary Force, he commanded the most powerful single military force ever assembled. On June 6, 1944, over 156,000 men invaded the beaches of Normandy. During the conquest of Europe, under Eisenhower's command, were General Omar N. Bradley, General George S. Patton, as well as British chief of staff Bernard L. Montgomery. The forces led by Eisenhower, now a five-star general, advanced through France but were held up in Belgium during the winter, until they finally smashed through to Germany in the spring.

The Germans signed an unconditional surrender on May 8, 1945, and Eisenhower headed the occupation forces for six months. He was then reassigned to Washington to succeed Marshall as army chief of staff. After completing the task of demobilizing the American army, he traveled, making speeches to promote national defense. His book *Crusade in Europe* (1948) was a best-seller, and he was urged by both the Democratic and Republican parties to accept a presidential nomination, but declined. In June 1948 he became president of Columbia University, holding that position until January 1953 but on leave of absence from December 1950 when he was appointed by President Harry S. Truman to be the supreme commander of the North Atlantic Treaty Organization (NATO).

The two major political parties continued to press Eisenhower to accept the presidential nomination. In 1952 he declared himself a Republican and in June of that year resigned his position as NATO supreme commander, returned to the United States, and began a hectic five-week preconvention campaign. He beat Robert A. Taft by a narrow margin on the first ballot at the Republican national convention.

Basically conservative, Eisenhower advocated a reduction in government controls and taxes, and in the presidential election he received 6.5 million more votes than the liberal Democratic candidate, Governor Adlai E. Stevenson of Illinois (442 to 89 votes in the electoral college). Riding in on the coattails of Ike's popularity, the Republicans captured both houses of Congress. The new president fulfilled one of his campaign promises by halting the fighting in Korea—where South Korea had been invaded by North Korea in 1950—but the ceasefire led to an uneasy truce rather than a genuine peace.

Eisenhower had a talent for getting people of diverse backgrounds to work together toward a common objective. Although he now drew on this and other capabilities he had shown as a military man, he did not prove to be a strong president. Day-to-day management of the government was left to his staff and he placed foreign policy decisions in the hands of Secretary of State John Foster Dulles. Among the achievements of Eisenhower's administration were the end of the Korean War and the creation of the Southeast Asia Treaty Organization and of the International Atomic Energy Agency.

In 1954 the Republicans lost their majority in both houses of Congress. At first, Congress continued to support the president, but opposition soon grew, and when Senator Robert Taft died, Eisenhower lost his main support in Congress. His attempts to balance the budget took three years, but were reversed shortly thereafter because of mounting expenditures for foreign aid and defense. He tried to end the cold war with the Soviet Union, but despite years of effort was unsuccessful in building mutual trust between the two countries.

Eisenhower was reelected in 1956 by an even greater majority, but his personal popularity did not help the Republican party, which lost in both houses of Congress. During the 1956 Suez crisis Eisenhower and Dulles forced Britain and France to break off their attack on Nasser's Egypt. Subsequently the president proposed the Eisenhower Doctrine, which pledged military help to any Middle Eastern country facing a communist threat. This policy was put into effect in 1968, when U.S. troops were sent to Lebanon. At home Eisenhower opposed racial segregation and sent federal troops to Little Rock, Arkansas, to enforce desegregation at a local school. In response to the 1957 Soviet launching of Sputnik, the first satellite, he created the National Aeronautics and Space Administration (NASA) in 1958. A planned meeting with the Soviet premier Nikita Kruschev in

Eisenhower created NASA in 1958 in response to the Soviet launching of Sputnik.

1960 was canceled by the latter after a U.S. spy plane was shot down over the USSR.

Eisenhower groomed Vice President Richard Nixon as his successor, but Nixon was defeated in the 1960 election. Upon retirement, Eisenhower was treated as a respected elder statesman. President John F. Kennedy frequently asked his opinions on international problems. In his later years, Ike suffered a series of heart attacks, and in August 1965 he ended his active participation in public affairs. He remained a very popular public figure and in the 1968 Gallup Poll topped the list of the Most Admired Americans. ◆

Eriksson, Leif

?–1020 ● Viking explorer

990s Eriksson imports Christianity he adopted in Norway to Greenland.

1001 Sailing south from Greenland, Eriksson discovers Baffin Island, Labrador, and "Vinland."

1020 Eriksson dies in Greenland, which sends settlers to Vinland to fish and harvest timber.

Eriksson, known as "Leif the Lucky," the younger son of Erik the Red, was apparently born in Iceland but emigrated to Greenland with his family when his father was exiled following a murder charge. Eriksson traveled to Norway in the early 990s to serve as a retainer at the court of King Olaf Trygvasson. There he adopted Christianity, which he brought back to Greenland on his return. That journey, however, was marked by harsh storm winds, causing Eriksson's ship to lose course. After sighting the coast of North America he managed to return to Greenland, where he reported on the new lands.

Although other Greenlanders, notably Bjarni Herjulfsson, had spotted the North American coastline, no one had set out to explore the region or examine settlement possibilities. In 1001, leading a crew of thirty-five, Eriksson sailed south from Greenland. The first land he encountered was an inhospitable mass of glaciers and rock slabs, generally identified as Baffin Island; he called the area Helluland ("Slab Land"). Sailing south, Eriksson discovered sandy beaches leading to dense forest. This area, apparently on the Labrador coast, he called Markland ("Forest Land"). The explorers then discov-

ered an island described as having the "sweetest dew we have ever tasted."

Eriksson spent the next day sailing around the opposite headland until he found a suitable harbor. The site, with lush pastureland and abundant salmon fishing, was chosen as a good place to make camp and the crew disembarked. According to the writer of the saga, in the commotion of making a campsite, they failed to notice that one of their members, Tyrkir, was missing. Just as Eriksson had organized a search party, a drunken Tyrkir staggered into the camp, explaining that he had eaten some wild grapes. After confirming Tyrkir's claim, Eriksson decided to call the country Vinland. In fact, Vinland comes from the old Norse meaning "meadow land" but was later misinterpreted.

Archeologists and scholars have argued over the precise location of Vinland. Claims range from as far north as Labrador and Newfoundland to as far south as Florida, and as far west as Minnesota. A number of clever forgeries of Viking remains and **runic** script were exposed in the 1960s, but the

Lief Eriksson spots the North American coastline, 1001 A.D.

runic: written with a Germanic alphabet used from about 200 to 1200 A.D.

Erik the Red

Erik the Red (ca. 950–ca. 1002) was a Viking explorer and founder of the first European settlement in Greenland. Erik was born in the Norwegian town of Jaeren. Around 960 he and his father Thorvald committed murder and were forced to flee the country. They headed for the prosperous settlement of Iceland, settling in the inhospitable northwest corner of the island. After some time they moved to the more comfortable Haukadale, but Erik's fierce temper led to several brawls, ending with the death of a neighbor. Erik then moved to the island of Breidafjord, but again found himself involved in a local feud, for which he was banished from Iceland for three years. Rather than risk a return to Norway, Erik decided to explore Greenland. Barely visible from Iceland's west coast, the island had first been mentioned around 900 by Gunbjor Ulfsson, who had approached several outlying islands when his ship was blown off course in a storm. Nevertheless, Icelanders ignored the island for almost eighty years until in 978, when a group of prospective settlers reached the island to escape overpopulation in Iceland; harsh weather conditions led to the abandonment of the colony, however.

Erik took his wife, Thjodhild, two sons, Thorstein and Leif Eriksson, and some thirty supporters to Greenland in 981. After exploring the western coast of the island, they settled in a southwest fjord, naming it Brattahlid. Climatic conditions on the island were considerably better than they are today and the small colony flourished. At the end of his term of exile, Erik returned briefly to Iceland to organize a group of settlers to join him in the new land. Twenty-five ships set out to Greenland, but only fourteen survived the four-day journey, some deciding to turn back, others being lost at sea. The 350 colonists were exceedingly successful in their first fifteen years, which encouraged more immigrants to join them. In 1002, an epidemic, apparently introduced by prospective new immigrants, wiped out a large part of the colony, including Erik himself. Despite the disaster, the colony recovered and continued to exist until the fifteenth century.

debate continues. Two possible locations are Quebec and Virginia.

After spending a year in Vinland, Eriksson returned home to Greenland. Attempts to settle the new lands failed, although the Greenland settlers apparently traveled to Vinland frequently to fish and harvest timber. Eriksson remained in Greenland until his death in 1020. ◆

Gallaudet, Thomas Hopkins

1787–1851 ● FOUNDER OF AMERICAN DEAF-MUTE INSTRUCTION

Thomas Hopkins Gallaudet was born in Philadelphia, Pennsylvania, on December 10, 1787, the son of Peter Wallace and Jane (Hopkins) Gallaudet. Early in the eighteenth century, a French Protestant, Peter Elisha Gallaudet, who some years previous had fled from his native country to escape persecution, settled at New Rochelle, New York. His family was an ancient one, and for generations had adhered to the reformed faith. Peter Wallace Gallaudet, a grandson of the emigrant, was a commission-merchant in Philadelphia for many years. He later lived in New York City and Hartford, Connecticut, and in 1824 took up residence in Washington, D.C., where in his eightieth year, he founded a manual-labor school and orphan asylum. Jane Hopkins, his wife, was descended from John Hopkins and Rev. Thomas Hooker, founders of Hartford, and by her ardent piety showed herself worthy of he Puritan ancestors.

Thomas Hopkins Gallaudet was the eldest of twelve children, and was precocious in his mental development. He was fitted for college at the Hopkins Grammar School in Hartford; in 1802 he entered the sophomore class at Yale and in 1805 was graduated with the highest honors. He spent a year in a law office in Hartford, another year in private study of English literature, and two years, 1808–10, as a tutor in Yale College, but ill health disarranged every plan, and in order to lead amore active, outdoor life, he became a traveling agent for a business house in New York city.

Suddenly, and before his mind was free from religious doubts that had depressed him for years, even before he had united with a church, although it was his purpose to do so, he decided to study for the ministry, and in 1812 entered Andover Theological Seminary. After a conscientious course of study for two years, he was licensed to preach in 1814, and soon received calls to important churches, but declined them, his health not having been established. During one of his vacations, while a theological student, he grew deeply interested in a deaf child, daughter of Dr. Mason Fitch Cogswell, an eminent physician of Hartford, and was convinced that he could impart to her a knowledge of simple words and sentences. The result of his first effort was so encouraging that he

Gallaudet University

In 1856, the politically connected Amos Kendall donated two acres of his Washington, D.C., estate for a school serving 12 deaf and 6 blind wards. The son of Thomas Hopkins Gallaudet, founder of the first U.S. school for deaf students, was its first superintendent. Eight years later, when President Abraham Lincoln signed the charter creating Gallaudet University, there were still fewer than 20 students. One building housed dorm rooms, classrooms, the library, and offices. Since then, Gallaudet has grown into the world's only four-year liberal arts university for deaf and hard-of-hearing students. Its 93-acre campus serves more than 1,300 undergraduate and 800 graduate students. Gallaudet also has pioneered demonstration programs for elementary and high school age deaf children. Its national and international reputation has grown through a network of outreach centers and public service and advocacy efforts on behalf of the deaf. Graduate studies, open to hearing students, feature cutting-edge research of interest to those working in the field of deaf education. In 1988, the student-led Deaf President Now movement closed the university for a week, forcing the selection of the school's first deaf president. Those protests generated worldwide awareness about the language and culture of deaf people.

gave considerable time to the task during the winter of 1814–15, aided by a publication of Abbe Sicard, of Paris.

Dr. Cogswell became eager to have a school for deaf people established in the United States and to have Gallaudet placed at its head. A meeting of influential citizens was called to establish a fund for the purposed of sending Gallaudet abroad to acquire the art of teaching the deaf in the schools of Great Britain and France, and not many weeks later, on June 25, 1815, the young clergyman landed in Liverpool. In spite of letters of introduction, intercessions of people in high life, and persistent personal efforts, he failed to achieve the object of his mission, so far as the schools in London and Edinburgh were concerned. These were under the control of a single family, which had for generations selfishly monopolized the work, and so many obstacles were thrown in Gallaudet's way, and so many galling conditions imposed, that he abandoned all hope of becoming acquainted with the English method, and departed for Paris. In Paris, Gallaudet met with a different reception. The Abbe Sicard gave him every possible facility for the study of his methods, and when, in June 1816 Gallaudet returned to the United States, he took with him Laurent Clere, a young deaf man who had been the abbe's most valued teacher.

In the meantime, the new institution had been incorporated with a grant of money obtained from the state legislature, and through Gallaudet's solicitations, liberal donations from individuals in different parts of the eastern and middle states had been received. The Hartford School for the Deaf was opened with seven pupils on April 15, 1817, and for fourteen years Gallaudet remained at it s head, overcoming difficulties and bearing burdens with a self-sacrifice that was not fully appreciated by the board of directors. He was overworked, underpaid, and owning to lack of a fixed policy on the part of the directors, was subjected to many annoyances. Although he had brought the institution to a state of property, an attempt to remove him was made in 1823; fortunately for the life of the school it was frustrated, and he kept on, bearing increasing burdens, until April 7, 1830, when, for the sake of his health, he resigned.

In addition to teaching classes, drilling new teachers, preparing annual reports, and conducting a large correspondence, he had spent a large part of his time in helping to

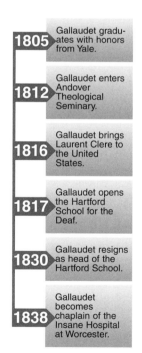

1805 Gallaudet graduates with honors from Yale.

1812 Gallaudet enters Andover Theological Seminary.

1816 Gallaudet brings Laurent Clere to the United States.

1817 Gallaudet opens the Hartford School for the Deaf.

1830 Gallaudet resigns as head of the Hartford School.

1838 Gallaudet becomes chaplain of the Insane Hospital at Worcester.

Gallaudet
opened the
Hartford School
for the Deaf
with seven
pupils on April
15, 1817.

found similar institutions, in delivering public addresses on deaf education, in making appeals to legislatures, and in preaching; moreover, "in most of the organized public movements of the day his support and active cooperation were considered essential." Of his work as a teacher, his son and biographer Edward M. Gallaudet, says: "His skill in adapting methods borrowed from France, to the needs of American children, was great. He possessed peculiar and natural endowments for the special work of instructing the deaf, prominent among which was a really marvelous grace and clearness in all kinds of pantomimic expression. He was the first to suggest and use in schools for the deaf the language of signs in religious exercises and lectures. His eloquence in this language has never been surpassed and rarely equaled."

Gallaudet ended his labors October 1, 1830. Meanwhile he had been invited to inaugurate in Boston the education of the blind in America; to accept professorships in several colleges, and to be come principal of various institutions, including the first normal school in America, and to inaugurate a professorship of the philosophy of education in the New York University. All of these he declined, to devote himself to the preparation of books for the young, for which he was peculiarly titled. Before the end of the year he had written the *Child's Book on the Soul,* and this was followed by the *Child's Book on Repentance,* the *Child's Book of Bible Stories,* the *Youth's Book on Natural Theology,* and eleven volumes of *Scripture Biography,* all of which were circulated to the extent of thousands of copies, and were translated into many languages. Assisted by Rev. Horace Hooker he prepared a *Practical Spelling Book,* and a *School and Family Dictionary and Illustrated Definer,* both of which had a large circulation. His work as an author covered a period of eight years. For eight years also he acted as agent of an association for the promotion of Protestantism in the West, especially in sections settled by Germans.

In 1838 he was invited to become chaplain of the Insane Hospital at Worcester, Massachusetts, and in the same year to accept a similar position in the Retreat for the Insane at Hartford. He accepted the latter position, and held it until his death. It was a field of labor for which he was admirably gifted, and supported by the love and confidence of his medical associates, he did work that was hardly inferior to that performed in the other institutions. Gallaudet's culture, his personal magnetism, his tact, his humor, were all brought into exercise, and his direct influence on the patients was considered a most important curative force.

Throughout his life Gallaudet was a member of the ancient First Church (Centre Congregational) of Hartford, but was broad-minded enough to sympathize with the gifted pastor of the North Congregational Church, Horace Bushnell, when the latter was under trial for so-called heterodoxy. His relations with clergymen of all denominations were of the most cordial nature. As a public speaker and as a preacher he had great popularity. His topics were logically arranged, his thoughts were set forth in polished language, the earnestness of his manner compelled attention, and his personal presence, in spite of the fact that he was undersized, had a gentle power of fascination. Gallaudet was married in 1821 to once of his pupils, Sophia, daughter of Miner and Rachel (Hall) Fowler. Attractive in person, vivacious in manner, and lovely in character, she endeared herself to everyone, and her sympathy and encouragement brought her husband through many a period of trial. She was of great aid to him and to her son Edward Miner in the schools of which they respectively had charge. She bore him four sons and four daughters, and survived him by twenty-six years. Gallaudet received the degree of LL.D. from Western Reserve College a short time before his death, which occurred at Hartford, September 10, 1851. In 1854 a monument, designed by two deaf artists, was created on the grounds of the Hartford School for the Deaf. ◆

Gandhi, Mohandas Karamchand (Mahatma)

1869–1948 ● INDIAN POLITICAL & SPIRITUAL LEADER

*"Nonviolence is the first article of my faith.
It is also the last article of my creed."*
Mahatma Gandhi, 1922

Born in Porbandar, the capital of a small principality in Gujarat, western India, where his father was chief minister, Mohandas Karamchand Gandhi grew up in a pious Hindu household. Gandhi took the doctrine of *ahimsa*—refraining from harming any living being—for granted; it was later to constitute an integral part of his personal philosophy of social and political action.

Married at thirteen, Gandhi overcame his mother's anxiety and ultraorthodox Hindu condemnation to sail to London to study law in 1888. Separated from his wife and family, the lonely youth was forced to question and justify such personal practices as his vegetarianism; becoming a member of the London Vegetarian Society's executive commitee, he came into contact with such radical figures as Edward Carpenter, George Bernard Shaw, and Annie Besant. He was also exposed for the first time to the Hindu spiritual classic the *Bhagavadgita*, which was to have a profound and lasting effect upon him.

Unable to make a satisfactory living as a lawyer in India, Gandhi remained there for only two years, sailing to South Africa in 1893 accept a position with an Indian firm. Journeying by train from Durban to Pretoria, Gandhi, despite his elegant Western dress and manner, was expelled from his first-class carriage at the insistence of a white passenger who objected to sharing it with an Indian. In later years, he was consistently to designate this as the single most important formative experience of his life; it moved him to determine to assert his dignity as an Indian and a man in a country where apartheid laws rendered him and his fellow Indians second-class citizens.

Gandhi soon became recognized as a leader of the South African Indian community, staying on to fight for its interests even after his original work was completed. His trip was to have lasted a few months; he remained in South Africa for a quarter of a century.

Founding the Natal Indian Congress, Gandhi organized demands for improved civil rights for the thousands of Indians living in the then-crown colony, most of whom were indentured laborers. In 1899, stressing duties as well as rights, he argued that as citizens of the British Empire, Indians should help defend Natal during the Boer War and formed an eleven-hundred-man Indian volunteer ambulance corps.

Gandhi's life constituted a continuous spiritual quest and in 1904, after reading *Unto This Last*, John Ruskin's avowal of the nobility of manual labor, he gave up his £5,000-a-year legal practice and, with some of his growing band of followers, renounced material possessions and strove to satisfy human needs in the simplest manner, with all labor considered equally valuable and all goods shared. Tolstoy Farm (named after Leo Tolstoy, whose *The Kingdom of God Is Within You* profoundly impressed Gandhi, and with whom he corresponded briefly) near Johannesburg became Gandhi's home and a center for communal living. Throughout his life he was to continue such "experiments with truth," which led him to simplify his diet, renounce sex, spend an hour each morning in careful study of the *Bhagavadgita* (which he came to regard as his "spiritual dictionary"), profess the unity of all religions, dress in the garb of a simple Indian peasant, and even extol the virtues of a daily salt water enema.

The opposition to the Transvaal government's 1906 registration ordinance, which required all Indians over the age of eight to be fingerprinted and carry an identity card, marked the first use of strategies based on the principle of *satyagraha* (literally "truth-firmness," passive resistance), which Gandhi

1888 Gandhi sails to London to study law.

1893 Gandhi moves to South Africa to practice law.

1914 Gandhi sails to India.

1919 Gandhi organizes nonviolent protests against India's Rowlatt Act.

1930 Gandhi marches to Dandi to collect sea salt as a protest.

1942 Gandhi's call for the British to leave India leads to his imprisonment.

1947 India becomes independent.

1948 Gandhi is assassinated.

"The moment the slave resolves that he will no longer be a slave, his fetters fall. He frees himself and shows the way to others. Freedom and slavery are mental states.
Mahatma Gandhi,
Non-Violence in Peace and War

had formulated. His religious convictions had led him to a complete disavowal of violence, but he still received a jail sentence for organizing a boycott of the registration process and peaceful picketing of registration centers.

While in prison, he read Henry Thoreau's *On Civil Disobedience*, which asserted the individual's right to ignore unjust laws and refuse allegiance to a government whose tyranny had become unbearable; the book acted as a catalyst for his ideas and motivated his strategy for opposing the 1913 decision by the Transvaal government to close its borders to Indians. Thousands of floggings and hundreds of jailings could not break the nonviolent movement, and in the face of international condemnation of its heavy-handed retaliatory measures, Jan Smuts's government engineered a compromise agreement with Gandhi. "The saint has left our shores, I hope for ever," observed Smuts when Gandhi sailed for India in 1914.

Hailed as "Mahatma" (great-souled) by Rabindranath Tagore, Gandhi played little active role in Indian politics until 1919, when he organized nonviolent protests against the Rowlatt Act, which sought to repress agitation for Indian freedom. The British authorities' response was nowhere more brutal than in the city of Amritsar, Punjab, where some fifteen hundred unarmed and nonviolent protesters were gunned down by troops. Indians reacted with shock and horror and calls for independence from British rule became even stronger.

superannuated: old and out-of-date.

Quickly recognized as the undisputed leader of the Indian nationalist movement, Gandhi succeeded in transforming the Indian National Congress from a **superannuated** body of anglicized Indian gentlemen into a genuinely representative mass organization, using it as the launching pad for a campaign of nonviolent noncooperation against British rule. To the dismay of many of his colleagues, he called off the hugely successful campaign in 1922, when outbreaks of violence convinced him that his followers did not fully understand the importance of the principle of nonviolence. He was arrested shortly thereafter, but was released due to ill health after serving three years in jail.

Convinced that self-sufficiency was an essential prerequisite for successful Indian self-government, he called for a boycott of British goods, a return to the wearing of rough homespun cotton clothing; he himself spent an hour each day at a spinning wheel and homespun soon became the unofficial uniform of nationalist political leaders, In 1930 he marched to Dandi on the Gujarat coast and collected sea salt in defiance of the government monopoly on its manufacture and sale. The wave of civil disobedience this action triggered resulted in 60,000 arrests, in cluding that of Gandhi himself, but the British government was eventually forced to acknowledge Indian nationalist aspirations. The man Winston Churchill derided as a "half-naked **fakir**" traveled to London to negotiate with the British government, but negotiations did not yield the timetable for a British withdrawal from India for which he had hoped.

fakir: a Hindu or Muslim holyman.

After his return to India, he was increasingly occupied with projects such as the uplift of India's tens of millions of untouchables (economically and socially the lowest of the low, whom he renamed *Harijans*, or "Children of God") and the promotion of village based economics as opposed to the economics of industrialization and urbanization, which he considered inappropriate to Indian needs. Nevertheless, even after leaving the Indian National Congress in 1934, he remained the spiritual leader of the nationalist movement and the Indian people, exerting a considerable practical and moral influence.

Gandhi's principles led him to staunchly refuse to approve Indian support for the British war effort, despite his acknowledgment that Nazi persecution of Jews meant that "if ever there could be justifiable war in the name of and for humanity, war against Germany to prevent the wanton persecution of a whole race would be completely justified." Meanwhile his 1942 call for the British to "Quit India" led to his imprisonment and that of the entire Congress leadership, but the writing was on the wall for British rule. Five years later, in August 1947, India became an independent state.

Gandhi had consistently struggled against separating the subcontinent into a Hindu India and a Muslim Pakistan, and the **sectarian** bloodbath that followed partition and claimed a million lives was a realization of his worst fears. He spent the night of the independence celebrations in Calcutta, where his presence successfully prevented the communal violence that had flared elsewhere. When violence did finally erupt there, Gandhi, seventy-seven years old and in poor health,

sectarian: prejudiced in favor of a certain group or sect.

"Nonviolence and truth (Satya) are inseparable and presuppose one another. There is no god higher than truth."
Mahatma Gandhi,
1939

expressed his intention of fasting until the fighting had completely stopped. He had fasted before to achieve spiritual or political ends, but never before had his life been so obviously at risk; within seventy-two hours hostilities in the city ceased.

In early January of the following year Gandhi arranged a truce in the riot-torn capital, Delhi; at the end of that same month he was assassinated by a Hindu fanatic at one of his own prayer meetings. He died with the words *"He, Ram"* ("O! God") on his lips. Among the thousands of tributes to him, none was more moving or heartfelt than Jawaharlal Nehru's representation of him as "that light that represented the living, the eternal truths, reminding us of the right path, drawing us from error, taking this ancient country to freedom."

The initiator of the twentieth century's struggles against colonialism, racism, and violence, Gandhi has also been an influential symbol of the moral and spiritual resources of the developing world, while his theory and practice of nonviolent direct action influenced many, including the African American civil rights leader, Martin Luther King Jr. ◆

Gagarin, Yuri Alexeyevich

1934–1968 ● Sovier cosmonaut

"I can see the earth's horizon. It has a very beautiful sort of halo, a rainbow!"
Yuri Gagarin,
1961

Yuri Gagarin became the first person to make a spaceflight when he rode a Vostok spacecraft on a single orbit of the earth on the morning of Wednesday, April 12, 1961.

It was a cloudless spring day at the Baikonur launch center on the arid steppes of Kazakhstan when the twenty-four rocket engines of the first stage of the R-7 rocket ignited. *"Poyekhali!"* Gagarin said as the rocket rose. "Here we go!" Within minutes he was in space reporting that he felt fine, that the Vostok was functioning. "I can see the earth's horizon," he said, describing sights no human had ever seen. "It

Yuri Alexeyevich
Gagarin, 1965.

has a very beautiful sort of halo, a rainbow!" He passed over
the Pacific Ocean and over America (and thought of Alan
Shepard, who Gagarin had believed would be the first to go
into space). Over Africa the Vostok retrorockets fired, nudg-
ing the spacecraft out of orbit. After the fiery reentry, made
tricky by the failure of the **retrorocket** package to separate as
commanded, Gagarin ejected as planned from Vostok and
parachuted safely to a field on a collective farm near Saratov.
Gagarin's flight lasted one hour and forty-eight minutes.

retrorocket: a small
rocket that produces
thrust opposite the
direction of the
spacecraft.

Gagarin was born March 9, 1934, in the village of
Klushino in the Smolensk Region west of Moscow. His father
was a carpenter, and the Gagarin family lived under German
occupation in the village of Gzhatsk for several years during
the Great Patriotic War. After graduating from secondary
school in 1949 Gagarin attended the Lyubertsy Agricultural
Machinery School for two years followed by the Saratov
Industrial Technical School. But while studying to become a
factory worker Gagarin joined an amateur pilot's club and
learned to fly. One of his instructors recommended him for air
force duty and Gagarin entered the Orenburg Higher Air
Force School in 1955.

After graduation in November 1957 Gagarin was offered
the chance to be an instructor at Orenburg, but he opted

instead for service with the Northern Fleet. For two years he was a pilot based at Zapolyarny, north of the Arctic Circle, until volunteering for the cosmonaut group in October 1959. The following March, after months of medical, psychological and political testing, Gagarin was one of young pilots who reported to the Frunze Central Airport in Moscow to begin training for manned flights into space.

Gagarin quickly established himself as one of the candidates for the first flight and in late March 1961 was advised by Lieutenant General Nikolai Kamanin, the director of cosmonaut training, that he would be the pilot of the first Vostok. A meeting of the State Commission for Space Flight on April 8, 1961, confirmed the appointment.

Following his historic flight Gagarin spent many days and weeks making public appearances and trips, visiting Czechoslovakia, Britain, and Canada. He found it difficult to devote time to his career as an active pilot and cosmonaut and so found himself in administrative jobs. He was, in fact, named commander of the cosmonaut team on May 25, 1961, a post he held until December 1963, when he was made deputy director of the Cosmonaut Training Center. In these posts he directed the training of the first women cosmonauts (who arrived at the Center in March 1962) and acted as communications operator for the twin flights of Vostok 3 and Vostok 4, Voskhod 1, and Voskhod 2. He was also active politically as a delegate to Party Congresses in 1961 and 1966.

1955 Gagarin enters Orenburg Higher Air Force School.

1959 Gagarin volunteers to be a cosmonaut.

1960 Gagarin becomes the first person to make a space flight.

1961 Gagarin becomes deputy director of the Cosmonaut Training Center.

1968 Gagarin dies in a plane crash.

As of June 1964 Gagarin was also forbidden to fly and train actively, a restriction he found increasingly frustrating. He made repeated requests to General Kamanin to be allowed to train again, and in April 1966 Kamanin-Vostokrelented, allowing Gagarin to join the group of cosmonauts beginning to train for manned Soyuz flights.

The preliminary crew assignments for the proposed Soyuz 1/Soyuz 2 mission, made in September 1966, originally didn't include Gagarin. But he fought for inclusion, and was finally named as second, or backup, pilot to Komarov on Soyuz 1. He was expected to fly a weeklong Soyuz mission later in 1967.

But following launch on April 23, 1967, Komarov's Soyuz 1 developed severe technical problems: one solar panel failed to unfold, leaving the spacecraft short of power. There were also problems with the attitude control system. The scheduled Soyuz 2 launch was scrubbed, and Soyuz 1 was ordered to land.

Following reentry, however, the parachute on Komarov's spacecraft failed to open properly. The vehicle smashed into the ground and burst into flames, killing Komarov and bringing the Soviet manned space program to a sudden halt. Gagarin took part in Komarov's memorial service, and hoped to involve himself in the investigation and return to flight. But five days after the accident General Kamanin again removed Gagarin from flight status.

Throughout 1967 Gagarin continued his studies at the Zhukovsky Air Force Engineering Academy (he would graduate in February 1968) and supervised training for not only the Earth orbit Soyuz, but also the Soyuz-Zond circumlunar missions.

On March 12, 1968, following completion of Gagarin's academic work, Kamanin was able to restore him to flight status. Gagarin immediately joined cosmonauts Shatalov, Volynov, Gorbatko, and others in weightless flights aboard the Tu-104, and set out to requalify himself as a jet pilot.

At 10:19 on the morning of March 27, 1968, Gagarin and flight instructor Vladimir Seregin took off from the Chkalov air base near the Center in a MiG-15. After one request from the pilots for a change of course, nothing further was heard. Ground controllers became alarmed. Search and rescue helicopters were ordered into the air. Other air bases in the region were alerted in case Gagarin and Seregin had had to land there. Hours passed without word. Finally wreckage was spotted in a forest little more than a mile from the village of Novoselovo. Kamanin himself flew to the site, wading through waist-deep snow to the crater, which had now filled with melted water. It was almost dusk and darkness made it impossible to tell what had happened. It wasn't until dawn the next day that Gagarin's remains were found.

An investigation and reconstruction of the accident twenty years later concluded that Gagarin and Seregin's MiG15 had been caught in the vortex of another jet and thrown into a spin. The pilots recovered, but found themselves in a steep dive at an altitude of not much more than 1,000 feet. They were unable to pull out or eject.

Gagarin has been the subject of several biographies published around the world, including *Orbits of a Life* by Oleg Nudenko (1971), *My Brother Yuri* by Valentin Gagarin (1973), *It Couldn't Have Been Otherwise* by Pavel Popovich

Gagarin and Seregin's MiG15 was caught in a vortex of another jet and thrown into a spin.

A crater on the far side of the moon has been named for Yuri Gagarin.

and Vasily Lesnikov (1980), *108 Minutes and an Entire Life* by his wife, Valentina (1981), *Words About a Son* by his mother, Anna (1983), and *Gargarin* by V. Stepanov (1986). His auto-biographies include *My Road to Sloace* (1961) and *Flame* (1968). Gagarin also co-authored several technical works, including *Survival in Space* (1969).

A crater on the far side of the moon, a Soviet space track-ing vessel, the Red Banner (Order of Kutuzov) Air Force Academy, the Cosmonaut Training Center, and his former hometown of Gzhatsk have all been named for Yuri Gagarin, the "first citizen" of space travel. ◆

Garrison, William Lloyd

1805–1879 ● ABOLITIONIST

"I am in earnest—I will not equivocate—I will not excuse—I will not retreat a single inch—and I will be heard."

William Lloyd Garrison

William Lloyd Garrison was the most outstanding and influential abolitionist writer and publisher in the United States. His weekly newspaper, *The Liberator*, which appeared for thirty-five years from 1830 to 1865, built up and encouraged antislavery feeling among abolitionists, and aroused reaction among slaveholders and their sympathizers.

Garrison began life in hardship. He was born on December 10, 1805, in Newburyport, Massachusetts. His father had been an alcoholic, and as a very young boy he was left fatherless. After brief formal schooling, he was apprenticed to a newspaper editor in Newburyport. His apprenticeship taught him printing and editing, and gave him a chance to develop skill in writing. He ran a small Newburyport newspa-per, the *Free Press*, in 1828. This was not a success, but he did become friendly with a struggling young poet, John Greenleaf Whittier. The two became lifelong friends. Garrison moved to Boston where he worked for a time on a newspaper devot-ed to the cause of temperance. He wrote articles on many kinds of reform—antidrinking, antigambling, antiwar. While in Boston, he met Benjamin Lundy, a Quaker who was already committed to the cause of abolition.

Garrison took up the abolitionist idea rapidly. He recognized this as his life work, and plunged into an absolute, "no-holds-barred" attack on the very idea of slavery. He spent part of 1829 and 1830 in Baltimore, writing strong, even violent, attacks on slavery and slaveowners. One man brought suit against him for libel and he went to jail when he couldn't pay his fine. This jail term lasted only briefly, for a New Yorker came to his help with money to pay the fine.

Garrison and a partner, Isaac Knapp, began to publish *The Liberator* on January 1, 1831. They had borrowed equipment, and they operated "on a shoestring" with very small subscription lists to support the publication. Garrison, however, set the tone for the drive on slavery in his opening issue. It included an editorial denouncing the evil of slavery and ending with his famous statement: "I am in earnest—I will not equivocate—I will not excuse—I will not retreat a single inch—and I will be heard." He lived on that principle for the next thirty-five years.

Garrison suffered personal injury and was in danger of death from mobs who opposed his uncompromising ideas. Accepting the southern argument that slavery was protected by the U.S. Constitution, he denounced the Constitution as a "covenant with death and an agreement with hell!" He argued that the free (and therefore good) northern states should secede from the Union and he went on a lecture tour through the midwestern states to argue this point. He publicly burned a copy of the Constitution and demanded the prompt and complete conversion of Americans to the doctrine of abolition. He acted more like a reforming clergyman than a political leader. He voted only once in his life, and he would have nothing to do with those who organized political parties to oppose slavery, or who supported efforts to abolish slavery gradually. He wanted immediate emancipation, with no reservations and no payments to slaveowners.

Given these positions, his approach to the Republican Party in 1860 was cool and detached. He did not fully support the Civil War effort until after Lincoln had published the Emancipation Proclamation. Then he did support Lincoln. Garrison's main objective was accomplished with the Thirteenth Amendment. He suggested that the antislavery

1828 Garrison runs the *Free Press*, a paper in Newburyport, Massachusetts.

1831 Garrison and Isaac Knapp begin producing *The Liberator*.

1865 Garrison discontinues *The Liberator*.

societies that he had organized and helped should be dissolved, and he discontinued *The Liberator* on December 29, 1865. Garrison was not especially active in the drive for civil rights for Negroes after the Civil War; his major interest was in emancipation and the end of formal slavery. He did take up a number of other reform movements after the war, and was especially active in the drives to curb alcoholic beverages, and to arrange for women's right to vote. Garrison was internationally famous. He had many friends and supporters among the English abolitionists (who had succeeded in ending slavery in the British Empire long before 1865), and with Irish and Canadian reformers as well. His single-minded drive on slavery was an extremely important and significant element in developing the antislavery movement in the United States. ◆

Grant, Ulysses Simpson

1822–1885 ● AMERICAN GENERAL & PRESIDENT OF THE UNITED STATES

"The war is over—the rebels are our country-men again."

Ulysses Simpson Grant, upon General Lee's surrender, 1865

Ulysses S. Grant was born in Point Pleasant, Ohio, but the year after his birth the family moved to Georgetown, Ohio. Grant showed little academic ability but was very good with horses and preferred to work on his father's farm rather than in his tannery. Against his will, his father sent him to the U.S. Military Academy in 1839. After a short time Grant decided that, "A military life has no charms for me." He graduated in 1843, ranking twenty-first in a class of thirty-nine, his main achievement being in horsemanship. He was commissioned a brevet second lieutenant and assigned to the Fourth U.S. Infantry, which was stationed at Jefferson Barracks near Saint Louis, Missouri.

From 1846 to 1848 Grant served with distinction in the Mexican War, where he was promoted to a full second lieutenant under General Zachary Taylor. In later years Grant

Ulysses Simpson Grant.

copied Taylor's informal dress and lack of military pretension. Grant's regiment was transferred to the army of Winfield Scott, under whom he was promoted, in battle, to first lieutenant and then to captain. For the next four years Grant was stationed in Sachets Harbor, New York, and Detroit, Michigan, but in 1852 he was transferred to the Pacific coast, where he spent two miserable years with an inadequate income and without his family. At that point he had to resign his commission and went to Missouri to try his hand at farming. This attempt proved unsuccessful and he went to work on his father's farm.

In August 1861 President Abraham Lincoln appointed Grant brigadier-general of volunteers. In January 1862, while in command of the Twenty-First Illinois Volunteers, he achieved the first major Union victory in the Civil War and subsequently participated in many battles as second in command. When his commander was called to Washington in July 1862, Grant led the forces to victory in several impressive battles. In October 1862 he was made commander of the Department of Tennessee and it was his aggressiveness, resilience, independence, and determination that made possible the final victory at Vicksburg, where he succeeded in cutting the Confederacy in half.

His successes brought him to Washington in 1864, where he received Lincoln's personal thanks and was voted a gold medal by Congress. He was promoted to lieutenant general and commander of all the armies of the United States. He then developed a plan of action for the armed forces which, together with their superior numbers, enabled them to defeat the Confederates and on April 9, 1865, General Robert E. Lee officially surrendered to Grant.

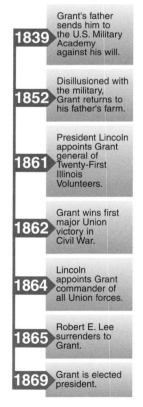

Late in 1865 Grant, who recommended a lenient Reconstruction policy, toured the South, where he was greeted with friendliness. In 1866 he was given the rank of general of the armies of the United States. He became a popular public figure and was the obvious candidate for the presidency, easily defeating Democrat Horatio Seymour; he assumed the presidency on March 4, 1869.

At the time of his election he was forty-six years old, the youngest man to achieve that office. He proved an inept politician; his cabinet consisted of friends, not strong leaders. He had formulated no policy and displayed no leadership in dealing with the Congress, and for the next eight years the country was run by his advisers, whose counsel was for the most part poor. During his second term in office, both his domestic and his foreign policies were in such disarray that the Republican party as a whole was discredited and he was defeated at the Republican convention in his attempt to run for a third term.

When he left the presidency Grant went on a world tour, during which he was received not as a discredited president but as the victor of the Civil War. He returned to the United States after two years of traveling and again tried for the presidential nomination. On the thirty-sixth ballot at the 1880 Republican national convention, James A. Garfield was nominated and Grant's political career came to an end.

Timeline (left margin):

1839 Grant's father sends him to the U.S. Military Academy against his will.

1852 Disillusioned with the military, Grant returns to his father's farm.

1861 President Lincoln appoints Grant general of Twenty-First Illinois Volunteers.

1862 Grant wins first major Union victory in Civil War.

1864 Lincoln appoints Grant commander of all Union forces.

1865 Robert E. Lee surrenders to Grant.

1869 Grant is elected president.

In 1881 he moved to New York and became involved with an investment firm in which his son was a partner. He invested heavily and encouraged friends to do the same, but a swindle by Ferdinand Ward left him with a debt of sixteen million dollars and a clouded reputation. Grant attempted to recoup some of his losses by becoming a partner in a brokerage firm but like all of his other business ventures, it failed, and in 1884 he was forced into bankruptcy.

He began to write reminiscences of his various battles and to prepare his memoirs. Suffering from throat cancer, he composed in his sickroom in Saratoga, New York, two volumes of his recollections and they remain one of the great war commentaries of all time. These memoirs, published by Mark Twain, brought the Grant family $450,000 in royalties. In 1885, the family moved to the Adirondacks, where Grant died. ◆

Greene, Nathanael

1742–1786 ● SOLDIER

Nathanael Greene was born on July 27, 1742, in Warwick, Rhode Island. He was a self-made soldier and military leader who overcame a permanent injury that made him lame and turned away from his religious upbringing as a Quaker to become one of the most important Revolutionary War generals.

Greene commanded Rhode Island's troops at the siege of Boston in 1775–1776. Thereafter, as a Continental officer, he became one of Washington's most trusted advisers and division commanders in battle. As Quartermaster-General for the years 1777–1780, he was responsible for securing and moving all army supplies. In 1780, Greene was assigned to command the army in the South. Lord Cornwallis had just defeated General Horatio Gates at the battle of Camden and Greene

> *"We fight, get beat, rise, and fight again."*
> Nathaniel Greene, 1781

took over a skeleton army. For the remainder of the war he built up its strength while he hacked away at Cornwallis's supply lines in a series of small actions, never allowing himself to be tricked into a major engagement. Greene's base of supplies was in Virginia, and it was an attempt to destroy Greene's supplies that drew Cornwallis and the British into the campaign that led to Yorktown. While Cornwallis was engaged in Virginia, Greene pushed his own army around the British and liberated the Carolinas and Georgia. Greene died on a plantation given him by the grateful legislature of Georgia. Greensboro, North Carolina, was named in his honor, for it is located at the site of his victory at Guilford Court House. ◆

Hale, Nathan

1755–1776 ● SOLDIER &
SECRET AGENT

Nathan Hale was born on June 6, 1755, in Coventry, Connecticut. He was one of six brothers who fought in the Revolutionary War. As a student at Yale (A.B., 1773), he was well known as an athlete and as a speaker. Both skills were useful in his brief career as a schoolteacher, from 1773 to 1775.

When news of the battles of Lexington and Concord reached him in New London, Connecticut, he made a stirring public speech demanding liberty and independence for the colonies. He then volunteered for the army and was commissioned a lieutenant of Connecticut troops on July 1, 1775. Six months later he was promoted to captain. He served at the siege of Boston, and during the battles around New York in the period from April to September 1776. Hale volunteered to gather information about the enemy for Washington's use, and slipped through the British lines disguised as a school teacher, using his Yale diploma as his credentials. After studying British strength on Long Island, he returned to New York City and was on his way back to the American headquarters when he was captured by the British on September 21. His own family and friends believed that he was betrayed by a Loyalist relative.

When Hale admitted he was an American agent, General Sir William Howe ordered his immediate execution. Just before he was hanged, he gave a speech from the gallows that ended: "I only regret that I have but one life to lose for my country." ◆

"I only regret that I have but one life to lose for my country."

Nathan Hale,
1776

1773 Hale begins a career as a schoolteacher.

1775 Hale becomes a lieutenant of Connecticut troops.

1776 Captain Hale serves at the siege of Boston.

1776 Hale is captured by the British.

1776 On the gallows, Hale states, "I only regret that I have but one life to lose for my country."

Hamilton, Alexander

1755–1804 ● AMERICAN STATESMAN

"Real liberty is neither found in despotism or the extremes of democracy, but in moderate governments."
Alexander Hamilton, 1787

Hamilton was born in Nevis, British West Indies. Hamilton began to work, at age eleven, as a clerk in a counting house of a firm of New York merchants who had set up a business on Saint Croix, and by 1772 he had advanced to the position of manager.

He so impressed his friends and associates on Saint Croix that they gathered funds to send him to the mainland to further his education. In 1773 he began studying at King's College in New York (subsequently Columbia University). His student days were shortlived, however, due to his involvement in the revolutionary cause. At King's College he joined a patriotic volunteer group known as the "Corsicans" and drilled in military exercises every morning before classes. In 1774 he made a widely reported speech and wrote a number of pamphlets attacking British policies.

Hamilton's military ability became apparent in 1776 when he received a captain's commission in the provincial artillery. At the second battle of Trenton his talents helped bar General Charles Cornwallis from crossing the Raritan River to attack Washington's main army, and in February 1777 he was made an aide-de-camp to General George Washington, with the rank of lieutenant colonel. He remained on Washington's staff for four years and even had a command of his own for the Yorktown campaign (Sept-ember–October 1781).

After the surrender of Cornwallis in 1781, Hamilton, now with a wife and family, proceeded to Albany, New York, to study law, and the following year was authorized to practice in New York. Also in 1782, he was elected to the Continental Congress by the New York legislature. Notwithstanding his extensive involvement in the Revolution, he defended Loyalists in actions brought against them, his strong feelings for justice even leading him to publish pamphlets asking that the Loyalists be treated justly and with moderation. He helped achieve the repeal of laws disbarring Loyalist lawyers and disenfranchising Loyalist voters.

In 1784 he became involved in the founding of the Bank of New York, becoming one of its directors, a move in line with his personal policy favoring a strong banking system.

May 1787 marked the U.S. Constitutional Convention in Philadelphia where Hamilton was a member of the three-man New York delegation. Having always favored a strong central government instead of thirteen small states in a confederacy, Hamilton did his utmost to promote the ratification of the U.S. Constitution. Toward that end he co-authored *The Federalist* together with John Jay and James Madison, which consisted of eighty-five essays (reputedly two-thirds were by Hamilton) that were to become classics of political literature. These went far in molding U.S. political institutions and con-cepts of justice, general welfare, and the rights of individual citizens. This presentation of the new federal system and the central government proposed in the new Constitution con-tributed significantly to securing support favoring replace-ment of the former Articles of Confederation with the Constitution.

Despite Hamilton's involvement, New York was the eleventh state to ratify and endorse the Constitution. At the New York ratification convention at Poughkeepsie, New York, in 1788. it was only Hamilton's skillful speeches and maneuvering that insured ratification by a vote of thirty to twenty-seven.

In 1789 George Washington became the first president of the United States and named Hamilton as the first secretary of the treasury, an office in which he served from 1789 to 1795. Hamilton realized that the United States must have

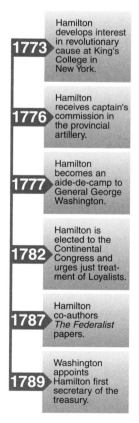

1773 Hamilton develops interest in revolutionary cause at King's College in New York.

1776 Hamilton receives captain's commission in the provincial artillery.

1777 Hamilton becomes an aide-de-camp to General George Washington.

1782 Hamilton is elected to the Continental Congress and urges just treat-ment of Loyalists.

1787 Hamilton co-authors *The Federalist* papers.

1789 Washington appoints Hamilton first secretary of the treasury.

"A national debt, if it is not excessive, will be to us a national blessing."

Alexander
Hamilton, 1781

financial credit for the normal operations of government as well as for commercial functions and industrial development. He believed the government had to arrange to pay off its entire national debt (Revolutionary War debt) as well as the unpaid debts of the several states incurred during the Revolution. However, some officials wanted to repudiate part or even all of the national debt.

Hamilton believed that the functions of paying debts and borrowing money would be helped by the establishment of a national bank of the United States that had the right to set up branches in different parts of the country. On this issue he clashed with the secretary of state, Thomas Jefferson. Hamilton therefore introduced a bill in Congress to establish a national bank. Jefferson maintained that this was unconstitutional, as the power to do so was not specifically noted in the Contitution and was therefore limited to the several states. Hamilton argued effectively that many powers were implied in such provisions as the one "authorizing Congress to make all laws which shall be necessary and proper" for carrying out such enumerated powers as the levying and collection of taxes, payment of debts, and borrowing of money. Obviously, he argued, a national bank would help such functions tremendously. Congress, in accepting this argument, established the precedent of "implied powers."

After 1795 Hamilton continued to be a major political voice and for a time served as second-in-command of the army. He was a bitter political enemy of Aaron Burr, thwarting Burr's ambitions on several occasions. After Hamilton criticized Burr at a dinner party, Burr challenged Hamilton to a duel in Weehawken, New Jersey. Hamilton had an aversion to duelling stemming from the death of his eldest son, Philip, three years earlier in a duel on the same site. However, he felt honor-bound to accept the challenge; Hamilton was reported to have shot in the air but Burr killed him. ◆

Hancock, John

1736–1793 ● REVOLUTIONARY
LEADER

> *"There, I guess King George will be able to read that."*
> John Hancock, after signing the Declaration of Independence, 1776

John Hancock presided over the Continental Congress when the Declaration of Independence was adopted. His signature, big and bold, heads the other signatures to that document, and is probably the best-known signature in all American history. In fact, "putting your John Hancock on it" has come to be a slang expression for autographing or signing a paper.

John Hancock was born on January 12, 1736, in Braintree, Massachusetts. He was adopted by his uncle Thomas Hancock, the richest merchant in Boston, and the uncle trained him to be a businessman. John Hancock made a visit to England after his graduation from Harvard College in 1754. A successful shipowner and importer, he came to be a leader of anti-British activity in Boston, especially after his sloop *Liberty* was seized by the British for smuggling. The charge was true but the Bostonians by this time justified any and all evasions of the British tax laws. After the *Liberty* incident, Hancock became a close associate of John Adams and Samuel Adams and an outspoken supporter of the various movements toward rebellion. The British patrols that were out at the time the battle of Lexington was fought were trying to lay hands on Hancock as a prime rebel.

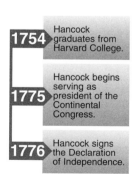

1754 Hancock graduates from Harvard College.

1775 Hancock begins serving as president of the Continental Congress.

1776 Hancock signs the Declaration of Independence.

He served Massachusetts as a delegate to the Continental Congress, and was president of Congress from 1775 to 1777. After the Revolution, he helped to get the U.S. Constitution approved by Massachusetts, and he was governor of that state for eight full terms. He died during his ninth term in office. ◆

Havel, Václav

1936–PRESENT ● HUMAN RIGHTS ACTIVIST

"Human rights are universal and indivisible. Human freedom is also indivisible; if it is denied to anyone in the world, it is therefore denied, indirectly, to all people."
Václav Havel, "Task of Independence," 1992

Václav Havel is a celebrated playwright and defender of human rights who helped lead the dissident movement that led to the overthrow of communism in Czechoslovakia in 1989. He became the first president of the newly democratic country and was later elected president of the new Czech Republic after the split of Czechoslovakia in 1992.

Havel was born in Prague, Czechoslovakia (now in the Czech Republic), on October 5, 1936, to Václav M. and Bozena (Vavrecka) Havel. His father was a wealthy building contractor and restaurateur. After the communist government came to power in the 1940s, all businesses and industries were nationalized, and the Havel businesses and properties were confiscated. Havel's father then became an office clerk and his mother took a job as a tour guide in Prague.

Because of his privileged background as a "bourgeois child," the Communist authorities made it difficult for Havel to continue his education beyond elementary school. He got a job as a laboratory assistant and managed to enroll in night school through a bureaucratic slip. The night school was intended for working-class managers who wanted to broaden their education. Havel completed his high school education by working days and going to school at night. After rejection from a number of arts schools, Havel studied briefly at the Czech University of Technology and then served in the army from 1957 to 1959. During his service, he became involved with theater and founded a regimental theater company. When he returned to Prague after the army, he worked as a stagehand at the ABC Theater in Prague, where he came to see theater as a place that could nurture social self-awareness. His experiences at the theater also inspired him to write plays. Havel later held various positions at the Theater on the Balustrade, an avant-garde troupe that helped form him as a playwright.

Havel's work as a writer began in his youth, and over the years he produced essays, articles, theater profiles, poems, and other pieces of writing. However, he is best known for his absurdist plays, in which plot, characterization, and thematic structure are distorted to dramatize the absurdity of the human condition in an irrational world. His first three plays—*The Garden Party*, *The Memorandum*, and *The Increased Difficulty of Concentration*—dealt with how bureaucracy can create a dehumanized society. They were first produced at the Theater on the Balustrade in the 1960s, and they garnered him considerable success as an avant-garde playwright.

In 1968, the Czechoslovakian government began a liberal reform movement sometimes called "Prague Spring." The reforms ended after the Soviet Union and other communist countries, fearing that such reforms would threaten the communist system, sent tanks and troops into Czechoslovakia to crush the movement. The head of the government was replaced and strong party controls were imposed on economic and political life in Czechoslovakia. Havel then began a campaign of protest against the government's repression and abuse of human rights.

In the years following the invasion, Havel continued to speak out against the government and to write plays and

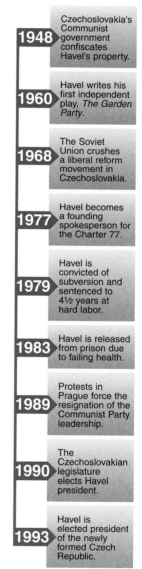

1948 Czechoslovakia's Communist government confiscates Havel's property.

1960 Havel writes his first independent play, *The Garden Party*.

1968 The Soviet Union crushes a liberal reform movement in Czechoslovakia.

1977 Havel becomes a founding spokesperson for the Charter 77.

1979 Havel is convicted of subversion and sentenced to 4½ years at hard labor.

1983 Havel is released from prison due to failing health.

1989 Protests in Prague force the resignation of the Communist Party leadership.

1990 The Czechoslovakian legislature elects Havel president.

1993 Havel is elected president of the newly formed Czech Republic.

> *"Society can be enriched and cultivated only through self-knowledge, and the main instrument of society's self-knowledge is its culture. Where total control over society is sought, the first thing to be suppressed is its culture."*
> Václav Havel, 1975

essays on totalitarianism and dissent. He became a leading voice of the dissident movement in Czechoslovakia, and the government confiscated his passport and kept the playwright and his family under surveillance as a result. He was also repeatedly interrogated by security police and jailed for his dissident activity. Theaters and publishers in the West performed and published his works, but his plays were banned in Czechoslovakia. Havel received a number of invitations to work abroad, but he declined them all because he was afraid that he would not be allowed back in the country.

In 1977, Havel became a founding spokesperson for the Charter 77, a manifesto that charged the Czechoslovakian government with human and civil rights violations and called for the government to abide by the rules of the Helsinki Covenant on Civil and Political Rights, to which it was bound. The government responded by jailing dissidents, including Havel. In 1979 Havel was convicted of subversion to the government and sentenced to four-and-a-half years at hard labor. Out of this period came a series of letters to his wife Olga, whom he had wed in 1964, which were published as *Letters to Olga* in 1988. Havel was given an early release from his sentence in 1983 due to failing health.

In November 1989, Havel founded the Civic Forum, a political group that sought a nonviolent, nonpartisan solution to the country's violations of human and civil rights. Opposition to the government grew, and in December massive protests on the streets of Prague forced the resignation of the Communist Party leadership. The end of communist rule was so smooth that it became known as the "Velvet Revolution." In 1990 free elections took place and the Civic Forum and an allied party won a majority of seats in the legislature. The legislature elected Havel president.

As president Havel oversaw the transformation from a state-controlled economy to a capitalist system. Meanwhile, a movement to split Czechoslovakia into two nations, one for the Czechs and one for the Slovaks, gained force. In July 1992, Havel, a Czech, resigned as president after failing to receive support for reelection from the Slovaks in the national legislature. Czechoslovakia split into the Czech Republic and Slovakia in 1992, and Havel was elected president of the Czech Republic in 1993. As Czech president Havel sought political stability and the support of human rights. He was regarded as a man who was committed to the future and to the long-term transformation of society. Havel was known throughout the world for his courtesy, his intelligence, and his decency. However he drew criticism in early years for relying on aides who were close friends and not members of a cabinet. In 1997 his government also suffered a slide in popularity after a financial crisis that led to austerity measures and after the collapse of the coalition government amidst charges of corruption.

In the late 1990s Havel suffered from repeated bouts of illness after undergoing surgery for lung cancer in 1997. He married the outspoken actress Dagmar Veskrnova in 1997 less than a year after the death of his wife Olga. In early 1998 Havel narrowly won reelection for a second five-year term. ◆

Hidalgo y Costilla, Miguel

1753–1811 ● MEXICAN REVOLUTION- ARY PRIEST

The son of a Creole estate manager, Miquel Hidalgo's studies for the priesthood at the Jesuit College de San Francisco Javier were disturbed by the proclamation of King Charles III of Spain banning the Jesuits from Mexico. He continued his clerical studies at the College of San

Nicolás Obispo, but also found time to learn local Indian languages and read the proscribed revolutionary literature of France. After his ordination in 1778 Hidalgo served as rector of the college until a scandal over mismanagement of funds led to his resignation.

Inquisition: a Roman Catholic court that sought out and suppressed heresy.

In his new position as curate of the village of San Felipe, Hidalgo came under the constant scrutiny of the **Inquisition**. Not only had he abandoned the spiritual welfare of his parishioners in favor of their physical well-being by encouraging forbidden agriculture and industry, but he was rumored to have abandoned important church dogma. In fact, he questioned the Virgin Birth and the authority of the pope, and took a mistress to flaunt his rejection of celibacy. His home was modeled after fashionable French salons, and a theater and orchestra were organized. Among his close friends was a liberal cavalry captain, Ignacio de Allende, with whom he organized a revolutionary society under the guise of a literary club. Together they established a newspaper, *El Despertador Americano*, and signed the first proclamation outlawing slavery in the New World.

Hidalgo ran to the church and rang its bell, summoning his parishioners to what they assumed was mass. Instead, he exhorted them to revolt.

Foremost on their minds were plans to overthrow the Spanish regime and declare Mexico's independence. A coup was planned for December 8, 1810, but by September news had leaked out, and the Spanish army came to arrest the conspirators. When, on September 16, Hidalgo and Allende discovered that they were about to be arrested, they decided to act immediately. Hidalgo ran to the church and rang its bell, summoning his parishioners to what they assumed was mass. Instead, he exhorted them to revolt.

The content of this speech, known as the *Grito del Dolores*, is still debated. It is unlikely that he called for "independence," as that term would have been incomprehensible to the peasant masses. He did call for a defensive war against the Spanish, ending with, "Long live Ferdinand VII [the Spanish king imprisoned by Napoleon]! Long live America! Long live the Catholic religion! Death to bad government!" The crowds cheered wildly.

Adopting the Virgin of Guadalupe, a humbly dressed Indian icon, as his standard, Hidalgo attracted a growing mob of peasants. The entire local militia of San Miguel joined the rebels in their assault on the provincial capital of Guanajuato. Hidalgo was a firm believer in the power of the masses and rejected Allende's warnings that such a mob, now numbering almost one hundred thousand men, could not be controlled without strict discipline. Allende was right; all towns on the road to Guanajuato were pillaged. While Hidalgo was convinced of his oratorical skills in controlling the frenzied masses, stories of atrocities reaching Guanajuato strengthened the locals' resolve to defend their city. Spanish troops fortified themselves in the govermment granary, but were no match for the waves of angry peasants. Even Hidalgo was forced to fire on his supporters to restore order.

Hidalgo reached Mexico City on November 1, 1810. Allende encouraged him to invade the city but Hidalgo realized that the revolutionary fervor of his supporters had waned. After several days' hesitation, he turned north to Morelia (present-day Guadalajara), chased by Spanish troops. His retreat was fatal. To Allende it seemed that Hidalgo's bloated ego bordered on insanity. As the self-proclaimed "Captain General of America," he insisted upon being addressed as "Serene Highness." Finally, Hidalgo was removed from his command and installed as a figurehead.

1778 After his ordination, Hidalgo serves as rector of the College of San Nicolas Obispo.

1810 Hidalgo foments peasant revolt against Spanish rule.

1811 Hidalgo is captured and executed, 10 years before Mexican independence.

In January 1811, the Spanish caught the rebels en route to the United States. The ensuing Battle of Calderón was a disaster for Hidalgo. Again, he had rejected Allende's advice and ordered all his men into battle. The rebels were routed and Allende and Hidalgo captured. Allende was executed immediately and Hidalgo was taken in chains to Chihuahua to face the Inquisition. Although he recanted, he was **defrocked** and sentenced to death by firing squad. His decapitated head was placed in a cage and suspended from the Guanajuato granary as a warning to all future insurgents. It remained there until 1821.

defrocked: deprived of priestly authority.

Today, Hidalgo is considered the "Father of Mexico." September 16, the anniversary of the Grito del Dolores, is the principal national holiday of Mexico, celebrating the achievements of a man who died ten years before independence. ◆

Inouye, Daniel Ken

1924–PRESENT ● WORLD WAR II HERO

"The story is not of covert activity alone, but of covert foreign policy. Not secret diplomacy, which Congress has always accepted, but secret policy-making, which the Constitution has always rejected."

Daniel Inouye, describing the Iran-Contra hearings, 1987

Daniel Ken Inouye, longtime United States Senator from Hawaii, is a hero of World War II, the first congressional representative from Hawaii, and the first Japanese-American ever to serve in the United States Congress. Inouye was born on September 7, 1924 in Honolulu to Kame and Hyotaro Inouye. His father, Hyotaro, had immigrated to Hawaii from Japan as a child and worked as a file clerk to support his family. As a boy, Daniel Inouye attended a Japanese-language school as well as the local public schools. He enjoyed raising homing pigeons, collecting stamps, and assembling crystal radio sets.

In 1941, when Inouye was seventeen years old, the Japanese attacked Pearl Harbor, forcing the United States to enter World War II. Because Inouye had been trained in first aid, he volunteered to lead a litter-team that helped carry civilian casualties to hospitals. Inouye graduated from high school in 1942, then enrolled in the premedical program at the University of Hawaii. He dropped out of college during his first year so he could join the U. S. Army's 442nd Regimental Combat Team, a unit whose members were all volunteers of Japanese heritage.

The 442nd regiment was sent to Europe, and become one of the most decorated combat units of World War II. Inouye was commissioned a 2nd Lieutenant on the battlefield after fighting bravely in the French Vosges Mountains. In the closing months of the war, he led an assault on a heavily defended German infantry position on a hill in Italy's Po Valley. Early in the assault Inouye caught a bullet in the abdomen, but continued advancing against heavy machine gun fire. He managed to toss two hand grenades into German machine gun nests before his right arm was shattered by an enemy grenade. Inouye threw a third grenade with his uninjured left hand when a bullet hit him in the leg and he was knocked down the hill. He spent the next 20 months in army hospitals, recovering from his injuries and from the loss of his right arm. For his wartime valor, Inouye was awarded numerous medals, including a Distinguished Service Cross, a Bronze Star, and a Purple Heart with clusters.

After the war, Inouye returned to Hawaii and reentered the University of Hawaii. The loss of his arm convinced him to give up medicine and turn to government and economics. In 1949, Inouye married Shinobu Awamura, with whom he

Hiram Leong Fong

Hiram Leong Fong was the first Asian American to serve in the United States Senate. Fong was born in 1906 in Honolulu, Hawaii, to Chinese immigrant parents. He had ten brothers and sisters, and had to begin working at an early age to help support his large family. Fong worked his way through college, eventually earning a Ph.D. from Harvard Law School in 1935. Closely following the career of fellow Hawaiian and fellow senator Daniel Inouye, Fong practiced as an attorney in Hawaii, and served in the Air Force during World War II. Fong was elected as a Republican to Hawaii's territorial House of Representatives in 1938, where he served for the next 16 years, including six years as Speaker of the House. When Hawaii became a state in 1959, Fong was elected to the United States Senate. He was reelected to the Senate in 1964 and 1970. In the Senate, Fong held seats on the Post Office and Civil Service, Appropriations, and Judiciary committees. He retired in 1976, setting off a scramble for his seat, with Japanese American Spark M. Matsunaga eventually succeeding him.

later had one son, also named Daniel. Inouye graduated from college in 1950, and moved to Washington D.C. to attend the George Washington University Law School. After receiving his law degree in 1952, Inouye returned to Hawaii and served as Honolulu's Deputy Public Prosecutor. He also became active in local Democratic Party politics. In 1954, Inouye was elected to Hawaii's territorial house of representatives. He moved up to Hawaii's territorial senate in 1958.

The following year, Hawaii joined the union, and Inouye become the new state's first representative in the United States House. When Inouye took his oath of office, the Speaker of the House, Sam Rayburn, not knowing of Inouye's wartime injury, asked the new congressman to raise his right hand. As Congressman Leo O'Brien later observed, "There was no right hand, Mr. Speaker. It had been lost in combat by that young American soldier in World War II. Who can deny that, at that moment, a ton of prejudice slipped quietly to the floor of the House of Representatives." Inouye raised his left hand to the admiration of his fellow members of Congress.

During his first term in the House, Inouye served on the Senate Banking and Commerce Committee, and become a strong supporter of civil rights and a spokesman for Asian American issues. He was reelected to the house in 1960, then won a seat in the United States Senate in 1962. In 1973, during Richard Nixon's administration, Inouye was appointed to the Senate's Select Committee that investigated the Watergate scandal. Inouye later served as the first Chairman of the Senate's Select Committee on Intelligence, which was formed in 1974 to monitor and investigate allegations of abuse of power by the Central Intelligence Agency, the Federal Bureau of Investigation, and other government intelligence agencies. In 1986, Inouye took on his most challenging and most public role as chairman of the Senate's Select Committee that investigated charges that President Ronald Reagan's administration had sold weapons to Iran and diverted some of the profits from the sale to anti-government rebels in Nicaragua.

After almost forty years in the United States Congress, Inouye has become one of the country's most powerful and respected politicians. He has built a reputation for integrity and is known for his moderate political views and his ability to compromise. ◆

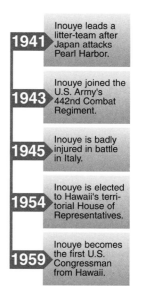

1941 Inouye leads a litter-team after Japan attacks Pearl Harbor.

1943 Inouye joined the U.S. Army's 442nd Combat Regiment.

1945 Inouye is badly injured in battle in Italy.

1954 Inouye is elected to Hawaii's territorial House of Representatives.

1959 Inouye becomes the first U.S. Congressman from Hawaii.

Jackson, Andrew

1767–1845 ● AMERICAN GENERAL & PRESIDENT OF THE UNITED STATES

"The brave man inattentive to his duty is worth little more to his country than the coward who deserts her in the hour of danger."
Andrew Jackson, 1815

Andrew Jackson was born in Waxhaw, South Carolina, to an Irish farmer who died before Andrew's birth. His mother, unable to manage alone, moved the family to the nearby home of her invalid sister.

As the youngest of eleven children, Jackson was given to excessive and wild behavior. In school he was taught to read and write, but little else; his grammar and spelling were atrocious throughout his life. His behavior was often violent and unpredictable, and he was not a particularly happy child.

During the War of Independence Jackson helped his mother tend to the wounded and dreamed of being a soldier like his brother Hugh, who was later killed in action. Jackson eventually had his chance to serve his country, but in the spring of 1781, he and his brother Robert were captured by British forces. In captivity they developed raging fevers, and though they escaped after a few weeks, Robert died from smallpox two days after they were liberated. His mother was sent to care for other sick cousins and she, too, became ill with fever and died.

Once over the illness, Jackson discovered he had inherited a small fortune of 400 pounds from his grandfather. After claiming it, however, he wasted it on a spending spree. He soon convinced himself that his life had been spared so that he could lead a life his mother would be proud of—a life of honor, courage, and order.

After moving from one set of relatives to another, Jackson decided to be a lawyer. He studied in Salisbury, North Carolina, and gained permission to practice law in 1787. He found a job as a prosecutor in a western district superior court on the frontier. Before arriving in Nashville, Tennessee, in 1788, he tried to establish a reputation for himself as a "civilized" man by buying a slave and fighting a duel.

Jackson aspired to be a judge but first he became a politician. Through the patronage of William Blount, the first governor of the Southwest Territory, Jackson was one of a five-member delegation to the constitutional convention in 1796 that promoted statehood for Tennessee. Blount, his patron, became the first U.S. senator from Tennessee, and Jackson became the first representative in the House. The beginnings of his political career were uneventful, and he soon resigned in 1798. He distrusted central government and was a great believer in personal loyalty, of which he did not see much in national politics.

In 1798 he returned to Tennessee, where he finally became a judge. In 1801 he was appointed major general of Tennessee, though he had little formal military training. He soon became embroiled in the Burr conspiracy, in which former vice president Aaron Burr visited him and asked him to build boats for a possible military excursion against Spain. Burr was accused of attempting to divide the union and, though he was later acquitted in court, the incident tarnished Jackson's reputation.

In the War of 1812 Jackson still held the position of major general of Tennessee. He proved himself to be an excellent military leader, developing the nickname Old Hickory because hickory was the hardest wood that the soldiers knew. The war was a disaster for the Americans, bringing into question the young nation's independence. In the battle of New Orleans on January 8, 1815, Jackson's troops repelled the invading British soldiers. Over two thousand enemy troops were killed or wounded, while fewer than a dozen Americans fell. "Through

1781 Jackson is captured by British forces during War of Independence.

1796 Jackson serves on five-member Tennessee delegation to the Constitutional Convention.

1815 "Old Hickory" repels British invaders at pivotal War of 1812 battle of New Orleans.

1828 Jackson, elected seventh president of the United States, institutes Indian "removal" policy.

1832 Jackson faces threatened secession of South Caroline during second term.

Andrew Jackson, the American people were vicariously purged of shame and frustration. At a moment of disillusionment, Andrew Jackson reaffirmed the young nation's self-belief; he restored its sense of national prowess and destiny," wrote John William Ward, one of his biographers.

In 1824, Jackson ran for president. He was regarded as the symbol of democracy and later, people spoke of Jacksonian democracy. Though he received more popular votes than his opponents, he did not obtain the necessary electoral votes, and the House of Representatives eventually chose John Quincy Adams. For the next four years Jackson devoted his time to becoming president, promising to rid the government of corruption.

In 1828 he received 56 percent of the vote, although he had not promised specific programs. The era came to be known as the Age of Jackson, and it stretched from his inauguration to the Civil War. Jackson brought in many of his own people to run the government, which his opponents called the spoils system.

During his first term he advocated the "voluntary" removal of the Indians, promising them a home in the southwest if they would relinquish their tribal lands in the east. Other events marking his presidency included his war against the Second Bank of America, in which he vetoed the bank's recharter, and his vast expansion of presidential powers. He was reelected in 1832 by 55 percent of the popular vote.

Shortly after his reelection, he faced the greatest challenge of his presidency. South Carolina was threatening to secede because it perceived existing tariff laws as a northern conspiracy. A long congressional fight ensued and finally in May 1833 a compromise bill was passed that settled the crisis. The remainder of Jackson's term was not as successful and his health began to fail. In February 1837 he left office, succeeded by Martin Van Buren, who was Jackson's personal choice. He lived at his home, the Hermitage, near Nashville, Tennessee, for the rest of his life. ◆

> *"One man with courage makes a majority."*
> Andrew Jackson, attributed

Jefferson, Thomas

1743–1826 ● PRESIDENT OF THE
UNITED STATES

"There is not a single crowned head in Europe whose talents or merits would entitle him to be elected a vestryman by the people of any parish in America."

Thomas Jefferson,
letter to George Washington, 1788

Jefferson's inventions included a stick that unfolded into a chair.

Known for his political sophistication, Thomas Jefferson authored the Declaration of Independence and the Virginia Statute for Religious Freedom. To this day he is regarded as the outstanding champion of political and spiritual freedom and, together with Benjamin Franklin, is viewed as the closest American approximation to the "universal man." He was a brilliant conversationalist and was regarded as one of the best-educated men of his time. He was also an inventor whose inventory included a reclining chair and a stick that unfolded into a chair.

Jefferson was born in Shadwell, Virginia, where his father, a man of legendary strength, was a successful planter, surveyor, explorer, and mapmaker. His mother, Jane Randolph, was a member of one of the most famous families in Virginia. Having grown up in a wealthy family, Jefferson was well educated, attending small private schools where he was taught the classics. He attended the College of William and Mary and had many exceptional instructors in mathematics, science, and law. He graduated in 1762 and until 1767 was an associate and read law with some of the finest legal minds of the time. He was admitted to the bar in 1767 and practiced law until 1774, when the courts were closed due to the American Revolution.

As a young lawyer, he worked toward the emancipation of the slaves, but was not successful. Even though he had a flourishing law practice, he did not depend on his income for maintaining his lifestyle, as he had inherited a considerable estate from his father.

Jefferson's interest in architecture grew out of his desire to build his own home at Monticello in central Virginia, a project he began in 1769. Private homes such as the one he wanted did not exist at the time, and he did much research before beginning construction. He was responsible for both design and construction, and when it was finished, he was considered an authority on house building.

Jefferson's emphasis on local government came from his own experiences. He had served as a magistrate and as county lieutenant of Albemarle County. When he was only twenty-five he was elected to the colonial House of Burgesses, serving from 1769 to 1775. There he proved his effectiveness as a committee member and drafter of legislation, but he was not an able orator.

He entered the revolutionary scene in 1769 and seven years later wrote the credo of the new nation. From the beginning of the struggle with England, he stood together with the most ardent patriots, and his knowledge of English history and political philosophy served him well. His best known early contribution to the House was his powerful pamphlet *A Summary View of the Rights of British America*, pleading for colonial self-government, which he wrote in 1774.

As a member of the second Continental Congress, Jefferson was chosen to write the Declaration of Independence (1776). He once said that his writing of the declaration and the Virginia Statute for Religious Freedom (1786) were more memorable than his presidency of the United States.

Because he wanted to be closer to his family he left the Congress in 1776, and served instead in the Virginia legislature until he was elected governor of Virginia in 1779. He remained as governor until 1781, and when the British overran Virginia, he galloped away ahead of them. This led the legislature to investigate charges of cowardice, which ended with his vindication. From 1783 to 1784 he once again served in the Continental Congress, where his proposal for a decimal monetary system was adopted.

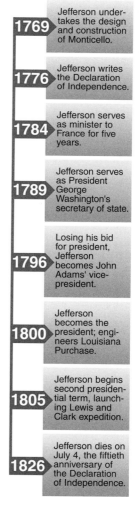

1769 Jefferson undertakes the design and construction of Monticello.

1776 Jefferson writes the Declaration of Independence.

1784 Jefferson serves as minister to France for five years.

1789 Jefferson serves as President George Washington's secretary of state.

1796 Losing his bid for president, Jefferson becomes John Adams' vice-president.

1800 Jefferson becomes the president; engineers Louisiana Purchase.

1805 Jefferson begins second presidential term, launching Lewis and Clark expedition.

1826 Jefferson dies on July 4, the fiftieth anniversary of the Declaration of Independence.

> *"The care of human life and happiness, and not their destruction, is the first and only legitimate object of good government."*
>
> Thomas Jefferson,
> 1809

In 1784 Jefferson became the minister to France, serving for five years, during which he won many concessions from the French. He welcomed the advent of the French Revolution and was sympathetic to the moderate revolutionaries. When he returned to the United States in 1789, he was informed that President George Washington had nominated him to serve as secretary of state. A letter from Washington followed, and after four days of soul-searching Jefferson decided that he could not refuse the president and accepted the offer. Before leaving for Washington he returned to his home at Monticello, where he was afforded a hero's welcome by his slaves, friends, and relatives. As secretary of state, a position he held from 1790 to 1793, he was in conflict with Alexander Hamilton, secretary of the treasury. Hamilton supported the British and Jefferson was pro-French. Washington mainly relied on Hamilton, and Jefferson resigned.

In 1794 he returned to Monticello and spent three years remodeling his beloved home. He wanted to retire to private life and spend his remaining years reading and studying, but this was not to be. In 1796 he ran for president but was defeated by John Adams by only three electoral votes. He automatically became vice president and in 1797 he was elected president of the American Philosophical Society.

Jefferson disagreed with Adams in many areas, which resulted in his running against Adams for the presidency in 1800, defeating him on the thirty-sixth ballot. The election campaign was based on Jefferson's contention that he was a stronger supporter of the U.S. Constitution than his opponent, and his victory marked the first time that the federalists were defeated by a Republican. He was inaugurated as president on March 4, 1801, with Aaron Burr as vice president.

The most notable achievement of Jefferson's first term was the Louisiana Purchase. As secretary of state he had recognized the importance of free navigation down the Mississippi River and was determined to incorporate the area, especially after it had been transferred from Spain to France. Throughout his lifetime Jefferson had his detractors, particularly regarding his attempts to separate church and state. He was quoted as saying, "I have no ambition to govern men. It is a painful, thankless office." This sentiment was proved when Aaron Burr's attempts at conspiracy were foiled.

Reelected and inaugurated on March 4, 1805, Jefferson began his second term with George Clinton as vice president. During this term, the Lewis and Clark expedition, which explored the territory of the Louisiana purchase and the country beyond as far as the Pacific, was concluded.

Jefferson continued his efforts to acquire west Florida, which turned out to be an "exercise in futility." His relations with Congress were good and remained stable until shortly before he completed his second term of office. When he left the presidency he was a discouraged man, and spent the last seventeen years of his life at Monticello. From there he continued to exert a strong influence on the government. He said, "The happiest moments of my life have been the few which I have spent in the bosom of my family."

Those final years were among his most productive. He founded the University of Virginia and held the position of first rector, and also designed its buildings. William Howard Taft once said that Jefferson was still spoken of there as if he were sitting in the next room.

Jefferson died at Monticello on July 4, 1826, just hours after the passing of John Adams, and on the fiftieth anniversary of the Declaration of Independence. The Jefferson Memorial in Washington was dedicated on the two hundredth anniversary of his birth. ◆

Throughout his lifetime Jefferson had his detractors, particularly regarding his attempts to separate church and state.

Jemison, Mae Carol

1956–PRESENT ● ASTRONAUT

Mae C. Jemison was born in Decatur, Alabama, but grew up in Chicago, Illinois. In 1977, she graduated from Stanford University with a B.S. in chemical engineering and a B.A. in African and Afro-American studies. She received an M.D. from Cornell University Medical College in 1981. After interning at the University of

Space shuttle mission specialist Mae Carol Jemison, 1992.

1981 Jemison receives her M.D. from Cornell.

1983 Jemison joins the Peace Corps.

1987 Jemison is named the first African American woman astronaut.

1992 Jemison becomes the first black woman in space.

1993 Jemison forms the Jemison Group.

Southern California Medical Center in Los Angeles, she worked in private practice until January 1983, when she joined the Peace Corps. She served in Sierra Leone and Liberia as a Peace Corps medical officer for two and a half years, returning in 1985 to Los Angeles to work as a general practitioner.

In 1987, Jemison's application to NASA's astronaut training program was accepted, and she was named the first African-American woman astronaut. After completing the one-year program, she worked as an astronaut officer representative at the Kennedy Space Center in Florida. In September 1992, Jemison became the first black woman in space when she flew as a payload specialist aboard the space shuttle *Endeavor*. During the seven-day flight, Jemison conducted experiments to determine the effects of zero gravity on humans and animals.

In March 1993, Jemison resigned from NASA in order to form her own company, the Jemison Group, which specializes in adapting technology for use in underdeveloped nations. Her historic spaceflight brought her much adulation. In Detroit a school was named after her. And in the spring of 1993, a PBS special, *The New Explorers*, focused on her life story, while *People* named her one of the year's "50 Most Beautiful People in the World." Also in 1993, Jemison made a guest appearance as a transport operator named Lieutenant Palmer on the television series *Star Trek: The Next Generation*. This was fitting, as Jemison claimed that she was inspired to become an astronaut by the actress Nichelle Nichols, who portrayed the black Lieutenant Uhura on the original *Star Trek*.

Jemison received the CIBA Award for Student Involvement in 1979, the Essence Award in 1988, the Gamma Sigma Gamma Woman of the Year Award in 1989, and the Makeda Award for community contributions in 1993. ◆

Joan of Arc (Jeanne d'Arc)

CA. 1412–1431 ● FRENCH NATIONAL HEROINE

The daughter of a peasant family of the village of Domremy on the Meuse river, in the Vosges, Joan of Arc was a taciturn, very pious girl, who could neither read nor write. Her fascination for military life worried her father and he tried to frighten her by threatening to drown her if she ran away with the soldiers, and ordered her brothers to drown her if he were not on the spot. From about the age of thirteen she had visionary experiences in which voices, which she identified as belonging to Saint Catherine, Saint Marguerite, and Saint Michael, urged her to assume the task of saving France from the English and see that the dauphin (Charles VII) was crowned.

France was in a critical situation at the time: the northern part of the kingdom was occupied by the English allied to the Burgundians. The French crown was contested: the dauphin's insane father, Charles VI, had declared his son illegitimate and had designated Henry V of England regent and future

> *"Good Prince, why do you not believe me. I tell you God pities you, he pities the kingdom and your people; for Saint Louis and Charlemagne are on their knees before him, praying for you."*
>
> Joan of Arc, attributed, to the dauphin, 1429

Joan of Arc

heir. Yet after Charles VI's death, his son was recognized as king by southern France. Five years after his father's death the dauphin Charles had not been crowned at Rheims, where the French kings were traditionally consecrated, as the town was within the occupied territory.

In 1428 Joan of Arc tried and failed to convince the commander of the French troops at Vaucouleurs, Robert of Beaudricourt, of the genuineness of her mission. However, in 1429, when some of her prophecies had been fulfilled, she was allowed to come before the dauphin (the future Charles VII)

who was at Chinon with his court. To test her, the dauphin
disguised himself as one of his courtiers, but Joan recognized
him immediately. Joan was submitted to the examination of a
commission of theologians and her views were found
untouched by heresy. In view of the desperate situation of
Orleans, besieged by the English army, she succeeded in convincing the dauphin and was sent at the head of a small expedition to lift the siege of the town (April–May 1429).
Wearing white armor and carrying a banner, she succeeded in
inspiring the French troops who finally entered the town.
Thanks to the popular national movement inspired by the
young woman the French king was able to recover the occupied territories and the way to Rheims was opened. On July
17, 1429, Joan, holding her white banner, was present at the
coronation of the king at the Cathedral of Rheims. In
September she was wounded during an attempt to recapture
Paris. She rejoined the French army in the spring of 1430 but
on May 24 was taken prisoner near Compiegne and in
November was sold to the English by the duke of Burgundy.
Charles VII did nothing to rescue her. Imprisoned at
Beaurevoir Castle she attempted to escape by jumping from a
tower and recovered from her fall after fasting for several days.
She was taken to Rouen in an iron cage where she was tried
for heresy and witchcraft in February 1431 by a court of
French ecclesiastics headed by the bishop of Beauvais, Pierre
Cauchon. After a long trial, she was found guilty on seventy
counts; among these was the accusation of blasphemy since
she claimed the authority of divine revelation; of prophesying
the future; of immodesty since she wore men's clothing. She
was also accused of daring to say that the saints who spoke to
her spoke in French and not in English! Joan answered with
simplicity and courage. The charges were reduced to twelve.
Pressured to recant under threat of torture, she did so. She
was condemned to life imprisonment but a few days later Joan
declared that Saint Catherine and Saint Margaret had condemned her abjurating. She was then condemned to be burnt
at the stake and handed over to the English secular authorities at Rouen for execution of the sentence. As the flames
engulfed her she maintained that the voices she had heard
were sent from God and were true.

Her sentence was revoked by Pope Calixtus III in 1456.
She was beatified in 1909 by Pope Pius X, and canonized in

1428 Joan attempts to convince Robert of Beaudricourt of the genuineness of her mission.

1429 Joan is allowed to come before the dauphin.

1430 Joan is taken prisoner near Compiegne.

1431 Joan is burned at the stake after conviction for heresy and witchcraft.

1456 Pope Calixtux III revoked Joan's sentence.

1920 Joan is canonized by Pope Benedict XV.

1920 by Pope Benedict XV. Her status as France's national heroine is a comparatively modern phenomenon, stimulated by French Catholics of the late nineteenth century. ◆

Jones, John Paul
1747–1792 ● AMERICAN NAVAL HERO

> *"Sir, I have not yet begun to fight."*
>
> John Paul Jones,
> 1778

John Paul Jones's indomitable courage and brilliant seamanship won him the title of father of the U.S. Navy. He was born John Paul, son of a gardener in Scotland, where he inherited the doggedness and cavalier attitude that were to serve him well at sea. After briefly attending school in the local parish, he was apprenticed to a shipowner out of Whitehaven, England. His first voyage, at the age of thirteen, was to Virginia, where his brother had established a tailoring business. In Virginia, Jones stayed with his brother for a short period, but eager to continue at sea, soon found a berth aboard a slaver. Taking jobs where he could find them, by the age of nineteen he had advanced to the rank of first mate. Jones received his first command at the age of twenty-one, of a small merchant vessel, the *John*, in which he made several voyages to Tobago. On one such voyage he flogged the ship's carpenter for neglect of duty; several weeks later, after a bout of malaria, the man died while on board another ship. Jones was charged with murder and briefly imprisoned. Although he subsequently proved his innocence, he earned a reputation as a harsh master

On a later command in 1773, Jones killed the ringleader of a mutiny. According to Jones, the man had rushed onto his sword. Advised by his friends to leave Tobago because of the hostility of the witnesses in the case, Jones traveled incognito to Virginia. At this time he attached "Jones" to his name. He passed the next two years in quiet obscurity, running the estates of a dead brother in Virginia.

The impending War of Independence was an opportunity for the young seaman to show his mettle. He traveled to

Philadelphia and made the acquaintance of a number of eminent congressmen, who were impressed with this small, intense Scotsman. In 1775 he received his first commission as a lieutenant on the frigate *Alfred* the first ship to fly the continental flag. The following year he was given command of the *Providence*, with overall command of a small fleet and promotion to the rank of captain soon following. He quickly established an unrivaled reputation for skill and strategy, achieving several resounding victories for the fledgling U.S. Navy. However, his common background rankled the naval establishment and, despite his obvious talent, Congress ranked him low on the captains' list. However, in clear deference to his ability, he was given command of the *Ranger*, and ordered to head for France.

The *Ranger* itself was a rather insubstantial ship when compared to the British man-o'-wars. Nevertheless Jones was determined to inflict serious punishment on the enemy in its own waters. His first attack at Whitehaven, a port he knew well from his youth, was not the total success he had sought. The most notable event of his first cruise was the capture of the *Drake,* the first British naval ship captured by the Continental navy. After twenty-eight days Jones returned triumphantly to port in Brest. The British for their part were rightly alarmed by the presence of an obviously formidable raider near their own territory. Jones was dubbed a renegade Scot pirate and a price was offered for his capture

Jones was eager to continue his adventures, hoping that after his early successes he would be given command of a more significant ship. What he received was an old and slow refitted merchantman, which he named the *Bonhomme Richard*. After several false starts, he set sail accompanied by a number of other smaller ships all under his command. Jones's squadron had captured seventeen small vessels around the coast of Great Britain when, in September 1779, they encountered the Baltic trade fleet of forty-two vessels being escorted by two British ships of war, the small *Countess of Scarborough* and the forty-four-gun *Serapis*. The *Scarborough* soon surrendered, leaving the *Richard* engaged in a tremendous battle with the *Serapis*, which carried more than twice its firepower. Hopelessly outclassed, Jones saw his only hope of victory in close quarters action. He skillfully maneuvered the *Richard* alongside the *Serapis* and lashed the two ships togeth-

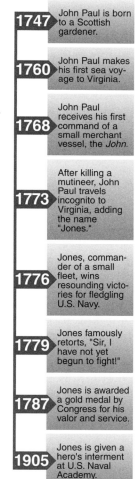

1747 John Paul is born to a Scottish gardener.

1760 John Paul makes his first sea voyage to Virginia.

1768 John Paul receives his first command of a small merchant vessel, the *John.*

1773 After killing a mutineer, John Paul travels incognito to Virginia, adding the name "Jones."

1776 Jones, commander of a small fleet, wins resounding victories for fledgling U.S. Navy.

1779 Jones famously retorts, "Sir, I have not yet begun to fight!"

1787 Jones is awarded a gold medal by Congress for his valor and service.

1905 Jones is given a hero's interment at U.S. Naval Academy.

Jones died in Paris and was placed in a lead coffin filled with alcohol in the hope that he would be accorded a hero's burial in the United States.

er. For hours the two crews savaged each other's vessel. The *Richard* was set on fire and began taking on water so badly that a British officer asked Jones if he would surrender, to which he made the famous retort "Sir, I have not yet begun to fight!" After some three hours of desperate skirmishing, the *Serapis* struck its colors. The unlikely victory of the *Richard* was credited wholly to Jones's valor and skill. The *Richard* sank the following day, its colors still flying.

Returning to Paris, Jones was feted as a national hero. He enjoyed his time ashore, plunging into French society wholeheartedly. This harsh seafarer even composed poetry for his lady friends, of whom there were many. Eventually, Jones set sail for America in 1781. There too he was paraded and lauded for his heroic efforts, yet still his rank was not raised, due to objections by other senior officers. By way of compensation, Jones was given command of the soon-to-be-completed ship of the line *America*, which conferred on him the *de facto* rank of rear admiral. However, before he took command, the vessel was given to the French government as a gift

Jones marked his time, writing on naval warfare and observing the maneuvers of the French fleet. He traveled to Europe for a few years where he negotiated the return of the booty he had captured from Britain. Returning to America in 1787, he was awarded a gold medal by Congress for his valor and service, but still had no place in an America at peace. In 1788 he received an offer to command a fleet for the Russian navy against the Turks, which he accepted, hoping to keep his hand in for future service in America. However, from the first his position was untenable. The other Russian officers were not happy to have this adventurer in their midst, and despite some notable battles his successes were credited to others. Then a scurrilous rumor was circulated that he had violated a young girl, and he unceremoniously returned to France in 1789. His disappointment in Russia affected his health badly. He took up comfortable lodgings in Paris, keeping company with a few close friends, his heroic days over. In 1792 the U.S. government appointed him commissioner to Algiers, but before the letter detailing the appointment reached him, he died, prematurely aged by his years at sea.

He was buried in a lead coffin, filled with alcohol and ready for shipping, in the hope that he would be accorded a hero's burial in the United States. However, over the years the cemetery was closed and forgotten. Only in 1905, after an intense search, was the coffin discovered, opened, and Jones's body positively identified. It was taken for its final interment at the U.S. Naval Academy in Annapolis, Maryland. ◆

Chief Joseph (Nez Percé)

CA. 1840–1904 ● NATIVE AMERICAN LEADER

Chief Joseph is best remembered for his leadership during the Nez Percé War of 1877 and for his eloquent surrender speech, which seemed to summarize the tragic history of conflict between Euro-Americans and Native Americans. Chief Joseph, also known as Young Joseph to distinguish him from his father, Joseph the Elder or Old Joseph, was born in the Wallowa Valley of Oregon. His Nez Percé name, variously transliterated as Heinmot Tooyalaket, In-muttoo-yah-lat-lat, Hin-mah-too-yah-lat-kekt, and Hin-maton-yalatkit, means "thunder coming from water over land." (Old Joseph, who had been Christianized, baptized his son Ephraim.)

Old Joseph was among the Nez Percé leaders who, in 1855, signed a treaty with Isaac Stevens, Washington's territorial governor. The treaty ceded much of Nez Percé land to the federal government in return for the guarantee of a large reservation in Oregon and Idaho. Stevens almost immediately violated the, treaty by pushing settlement into the reservation, provoking the Yakima War of 1855 to 1856. Old Joseph managed to keep the Nez Percés out of the conflict until 1861, when gold prospectors encroached on the Wallowa Valley. Demanding a revision of the 1855 treaty, government negotiators at the Lapwai Council called for a great reduction in the size of reservation in 1863. For the most part, those Nez Percés whose homes remained undisturbed by the proposed

> *"Hear me, my chiefs. I am tired; my heart is sick and sad. From where the sun now stands I will fight no more forever."*
>
> Chief Joseph, upon his surrender, 1877

revision signed the new treaty and agreed to sell the old lands, while those—such as Chief Joseph the Elder—whose homes lay outside the new boundary resisted and refused to sign. Those so-called nontreaty Nez Percés nevertheless lived in relative peace because Euro-American settlement was slow to invade the Wallowa Valley, and there was no attempt to move the nontreaty bands by force.

In 1871, Chief Joseph the Elder died, and Young Joseph continued his father's policy of passive refusal to move. Shortly after the death of Chief Joseph the Elder, homesteaders began pushing into the Wallowa Valley, and Young Joseph gained prestige by successfully protesting the incursion to the Indian Bureau. The result, in 1873, was a proclamation by President Ulysses S. Grant establishing the Wallowa Valley as a reservation.

Chief Joseph's triumph was short lived. Settlers ignored the reservation boundaries, established homesteads at will, and soon became a political constituency powerful enough to prompt Grant in 1875 to reverse his decision. Although a number of other Nez Percé chiefs, older and more established, outranked Chief Joseph, he was recognized by U.S. authorities as the most influential of the Indian leaders, and it was with him that General Oliver Otis Howard decided to negotiate. He met with Chief Joseph and another leader, Toohoolhoolzote, at Fort Lapwai on November 13 and 15, 1876. Chief Joseph succeeded in winning Howard's sympathy as well as his acknowledgment that Old Joseph had never sold the Wallowa Valley, yet the general persisted in his mission and gave the Indians one month to move to a reservation or be driven off by force.

Chief Joseph demonstrated great restraint in resisting tribal pressure (especially from his own brother, Ollokot) to fight because he realized that war against the far more numerous settlers would be fruitless. However, on June 13 and 14, 1876, a number of young disheartened and drunk warriors, led by Wahlitits, murdered four whites who were implicated in the death of Wahlitits's father. Despite Chief Joseph's protests to authorities that the killings had not been sanctioned by the tribal council, Howard dispatched one hundred cavalrymen to pursue the nontreaty Nez Percés, who had begun to move south toward the Salmon River. The killing of fifteen more settlers increased the urgency of the mission, yet the Indians

1873 Chief Joseph's protests persuade President Grant to establish Wallowa Valley reservation.

1875 Grant reverses his decision.

1876 Chief Joseph leads eight hundred Nez Percé over seventeen hundred miles.

1877 Chief Joseph makes his famous surrender speech.

1904 Chief Joseph dies on the Colville Reservation in Washington.

Chief Joseph.

consistently eluded the pursuers. It was at Chief Joseph's insistence that a delegation of Nez Percés met with Captain David Perry on June 17. The first to encounter the Indian party were undisciplined civilian volunteers, who opened fire, thereby igniting general warfare between the Nez Percés and the U.S. Army.

The first battle went to the Indians, and a series of Nez Percé victories followed, always against superior numbers, as

Chief Joseph led his band of eight hundred over seventeen hundred miles of the most forbidding terrain the West had to offer. At each turn, Chief Joseph eluded the pursuing army, and when an engagement took place, it was the army that took the greater punishment.

Yet the pursuit steadily took its toll on the Nez Percés. Chief Joseph sought haven for his people among the Crows, but when he discovered that Crow scouts had been working for Howard, he determined to press on to Canada. He hoped that the great Hunkpapa leader Sitting Bull, self-exiled there, would welcome the Nez Percés as his brothers. On September 30, 1877, Chief Joseph and his followers were encamped on the northern edge of the Bear Paw Mountains, a mere forty miles south of the Canadian border. Three hundred fifty to four hundred troopers commanded by Nelson Appleton Miles attacked in a bitter, snow-whipped battle that developed into a six-day siege. Realizing that the situation was hopeless, Chief Joseph counseled surrender but was resisted by two other leaders, Looking Glass and White Bird, who wanted to fight to the end. When Looking Glass was struck in the head and killed by a stray bullet on October 5, Chief Joseph at last spoke to Miles in a speech of extraordinary sorrow and dignity:

> *I am tired of fighting. Our chiefs are killed. Looking Glass is dead. Toohoolhoolzote is dead. The old men are all dead. It is the young men who say yes or no. He who led on the young men [that is, Olikut] is dead. It is cold and we have no blankets. The little children are freezing to death. My people, some of them, have run away to the hills, and have no blankets, no food; no one knows where they are—perhaps freezing to death. I want to have time to look for my children and see how many of them I can find. Maybe I shall find them among the dead. Hear me, my chiefs! I am tired; my heart is sick and sad. From where the sun now stands I will fight no more forever.*

Consigned with his followers to a reservation, Chief Joseph spent many years petitioning the government for permission to return to the Wallowa Valley. In these efforts, he was aided by the military adversaries whose respect and admiration he had won: generals O. O. Howard and Nelson Miles. The petitions nevertheless proved fruitless, and Chief Joseph died on the Colville Reservation in the state of Washington. ◆

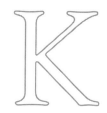

Keller, Helen Adams

1880–1968 ● AMERICAN AUTHOR & LECTURER

"The mystery of language was revealed to me. I knew then that 'w-a-t-e-r' meant the wonderful cool something that was flowing over my hand. That living word awakened my soul, gave it light, joy, set it free!"
Helen Keller, *The Story of My Life*, 1902

Helen Keller was born in Tuscumbia, Alabama. At the age of nineteen months she became ill with acute congestion of the stomach and brain and lost the senses of sight and hearing, and was also rendered mute by her new disabilities. Until the age of seven she was totally dependent on her parents, who loved her but had no idea how to educate her and who let her run wild. When Anne Sullivan from the Perkins Institute for the Blind, herself a former victim of blindness. was hired as her tutor in 1887, she found that her first task was to teach Helen obedience. It was a difficult battle but Anne (who came to be called Annie) triumphed and so opened the door to Keller's initiation into the joys of language.

"We walked down the path to the well house. . . . Someone was drawing water and my teacher placed my hand under the spout. As the cool stream gushed over one hand she spelled into the other the word water, first slowly, then rapidly. I stood still, my whole attention fixed upon the motions of

Americans with Disabilities Act

Since 1973, Americans with disabilities such as deafness, blindness, and paralysis have been legally protected in public schools, federal agencies, and businesses receiving federal funds. This protection was extended to the private sector in 1990, when President George Bush, in the face of strong opposition from small business owners, signed the Americans with Disabilities Act (ADA), the most sweeping civil rights legislation since the 1960s. ADA mandated that new buildings or buildings undergoing major renovations must be made wheelchair-accessible. In addition, businesses with fifteen or more employees cannot use a person's handicap as a factor in making hiring decisions and must make reasonable accommodations for their disabled employees. In the communications industry, all telephone companies must offer services to assist those with hearing or speech impairments. In transportation, all new buses must be wheelchair accessible, and several categories of rail and bus companies must expand their services for disabled customers. Since ADA was passed in 1990, U.S. courts have broadened the definition of who is covered by the act to include, for instance, persons who are HIV-positive.

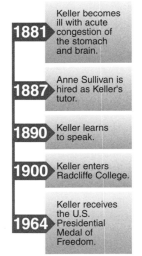

1881 Keller becomes ill with acute congestion of the stomach and brain.

1887 Anne Sullivan is hired as Keller's tutor.

1890 Keller learns to speak.

1900 Keller enters Radcliffe College.

1964 Keller receives the U.S. Presidential Medal of Freedom.

her fingers. Suddenly I felt a misty consciousness as of something forgotten—a thrill of returning thought; and somehow the mystery of language was revealed to me. I knew then that "w-a-t-e-r" meant the wonderful cool something that was flowing over my hand. That living word awakened my soul, gave it light, hope, joy, set it free!"

Sullivan was a dedicated and talented teacher and Keller was a bright pupil. She quickly learned to read by the Braille system and to write with a typewriter. In 1890 she learned to speak. She wrote in her autobiography that the impulse to utter audible sounds had always been strong in her, and before her illness she had already been learning to talk. Once she learned to communicate it did not take her long to realize that other people communicated differently, and a determination to speak like them began to prevail in her. Despite discouragement from her friends she was determined to try, and engaged the assistance of Sarah Fuller, principal of the Horace Mann School. Within a brief period she had begun to realize her ambitions.

In 1900 Helen entered Radcliffe College, graduating in 1904 with honors. She served on the Massachusetts Commission for the Blind and lectured all over the world. After World War II she visited wounded veterans in hospitals and spoke throughout the United States and Europe on behalf of the physically handicapped. In 1964 she received the U.S. Presidential Medal of Freedom. Her books include *The Story of My Life* (1902), *The World I Live In* (1908), *Out of the Dark* (1913), *Mid-stream—My Later Life* (1930), *Let Us Have Faith* (1940), *Teacher: Anne Sullivan Macy* (1955) and *The Open Door* (1957). *The Miracle Worker*, a play by William Gibson based on her life, was produced in 1957. ◆

Kenyatta, Jomo

CA. 1894–1978 ● KENYAN NATIONAL HERO

> *"We want our cattle to get fat on our land so that our children grow up in prosperity; and we do not want the fat removed to feed others."*
>
> Jomo Kenyatta, in a speech, 1952

A member of the Kikuyu tribe, Jomo Kenyatta's given name was Kamau wa Ngengi, and from an early age he was assigned the duty of looking after his family's livestock; he also often accompanied his grandfather, a prophet and magician, on his travels around Kikuyuland. At about age thirteen Kenyatta left home for the Church of Scotland Mission, where he received treatment for a spinal disease and remained for five years, studying and assisting with the first translation of the New Testament into Kikuyu.

On being baptized he changed his name to Johnstone Kamau, and in 1914 moved to Nairobi, where he began working as an interpreter at the Supreme Court, and later as an inspector of water supplies, a post that gained him status among Africans. He adopted the name Kenyatta from "Muibi wa kinyata," the name of a beaded belt he wore, and became involved in politics, joining the Young Kikuyu Association. In 1928 he was elected general secretary of the Kikuyu Central Association (KCA) and edited the party newspaper, formulating the African case against exclusive European occupation of the Kenya Highlands.

Kenyatta visited London in 1929, and again in 1931 on behalf of the KCA. Interested in communism, he made a four-month visit to Russia in 1933, returning to London where he worked as an assistant in phonetics and taught Kikuyu at London University. He represented Kikuyu grievances against colonialism and campaigned for his people's right to self-determination by presenting petitions to government officials and voicing his opinions in the British press. He studied social anthropology under Bronislav Malinowsky at the London School of Economics, publishing his thesis in 1938 in the form of a book, *Facing Mount Kenya*, which, as well as being a pioneering work of anthropology, was also a perceptive criticism of British colonialism.

Through the Workers' Educational Association, Kenyatta lectured on Kenya and imperialism, and met his second wife. With the outbreak of war the couple moved to a small village in Sussex, where Kenyatta worked as a farm laborer, adopting the forename "Jomo" from the nickname "Jumbo," which the villagers called him on account of his stature. In 1945 he helped to form the Pan-African Federation and the following year organized the fifth Pan-African Congress in Manchester.

Leaving his English family behind, Kenyatta returned to Kenya in 1946, where he was made president of the KCA— by now banned by the British—and of the Kenya African Union (KAU), and campaigned for independence through peaceful means, emerging as a much loved national figure.

In 1952 he was arrested by the colonial authorities and charged with managing Mau Mau, the violent nationalist movement opposing colonialism. Although no evidence was found linking him to this cause, he was nonetheless convicted and imprisoned at Lokitaung. His arrest sparked off bloody

1928 As general secretary of KCA, Kenyatta argues against European occupation.

1933 In London, Kenyatta presents Kikuyu grievances against colonialism.

1938 Kenyatta publishes *Facing Mount Kenya*.

1946 Kenyatta returns to Kenya, becoming president of KCA.

1952 Kenyatta's arrest on terrorist charges touches off bloody rebellion.

1961 Kenyatta is freed from prison.

1963 Kenyatta becomes Kenya's first prime minister.

1964 Kenyatta becomes first president of republic of Kenya.

rebellion and unrelenting pressure for his release, until he was finally freed in 1961.

In 1962 he was elected to the legislative council, becoming Kenya's first prime minister in May 1963, and then president upon the declaration of Kenya as a republic in December 1964.

As a proponent of African socialism, Kenyatta believed that traditional tribal values of individual responsibility and cooperation within the extended family could serve as a model for the governance of and organization within the nation-state, and, under the slogan of "Harambee" ("pulling together"), called upon all Kenyans, regardless of race or tribal affiliation, to cooperate in developing Kenya. Black Kenyans were allowed rights to purchase land that had formerly been reserved exclusively for whites, improvements were made in education, the economy grew rapidly, and agriculture, industry, and tourism were expanded.

Fostering resentment toward colonialists for past wrongs was futile, Kenyatta felt; he allowed white settlers to stay on their farms and kept British advisers within his government. He rejected Soviet communism as just another form of imperialism, and his maintenance of ties with the West brought an inflow of investment; he came to be thought of by Western countries as an important source of stability within Africa.

Other Kenyans resented Kikuyu predominance both in government and in society at large; the Luo tribe in particular resented the dismissal of one of its members, Oginga Odinga, from his post as vice president, after he adopted a communist stance, the assassination of their leader, Tom Mboya, in 1969 almost led to tribal warfare between the Kikuyu and Luo. Kenyatta, however, refrained from using violence to suppress hostilities and the atmosphere eventually calmed.

Kenyatta was instrumental in forming the East African Community in 1965, which operated mainly as a customs union between Kenya, Uganda, and Tanzania. The refusal of Julius Nyerere, president of Tanzania, to continue relations with Uganda after General Idi Amin's coup in 1971, led to a near state of war between the two countries; Kenyatta's mediation was a crucial factor in resolving the conflict.

Toward the end of his life, "Mzee," or "Father of the Nation," as Kenyatta was fondly known, confined himself largely to ceremonial duties. ◆

"The African is conditioned, by the cultural and social institutions of centuries, to a freedom of which Europe has little conception, and it is not in his nature to accept serfdom forever."
Jomo Kenyatta, 1938

Kerrey, Joseph Robert

1943–PRESENT ● VIETNAM WAR HERO

Joseph Robert (Bob) Kerrey, United States senator from Nebraska, is a highly decorated veteran of the Vietnam War. Kerrey was born on August 27, 1943. He grew up in Lincoln Nebraska and attended the University of Nebraska at Lincoln as a pharmacy major. He graduated in 1965, intending to become a pharmacist. But the Vietnam War had begun, and Kerrey decided to enlist in the United States navy, in part to avoid being drafted into the army. After completing Officer Candidate School in Newport, Rhode Island, Kerrey volunteered for the elite U.S. Navy SEALs (Sea, Air, and Land).

Kerrey was sent to Vietnam in January 1969, where he served as a lieutenant junior grade in charge of a SEAL platoon. On March 14, 1969, Lieutenant Kerrey led his SEAL team on a secret mission to capture important members of a Viet Cong political unit who were believed to be hiding on an

The Medal of Honor

The Medal of Honor is the highest award for heroism that can be given to a man or woman serving in the U.S. armed forces. Congress established the Medal of Honor in 1862 during the Civil War. Initially, only enlisted personnel were eligible, but Congress later made officers eligible as well. The medal is awarded to a soldier, sailor, airman, marine, or coast guardsman who risks of his or her life above and beyond the call of duty while engaged in military action against an enemy of the United States or while serving with foreign forces engaged in an armed conflict. The deed of the nominated person must be proven beyond any doubt by testimony of at least two eye-witnesses. On March 25, 1863, Private Jacob Parrot of the U.S. Army became the first person to receive a Medal of Honor. Parrot was recognized for penetrating nearly 200 miles into enemy territory and capturing a railroad train at Big Shanty, Georgia, in an attempt to destroy the bridges and tracks between Chattanooga and Atlanta. More recently, Master Sergeant Gary Gordon and Sergeant First Class Randall Shughart of the U.S. Army were awarded posthumous Medals of Honor for bravery in action in Somalia in 1993. As of 1998, the total number of Medal of Honor recipients was 3,408. Twenty people have received two Medals of Honor.

island in the bay of Nha Trang. To surprise the enemy, Kerrey and his team scaled and then descended a 350-foot cliff to reach a ledge where the enemy was encamped. Just as Kerrey and his team were nearing the enemy camp, they were discovered and the Viet Cong directed intense fire at them. Kerrey was badly wounded when a grenade exploded at his feet and threw him backward onto jagged rocks. The grenade had blown off the lower half of his right leg. Although he was in great pain and bleeding profusely, Kerrey remained calm and continued to direct his troops until they had suppressed the enemy's fire and captured several enemy soldiers. Kerrey was eventually evacuated by helicopter and spent nine months recuperating in a Naval hospital. He was awarded the Congressional Medal of Honor for courage beyond the call of duty during this incident.

Upon his return to the United States, Kerrey became an outspoken opponent of the war in Vietnam and began helping peace activists register antiwar voters. Kerrey considered refusing to accept the Medal of Honor because he believed that the United States government's intervention in Indochina was unjustified. In 1972, Kerrey and his brother-in-law opened a small restaurant in Omaha, Nebraska. Over the next few years, they expanded their business until they had a chain of restaurants and several health clubs.

In 1982, Kerrey ran as the Democratic candidate for governor of Nebraska. Although he had no political experience, he defeated the incumbent Republican governor. He served one four-year term as governor, where he was noted for balancing the state's budget and leaving office with a 7 percent budget surplus. As governor, Kerrey also implemented programs to reform welfare and education, and stressed job training and environmental protection in Nebraska.

Kerrey ran for the United States Senate in 1988 and easily defeated the incumbent Republican senator. During his first term in the Senate, Kerrey advocated fiscal responsibility, and education and health care reform. In 1991, he entered the race for the Democratic presidential nomination. During the campaign he stressed the need for a national health care system, which would be funded with higher taxes. Kerrey did not win the Democratic nomination, but he was reelected to the Senate in 1994. ◆

"Fear is a natural reaction, but fear is also the great debilitator. Fear keeps us from taking necessary action."
Bob Kerrey, 1998

King, Martin Luther Jr.

1929–1968 ● Minister & Civil Rights Leader

> *"I have a dream that my four little children will one day live in a nation where they will not be judged by the color of their skin, but by the content of their character."*
>
> Martin Luther King, 1963

Born Michael King Jr. in Atlanta on January 15, 1929, he was the first son of a Baptist minister and the grandson of a Baptist minister, and his forebears exemplified the African-American social gospel tradition that would shape his career as a reformer. King's maternal grandfather, the Rev. A. D. Williams, had transformed Ebenezer Baptist Church, a block down the street from his grandson's childhood home, into one of Atlanta's most prominent black churches. In 1906, Williams had joined such figures as Atlanta University scholar W. E. B. Du Bois and African Methodist Episcopal (AME) bishop Henry McNeal Turner to form the Georgia Equal Rights League, an organization that condemned lynching, segregation in public transportation, and the exclusion of black men from juries and state militia. In 1917, Williams helped found the Atlanta branch of the NAACP, later serving as the chapter's president. Williams's subsequent campaign to register and mobilize black voters prodded white leaders to agree to construct new public schools for black children.

After Williams's death in 1931, his son-in-law, Michael King Sr., also combined religious and political leadership. He became president of Atlanta's NAACP, led voter-registration marches during the 1930s, and spearheaded a movement to equalize the salaries of black public school teachers with those of their white counterparts. In 1934, King Sr.—perhaps inspired by a visit to the birthplace of Protestantism in Germany—changed his name and that of his son to Martin Luther King.

Despite the younger King's admiration for his father's politically active ministry, he was initially reluctant to accept his inherited calling. Experiencing religious doubts during his early teenage years, he decided to become a minister only after he came into contact with religious leaders who combined theological sophistication with social gospel advocacy. At Morehouse College, which King attended from 1944 to 1948, the college's president, Benjamin E. Mays, encouraged him to believe that Christianity should become a force for progressive social change. A course on the Bible taught by Morehouse professor George Kelsey exposed King to theological scholarship. After deciding to become a minister, King increased his understanding of liberal Christian thought while attending Crozer Theological Seminary in Pennsylvania. Compiling an outstanding academic record at Crozer, he deepened his understanding of modern religious scholarship and eventually identified himself with theological personalism. King later wrote that this philosophical position strengthened his belief in a personal God and provided him with a "metaphysical basis for the dignity and worth of all human personality."

At Boston University, where King began doctoral studies in systematic theology in 1951, his exploration of theological scholarship was combined with extensive interactions with the Boston African American community. He met regularly with other black students in an informal group called the Dialectical Society. Often invited to give sermons in Boston-area churches, he acquired a reputation as a powerful preacher, drawing ideas from Aftican American Baptist traditions as well as theological and philosophical writings. The academic papers he wrote at Boston displayed little originality, but King's scholarly training provided him with a talent that would prove useful in his future leadership activities: an exceptional ability to draw upon a wide range of theological and philosophical texts to express his views with force and precision. During his stay in Boston, King also met and began dating Coretta Scott, then a student at the New England

1955 King becomes president of the Montgomery Improvement Association.

1957 King founds the Southern Christian Leadership Conference.

1961 King is arrested during a protest in Atlanta.

1963 King heads the Birmingham demonstrations.

1963 King makes his famous "I Have a Dream" speech in Washington.

1964 King is awarded the Nobel Peace Prize.

1967 King forms the Poor People's Campaign.

1968 King is assassinated in Memphis.

> *"Returning violence for violence multiplies violence, adding deeper darkness to a night already devoid of stars. Darkness cannot drive out darkness; only light can do that. Hate cannot drive out hate; only love can do that."*
>
> Martin Luther King, 1967

Conservatory of Music. On June 18, 1953, the two students were married in Marion, Alabama, where Scott's family lived. During the following academic year, King began work on his dissertation, which was completed during the spring of 1955.

Soon after King accepted his first pastorate at Dexter Avenue Baptist Church in Montgomery, Alabama, he had an unexpected opportunity to utilize the insights he had gained from his childhood experiences and academic training. After NAACP official Rosa Parks was jailed for refusing to give up her bus seat to a white passenger, King accepted the post of president of the Montgomery Improvement Association, which was formed to coordinate a boycott of Montgomery's buses. In his role as the primary spokesman of the boycott, King gradually forged a distinctive protest strategy that involved the mobilization of black churches, utilization of Gandhian methods of nonviolent protest, and skillful appeals for white support.

After the U.S. Supreme Court outlawed Alabama bus segregation laws in late 1956, King quickly rose to national prominence as a result of his leadership role in a successful boycott movement. In 1957, he became the founding president of the Southern Christian Leadership Conference (SCLC), formed to coordinate civil rights activities throughout the South. Publication of King's *Stride Toward Freedom: The Montgomery Story* (1958) further contributed to his rapid emergence as a nationally known civil rights leader. Seeking to forestall the fears of NAACP leaders that his organization might draw away followers and financial support, King acted cautiously during the late 1950s. Instead of immediately seeking to stimulate mass desegregation protests in the South, he stressed the goal of achieving black voting rights when he addressed an audience at the 1957 Prayer Pilgrimage for Freedom. During 1959, he increased his understanding of Gandhian ideas during a month-long visit to India as a guest of Prime Minister Jawaharlal Nehru. Early in 1960, King moved his family—which now included two children, Yolanda Denise (born 1955) and Martin Luther III (born 1957)—to Atlanta in order to be nearer SCLC's headquarters in that city and to become copastor, with his father, of Ebenezer Baptist Church. The Kings' third child, Dexter Scott, was born in 1961; their fourth, Bernice Albertine, was born in 1963.

Soon after King's arrival in Atlanta, the lunch counter sit-in movement, led by students, spread throughout the South and brought into existence a new organization, the Student Nonviolent Coordinating Committee (SNCC). SNCC activists admired King but also pushed him toward greater militancy. In October 1960, his arrest during a studentinitiated protest in Atlanta became an issue in the national presidential campaign when Democratic candidate John F. Kennedy intervened to secure his release from jail. Kennedy's action contributed to his narrow victory in the November election. During 1961 and 1962, King's differences with SNCC activists widened during a sustained protest movement in Albany, Georgia. King was arrested twice during demonstrations organized by the Albany Movement, but when he left jail and ultimately left Albany without achieving a victory, his standing among activists declined.

King reasserted his preeminence within the African-American freedom struggle through his leadership of the Birmingham, Alabama campaign of 1963. Initiated by the SCLC in January, the Birmingham demonstrations were the most massive civil rights protests that had occurred up to that time. With the assistance of Fred Shuttlesworth and other local black leaders, and without much competition from SNCC or other civil rights groups, SCLC officials were able to orchestrate the Birmingham protests to achieve maximum national impact. During May, televised pictures of police using dogs and fire hoses against demonstrators aroused a national outcry. This vivid evidence of the obstinacy of Birmingham officials, combined with Alabama governor George C. Wallace's attempt to block the entry of black students at the University of Alabama, prompted President John F. Kennedy to introduce major new civil rights legislation. King's unique ability to appropriate ideas from the Bible, the Constitution, and other **canonical** texts manifested itself when he defended the black protests in a widely quoted letter, written while he was jailed in Birmingham.

canonical: authorized; accepted.

King's speech at the August 28, 1963, March on Washington, attended by over 200,000 people, provides another powerful demonstration of his singular ability to draw on widely accepted American ideals in order to promote black objectives. At the end of his prepared remarks, which announced that African Americans wished to cash the "promissory note" signified in the words of the Constitution and the Declaration of Independence, King began his most quoted oration: "So I say to you, my friends, that even though we must face the difficulties of today and tomorrow, I still have a dream. It is a dream deeply rooted in the American dream that one day this nation will rise up and live out the true meaning of its creed—we hold these truths to be self-evident, that all men are created equal." He appropriated the familiar words of the song "My Country 'Tis of Thee" before concluding: "And when we allow freedom to ring, when we let it ring from every village and hamlet, from every state and city, we will be able to speed up that day when all of God's children—black men and white men, Jews and Gentiles, Catholics and Protestants—will be able to join hands and to sing in the words of the old Negro spiritual, 'Free at last, free at last, thank God Almighty, we are free at last.' "

After the march on Washington, King's fame and popularity were at their height. Named *Time* magazine's Man of the Year at the end of 1963, he was awarded the Nobel Peace Prize in December 1964. The acclaim he received prompted FBI director J. Edgar Hoover to step up his effort to damage King's reputation by leaking information gained through surreptitious means about King's ties with former communists and his extramarital affairs.

King's last successful civil rights campaign was a series of demonstrations in Alabama that were intended to dramatize the denial of black voting rights in the deep South. Demonstrations began in Selma, Alabama, early in 1965 and reached a turning point on March 7, when a group of demonstrators began a march from Selma to the state capitol in Montgomery. King was in Atlanta when state policemen, carrying out Governor Wallace's order to stop the march, attacked with tear gas and clubs soon after the procession crossed the Edmund Pettus Bridge on the outskirts of Selma. The police assault on the marchers quickly increased national support for the voting rights campaign. King arrived in Selma to join several thousand movement sympathizers, black and white. President Lyndon B. Johnson reacted to the Alabama protests by introducing new voting rights legislation, which would become the Voting Rights Act of 1965. Demonstrators were finally able to obtain a court order allowing the march to take place, and on March 25 King addressed the arriving protestors from the steps of the capitol in Montgomery.

After the successful voting rights campaign, King was unable to garner similar support for his effort to confront the problems of northern urban blacks. Early in 1966 he launched a major campaign in Chicago, moving into an apartment in the black ghetto. As he shifted the focus of his activities north, however, he discovered that the tactics used in the South were not as effective elsewhere. He encountered formidable opposition from Mayor Richard Daley, and was unable to mobilize Chicago's economically and ideologically diverse black populace. He was stoned by angry whites in the suburb of Cicero when he led a march against racial discrimination in housing. Despite numerous well-publicized protests, the Chicago campaign resulted in no significant gains and undermined King's reputation as an effective leader.

His status was further damaged when his strategy of nonviolence came under renewed attack from blacks following a major outbreak of urban racial violence in Los Angeles during August 1965. When civil rights activists reacted to the shooting of James Meredith by organizing a March Against Fear through Mississippi, King was forced on the defensive as Stokely Carmichael and other militants put forward the Black Power slogan. Although King refused to condemn the mili-

The National Civil Rights Museum

On April 4, 1968, Dr. Martin Luther King Jr. was assassinated while standing on a balcony of the Lorraine Motel in Memphis, Tennessee. Since 1991 the motel has housed the National Civil Rights Museum. On the balcony is a wreath laid where King fell. Rooms 306 and 307, where King and his followers stayed, have been preserved as they were The museum's 10,000 square feet are devoted primarily to a series of exhibits that graphically depict many key events of the civil rights struggles of the King era and afterward. The exhibits use photographs, artifacts, documents, graphics, and audiovisual media. The Montgomery Bus Boycott led by King in 1955 and 1956 includes a Montgomery, Alabama, bus of mid-1950s vintage. Visitors who sit in the front are told by a recorded voice to move back, and if they do not, the bottom of their seats are rapped. Another exhibit is a replica of the cell in which King wrote his famous "Letter from a Birmingham Jail" in 1963. Among the many other dramatic events represented are the student lunch-counter sit-ins of 1960 and the Freedom Rides that began in 1961.

> *"I believe that unarmed truth and unconditional love will have the final word in reality."*
>
> Martin Luther King, 1964

tants who opposed him, he criticized the new slogan as vague and divisive. As his influence among blacks lessened, he also alienated many white moderate supporters by publicly opposing United States intervention in the Vietnam War. After he delivered a major antiwar speech at New York's Riverside Church on April 4, 1967, many of the northern newspapers that had once supported his civil rights efforts condemned his attempt to link civil rights to the war issue.

In November 1967, King announced the formation of a Poor People's Campaign designed to prod the nation's leaders to deal with the problem of poverty. Early in 1968, he and other SCLC workers began to recruit poor people and antipoverty activists to come to Washington, D.C., to lobby on behalf of improved antipoverty programs. This effort was in its early stages when King became involved in a sanitation workers' strike in Memphis. On March 28, as he led thousands of sanitation workers and sympathizers on a march through downtown Memphis, violence broke out and black youngsters looted stores. The violent outbreak led to more criticisms of King's entire antipoverty strategy. He returned to Memphis for the last time early in April. Addressing an audience at Bishop Charles H. Mason Temple on April 3, he sought to revive his flagging movement by acknowledging: "We've got some difficult days ahead. But it doesn't matter with me now. Because I've been to the mountaintop. . . . And I've seen the promised land. I may not get there with you. But I want you to know tonight that we, as a people, will get to the promised land."

The following evening, King was assassinated as he stood on a balcony of the Lorraine Motel in Memphis. A white segregationist, James Earl Ray, was later convicted of the crime. The Poor People's Campaign continued for a few months but did not achieve its objectives. King became an increasingly revered figure after his death, however, and many of his critics ultimately acknowledged his considerable accomplishments. In 1969 his widow, Coretta Scott King, established the Martin Luther King, Jr., Center for Nonviolent Social Change, in Atlanta, to carry on his work. In 1986, a national holiday was established to honor his birth.

More than twenty-five years after his assassination, the militant political legacy of the Rev. Dr. Martin Luther King Jr. is in eclipse. Simultaneously, King's historical reputation is frequently distorted by the popular misconception that he was primarily a philosophical "dreamer," rather than a realistic and often courageous dissident.

King's true legacy is not the 1963 March on Washington and his grandly optimistic "I Have a Dream" speech; it is instead his 1968 plan for a massively disruptive but resolutely nonviolent "Poor People's Campaign" aimed at the nation's capital, a protest campaign that came to pass only in a muted and disjointed form after his death.

Some of the distortion of King's popular image is a direct result of how disproportionately he nowadays is presented as a gifted and sanguine speechmaker whose life ought to be viewed through the prism of his "dream." King had used the "I Have a Dream" phrase several times before his justly famous oration, but on numerous occasions in later years King invoked the famous phrase only to emphasize how the "dream" he had had in Washington in 1963 had "turned into a nightmare."

Both the dilution of King's legacy and the misrepresentation of his image are also in part due to the stature accorded his birthday, now a national holiday. Making King an object of official celebration inescapably leads to at least some smoothing of edges and tempering of substance that otherwise would irritate and challenge those Americans who are just as eager to endorse "I Have a Dream" as they are to reject any "Poor People's Campaign."

But another facet of King's erroneous present-day image as a **milquetoast** moderate, particularly among young people, is directly tied to the greatly increased prominence of Malcolm X. Even before the media boomlet that accompanied Spike Lee's 1992 movie *Malcolm X*, popular appreciation of Malcolm X had expanded well beyond anything that had existed in the first two decades following his 1965 death. Even if young people's substantive understanding of Malcolm X's message is oftentimes faulty or nonexistent, among youthful Americans of all races the rise of Malcolm X has vastly magnified the mistaken stereotype that "Malcolm and Martin" were polar opposites.

Far too many people assume that if Malcolm personified unyielding tenacity and determination, King, as his supposed opposite, was no doubt some sort of **vainglorious** compromiser who spent more time socializing with the Kennedys than

milquetoast: very timid.

vainglorious: very proud and boastful.

> *"Man must evolve for all human conflict a method which rejects revenge, aggression, and retaliation. The foundation of such a method is love."*
>
> Martin Luther King Jr., 1964

fighting for social change. Hardly anything could be further from the truth, for while Malcolm's courageous selftransformation is deserving of far more serious attention and study than it has yet received, King was as selflessly dedicated and utterly principled a public figure as the United States has seen in this century.

Perhaps King's most remarkable characteristic was how he became a nationally and then internationally famous figure without ever having any egotistical desire to promote himself onto the public stage, as is otherwise the case with virtually every luminary in contemporary America. Drafted by his colleagues in Montgomery, Alabama, in 1955 to serve as the principal spokesperson for the black community's boycott of municipal buses, King was far from eager to be any sort of "leader," and only a deeply spiritual sense of obligation convinced him that he could not refuse this call.

King's resolutely selfless orientation gave his leadership both a public integrity and a private humility that are rare, if not wholly unique, in recent U.S. history. Perhaps the greatest irony generated by the hundreds upon hundreds of King's ostensibly private telephone conversations that were preserved for history by the FBI's indecently intrusive electronic surveillance—and released thanks to the Freedom of Information Act—is that one comes away from a review of King's most unguarded moments with a distinctly heightened, rather than diminished, regard for the man. Time and again, those transcripts show King as exceptionally demanding of himself and as an overly harsh judge of his own actions. How many other public figures, lacking only an FBI director like J. Edgar Hoover to preserve their off-the-cuff comments for posterity, could hope to pass such an ultimate test of civic character?

King's remarkable political courage and integrity were just as dramatically visible on the public stage, however, as in his self-critical private conversations. Unlike almost every other public figure in the country both then and now, King had no interest in assessing which position on which issue would be the most popular or the most **remunerative** for organizational fund-raising before he decided how and when to speak his mind.

Nowhere was this more starkly apparent than in King's early decision to speak out against U.S. involvement in

remunerative: profitable.

Vietnam at a time when President Lyndon B. Johnson's war still had the support of most progressive Democrats. Many liberal newspapers—and even several "mainstream" civil rights organizations—harshly attacked King for devoting his attention to an issue that did not fall within the "black" **bailiwick**, and while in private King was deeply hurt by such criticism, he had decided to confront the Vietnam issue knowing full well that just such a reaction would ensue.

"Leadership" to King did not mean tailoring one's comments to fit the most recent public opinion poll or shifting one's positions to win greater acclaim or support. King realized, too, that real leadership did not simply comprise issuing press releases and staging news conferences, and he was acutely aware that most real "leaders" of the southern civil rights struggle were unheralded people who performed the crucial task of encouraging others to stand up and take an active part in advancing their own lives and communities—got none of the public attention and awards that flowed to King and a very few others.

King understood that in our culture of publicity, the recognition of an individual symbolic figure such as he was inevitable and essential to the movement's popular success, but he always sought to emphasize, as in his Nobel Peace Prize lecture, that he accepted such applause and honors only as a "trustee" on behalf of the thousands of unsung people whose contributions and aspirations he sought to represent. King realized, better than many people at the time, and far better than some subsequent disciples, that the real essence of the movement was indeed the local activists in scores of generally unpublicized locales. In private, King could be extremely self-conscious about how he personally deserved only a very modest portion of all the praise and trophies that came his way.

King would very much welcome the newfound appreciation of Malcolm X, but King likewise would be intensely discomfited by a national holiday that in some hands seems to encourage celebration of King's own persona rather than the movement he came to symbolize. King also would rue how our culture of celebrity has become more and more a culture of violence, and how economic inequality in America is even more pronounced in the 1990s than it was at the time of his death in 1968.

> *"We must learn to live together as brothers or perish together as fools."*
> Martin Luther King Jr., 1964

bailiwick: a distinct field of authority.

proffer: to offer.

King likewise would rue his legacy being too often shorn of his post-1965 nonviolent radicalism, and the celebration of his image by people who **proffered** him and the movement no support when he was alive. But King would not worry about any decline in his own reputation or fame, for he would greatly welcome increased credit and appreciation for those whom the media and history habitually overlook. If in the next several decades Martin Luther King Jr.'s individual image continues gradually to recede, King himself would be happy rather than sad, for personal fame and credit were not something that he sought or welcomed either in 1955 or in 1968. ◆

Lawrence, Thomas Edward (Lawrence of Arabia)

1881–1935 ● BRITISH SOLDIER & AUTHOR

> *"In October, 1913, when England launched the 'Queen Elizabeth,' first of the cruisers to burn crude oil, I knew then that it was up to me to concern myself with the supply of oil for my country and not with archeology."*
>
> T. E. Lawrence, 1916

Thomas Edward Lawrence was the second of five sons born to Sir Thomas Chapman and Sarah Maden. Chapman, a former land-owning Irish noble, fled Ireland with Maden, the governess to his daughters. Although the couple never married, they lived in Wales as Mr. and Mrs. Lawrence. In 1896, the family moved to Oxford, where Lawrence attended high school and Jesus College, Oxford University, where he studied medieval military architecture.

After traveling to France to study Crusader castles, Lawrence went on to Mesopotamia, where, from 1911 to 1914, he participated in an archeological expedition on the Euphrates River. While working on the dig, he learned fluent Arabic. Immersing himself deeply in the local culture, he adopted Arab dress and manners (retaining them even after his return to England) and became so well accepted that the people of the area often turned to him for advice on topics ranging from legal matters to marital matchmaking.

In 1914 Lawrence accompanied a map-making expedition to the northern Sinai desert, and was then drafted into military service, first as a map-maker for the British war department, later as an Arab affairs expert for the intelligence service in Cairo. In 1916 he was sent on an expedition to Arabia with Sir Ronald Storrs, entrusted with the mission of encouraging Arab revolt against the Ottoman Turks.

Persuading Faisal Husseini, a son of the emir of Mecca, to lead the revolt, Lawrence became its organizer and military technician. He proved himself a master of hit-and-run guerrilla tactics, specializing in blowing up trains and railroads and in mining bridges; his bands made the Damascus-Medina railway inoperable. The Arabs succeeded in capturing Aqaba in July 1917 by attacking through the desert after a dangerous crossing on camels. The Turks, expecting an attack from the sea, had all their heavy artillery facing the wrong way and were completely wrong-footed. Lawrence was captured and tortured by Turkish officers, but was not recognized, which was fortunate for him as by this time he had a price on his head and would have been killed if his identity had been revealed.

Upon his release Lawrence led the Arabs to Damascus, the ultimate target of their campaign, in October 1918. Lawrence, who had been promoted to lieutenant colonel, soon returned to England. There, he was nominated for the Distinguished Service Order, a decoration he turned down in order to express his disapproval of British government treatment of its Arab allies.

Demobilized in 1919, Lawrence attended the Paris Peace Conference to lobby for the Arab cause. Throughout the conference, at which he served as an adviser and interpreter to Faisal, he wore Arab dress. Disillusioned with the treatment of the Arabs by the British and French, he returned to England. After a period spent teaching and beginning working on his book *The Seven Pillars of Wisdom* (published in 1926), he became an adviser on Arab affairs in Cairo to the then-colonial minister Winston Churchill. Many of his contemporaries were surprised that such a restless adventurer would accept a desk job, asking of Churchill: "What! Wilt thou bridle the wild ass of the desert?"

1911 Lawrence begins work on an archeological expedition on the Euphrates River.

1914 Lawrence accompanies a map-making expedition to the Sinai desert.

1916 Lawrence makes an expedition to Arabia.

1919 Lawrence attends the Paris Peace Conference to lobby for the Arabs.

1926 Lawrence publishes *The Seven Pillars of Wisdom.*

1935 Lawrence dies in a motorcycle accident.

As Churchill had anticipated, Lawrence performed well in the position, earning the praise and admiration of his minister. He proved a good team member and made a significant impact on the developing British policy in the Middle East, realizing some of the goals he had failed to achieve in Paris. When he considered his job well done, he left, telling his colleagues that "all you will see of me is a small cloud of dust on the horizon." He returned to England to finish work on *The Seven Pillars*. Churchill considered the work "unsurpassed as a portrayal of the Arabs," adding that "it ranks with the greatest books ever written in the English language."

In later years, Lawrence sought privacy and anonymity through a return to the military, enlisting in the British Royal Air Force as a private under the alias John Hume Ross. However, after a London newspaper found him out and published his story, he was released from the air force. He then enlisted in the tank corps in 1923, calling himself T. E. Shaw (which legally became his name in 1927). In 1925 he rejoined the air force, from which he was discharged in 1935. He died in a motorcycle accident a few months later.

His idiosyncrasies notwithstanding, Lawrence combined a rare blend of outstanding qualities: archeologist, scholar, philosopher, soldier, statesman and writer. He was also a man who consistently backed up his strong beliefs with determined action. ◆

Lee, Robert Edward

1807–1870 ● CONFEDERATE GENERAL

Best known for his role as an almost-legendary Civil War general, Robert E. Lee is one of the few military geniuses who gained fame mainly through his actions in defeat. He was born in Westmoreland County, Virginia, the son of a famous American Revolution cavalry officer,

"It is well that war is so terrible, or we should grow too fond of it."
Robert E. Lee, 1862

Henry "Lighthorse Harry" Lee. Lee was raised as a Southern gentleman, albeit in near poverty because his father had squandered his and both his wives' family fortunes, even spending some time in prison because of his debts. After his father's death when he was only eleven, Lee took over family responsibility, caring for his mother and sisters. He was a pious and honest man, never smoked or drank and was friendly and even-tempered, his private life untouched by any hint of scandal.

At the age of eighteen Lee entered West Point, where he graduated second in his class, never having received a single demerit. He entered the army's prestigious Corps of Engineers and distinguished himself through his service in Mexico in 1846. Meanwhile, in 1831 Lee had married Mary Anne Randolph Custis, the daughter of George Washington's adopted son. The couple had seven children; their three sons all later served as Confederate soldiers. In 1857 Mary's father died, and the Lee family took up residence at her family estate in Arlington, Virginia.

After the Mexican War, Lee took charge of the construction of Fort Carroll in Baltimore Harbor. Following this assignment, Lee became superintendent of West Point in 1852. He soon tired of academic life and in 1855, transferred to the Second Cavalry Division, serving in Missouri, Kansas, and Texas, where the cavalry protected settlers from roving bands of Indians.

Home on leave in Arlington in 1859, Lee was appointed to lead the troops that put down abolitionist John Brown's raid on Harper's Ferry. He then went back to Texas, remaining until February 1861. On his return to Arlington, Lee realized that the growing tension between North and South meant that he would have to decide whether he owed greater loyalty to his country or to his native state. Lee disapproved of slavery and had freed his own slaves years before the war. He was deeply distressed by the thought of the dissolution of the Union, but nonetheless decided that his primary duty lay in loyalty to his home state. Therefore in April 1861, when Lee was offered field command of the United States Army, he declined the position and resigned his commission in the army. He intended to remain a private citizen and wrote to his brother that, "Save in defense of my native state, I have no desire ever again to draw my sword." Soon after the governor

"Save in defense of my native state, I have no desire ever again to draw my sword."

Robert E. Lee

Robert Edward Lee.

of Virginia offered him command of that state's army, which he accepted.

In the field, Lee eschewed the privileges generally taken by officers. Not wanting to displace civilians from their homes, he lived in a tent and kept a minimum of aides-de-camp and servants. Lee's first field test came in June 1862 when, after he took over command from the wounded General A. E. Johnston, the army of Northern Virginia forced General George B. McClellan's Union troops to withdraw from their siege of Richmond. In August of the same year Lee, aided by generals Thomas J. "Stonewall" Jackson and James Longstreet, faced the Union's General John Pope at Second

Bull Run. Lee devised a bold plan for his greatly outnumbered troops, dividing the army and sending Jackson, with three divisions, around Pope's army to a point twenty-four miles behind the line of battle. Lee's daring strategy gained him his first decisive field victory.

Lee then moved his troops into Maryland and attempted to gain Marylanders' support for the South; the response was less enthusiastic than he had hoped. In a further stroke of bad luck, Union soldiers found a copy of Lee's orders for the invasion of Maryland, giving McClellan a valuable edge in the upcoming confrontation at Antietam (Sharpsburg). Despite that setback, Lee swiftly and elegantly maneuvered his troops in what historians call his most brilliant performance ever. The Antietam campaign, which included "the bloodiest single day of the war," on which over twenty-three thousand soldiers were killed and wounded and over twenty-seven hundred were missing (on both sides), could have resulted in the destruction of the Confederate army and the end of the war. But Lee's brilliance, coupled with McClellan's indecisiveness, turned what could have been annihilation into a mere defeat, with Lee withdrawing to Virginia.

His next two engagements, against General Ambrose E. Burnside at Fredericksburg in November and at Chancellorsville in May 1863, brought victories to the South. Lee then decided to invade the North and drove his troops up the Shenandoah Valley, through Maryland and into Pennsylvania, where his next major battle took place at Gettysburg in July 1863. Bad judgment and delays by Lee's subordinate officers in carrying out his orders cost him severely. The end of the first day's fighting saw a decided Confederate victory, with Union troops retreating in disarray and panic. It was here that the Confederacy could have won the battle and, possibly, the war. Lee saw that the Union troops were beaten and tired and he knew that they could not withstand another assault. He also understood that whoever controlled the hills would command the battle. Knowing this, he told General Richard Ewell to "take that hill if at all practicable" but Ewell had made the fateful decision to wait until morning, giving the Union army all night to receive reinforcements and build barricades. On the second day of the battle Lee tried to crack the Union flanks. By then, however, they were well anchored and fortified and the assaults failed. On the third and final day

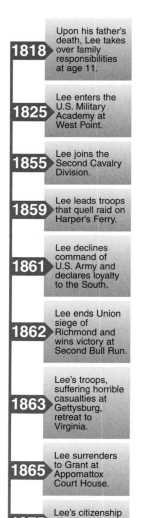

1818 Upon his father's death, Lee takes over family responsibilities at age 11.

1825 Lee enters the U.S. Military Academy at West Point.

1855 Lee joins the Second Cavalry Division.

1859 Lee leads troops that quell raid on Harper's Ferry.

1861 Lee declines command of U.S. Army and declares loyalty to the South.

1862 Lee ends Union siege of Richmond and wins victory at Second Bull Run.

1863 Lee's troops, suffering horrible casualties at Gettysburg, retreat to Virginia.

1865 Lee surrenders to Grant at Appomattox Court House.

1975 Lee's citizenship is restored by Congress.

Lee, feeling that he had no alternative, took a big gamble, sending 15,000 men in a charge (Pickett's Charge) against the Union center. The men broke through briefly but, to Lee's horror, the surviving gray troops soon came wearily down the hill and Lee conceded, "This is all my fault." The Southern forces retreated to Virginia to regroup, expecting a counterattack, which never came. Casualties at Gettysburg numbered more than one third of the Virginia army's troops. Lee accepted blame for the defeat and offered his resignation, which was refused.

Lee's troops were severely lacking in supplies and rations throughout the rest of 1863 and early 1864 but resumed fighting in May 1864, sparring with General Ulysses S. Grant in the battle of the Wilderness and forcing the Union troops to a standstill. The Petersburg campaign began in June and dragged on for months, wearing down the poorly fed and badly equipped Confederate troops. In February 1865, Lee became general-in-chief of all Confederate armies, by then an almost meaningless title. In April, as Federal troops closed in, Lee ordered the evacuation of Petersburg and Richmond. He remained in retreat until his surrender to Grant at Appomattox Court House.

Lee had lost his United States citizenship because he had served as a Confederate officer and, after the war, was indicted for treason, but the case was allowed to lapse. Lee urged his troops and all Southerners to accept the Union victory and help to rebuild their country. He applied for the restoration of his citizenship and swore a loyalty oath before a notary, but by accident his citizenship was not restored until an act of Congress in 1975 corrected the oversight.

After the war Lee accepted the presidency of Washington College (later renamed Washington and Lee University) in Lexington, Virginia. He rebuilt and revitalized the war-ravaged college and after his death on October 12, 1870, was buried in the university chapel. ◆

After the war, Lee urged his troops and all Southerners to accept the Union victory and help to rebuild their country.

Lewis, Meriwether

1774–1809 ● EXPLORER

Famed explorer of the Lewis and Clark Expedition, Meriwether Lewis was born in Ablemarle County, Virginia, near the home of Thomas Jefferson. Lewis entered military service in the militia during the Whiskey Rebellion in 1794, joined the regular army, and quickly rose to a captain's rank. During those years, he met William Clark, with whom he became lifelong friends.

In 1801, Lewis became President Jefferson's private secretary, and the two began planning the Western exploration. As Lewis headed west in 1803 to meet Clark, the Louisiana Purchase was completed, and the transaction made the expedition all the more important.

After wintering in Illinois across from St. Louis, the Corps of Discovery set out up the Missouri River on May 14, 1804. Lewis and Clark initially commanded a force of about forty men, including regular army enlistees and French boatmen. The summer's trip, laborious but exhilarating, was marked by friendly relations with Indians except for one tense encounter with Teton Sioux. During the summer, one of the men died, apparently of a ruptured appendix. No other such losses occurred during the trip. By late fall, the explorers reached the Mandan and Hidatsa Indians living near present-day Bismarck, North Dakota, and settled in for the winter. In the spring of 1805, the corps, now numbering thirty-three people, including the Shoshone woman Sacagawea, continued up the Missouri. The explorers crossed the Rockies in late summer with the help of Sacagawea's people and found streams that carried them to the coast. Along the way, they met natives who had never seen white people, most notably Nez Percés, with whom they made friendly contact.

They spent the winter of 1805 to 1806 on the Oregon coast among Clatsop Indians and began their return trip in March 1806. The captains split the command in July on the crest of the Rockies. Lewis and a small detachment followed a short cut to the Missouri River and explored its northern tributaries, while Clark descended the Yellowstone River with the main party. On Lewis's excursion, the corps had its only

1801 Lewis becomes President Thomas Jefferson's secretary.

1804 Lewis sets out to explore the West with William Clark.

1806 Lewis and Clark return to St. Louis.

1807 Jefferson appoints Lewis governor of the Louisiana Territory.

1809 Lewis kills himself along the Natchez Trace in Tennessee.

deadly engagement with natives; Lewis and his men killed two Piegan Blackfoot Indians who were stealing horses and guns. Later, Lewis was accidentally shot in the hip by one of his men, but he mended quickly under Clark's care. The reunited corps reached St. Louis in September 1806.

Lewis was the nominal leader of the expedition, although Clark was given equal authority. Lewis served as the party's naturalist and astronomer and performed most of the scientific tasks. He is praised for his ecological descriptions and is credited with a host of natural history discoveries. As reward for his work, he was appointed governor of the Louisiana Territory in 1807. Jefferson also looked to him to write a report of the expedition, but it was barely begun when Lewis killed himself along the Natchez Trace in Tennessee in October 1809. Although some believe he was murdered, it is more likely that personal problems and professional difficulties drove him to suicide. ◆

Lincoln, Abraham

1809–1865 ● PRESIDENT OF THE UNITED STATES

Abraham Lincoln was born in a log cabin in the slave-owning state of Kentucky, but when he was small the family moved to Indiana, and then he settled in Illinois (first New Salem, then Springfield). Lincoln's father was a hardworking man, but lacked money sense and was always moving his family to another, supposedly better, farm further west. Lincoln's mother died when he was eight and he was cared for by his elder sister until his father remarried. His stepmother encouraged his studies, but even so he was able to attend school for a total of only twelve months, accumulated during the times they happened to live near a school. Ambitious and extremely intelligent, he taught himself read-

"As I would not be a slave, so I would not be master. This expresses my idea of democracy."
Abraham Lincoln, 1858

ing, writing, arithmetic, and later law, spending every spare moment reading.

Lincoln was very tall, thin, and extremely strong. He became known for amazing feats of strength, an attribute he needed as many of the jobs on the frontier (and young Lincoln worked at different times as a storekeeper, casual laborer, rail-splitter, waterman, and soldier) required great physical strength. In many ways the frontier had a lifelong influence on him. His everyday speech and sense of humor, though witty, at times were coarse and homely—typical of the time, place, and people with whom he lived as a boy and young man. Yet his morals and character were atypical. For example, although hunting was common on the frontier, he never hunted again after shooting a turkey when he was eight. He never smoked or drank.

At the age of thirty-three he married Mary Todd, an ambitious, supportive woman with a temper and a gift for graceful hospitality. She faced their poverty with spirited resolution but disliked his uncouth appearance and ways. Their relationship was marked by a common love for their children, a lack of serious quarrels, and his avoidance of conflict, which sometimes meant an avoidance of her.

At twenty-five he was elected to the Illinois state legislature, where he served for three undistinguished terms. He did, however, present a pioneer statement endorsing female suffrage. In 1847 he was elected to the U.S. House of Representatives. He never ceased working as a lawyer and had an excellent reputation for kindness and honesty as well as ability. One of the shrewdest, most experienced politicians in Illinois, he knew how to turn situations to his political advantage. Lincoln tried twice to run for the U.S. Senate. He withdrew from the first race in 1856 to ensure the victory of a third, antislavery candidate from a different party. His second attempt was unsuccessful and the next public office he held was that of president of the United States. Previous to that, in 1858, he won a great reputation in his seven public debates with the proslavery senator Stephen A. Douglas, in which he contended that slavery, apart from being morally wrong, threatened all workers.

In 1860 Lincoln was elected president. At first the new president did not make a favorable impression on the government in Washington. While it was never suggested that he

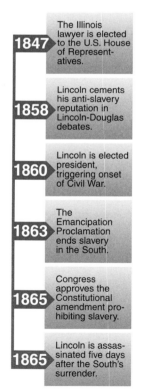

1847 The Illinois lawyer is elected to the U.S. House of Representatives.

1858 Lincoln cements his anti-slavery reputation in Lincoln-Douglas debates.

1860 Lincoln is elected president, triggering onset of Civil War.

1863 The Emancipation Proclamation ends slavery in the South.

1865 Congress approves the Constitutional amendment prohibiting slavery.

1865 Lincoln is assassinated five days after the South's surrender.

Abraham Lincoln.

was untrustworthy or motivated by personal aims. Lincoln did not inspire confidence in anything but his good intentions. His peculiar appearance and eccentric ways were regarded by many with embarrassment or condescending amusement. **Idiosyncrasies** such as his tactlessness, his insistence on standing back to back with other tall men to see who was tallest, and his way of beginning a conversation by telling a little story, were regarded with affection by those who came to know and appreciate the inner Lincoln. For many that knowledge, appreciation. and affection came only after his death.

idiosyncrasy: a personal peculiarity.

The South **extolled** the beauty and virtue of the Southern way of life based on slavery, which they wanted to see extended into the territories. Lincoln was the candidate of the Republican party in 1860. The Republican Party, founded in 1854, believed that while slavery had to be tolerated where it

extol: to praise highly.

When Lincoln was inaugurated for the second time, he had a battalion of black soldiers in his escort.

already existed to maintain the Union (it was constitutional), it was nevertheless fundamentally wrong and should not be extended. Lincoln's election was the first time that a united North succeeded in outvoting the South. The South considered Lincoln's antislavery stand a threat to its way of life. The first steps toward secession were taken shortly after the November elections. In his inaugural address Lincoln assured the Southerners: "The Government will not assail you. You have no conflict without yourselves being the aggressors."

Secession changed the basic issue between North and South from slavery to unity. The North viewed secession as outright rebellion, holding that the national government, the Union, had authority over the states. The South held that the Union was merely an agreed-upon alliance of the individual states, with states' rights (including withdrawal from the Union) having priority over those of the national government. Once the war began, slavery ceased to be an issue in the South: Southerners were fighting for their freedom and nothing else. Most Northerners, on the other hand, were willing to fight a war to preserve the Union but not to end slavery (four of the states on the Northern side were slave states).

This shift in issues presented Lincoln with a dilemma. He had hated slavery ever since he first encountered it as a young man on a visit to New Orleans. Yet he would have continued to tolerate an institution he hated, to preserve one he loved—the Union. Afraid that turning the war into an antislavery crusade would split the North, Lincoln resisted emancipating the slaves and let the individual generals decide the status of runaway slaves fleeing to Union forces. He favored a gradual emancipation that provided compensation for owners and opened ways for blacks to advance, such as education of black children or resettlement in Africa. He encouraged bills for gradual emancipation in the Congress and state legislatures, but none of them passed. The Emancipation Proclamation of 1863 ended slavery only in the South; it did not affect the Northern slave states. Two more years were to pass before, in January 1865, Congress voted for a constitutional amendment prohibiting slavery in the United States, with Lincoln putting a great deal of pressure on certain congressmen to ensure a sufficient number of votes. When Lincoln was inaugurated for the second time as president in March, 1865, he had a battalion of black soldiers in his escort. His reelection had not been easy; radical elements, feeling he was too moderate, had talked of dumping him. Lincoln called on the nation not to "swap horses while crossing a stream," and won the election.

Lincoln's greatest task was to preserve Northern unity. His handling of the powerful men in his cabinet (only Lincoln could have brought them to work so long and well together) illustrates how he accomplished this. Happy to delegate authority to men whose capabilities and judgment he trusted, Lincoln intervened very little unless he was unhappy with results (as with the Northern generals before Ulysses S. Grant). It was said that Lincoln's was the only real vote in his cabinet, but he preferred to bring his cabinet to agree on the best course of action rather than dictate to them. Sometimes he deferred to its superior knowledge of a subject or to public opinion, and there were also occasions when he made important decisions on his own, without consulting anyone. Lincoln used whatever methods he felt necessary to keep the North united sufficiently to fight the war until the end. No one else could have done it.

As the Civil War drew to a conclusion the question of the treatment of the defeated rebel states was debated. Lincoln wanted reunification, not revenge, and he might have got it but for a plot to kill important government figures by a small group of fanatical Southerners. Only one of their attempts succeeded: on Good Friday, April 14, 1865, Abraham Lincoln was assassinated by a Confederate sympathizer, the actor John Wilkes Booth, while watching a play at Ford's Theatre in Washington. The Confederate forces had surrendered at Appomattox Court House just five days before. ◆

"To give victory to the right, no bloody bullets, but peaceful ballots only, are necessary."
Abraham Lincoln, 1858

Lindbergh, Charles Augustus

1902–1974 ● PIONEER AVIATOR

Charles Augustus Lindbergh was born in Detroit, Michigan. His father served as a member of Congress for Minnesota from 1907 to 1917 and held a unique set of principles: stoic self-reliance, opposition to the Eastern banking system, opposition to American entrance into World War I, and affirmation of the anti-Catholic Free Press Defense League. Although these values cost him the governorship of Minnesota in a rowdy campaign in 1918, they were inherited by his son.

Charles A. Lindbergh Jr. early displayed mechanical skills. He began college studies in engineering at the University of Wisconsin in 1920, but dropped out after two years to do stunt flying. In 1924 he joined the U.S. army to train as an army air service reserve pilot, graduating the next year as the best pilot in his class. Lindbergh was hired to fly the mail between Saint Louis and Chicago, giving him the opportunity to develop his initial, limited reputation as a serious pilot.

A prize was offered for the first aviator to fly nonstop between Paris and New York by Raymond Orteig, a New York City hotelier, in 1919 and again in 1926. Although a number of men had sought it and had been either injured or killed in the attempt, none had succeeded. Lindbergh decided to try for the prize and on May 20, 1927, upon suddenly hearing a good weather report, he prepared to take off from Roosevelt Field, New York. Two other planes were also on the runway, ready to compete for the prize, but the pilots let Lindbergh go ahead. His plane, the *Spirit of Saint Louis*, was manufactured according to Lindbergh's own specifications, costing $10,580, which was paid for by nine Saint Louis businessmen. Lindbergh landed in Paris, a distance of thirty-six hundred miles, after a flight of 33.5 hours, some of it through treacherous sleet and ice clouds—to the greetings of an exuberant crowd of 20,000. He said his experience with the mob was the most dangerous part of the flight.

1922 Lindbergh drops out of college engineering studies to do stunt flying.

1927 Lindbergh completes first non-stop solo flight across the Atlantic Ocean.

1932 The Lindberghs' 20-month-old son is kidnapped and killed.

1938 Lindbergh is condemned as Nazi sympathizer after accepting German medal of honor.

1953 His book, *The Spirit of St. Louis*, receives Pulitzer Prize.

His feat made him a popular hero and spawned a love-hate relationship between the handsome aviator and the public that idolized him. Reticent by nature, he spent subsequent years avoiding reporters and photographers. President Calvin Coolidge presented him with the Congressional Medal of Honor and the first American Distinguished Flying Cross. As a result of his popularity, he was sent on a good will mission to Latin America. In Mexico he met and fell in love with Anne Spencer Morrow, the daughter of the U.S. ambassador, Dwight M. Morrow. Their courtship, engagement, wedding, and honeymoon were all spent in an intricate game of hide-and-seek with a persistent press. The young Lindberghs wore disguises, wrote in code to each other, and tried various escapes from the public eye, often to no avail.

Reticent by nature, Lindbergh spent years avoiding reporters and photographers.

Lindbergh taught his wife to fly and they went on a number of expeditions together. They inaugurated the transcontinental air passenger service and flew over Alaska to Siberia, Japan, and China. At each stop along the way they were quoted and photographed.

Anne Morrow Lindbergh was pregnant with her second child in Hopewell, New Jersey, when on March 1, 1932, their twenty-month-old son was kidnapped from the family home. The national press hounded the couple during the ten weeks of police investigation before the baby's body was found. The Lindberghs received an outpouring of compassion from the nation via thousands of letters during and after their ordeal. Two years later the police arrested Bruno Richard Hauptmann, a carpenter, who was tried, convicted, and executed for the murder. From diary entries and letters she wrote from 1929 to 1932, Anne Lindbergh described the early years of her marriage, both the romance and the suffering, in *Hour of Gold, Hour of Lead* (1973).

Their desire for privacy now became an obsession and the Lindberghs relocated to Europe for the rest of the 1930s, moving from place to place. They had five more children. While on the continent, Lindbergh toured the French and Nazi German aircraft industries, and was impressed by the latter. In 1938 he accepted a German medal of honor from the Nazi leader Hermann Goring, which brought the Lindberghs severe criticism upon their return to the United States in 1939. Lindbergh's advocacy of the America First Committee and his open criticism of "the three most important groups which have

> *"The price of peace is to be a strong nation, not only physically but also morally and spiritually."*
> Anne Morrow Lindbergh, *The Wave of the Future*, 1940

been pressing this country toward war . . . the British, the Jewish, and the [Franklin] Roosevelt Administration," did nothing to alleviate his image as a Nazi sympathizer.

Lindbergh was denied reenlistment during World War II, although he did serve as a civilian consultant in the Pacific zone and as such flew a number of combat missions. After the war he retired from public view. Anne Morrow Lindbergh, a poet and essayist, published several books in the 1950s and 1960s. Lindbergh, who became a consultant for Pan American World Airways and helped design the Boeing 747, took an interest in the conservation movement during the last years of his life. He died at his home on the Hawaiian island of Maui. His book *The Spirit of Saint Louis* (1953) received the 1953 Pulitzer Prize. *An Autobiography of Values* was published posthumously in 1978. ◆

Luthuli, Albert John Mvumbi

CA. 1898–1967 ● CIVIL RIGHTS LEADER

> *"To remain neutral in a situation where the laws of the land virtually criticized God for having created men of color was the sort of thing I could not, as a Christian, tolerate."*
> Albert Luthuli, 1961

Albert John Mvumbi Luthuli was born in Rhodesia (now Zimbabwe) and raised at the Groutville Mission (Umvoti), Natal, where his grandfather, chief of the Abasemakholweni Zulu, had been the first convert to the Methodist church, and his father a missionary. Luthuli himself was a devoutly religious man and Methodist lay preacher throughout his life. In 1917 he qualified as a primary school teacher and taught for fifteen years.

In 1936 he was elected tribal chief of the five thousand member Abasemakholweni tribe in Groutville, a post that afforded him a good opportunity to promote the economic and social position of his people. He presided over the councils, put down disturbances in the sugar fields, arbitrated disputes, and imposed laws. He also strengthened his ties with organized Christianity.

South African Albert
Luthuli receives Nobel
Prize.

In 1946 he joined the ineffectual, government sponsored
Native Representatives Council. He was already a member of
the African National Congress, then still a small organization
of some one thousand members devoted to achieving equality for South Africa's blacks. The legal aspects of apartheid
were only then being formulated by Daniel Malan's government, and the black majority responded with a vocal defiance
campaign, patterned after the nonviolent protest of Mahatma
Gandhi. In the course of the campaign, Luthuli, a soft-spoken
moderate, quickly rose to national prominence. He was dismissed from his state-appointed position as tribal chief and
briefly arrested. Rather than prosecute him, however, the government enacted the Criminal Laws Amendment Act, calling
for severe penalties for anyone breaking the law in protest of
government policies. In another protest, Luthuli challenged
the government over the unequal division of land between
blacks and whites, contrary to the Group Areas Act. In
response, the government legitimized its discriminatory policies in the Separate **Amenities** Act.

In 1952 Luthuli was elected president general of the
African National Congress. He held the post until his death,
at which time membership was over one hundred thousand.
Although he was regularly banned, he played an active role in

amenity: something
that makes life more
pleasant.

1917 Luthuli qualifies as a primary school teacher.

1936 Luthuli is elected tribal chief of the Abasemakholweni tribe.

1946 Luthuli joins the government of the Native Representatives Council.

1952 Luthuli is elected president of the ANC.

1960 Luthuli becomes the first black African to win the Nobel Peace Prize.

1962 Luthuli's autobiography, *Let My People Go*, is published.

1967 Luthuli dies after being struck by a train.

black politics and helped formulate the Freedom Charter of 1956 declaring South Africa the inheritance of all its inhabitants regardless of race. The government regarded the charter as a serious threat, and Luthuli, along with 155 others, was arrested and tried for treason. He was soon acquitted; no proof could be found that he had plotted the violent overthrow of the white government.

Just prior to the 1960 Sharpeville massacre, Luthuli was restricted to his tribal reservation for five years. He nonetheless burned his passbook, the document that, under the policies of apartheid, South African blacks had to carry on their persons at all times and which severely restricted their movements within the country. For this he was arrested and fined. Other black leaders were calling for armed violence against the oppressive white regime, but Luthuli remained dedicated to nonviolence. In 1960 he was awarded with the Nobel Prize for Peace, the first black African to win the award. At first, the government was reluctant to permit him to attend the prize ceremony in Oslo, but finally agreed to allow him one week abroad. Money from the prize was used to establish shelters in Swaziland for political exiles.

In 1964 the ban on Luthuli was extended for another five years. Although he was forbidden to publish, his impassioned autobiography, *Let My People Go*, appeared in 1962. Luthuli died in 1967 when he was struck by a train while crossing a railroad track near his home. ◆

Lutz, Carl (Charles)

1895–1975 ● RESCUER OF JEWS DURING WORLD WAR II

Born in Switzerland, Carl Lutz studied in the United States, and in 1935 served as head of the Swiss consulate in Tel Aviv. At the outbreak of World War II in September 1939, he interceded on behalf of the twenty-five hundred German settlers in Palestine who were being deported as enemy aliens by the British. This stood him in good stead with German authorities in Hungary years later. On January 2, 1942, he arrived in Budapest to represent the interests of the United States, the United Kingdom, and other countries that had severed relations with Miklós Horthy's Hungary, a member of the Axis nations.

During the fall of 1942, in his capacity as the representative of British interests, Lutz, in coordination with Moshe (Miklós) Krausz (who represented the Jewish Agency in Budapest), drew up lists of children and gave them certificates of immigration to Palestine. Nearly two hundred children and their adult chaperons were able to leave for Palestine before the German occupation of Hungary.

When the Germans invaded Hungary on March 19, 1944, Lutz invited Krausz to move into a Swiss office on Szabadsag Ter and continue his work from there. Under Lutz's protection, from this office and later from the Glass House at 29 Vadasz Utca, Krausz continued to promote various schemes for immigration to Palestine and related rescue projects.

The protection of Hungarian Jews with documents that certified them as foreign nationals had begun somewhat before the German occupation. The Geneva representative of the El Salvador government, George Mantello, had granted papers to thousands of Hungarian Jews that certified them as Salvadoran nationals. Lutz, who also represented Salvadoran interests in Budapest, was responsible for the distribution of these certificates. Perhaps this is what inspired Moshe Krausz to urge the Jewish Agency and the Swiss to persuade the British to declare that all bearers of Palestinian certificates of immigration were to be treated as potential British nationals. By the end of June 1944, the British had accepted the proposal. In the meantime, various diplomats in Budapest and abroad, including Lutz, pressured the Hungarian government to stop the **deportations** that had begun in mid-May. Early in July, Horthy ordered the deportations stopped, and soon thereafter declared his government's willingness to allow some seventy-five hundred bearers of certificates to leave for Palestine. The stage was now set to bring these Jews under Swiss protection.

With the help of Krausz, a group of fifty Jews was assembled in the Glass House to work with Lutz. Photos were collected from four thousand persons, and Lutz issued four collective passports, each with one thousand names. Each person

1942 Lutz is sent to Budapest to represent Allied interests in Hungary.

1944 Lutz works with Jewish Agency to relocate 50,000 Hungarian Jews.

1945 Lutz stays in Budapest under Soviet siege to ensure protection of remaining Jews.

1965 Lutz is recognized as "Righteous Among the Nations."

deportation: forced removal from a country.

was then issued a "protective letter" (*Schutzbrief*) guaranteeing that person's safety until his or her eventual departure for Palestine. To add as many people as possible to these *Schutzbriefe*, Lutz interpreted the permits as representing family units and not individuals. Eventually, protective letters were drawn up for fifty thousand Jews.

At the same time, Lutz instructed the recently arrived Swedish diplomat Raoul Wallenberg on the best uses of the protective passes, and gave him the names of persons in the government hierarchy with whom to negotiate. This idea served as a model for various types of protective letters issued by other neutral countries and by the International Red Cross through Friedrich Born, its representative in Budapest. In addition, after the pro-Nazi Arrow Cross Party came to power in mid-October of 1944, the Zionist youth underground manufactured and distributed tens of thousands of false documents, perhaps more than one hundred thousand, mostly in the name of Switzerland. Owing to the proliferation of false protective papers, the authorities pressured Lutz and Wallenberg to affirm the validity of the documents they had distributed. Lutz acquiesced so as to preclude the collapse of the entire rescue project. Late in November, he and his wife

Yad Vashem Righteous Among the Nations Award

Yad Vashem is Israel's national Holocaust memorial. Located in Jerusalem, Yad Vashem includes a library, an auditorium, an archive, a synagogue, a historical museum, an art museum, and several other monuments, all dedicated to preserving the memory of the six million Jews who died during the Holocaust. Under a program established in 1953, Yad Vashem has identified and honored close to 15,000 persons as "Righteous among the Nations." The Righteous among the Nations award is given to non-Jews who risked their lives to extend aid to Jews who were helpless or threatened with death or deportation to concentration camps. Many of the Righteous helped Jews during the Holocaust by sheltering them in their homes or religious institutions, helping them pass as a non-Jews by providing false credentials or baptismal certificates, and helping them flee to safer locations or across the border to a safer country. Those recognized as Righteous among the Nations are awarded the Righteous Medal and their names are inscribed on the Wall of Honor in the Garden of the Righteous at Yad Vashem. The garden is lined with carob tress that were planted by many of the rescuers when they visited Israel as guests of the Holocaust survivors whom they saved.

sorted out the bearers of legitimate passes from those holding forged papers at the assembly point in the Óbuda brickyard.

In the meantime, Lutz and other neutral diplomats, including Wallenberg and the papal **nuncio**, Angelo Rotta, interceded to have the new Hungarian government recognize the protective documents, using as bait the recognition of the regime by their governments. With the establishment of two ghettos, one for holders of protective passes and one for the rest of the Jews, Lutz procured twenty-five high-rise apartment buildings for concentrating the people under his protection. The Glass House and its annex also became a refuge for about three thousand Jews.

nuncio: an official representative of the Pope.

During the notorious death march of November 10 to 22, 1944, when over seventy thousand Jews were forcibly marched toward the Austrian border under the most inhumane conditions, Lutz and his fellow diplomats interceded on behalf of many Jews. Lutz made use of Salvadoran certificates still in his possession, following the deportees on their march and filling in many of their names on the documents. Those saved in this way were allowed to return to Budapest, which was already under siege by the Red Army. Ernst Kaltenbrunner, the Gestapo head, in a dispatch to the German Foreign Ministry complained about the disappearance of many Jews on this march as a result of intervention by the Swiss **legation**, as well as by the representatives of Sweden, Spain, Portugal, and the Vatican.

legation: a group of diplomats.

With the tightening of the Soviet siege of Budapest in December 1944, all foreign representatives were ordered to leave the beleaguered capital. Maximilian Jaeger, the head of the Swiss legation in Budapest, had already departed on November 10. But Lutz, not willing to abandon his protégés, decided to remain behind. Over thirty thousand Jews (out of a total of some one hundred thousand) with various protective passes—Swiss, Swedish, Red Cross, and Vatican—were housed in the so-called international ghetto.

Lutz later related that a German diplomat revealed to him that the Arrow Cross had received instructions not to harm the protected houses so long as Lutz remained in Budapest, as a token of Germany's gratitude to him for having looked after the interests of German expatriates in Palestine in 1939 and 1940. For three months thereafter, Lutz, together with his wife and a group of Jewish refugees, lived a precarious existence in the basement of the abandoned, but bombarded, British legation, almost without food and water. When the Russians stormed the building, Lutz jumped through the window and managed to reach Buda, the section of the city occupied only in February 1945.

In 1965, Lutz was recognized by Yad Vashem as a "Righteous Among the Nations." ◆

MacArthur, Douglas

1880–1964 ● AMERICAN MILITARY LEADER

> *"The soldier, above all other people, prays for peace, for he must suffer and bear the deepest wounds and scars of war."*
> Douglas MacArthur, 1962

D ouglas MacArthur's father, who had been awarded the Congressional Medal of Honor for exceptional brav-ery during the Civil War, constantly reminded his son that he received the award for an assault he led without hav-ing received an order to do so, and encouraged his son to take similar initiatives. MacArthur's mother saw her two older sons die prematurely, perhaps explaining the curious bond she maintained with MacArthur until her death. She even fol-lowed him to West Point Military Academy, keeping a hotel room near the campus to support her son's diligence and to remove any external distractions, notably women, that might interfere with his progress. His father, Arthur, was a haughty and often flamboyant commander who served in such presti-gious military positions as military **attaché** to China and commander of the Philippines. Douglas MacArthur excelled at West Point, finishing with a record average. He graduated with the rank of second lieutenant and chose to serve in the Philippines to be close to his father.

attaché: a technical expert serving a foreign government.

209

MacArthur found the Philippines alluring and befriended many prominent local leaders, including Manuel Quezon, later first president of that country. On the family's return to the United States, Douglas MacArthur studied engineering. He distinguished himself in the Spanish-American War for several daring assignments. In one, according to his own account, he single-handedly killed seven enemy gunmen. He was startled to discover that his bravery would not be rewarded since there was no verification of his feat and that the story, if true, was dismissed as an "error in judgment." He later served as military adviser to President Theodore Roosevelt.

During World War I MacArthur reached the rank of colonel and got the opportunity to command the Rainbow Division, formed, at his instigation, of National Guardsmen. In his two years in Europe he was the recipient of numerous medals and decorations. His troops fought in eight major battles. Yet despite his acknowledged bravery, MacArthur was regarded as an eccentric. He refused to wear a gas mask or helmet and carried no weapon but his riding crop. After a mission, he returned to base one night leading a high-ranking German officer with his crop.

After returning to America MacArthur was appointed superintendent of West Point, but was soon removed. Officially, his dismissal was attributed to the radical changes he had made in that institution, but he always ascribed his removal to the mutual distrust between himself and the commander of the army, General John J. Pershing. MacArthur was returned to the Philippines with the rank of major general.

In 1930 he was appointed army chief of staff. The depression-era posting saw enormous cuts in the military budget, including a cut in military pensions. Disgruntled veterans marched on Washington but were dispersed with considerable violence by MacArthur. Presidential candidate Franklin Delano Roosevelt responded to the attack on unarmed veterans by calling MacArthur "one of the most dangerous men in the country."

Rather than settle for a lesser post, MacArthur accepted the position of military adviser to his old friend Quezon, soon to be president of an independent Commonwealth of the Philippines.

In return for his encouraging Quezon to assert full independence for the Philippines, MacArthur was appointed field

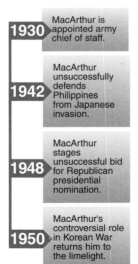

1930 MacArthur is appointed army chief of staff.

1942 MacArthur unsuccessfully defends Philippines from Japanese invasion.

1948 MacArthur stages unsuccessful bid for Republican presidential nomination.

1950 MacArthur's controversial role in Korean War returns him to the limelight.

marshal of the Philippine army, a force whose creation had been the result of his own devoted efforts in the face of official American opposition. Roosevelt came to detest MacArthur, who, in turn, took every opportunity to deride the president. In 1937, two years before his tour of duty in the Philippines was to end, MacArthur was finally convinced to retire from active service. He remained in the Philippines at the request of President Quezon, who continued to employ him as adviser, but the relationship between the two men degenerated and Quezon sought unsuccessfully to have MacArthur replaced by his rival and former aide General Dwight D. Eisenhower. MacArthur was, however, still recognized as an authority on East Asia; with the rising threat of Japan to the region, Roosevelt requested MacArthur to remain in Manila.

Following the Japanese occupation of French ports in Indochina, the new chief of staff, General George C. Marshall, persuaded Roosevelt to appoint MacArthur supreme commander of the armed forces in the Far East. MacArthur encouraged the American administration to abandon its original plan to defend only Manila and Subic Bay in favor of a comprehensive defense policy for the entire archipelago. The islands soon had the largest force of fighter planes outside the United States. When the Japanese invaded the Philippines in 1942, the local army crumbled in just two days. MacArthur evacuated Manila and moved his troops to the Bataan Peninsula and Corregidor Island. He defended the area for five months until, upon realizing that the Americans had chosen to abandon the front, he too made plans to retreat. His own press releases from the embattled island had already assured his entry into the pantheon of American heroes. After accepting a $500,000 gift from Quezon as a token of their friendship, MacArthur led his family and troops to Mindanao, where a plane took them to Australia. Arriving in Darwin, he issued his famous statement, "I shall return!"

Despite his growing fame among the masses, MacArthur's popularity waned in the administration. It was said that some would have preferred "to see MacArthur lose a battle than America win the war." He differed with the administration over wartime priorities and questioned the emphasis placed on the European rather than the Pacific front, claiming that

> *"Duty, honor, country: Those three hallowed words reverently dictate what you ought to be, what you can be, what you will be."*
>
> Douglas MacArthur, address at West Point, 1962

MacArthur
showed great
respect for
Japanese
Emperor
Hirohito, and
rejected all
attempts to try
him as a war
criminal.

life under the Nazis would be "tolerable; after all, the Germans are a civilized people."

Shortly before the Allied assault on Japan, MacArthur was appointed general of the army, empowered to lead the ground assault on Japan. To his dismay, this opportunity was "stolen" from him after the nuclear attacks on Hiroshima and Nagasaki. He did, however, conclude the armistice treaty with Japan and served as military governor of the country, overseeing its transformation into a democratic society. He showed great respect for Emperor Hirohito, and rejected all attempts to try him as a war criminal. His new constitution for Japan, drawn up in just six days, rejected militarism and redefined the role of the emperor. Although he was their conqueror, MacArthur won the esteem of the local population. From Japan MacArthur ran an unsuccessful bid for the Republican presidential nomination in 1948, but was defeated in the first two primaries and abandoned the race.

The Korean War in 1950 returned MacArthur to the forefront of American life. It was MacArthur who encouraged President Harry S. Truman to place American troops in combat and who planned the successful invasion of the port of Inchon, behind enemy lines. MacArthur was skeptical of the Chinese threat to enter the war, and when three hundred thousand Chinese troops swept down against American advances, he attributed it to faulty intelligence and refused to assume responsibility. MacArthur's support of an invasion of Communist China ran contrary to the plans of the American administration. His threat to disobey orders and carry out his plan forced Truman to recall him to the United States. It was there he made his last important public appearance, a farewell address to Congress interrupted by thirty ovations.

Three years before his death he made a last visit to the Philippines as the guest of honor at Independence Day celebrations. ◆

Madison, James

1751–1836 ● AMERICAN PRESIDENT
& FOUNDING FATHER

Born in King George County, Virginia, James Madison was taken as an infant to Orange County, Virginia, which was to be his home throughout his life. Little is known about his childhood. His early education came from local clergymen. In 1771 Madison received his bachelor of arts degree from the College of New Jersey at Princeton.

After graduation Madison became one of the principal writers of the Whig party. From 1774 to 1776 he served on the Orange County Committee for Safety and during this period wrote papers defining and defending the concept of religious liberty. His writings also sought to define the authority of the king of England.

In 1776 he was elected to represent the Orange County Committee at the Virginia Convention. His drafting of the guarantee of religious freedom was a pioneering document in modern history and became the model for other states. The convention had a lasting effect on Madison, becoming the foundation of the beliefs he adhered to for the rest of his life. However, he was not reelected because he failed to provide the electors with free whiskey.

In 1776 he was involved in the drafting of the Declaration of Independence; a delegate to the Continental Congress in 1780, he became one of its leading figures. A plan he introduced in Virginia became the basis for the Constitution of the United States and was adopted by the national government, giving it the power of taxation and law enforcement. Madison became known as "the father of the Constitution" and was co-author of *The Federalist*, the essays on the Constitution that played an important role in its adoption by the States.

When he was forty-three he married the widow Dolley Todd, a lively Washington hostess, whose magnificent entertaining became legendary and whose personality often overshadowed that of her quiet husband.

From 1789 to 1797 he was a member of Congress, where he was responsible for the first ten amendments to the Constitution. Madison worked closely with Thomas Jefferson,

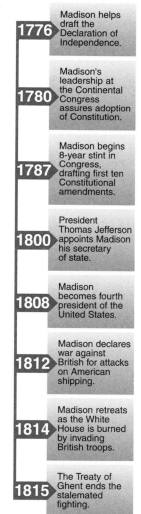

1776 Madison helps draft the Declaration of Independence.

1780 Madison's leadership at the Continental Congress assures adoption of Constitution.

1787 Madison begins 8-year stint in Congress, drafting first ten Constitutional amendments.

1800 President Thomas Jefferson appoints Madison his secretary of state.

1808 Madison becomes fourth president of the United States.

1812 Madison declares war against British for attacks on American shipping.

1814 Madison retreats as the White House is burned by invading British troops.

1815 The Treaty of Ghent ends the stalemated fighting.

> *"I believe there are more instances of the abridgment of the freedom of the people by gradual and silent encroachments of those in power than by violent and sudden usurpations."*
> James Madison, 1788

whom he helped gain the presidency in 1800. Jefferson appointed Madison his secretary of state and he served through both of Jefferson's terms, becoming heavily involved in the negotiations and agreement which enabled the country to make the Louisiana Purchase. He was instrumental in the enactment of the Embargo Act and obtained American ownership of the Gulf coast between Florida and New Orleans.

Madison was Jefferson's own choice as successor and was easily elected president in 1808. For three years he tried to negotiate rather than go to war over English attacks on American shipping but on June 12, 1812, war against Great Britain was declared. He was reelected the same year although this time the election was more closely contested by the Federalist party. In the war the United States at first sustained a series of defeats culminating in the burning of the White House in 1814. He was the only American president to have faced gunfire while in office: when the British entered Washington, Madison took command of an artillery battery for a time but as the situation deteriorated he returned to his carriage and drove off in the other direction. However, the tide of war turned somewhat and when neither side found it could gain the advantage, the 1815 Treaty of Ghent ended the fighting. During the remaining years of Madison's presidency he was immensely popular and many of his domestic programs were passed into law.

He spent his last years in retirement on his Virginia farm, supervising its operations and introducing various agricultural innovations. He also served as rector of the University of Virginia. ◆

Malcolm X

1925–1965 ● Civil rights activist

Malcolm X, born Malcolm Little and also known by his religious name, El-Hajj Malik El-Shabbazz, was the national representative of Elijah Muhammad's Nation of Islam, a prominent black nationalist, and the founder of the Organization of Afro-American Unity. He was born in Omaha, Nebraska. His father, J. Early Little, was a Georgia-born Baptist preacher and an organizer for Marcus Garvey's Universal Negro Improvement Association. His mother, M. Louise Norton, also a Garveyite, was from Grenada. At J. Early Little's murder, Malcolm's mother broke under the emotional and economic strain, and the children became wards of the state. Malcolm's delinquent behavior landed him in a detention home in Mason, Michigan.

Malcolm journeyed to Boston and then to New York, where, as "Detroit Red," he became involved in a life of crime—**numbers**, peddling dope, con games of many kinds, and thievery of all sorts, including armed robbery. A few months before his twenty-first birthday, Malcolm was sentenced to a Massachusetts prison for burglary. While in prison, his life was transformed when he discovered through the influence of an inmate the liberating value of education, and through his family the empowering religious/cultural message of Elijah Muhammad's nation of Islam. Both gave him what he did not have: self-respect as a black person.

After honing his reading and debating skills, Malcolm was released from prison in 1952. He soon became a minister in the Nation of Islam and its most effective recruiter and **apologist**, speaking against black self-hate and on behalf of black self-esteem. In June 1954, Elijah Muhammad appointed him minister of Temple Number 7 in Harlem. In the temple and from the platform on street corner rallies, Malcolm told Harlemites, "We are black first and everything else second." Initially his black nationalist message was unpopular in the African-American community. The media, both white and black, portrayed him as a teacher of hate and a promoter of violence. It was an age of integration, and love and nonviolence were advocated as the only way to achieve it.

> *"We are not fighting for integration, nor are we fighting for separation. We are fighting for recognition as human beings."*
> Malcolm X, 1964

numbers: an illegal lottery.

apologist: a person who defends an idea or religion.

Malcolm did not share the optimism of the Civil Rights Movement and found himself speaking to unsympathetic audiences. "If you are afraid to tell truth," he told his audience, "why, you don't deserve freedom. " Malcolm relished the odds against him; he saw his task as waking up "dead Negroes" by revealing the truth about America and about themselves.

The enormity of this challenge motivated Malcolm to attack the philosophy of the Rev. Dr. Martin Luther King Jr. and the civil rights movement headon. He rejected integration: "An integrated cup of coffee is insufficient pay for 400 years of slave labor." He denounced nonviolence as "the philosophy of a fool": "There is no philosophy more befitting to the white man's tactics for keeping his foot on the black man's neck." He ridiculed King's 1963 "I Have a Dream" speech: "While King was having a dream, the rest of us Negroes are having a nightmare." He also rejected King's command to love the enemy: "It is not possible to love a man whose chief purpose in life is to humiliate you and still be considered a normal human being." To blacks who accused Malcolm of teaching hate, he retorted: "It is the man who has made a slave out of you who is teaching hate. "

As long as Malcolm stayed in the Black Muslim movement, he was not free to speak his own mind. He had to represent the "Messenger," Elijah Muhammad, who was the sole and absolute authority in the Nation of Islam. When Malcolm disobeyed Muhammad in December 1963 and described President John F. Kennedy's assassination as an instance of "chickens coming home to roost," Muhammad rebuked him and used the incident as an opportunity to silence his star pupil. Malcolm realized that more was involved in his silence than what he had said about the assassination. Jealousy and envy in Muhammad's family circle were the primary reasons for his silence and why it would never be lifted.

Malcolm reluctantly declared his independence in March 1964. His break with the Black Muslim movement represented another important turning point in his life. No longer bound by Muhammad's religious structures, he was free to develop his own philosophy of the black freedom struggle.

Malcolm had already begun to show independent thinking in his "Message to the Grass Roots" speech, given in

1929 White supremacists burn down the Little family's house.

1931 The white vigilante Black Legion kills Malcolm X's father.

1952 Released from jail, Malcolm X joins Elijah Mohammed's Nation of Islam.

1953 Malcolm X begins preaching his message of black power.

1963 Malcolm X is dismissed from the Nation of Islam.

1965 Black Muslims assassinate Malcolm X.

Detroit three weeks before his silence. In that speech he endorsed black nationalism as his political philosophy, thereby separating himself not only from the civil rights movement, but more important, from Muhammad, who had defined the Nation as strictly religious and apolitical. Malcolm contrasted "the black revolution" with "the Negro revolution." The black revolution, he said, is international in scope, and it is "bloody" and "hostile" and "knows no compromise." But the so-called "Negro revolution," the civil rights movement, is not even a revolution. Malcolm mocked it: "The only revolution in which the goal is loving your enemy is the Negro revolution. It's the only revolution in which the goal is a desegregated lunch counter, a desegregated theater, a desegregated public park, a desegregated public toilet; you can sit down next to white folks on the toilet."

After his break, Malcolm developed his cultural and political philosophy of black nationalism in "The Ballot or the Bullet." Before audiences in New York, Cleveland, and Detroit, he urged blacks to acquire their constitutional right to vote, and move toward King and the civil rights movement. Later he became more explicit: "Dr. King wants the same thing I want—freedom." Malcolm went to Selma, Alabama, while King was in jail in support of King's efforts to secure voting rights. Malcolm wanted to join the civil rights movement in order to expand it into a human rights movement, thereby internationalizing the black freedom struggle, making it more radical and more militant.

During his independence, which lasted for approximately one year before he was assassinated, nothing influenced Malcolm more than his travel abroad. His pilgrimage to Mecca transformed his theology. Malcolm became a Sunni Muslim, acquired the religious name El-Hajj Malik El-Shabbazz, and concluded that "Orthodox Islam" was incompatible with the racist teachings of Elijah Muhammad. The sight of "people of all races, colors, from all over the world coming together as one" had a profound effect upon him. "Brotherhood," and not racism, was seen as the essence of Islam.

Malcolm's experiences in Africa also transformed his political philosophy. He discovered the limitations of skin-nationalism, since he met whites who were creative participants in liberation struggles in African countries. In his travels abroad, Malcolm focused on explaining the black struggle

> *"An integrated cup of coffee is insufficient pay for 400 years of slave labor."*
> Malcolm X

"You can't understand what is going on in Mississippi, if you don't know what is going on in the Congo."

Malcolm X

for justice in the United States and linking it with other liberation struggles throughout the world. "Our problem is your problem," he told African heads of state: "It is not a Negro problem, nor an American problem. This is a world problem; a problem of humanity. It is not a problem of civil rights but a problem of human rights."

When Malcolm returned to the United States, he told blacks: "You can't understand what is going on in Mississippi, if you don't know what is going on in the Congo. They are both the same. The same interests are at stake." He founded the Organization of Afro-American Unity, patterned after the Organization of African Unity, in order to implement his ideas. He was hopeful of influencing African leaders "to recommend an immediate investigation into our problem by the United Nations Commission on Human Rights."

Malcolm X was not successful. On February 21, 1965, he was shot down by assassins as he spoke at the Audubon Ballroom in Harlem. He was thirty-nine years old.

No one made a greater impact upon the cultural consciousness of the African-American community during the second half of the twentieth century than Malcolm X. More than anyone else, he revolutionized the black mind, transforming docile Negroes and self-effacing colored people into proud blacks and self-confident African Americans. Preachers and religious scholars created a black theology and proclaimed God as liberator and Jesus Christ as black. College students demanded and got Black Studies. Artists created a new black esthetic and proclaimed, "Black is beautiful."

No area of the African-American community escaped Malcolm's influence. Even mainstream black leaders who first dismissed him as a rabble-rouser, embraced his cultural philosophy following his death. Malcolm's most far-reaching influence, however, was among the masses of African Americans in the ghettos of American cities. Malcolm loved black people deeply and taught them much about themselves. Before Malcolm, most blacks did not want to have anything to do with Africa. But he reminded them that "you can't hate the roots of the tree and not hate the tree; you can't hate your origin and not end up hating yourself, you can't hate Africa and not hate yourself "

Malcolm X was a cultural revolutionary. Poet Maya Angelou called him a "charismatic speaker who could play an audience as great musicians play instruments." Disciple Peter Bailey said he was a "master teacher." Writer Alfred Duckett called him "our sage and our saint." In his eulogy, actor Ossie Davis bestowed upon Malcolm the title "our shining black prince." Malcolm can be best understood as a cultural prophet of blackness. African Americans who are proud to be black should thank Malcolm X. Few have played as central a role as he in making it possible for African Americans to claim their African heritage. ◆

Mandela, Nelson

1918–PRESENT ● SOUTH AFRICAN PRESIDENT & CIVIL RIGHTS ACTIVIST

> *"I have cherished the ideal of a democratic and free society in which all persons will live together in harmony and with equal opportunities. It is an ideal which I hope to live for and achieve. But, if needs be, it is an ideal for which I am prepared to die."*
>
> Nelson Mandela, 1964

Nelson Mandela was born to Henry Gadla Mphakan-yiswa and Nosekeni Fanny Mandela at Mbhashe in the Umtata district of the Transkei. Though a scion of the Thembu royal house, Henry Gadla was not in line for the succession. Nonetheless, he was a chief, albeit later deposed for insubordination. Fanny Mandela, a devout Methodist, was his third wife, which meant that her son,

Nelson, could not inherit the chieftainship. This set the young Mandela on the course of education and urban politics and paved the way for his presidency of South Africa.

After his father's death, the nine-year-old Nelson Mandela, as arranged by his father, traveled to Mqekezweni, where the acting chief of the Ama-Thembu, Jongintaba David Dalindyebo, took charge of his education. He enrolled at the local school and eventually gained admission to Fort Hare College in 1938 but was expelled in 1940 for engaging in a strike action. In 1941 he traveled to Johannesburg, where he took up temporary employment as a policeman at the mines and met Walter Sisulu, who encouraged him to study law. Mandela simultaneously enrolled for a B.A. degree by correspondence, which he obtained in 1942, and went on to study law at Witwatersrand University. Here he was exposed to Indian and white students and to radical, liberal, and Africanist thought. He joined the African National Congress (ANC) and in 1944 founded the ANC Youth League with Walter Sisulu and Oliver Tambo.

In 1948 the Afrikaner National Party came into power and began institutionalizing racism as apartheid. A spate of racist laws were passed in quick succession, among them the Group Areas Act of 1950, which ultimately resulted in the uprooting of millions of Black, Coloured, and Indian people, and the Bantu Education Act of 1953, designed to make sure that Africans remained menial laborers.

The ANC responded by adopting a program of militant action against the Nationalists. With Mandela on its executive committee, the ANC in 1951 organized a national work stoppage in cooperation with the Indian Congress. This was followed in 1952 with the Defiance of Unjust Laws Campaign, in which 8,577 volunteers defied racist laws and were imprisoned. The outbreak of violence and the six-month banning of fifty-two leaders, among them Mandela and the newly elected president-general of the ANC, Albert Luthuli, ended that campaign. Banning orders restricted the rights of movement and association. In 1953 Mandela was served with his second such order, this one for two years. A third, five-year, banning order came in 1956.

On 25–26 June 1955 the ANC and other antiapartheid organizations convened the Congress of the People in Kliptown, just outside Johannesburg, at which some three thousand delegates adopted the Freedom Charter as a blueprint for a nonracial, democratic South Africa. Discontent within the ANC over the charter and alleged White and communist influence resulted in a split in 1958 and led to the formation of the Pan-African Congress (PAC) under the leadership of Robert Sobukwe. Meanwhile, the government declared the Freedom Charter a treasonable document and in 1956 brought to trial 156 key figures, among them Mandela and Luthuli. The trial continued until March 1961, when all of the accused against whom charges had not already been dropped were acquitted.

In 1960 a peaceful anti-pass demonstration organized by the PAC resulted in the massacre at Sharpeville, in which police killed 69 protestors and injured 180. Blacks responded with a massive work stoppage; the government retaliated by declaring a state of emergency, banning the ANC and PAC and detaining thousands throughout the country, among them Mandela. After his release, he participated in the organization of a national conference of antiapartheid groupings against the government's intention to leave the British Commonwealth and establish a racist republic. In the campaign which followed the conference, he went underground to facilitate his work and avoid arrest and came to be known as the Black Pimpernel.

In 1961 Mandela, having reached the conclusion that the power of the Nationalists would never be broken through mass civil action alone, initiated Umkhonto we Sizwe (the Spear of the Nation) to organize sabotage against key state installations. December 1961 saw the first bomb blasts in South Africa against apartheid. Mandela left the country secretly and traveled to African nations incognito to raise funds and set up training bases for Umkhonto cadres. He himself underwent military training in Algeria and Tunisia.

Mandela returned to South Africa in July 1962, was arrested in August, and was sentenced in November to five years imprisonment, three for incitement to strike and two for leaving the country without a passport. In June 1964, he was sentenced to life imprisonment for sabotage and attempting to overthrow the state through violent revolution.

Mandela's personal life had seen drastic changes from 1957 to 1960. He and his first wife, Eveline, divorced in 1957. He married Winnie Madikizela in 1958, and by early 1960

> *"I will not leave South Africa, nor will I surrender. Only through hardship, sacrifice, and militant action can freedom be won. The struggle is my life. I will continue fighting for freedom until the end of my days.*
> Nelson Mandela, 1961

they had two daughters. Imprisoned numerous times beginning in the late 1950s and subjected to a long series of bans, Winnie nonetheless persisted in her antiapartheid activities and contributed significantly in keeping her husband in the public eye. (The Mandelas were divorced in 1995. That year, Winnie Mandela was dismissed from her government position amid controversial charges of abuse of power.)

The antiapartheid struggle escalated in 1976 when African youth in the township of Soweto revolted against the enforcement of Afrikaans as a medium of instruction. The revolt spread to other parts of the country and brought out the workers. By 1985 the government was in crisis. In 1988 Mandela's condition of imprisonment improved significantly, and the government began negotiating with him. The last Afrikaner president, F. W. de Klerk, unbanned the ANC, PAC, and the South African Communist Party and released Mandela in 1990. (The two men shared the Nobel Prize for peace in 1993.) The first nonracial democratic elections followed in 1994, and Mandela was inaugurated as the first democratically elected president of the country. ◆

> In 1994, Mandela became the first democratically elected president of South Africa.

Marshall, George Catlett

1880–1959 ● AMERICAN MILITARY
LEADER & STATESMAN

Georg Catlett Marshall was born in Uniontown, Pennsylvania, to a family of Virginia settlers; by the time Marshall entered Virginia Military Institute in 1897, his father, a coal merchant, had lost most of his money. He graduated in 1901 and was commissioned a second lieutenant in the cavalry.

After graduation, Marshall was sent to the Philippines for a year and a half. Early in his military career, he developed the habit of rigid self-discipline, and his attitude toward command soon won him the respect both of his soldiers and of civilians. His quiet self-confidence brought out the best in those under his command.

Marshall attended school at Fort Leavenworth, Kansas, at that time the center of the army's advanced educational program, and graduated first in his class. He then served there as an instructor from 1908 to 1910. In 1913 Marshall was sent back to the Philippines, where he remained until being called, in 1916, to serve in San Francisco and on Governor's Island in New York Harbor. During World War I Marshall was sent to France as the chief of operations. From 1919 to 1924 he was General John Pershing's senior aide, and then assistant commandant in charge of instruction at the infantry school.

Although Marshall was by then a lieutenant colonel, Pershing felt that he had not been promoted quickly enough and said of him, "He is the best goddamned officer in the U.S. Army." In 1933 Marshall was promoted to full colonel. He was made the senior instructor of the Illinois National Guard and served as a brigade commander in Vancouver Barracks for two years.

In 1938, Marshall moved to Washington and served as chief of war plans and then deputy chief of staff. President Franklin D. Roosevelt then nominated him as the head of the army and on September 1, 1939, the day the war began in Europe, Marshall took full command, a position he held for six years. Under Marshall's command, the army grew from two hundred thousand to almost eight and a half million. When President Harry S. Truman, considering an alternative to dropping the atomic bomb, was weighing the possibility of a blockade coupled with heavy bombing of Japan, Marshall pointed out that similar action in Germany had not brought about an end to the war in Europe.

Marshall attended all the great conferences and was deeply involved in directing Allied strategy during the invasion of Europe. Paying tribute to his efforts in planning, training, and supplying the Allied troops, Britain's Winston Churchill said, "General Marshall was the true organizer of victory."

Marshall resigned as chief of staff on November 21, 1945, and Truman appointed him ambassador to China, where he served from 1945 to 1947. Despite his lack of success in mediating the Chinese civil war, he had proved himself an able

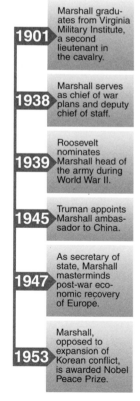

1901 Marshall graduates from Virginia Military Institute, a second lieutenant in the cavalry.

1938 Marshall serves as chief of war plans and deputy chief of staff.

1939 Roosevelt nominates Marshall head of the army during World War II.

1945 Truman appoints Marshall ambassador to China.

1947 As secretary of state, Marshall masterminds post-war economic recovery of Europe.

1953 Marshall, opposed to expansion of Korean conflict, is awarded Nobel Peace Prize.

"It is not enough to fight. It is the spirit which we bring to the fight that decides the issue. It is morale that wins the victory."

George Catlett Marshall, 1948

statesman and was appointed secretary of state in January 1947. In a speech delivered at Harvard in June of that year he outlined what came to be known as the Marshall Plan for the economic recovery of Europe, based on his belief that Russia was taking advantage of Europe's economic problems to control the area. During this period, representing the United States, he worked diligently in the United Nations and spent time in South America developing greater cooperation between Latin American countries and the United States. Marshall resigned as secretary of state in 1949 due to ill health.

Unwilling to let Marshall retire, Truman appointed him secretary of defense in 1950, when Marshall was almost seventy. This position gave Marshall the freedom to criticize General Douglas MacArthur's statements and actions. He opposed MacArthur in the controversy between Truman and MacArthur.

The Korean War had begun. Marshall again enlarged the United States army and helped to develop the North Atlantic Treaty Organization (NATO). As secretary of defense, Marshall strove to stop the expansion of the Korean conflict. While he obviously favored a strong America, he still sought peaceful solutions in Asia. In December of 1953 he was awarded the Nobel Peace Prize, after which he returned to private life.

In recognition of his service to the American people. the George C. Marshall Library was dedicated in Lexington, Virginia, in 1964, five years after his death. President Lyndon B. Johnson and former president Dwight D. Eisenhower both spoke at the dedication ceremony. ◆

Marshall, Thurgood

1908–1993 ● CIVIL RIGHTS LAWYER
& U.S. SUPREME COURT JUSTICE

"Lawlessness is lawlessness. Anarchy is anarchy is anarchy. Neither race nor color nor frustration is an excuse for either lawlessness or anarchy."

Thurgood Marshall, 1966

Thurgood Marshall distinguished himself as a jurist in a wide array of settings. As the leading attorney for the National Association for the Advancement of Colored People (NAACP) between 1938 and 1961, he pioneered the role of professional civil rights advocate. As the principal architect of the legal attack against **de jure** racial segregation, Marshall oversaw the most successful campaign of social reform litigation in American history. As a judge on the United States Court of Appeals, solicitor general of the United States, and associate justice of the Supreme Court, he amassed a remarkable record as a public servant. Given the influence of his achievements over a long span of time, one can reasonably argue that Thurgood Marshall may have been the outstanding attorney of twentieth-century America.

Marshall was born in Baltimore, Maryland, where his father was a **steward** at an exclusive, all-white boat club, and his mother was an elementary school teacher. He attended public schools in Baltimore before proceeding to Lincoln University in Pennsylvania where he shared classes with, among others, Cabell "Cab" Calloway, the entertainer, Kwame Nkrumah, who became president of Ghana, and Nnamdi Azikiwe, who became president of Nigeria. After graduating, he was excluded from the University of Maryland

de jure: by right; by law.

steward: a servant on a ship.

School of Law because of racial segregation. Marshall attended the Howard University School of Law, where he fell under
the **tutelage** of Charles Hamilton Houston. Houston elevated academic standards at Howard, turning it into a veritable
hothouse of legal education, where he trained many of those
who would later play important roles in the campaign against
racial discrimination. Marshall graduated in 1933, first in his
class.

tutelage: instruction.

After engaging in a general law practice for a brief period,
Marshall was persuaded by Houston to pursue a career working as an attorney on behalf of the NAACP. Initially he
worked as Houston's deputy and then, in 1939, he took over
from his mentor as the NAACP's special counsel. In that
position, Marshall confronted an extraordinary array of legal
problems that took him from local courthouses, where he
served as a trial attorney, to the Supreme Court of the United
States, where he developed his skills as an appellate advocate.
Over a span of two decades, he argued thirty-two cases before
the Supreme Court, winning twenty-nine of them. He convinced the Court to invalidate practices that excluded blacks
from primary elections (Smith *v.* Allwright, 1944), to prohib-

Sandra Day O'Connor

Sandra Day O'Connor, the first woman appointed to the U.S. Supreme Court, has made
a career of trailblazing. Born in 1930, she lived with her grandmother in El Paso, Texas, to
attend better schools than those near her family's sprawling Arizona ranch. She ranked
third in her Stanford Univeristy law school class, yet had trouble finding a law firm willing
to hire a woman. Soon after graduation in 1952, she married John Jay O'Connor. They
have three sons. In the mid-'50s, she landed her first political job as a deputy county
attorney in California. During the 1960s, O'Connor served as an Arizona assistant attorney general and state senator. In 1972, she became the first woman appointed State
Senate majority leader. In 1974, O'Connor won the Maricopa County Superior Court
Judgeship, followed by her appointment in 1979 to the Arizona Court of Appeals. In 1981,
President Ronald Reagan nominated her to the Supreme Court. Although viewed as a
conservative, O'Connor is part of the court's centrist core, often providing critical swing
votes. An Equal Rights Amendment supporter, she has diverged from conservative positions as the deciding vote for controversial decisions such as a constitutional right to
abortion, state affirmative action, and school prayer. Other positions include support of
the death penalty, limiting employment discrimination suits, and limiting affirmative action.

it segregation in interstate transportation (Morgan *v.* Virginia, 1946), to nullify convictions obtained from juries from which African Americans had been barred on the basis of their race (Patton *v.* Mississippi, 1947), and to prohibit state courts from enforcing racially restrictive real estate covenants (Shelley *v.* Kraemer, 1948).

Marshall's greatest triumphs arose, however, in the context of struggles against racial discrimination in public education. In 1950, in Sweatt *v.* Painter, he successfully argued that a state could not fulfill its federal constitutional obligation by hurriedly constructing a "Negro" law school that was inferior in tangible and intangible ways to the state's "white" law school. That same year he successfully argued in McLaurin *v.* Oklahoma State Regents that a state university violated the federal constitution by admitting an African-American student and then confining that student, on the basis of his race, to a specified seat in classrooms and a specified table in the school cafeteria. In 1954, in Brown *v.* Board of Education, Marshall culminated his campaign by convincing the Court to rule that racial segregation is invidious racial discrimination and thus invalid under the Fourteenth Amendment to the federal constitution.

In 1961, over the objections of white supremacist southern politicians, President John F. Kennedy nominated Marshall to a seat on the United States Court of Appeals for the Second Circuit in New York. Later, President Lyndon B. Johnson appointed Marshall to two positions that had never previously been occupied by an African American. In 1965, President Johnson appointed Marshall as Solicitor General, and in 1967 he nominated him to a seat on the Supreme Court.

Throughout his twenty-four years on the Court, Marshall was the most insistently liberal of the Justices, a stance that often drove him into dissent. His judgments gave broad scope to individual liberties (except in cases involving asserted claims to rights of property). Typically he supported claims of freedom of expression over competing concerns and scrutinized skeptically the claims of law enforcement officers in cases implicating federal constitutional provisions that limit the police powers of government. In the context of civil liberties, the most controversial positions that Marshall took involved rights over reproductive capacities and the death

1933 Marshall graduates from Howard University School of Law.

1938 Marshall becomes an attorney for the NAACP.

1954 The U.S. Supreme Court rules in Marshall's favor in Brown v. Board of Education.

1965 Marshall becomes U.S. Solicitor General.

1967 President Lyndon Johnson appoints Marshall to the U.S. Supreme Court.

1991 Marshall retires from the Supreme Court.

penalty. He viewed as unconstitutional laws that prohibit women from exercising considerable discretion over the choice to continue a pregnancy or to terminate it through abortion. Marshall also viewed as unconstitutional all laws permitting the imposition of capital punishment.

jurisprudential: having to do with the science of law.

The other side of Marshall's **jurisprudential** liberalism was manifested by an approach to **statutory** and constitutional interpretation that generally advanced egalitarian policies. His judgments displayed an unstinting solicitude for the rights of labor, the interests of women, the struggles of oppressed minorities, and the condition of the poor. One particularly memorable expression of Marshall's empathy for the **indigent** is his dissent in United States *v.* Kras (1973), a case in which the Court held that a federal statute did not violate the Constitution by requiring a $50 fee of persons seeking the protection of bankruptcy. Objecting to the Court's assumption that, with a little self-discipline, the petitioner could readily accumulate the required fee, Marshall wrote that

statutory: having to do with formally established laws/

indigent: needy or poor.

> It may be easy for some people to think that weekly savings of less than $2 are no burden. But no one who has had close contact with poor people can fail to understand how close to the margin of survival many of them are . . . It is perfectly proper for judges to disagree about what the Constitution requires. But it is disgraceful for an interpretation of the Constitution to be premised upon unfounded assumptions about how people live.

Marshall retired from the Court in 1991, precipitating the most contentious confirmation battle in the nation's history when President George Bush nominated as Marshall's successor Clarence Thomas, an ultraconservative African-American jurist.

Marshall died on January 24, 1993. His extraordinary contributions to American life were memorialized in an outpouring of popular grief and adulation greater than that expressed for any previous justice. ◆

McCain, John Sidney

1936–PRESENT ● VIETNAM WAR HERO

John Sidney McCain, a Republican senator from Arizona, was a prisoner of war for six years during the Vietnam War. McCain was born in the Panama Canal Zone in 1936. His grandfather, Admiral John S. McCain Sr., was the commander of all aircraft carriers in the Pacific Fleet during World War II. McCain's father, Admiral John S. McCain Jr., commanded all United States naval forces in the Pacific during the Vietnam War.

McCain grew up at various military bases in the United States and abroad. He entered the United States Naval Academy at Annapolis in 1954, graduating in 1958 with a degree in electrical engineering. He was not a strong student and graduated fifth from the bottom of his class. He was nonetheless commissioned a naval ensign and began training as a navy pilot.

During the Vietnam War, McCain flew carrier-based bombers on dangerous missions over enemy territory. On October 26, 1967, while flying over the North Vietnamese capital of Hanoi, McCain's plane was hit by a surface-to-air missile and he was forced to eject. He landed in a lake, breaking both arms and one leg. An angry crowd on the ground pulled him out of the water, then beat and stabbed him. McCain remained in Vietnam prison camps for the next five and a half years. While he was a prisoner of war, McCain was denied medical attention and was routinely tortured by his captors. He was also forced to spend over three years in solitary confinement and was not permitted to receive and send mail. At one point, the Vietnamese offered to release McCain ahead of other prisoners because of his father's status as an important military commander. When McCain refused this privilege, the prison officials beat him severely. He was finally released with other prisoners of war in 1973. After four months of recuperation, McCain resumed his navy career. He received many military awards for his wartime service, including the Bronze Star, the Silver Star, the Legion

> *"Walk away from the horror and suffering, and back to the land of the free. You will know to the end of your days what it means to be free."*
>
> John S. McCain, 1998

1958 McCain graduates from the U.S. Naval Academy.

1967 McCain's plane is shot down in Vietnam.

1973 McCain is released from a Vietnamese prison camp.

1982 McCain is elected to the U.S. Congress.

of Merit, the Purple Heart, and the Distinguished Flying Cross.

McCain married Cindy Hensley in 1980. He retired from the Navy in 1981 as a captain. Turning to politics he was elected as a Republican United States representative from Arizona in 1982. In 1987, McCain was elected to the United States Senate. As a senator, McCain continued to push for a full accounting of all United States military personnel still listed as missing-in-action from the Vietnam War. ◆

Menchú Tum, Rigoberta

JANUARY 1959–PRESENT? ●
GUATEMALAN CIVIL RIGHTS ACTIVIST

"Let us not forget that when the Europeans came to America, there were flourishing and strong civilizations there. One cannot talk about a discovery of America because one discovers that which one does not know about or that which is hidden."
Rigoberta Menchú Tum, 1992

indigenous: native to a country.

Rigoberta Menchú is a Maya-Quiché Indian woman from Guatemala and the first **indigenous** Latin American woman to win the Nobel Peace Prize. She is a member of the Coordinating Commission of the Committee of Peasant Unity (CUC) and a founding member of the United Representation of the Guatemalan Opposition (RUOG).

Menchú was born in Chimel, near San Miguel de Uspantán, to Vicente Menchú and Juana Tum, Maya peasants and Catholic lay leaders. Self-educated, from the age of eight she accompanied her parents to harvest export crops on south coast plantations, and later worked for two years as a domestic in Guatemala City. She participated with her parents in local pastoral activities.

In the 1970s, expropriation of Indian land in El Quiché threatened Maya subsistence and prompted her family's political activism and involvement with the CUC. In the late 1970s, Menchú organized local self-defense groups, armed with rocks and machetes, in response to the government's escalated counterinsurgency war in the highlands. In January 1980, her father was burned to death in the occupation of the Spanish embassy in Guatemala City by campesinos with the support of trade unionists and students. Menchú continued organizing efforts in local Maya communities until forced to flee in 1981; since then she has lived in Mexico City.

A powerful speaker, Menchú has continued to work for peace and the rights of indigenous people in Guatemala in international forums. She has participated in the U.N. Working Group on Indigenous Populations, the U.N. Subcommission on Prevention of Discrimination and Protection for Minorities, and the U.N. Conference on the Decade of Women. She is a credentialed observer of the U.N. Human Rights Commission and the General Assembly. She serves on the board of the International Indian Treaty Council and was a member of honor at the Second Continental Gathering of the "500 Years of Resistance" Conference. Among other awards, she has received the 1988 Nonino Prize special award, the 1990 Monseñor Proaño Human Rights Prize, the 1990 UNESCO Education for Peace Prize, and the 1991 French Committee for the Defense of Freedoms and Human Rights prize. In 1992, she was awarded the Nobel Prize for Peace. ◆

1980 Menchú's father is burned to death in Guatemala City.

1981 Menchú flees Guatemala for Mexico.

1990 Menchú receives the UNESCO Education for Peace Prize.

1991 Menchú receives a French human rights prize.

Mendes Filho, Francisco (Chico) Alves

1944–1988 ● BRAZILIAN UNION LEADER & ECOLOGIST

Francisco Alves Mendes Filho, from Xapuri, Acre, in Brazil, began his career as a rubber tapper at the age of eight, when he assisted his father in gathering rubber. After working twenty-eight years in this profession, Mendes founded the Xapuri Rural Workers' Union in 1977. As its quietly persuasive president, he sponsored education for members and their children, and he helped establish health posts in Acre. Ten years later, Mendes assisted by anthropologist Mary Allegretti, formed the National Council of Rubber Tappers (CNS). Through the CNS, Chico helped organize *Projeto Seringueiro* (Rubber Tapper Project), which promoted cooperatives whose literate members learned to manage their own finances. Mendes also led the Xapuri Rural Workers in their tactic of *empate* (standoff). Large landowners who hired workers to clear the Amazonian rain forest were faced with groups of rubber workers who assembled en masse and barricaded the area to be cleared. Although large landowners often removed them at gunpoint, the union achieved success through *empates* about one-third of the time. *Empates* brought worldwide attention to the rubber workers' social and environmental battles. Mendes won international recognition for his efforts and became a consultant to the World Bank and to the U.S. Senate on matters of investments in Amazónia.

1977 Mendes founds the Xapuri Rural Workers' Union.

1987 Mendes helps found the CNS.

1988 Mendes is assassinated.

1990 Mendes's murderer is convicted.

Mendes promoted extractive reserves, the union's innovative alternative to deforestation, which allows workers to live on and extract products from the rain forest while leaving it intact. In 1988, when the Brazilian government expropriated land from powerful owners for three extractive reserves, Mendes began receiving death threats. He was shot to death on December 22, 1988. News of his death made headlines throughout the world, and he became a martyr in the fight to preserve the Amazonian rain forest. In December 1990, a jury found landowner Darly Alves da Silva and his son, Darci, guilty of Chico's murder. ◆

Monroe, James

1758–1831 ● PRESIDENT OF THE
UNITED STATES

"National honor is national property of the highest value."

James Monroe, 1817

James Monroe was born in Westmoreland County, Virginia, carrying on the tradition of American presidents whose place of residence was the state of Virginia. In 1776 he dropped out of William and Mary College to serve in the Continental army, rising to the rank of major. Harlem Heights, White Plains, Trenton, Brandywine, Germantown, and Monmouth are some of the battles in which he fought.

Monroe left the army in 1780 to study law under Thomas Jefferson, who was then governor of Virginia and who became a close friend and political adviser to Monroe. Although not an equal intellectually with Jefferson and James Madison, Monroe worked well with both of them. He studied with Jefferson for three years and in 1782 became a member of the House of Delegates of Virginia and served in the Continental Congress from 1783 to 1786.

In 1788, as a member of the Virginia House of Delegates, Monroe opposed the proposed state constitution. Politically aligned with Jefferson, Monroe became involved in the organization and advancement of the Republican party.

President George Washington, although representing an opposing political party, appointed Monroe minister to France in 1794, where he spent two years. His work was considered less than satisfactory and he was recalled. From 1799

Although not an equal intellectually with Jefferson and Madison, Monroe worked well with both of them.

1776 ▶ Monroe drops out of William and Mary College to serve in Continental army.

1780 ▶ Monroe studies law under Thomas Jefferson, then governor of Virginia.

1799 ▶ Monroe proves an able administrator as governor of Virginia until 1802.

1816 ▶ Monroe defeats Federalist party to become fifth president.

1819 ▶ Monroe initiates purchase of Florida from Spain.

1820 ▶ Monroe's Missouri Compromise presages Missouri's statehood.

1823 ▶ The Monroe Doctrine establishes U.S. autonomy from European interests.

to 1802 he served as governor of Virginia and in this position demonstrated an aptitude as an administrator.

In 1803 Jefferson sent Monroe back to France, this time to negotiate the Louisiana Purchase, and Monroe established himself as a person with future presidential capabilities. From 1803 to 1807 he served in various posts abroad.

Despite their political differences, President Madison, who defeated Monroe in his first presidential bid, appointed him to serve as secretary of state, and for a six-month term as secretary of war. Monroe held both positions during the War of 1812, doing an excellent job and winning the respect of Congress.

In 1816 the Federalist party was in a state of collapse. Monroe was easily elected president as the Democratic-Republican candidate, inaugurating the "era of good feelings" between the Republicans and the Federalists. His major cabinet choices were wise selections and continued to serve during both of his terms. He was reelected to his second term, winning all but one electoral vote.

Foreign relations was Monroe's strong point. The Monroe Doctrine, introduced in 1823 as part of a presidential message, sought to establish the autonomy and independence of the New World, rejecting European intervention and proclaiming that the United States would not intervene in European politics. During Monroe's term of office, Florida was acquired from Spain (1819–1821) and the Missouri Compromise of 1820 paved the way for the state of Missouri to join the Union.

After completing his presidency in 1825, Monroe served as the presiding officer of the Virginia Constitutional Convention. ◆

Mother Teresa

1910–1997 ● NOBEL PRIZE WINNER
& MISSIONARY

Mother Teresa was a Roman Catholic nun who received the 1979 Nobel Peace Prize for her work with the poor. She was admired around the world for her compassion and for her commitment to providing care and comfort to the poor, the sick, the destitute, and the dying.

Mother Teresa was born Agnes Gonxha Bojaxhiu on August 26, 1910, to Nikola and Dranafile (Bernai) Bojaxhiu in Skopje, in what is now Macedonia. Her father was a building contractor and merchant, and her family was among the small minority of Roman Catholics in a predominantly Muslim region. Dranafile was deeply religious and she took her three children to church daily. She was known for her hospitality to the poor, who would frequently join the Bojaxhiu family for meals. In 1917 Agnes's father died, and her mother, left to support three children, set up a business selling embroidered red cloth.

As a child, Agnes was tidy, obedient, and thoughtful. She enjoyed praying and liked to be in church. After school hours she was engaged in church activities. She joined a Christian society for girls, and at meetings she learned about the lives of saints, and sometimes heard inspiring letters from missionaries who worked among the poor and sick in India.

Agnes first felt that her life's calling as a nun at the age of twelve. She decided to become a missionary nun in India, and at eighteen, she left home to join the Sisters of Loreto, an Irish Catholic order with a mission in Calcutta, India. After a few months of training and learning English in Dublin she was sent to Darjeeling at the foot of the Himalaya in India, where she took her initial vows as a nun in 1929 and took the name Teresa. In 1937 she committed herself to her vows of poverty, chastity, and obedience, and became Sister Teresa.

After taking her vows Sister Teresa taught at St. Mary's High School outside Calcutta. The suffering and poverty she witnessed on the streets of Calcutta deeply impressed her, and she felt inspired to work among the poor in the slums of Calcutta. In 1948 she left the Loreto community, exchanged

> *"How can you love God whom you do not see, if you do not love your neighbor whom you see, whom you touch, with whom you live?"*
>
> Mother Teresa

1928 — Agnes Gonxha Bojaxhiu joins the Loretto order and takes the name Teresa.

1929 — Sister Teresa arrives in Calcutta to teach at St. Mary's High School.

1937 — Sister Teresa took final vows as a nun and became Mother Teresa.

1946 — Mother Teresa experienced a calling to work among the poor.

1950 — Mother Teresa founded the order of Missionaries of Charity.

1979 — Mother Teresa won the Nobel Peace Prize.

her convent habit for a simple white sari with a blue border, and began her life's work among the poor. She became an Indian citizen that year at the age of thirty-eight.

Mother Teresa began her work by first learning nursing, feeling that medical training was indispensable to her task of caring for people. Her first facility for the poor was an open-air school for homeless children. She gradually expanded her work, joined by volunteers and supported by donations from various religious organizations, individuals, and the government.

In 1950, Mother Teresa received permission from the church to start her own order, "The Missionaries of Charity," whose main task was to love and care for people in need. Over the years she set up orphanages, schools in slums, and homes for sick and dying homeless people. In all her endeavors Mother Teresa emphasized the importance of giving the deprived and the sick a feeling of dignity through personal contact. The order grew tremendously and by the early 1990s, it comprised about 4,000 nuns and novices, 400 priests and brothers, and hundreds of thousands of lay workers. It worked at 450 sites throughout the world, including shelters for the homeless, centers for the malnourished, hospices for lepers, mobile health clinics, homes for drug addicts and alcoholics, and relief centers for people hit by natural catastrophe.

One of her best known missions abroad occurred in 1982 when Mother Teresa traveled to war-torn Beirut to assist the war victims there. At that time the city was crippled by fighting between the Muslims and the Christians. Crossing the line that separated Christian East Beirut from Muslim West Beirut, she rescued dozens of mentally ill Muslim children who were trapped in a hospital without food or water.

Mother Teresa's work drew considerable attention throughout the world, and she received a number of awards, including the Pope John XXIII Peace Prize in 1971 and India's Jawaharlal Nehru Award for International Understanding in 1972 for her promotion of international peace and understanding. She also received the 1979 Nobel Peace Prize for her work to overcome poverty and distress in the world, which the Nobel Committee recognized as a constant threat to peace. Mother Teresa used the prize money that accompanied the award—the equivalent of $190,000—for building homes for the destitute.

Mother Teresa, of
Calcutta, at London
Airport in 1979, hold-
ing a child who had
been named after her.

Mother Teresa was not without critics. Some were concerned that she was trying to idealize poverty. Others were
dismayed by her strong opposition to abortion, divorce, and
the use of contraceptives. She was also criticized for her view
that women belonged in the home.

Most people, however, knew Mother Teresa for her piety,
humility, organizational talents, energy, and practicality.
Throughout the years she declined offers of regular income,
because she did not want her work to become a business. She
also forbade fund-raising at her order, partly because such an
activity would require accounting and would take away from
time spent with the needy. She and her order lived a life of
poverty, eating the same food as the poor and typically rising
at 4:40 a.m. and working until 9 p.m. with only 30 minutes
rest. The women who joined her order were expected to sever
family ties and only return home on a rare occasion to attend
an important family event. A cheerful disposition was

Religious Devotion and Social Action

In some religious traditions, charitable service to one's fellow human beings is considered the most perfect form of devotion to the divine. In Christianity, several movements with a strong devotional bias have emphasized works of charity as central to the devotional life. With the inauguration of active religious orders for men by Francis of Assisi in the 13th century, and for women by Mary Ward and Vincent de Paul in the 17th century, the focus of the religious life, which had earlier been cloistered, shifted from the cultivation of one's spiritual predilections in isolation from society to serving the poor and needy in the world. Several religious brotherhoods and sisterhoods have been founded in Protestant Christianity that aim at serving the poor, while the Social Gospel movement of the nineteenth century in America represents an attempt to provide theological justification for social involvement as central to the Christian life. A dramatic example of devotion as inextricably associated with social service is the life of Mother Teresa of Calcutta and her Sisters of Charity, who minister to the "poorest of the poor" as a way of life. Mother Teresa taught the women who joined her order to see Jesus in each person they served; in serving men and women, they served Jesus. The theme of service to human beings being equated with the service of god exists in non-Christian traditions as well. The Indian Hindu leader Mahatma Gandhi, for example, was once asked why he did not withdraw from the world in his search for god. He replied that if he thought for one moment that god might be found in a Himalayan cave, he would go there at once, but he was convinced that God could only be found among human beings and in their service.

required of all who worked with her, as was a show of respect for the worth and dignity of the individual human being.

In 1990 Mother Teresa experienced heart problems that caused her to resign as head of her order. But the order could not agree on a successor and reelected her to her post. In March 1997 her failing health caused her to step down from her post. She died in Calcutta on September 5, 1997, after suffering cardiac arrest. ◆

Nelson, Lord Horatio

1759–1805 ● BRITISH NAVAL HERO

"Firstly you must always implicitly obey orders, without attempting to form any opinion of your own respecting their propriety. Secondly, you must consider every man your enemy who speaks ill of your king; and thirdly you must hate a Frenchman as you hate the devil."
Horatio Nelson, to a subordinate, 1793

Born in Burnham Thorpe, Norfolk, Horatio Nelson, whose mother died when he was eight years old, was one of the eight children of a parson. Horatio (he preferred to call himself Horace) often went to view vessels plying the Norfolk coastal trade. At twelve, he enlisted as a midshipman on the warship *Raisonnable*, captained by his uncle Maurice Suckling—a veteran of many battles and a figure young Horatio looked up to.

Nelson learned to handle the ship's boat ferrying men and supplies to and from his uncle's man-of-war. Still in his teens he sailed in the *Carcass* on an exciting expedition to discover the northeast passage through the Atlantic to the Orient. His ship was trapped in ice flows and Nelson almost lost his life in a foolhardy attempt to get a polar bear skin for his father.

After his return, Nelson did not stay in the safety of England long but was soon off on a voyage in a warship to India. He caught malaria and had to return to England. During the voyage he had a mystical experience sighting a "radiant orb," a vision that inspired him with a heroic mission to serve king and country. While he was abroad, his uncle Maurice had been promoted to naval comptroller and could use patronage to advance his nephew's career, but it was rather Nelson's more proven skills as a ship's officer that won him a commission as lieutenant at the age of eighteen.

Nelson served in several theaters of conflict. He took part in an ill-fated attempt to seize territory in Nicaragua, aimed at dividing Spanish America in two. Transporting troops up river through the jungle was a severe test of his resourcefulness and the monkey stew cooked by the Indians a test for his stomach.

During service in the Caribbean Islands, he made enemies by vigorously pursuing ships from rebel America illegally trading with Britain's colonies. The colonists resented interference in their business, and Nelson and fellow officers were excluded from the plantation social life that was their chief diversion. Despite unpopularity with merchants, he received a hospitable reception from the president of Nevis, John Herbert. He was attracted to Herbert's niece, a young widow named Frances Nisbit, and they were married in 1787.

Following the wedding the Nelsons returned to Norfolk. His activities against illegal trading had also made enemies in London, thus he had to settle down to the quiet life of a gentleman farmer on land around Burnham Thorpe. Efforts to get a naval command met with failure until the outbreak of war with France.

In 1793 Nelson was assigned to the Mediterranean where the siege of Toulon and the capture of Corsica offered ample opportunity for the initiative and gallantry that became his trademark. In an attack on Calvi he suffered serious injury to his right eye. In 1797 a battle with the Spanish off Cape Saint Vincent brought him national fame. Ignoring naval regulations, he broke from the squadron and succeeded in capturing two Spanish warships after **broadsides** disabled them; Nelson personally led a boarding party, sword drawn.

Honored with appointment as a rear admiral and a knighthood, he was in a confident mood and underestimated the strength of the Spanish garrison of Tenerife in the Canary Islands. The landing party he was courageously leading was ambushed and Nelson was shot in his right arm; the wound necessitated amputation with a cold knife and opium

1793 Nelson distinguishes himself during war with France.

1797 Nelson's capture of two Spanish warships earns him national fame.

1798 Nelson vanquishes French fleet in Mediterranean, stranding Napolean's army in Egypt.

1805 Nelson is shot during Cape Trafalgar battle that secures British command of the seas.

broadsides: the firing at the same time of all the guns from one side of a ship.

to dull the pain. The attack was repulsed but Nelson still returned to England with a hero's welcome. Besides being an honored guest in homes of aristocrats, he had won a place in the hearts of ordinary sailors, showing concern that they should be promptly paid and families compensated in the event of a death. Although a strict disciplinarian not averse to the use of floggings, sailors knew he never asked of them anything he was not prepared to do himself; he would challenge nervous trainee officers to a race up the masthead, encouraging them not to fear one of the most daunting of the sailor's duties.

In 1798 Nelson pursued the French fleet around the Mediterranean. In August he caught up with the ships moored in the Nile **estuary** and with skillful maneuvering the British squadron placed itself in a position from where it destroyed or captured almost all the enemy ships. This sensational victory left Napoleon's army stranded in Egypt with the Royal Navy controlling Mediterranean sea-lanes.

estuary: the mouth of a river.

Nelson delighted in his own praises, and the British government's were usually not sufficiently generous to satisfy his ego. In Naples he received a grand welcome. Most enthusiastic was the famous courtesan Emma Hamilton, wife of the British ambassador; she wore a ribbon round her forehead proclaiming "Nelson and Victory." He was soon infatuated with her and was delighted when she bore him a daughter. Her husband, Sir William Hamilton, did not seem in the least perturbed but Mrs. (now Lady) Nelson was understandably averse to her husband's new affection. When the Nelsons and Hamiltons met in London, the confrontation between the women left Nelson's marriage to Fanny **extant** on paper only. He set up home with Emma and Sir William, in a house Emma found for them in Merton outside London. Nelson's behavior provided abundant material for gossip writers and cartoonists and distanced him from his elderly father. When his father died in 1802 he did not go to the funeral in order to avoid his wife, who had remained close to her father-in-law.

extant: still existing.

The end of the short-lived peace with France in 1802 increased fears of invasion. For several years Admiral Nelson chased the French fleet round the Mediterranean and across the Atlantic engaging in skimishes, trying to bring them out into a full-scale battle, convinced he would break their power once and for all.

On October 21, 1805 the long-awaited confrontation came off Cape Trafalgar. He signaled to his captains the famous message "England expects that every man will do his duty" and they did; the superiority of British gunnery and seamanship won the day, effectively ending French naval power and leaving Britain in command of the seas. Nelson knew of the triumph but did not live to celebrate. Ignoring his colleagues' advice he remained at his command post on the deck of H.M.S. *Victory* wearing numerous shiny medals on his uniform, an obvious target for the French sniper who cut him down. His last words were "Thank God I have done my duty." Nelson's greatest glory came posthumously. He was buried under the cupola of Saint Paul's Cathedral and became a legend. His statue stands on a high pillar in London's Trafalgar Square, although a similar pillar that long stood in Dublin's main street was blown up by Irish nationalists. ◆

Ness, Eliot

1903–1957 ● GANGBUSTER

Eliot Ness was an American crime fighter. He was known for heading a team of dedicated law enforcement officers who investigated the bootlegging activities of Chicago gangster Al Capone. Ness and his men were called "The Untouchables" because, unlike many other law officials of the time, they could not be bribed.

Ness was born in Chicago on April 19, 1903. His parents were Norwegian and his father was a baker. From his parents he learned an appreciation of Shakespeare, whom he continued to read through much of his life. He attended the University of Chicago and graduated in 1925 with a degree in commerce and business administration. But life behind a desk as an administrator did not appeal to him, and he pursued his boyhood dream to become a detective. In 1928 he joined the U.S. Department of Justice as a special agent. He was soon chosen to lead a team that was put together to enforce the

**Ness and his
men were called
"Untouchables"
because they
could not be
bribed.**

Eliot Ness.

prohibition law, a constitutional ban on alcoholic beverages that had been in effect since 1920. Despite this ban, the illegal distribution of alcoholic beverages continued. Bootleggers provided much of the illegal alcohol, and Chicago mobster Al Capone was probably the most famous bootlegger of his time. For more than two years, Ness and his team of about 10 agents raided Capone's bootlegging operations and seized barrels of illegal liquor, and beer delivery trucks, stills, and other equipment. With the Untouchables, Ness raided many of Capone's breweries. Although he's been given credit for bringing Capone down, Ness was never able to arrest Capone for bootlegging. Rather, Capone was arrested and convicted by the Internal Revenue Service (IRS) for income tax evasion.

Ness died, destitute and an alcoholic, at 54. He had spent seven years as Cleveland's director of public safety (overseeing both the police and fire departments) after retiring from the Justice Department's gangbusting Untouchables in Chicago. Ness's ashes, along with those of his third wife and their adopted son, a leukemia victim, were scattered in a lagoon at Cleveland's Lake View Cemetery. Ness published his autobiography, *The Untouchables*, posthumously in 1957, which later inspired the television series and the 1987 film. ◆

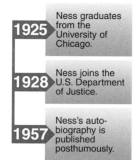

1925 Ness graduates from the University of Chicago.

1928 Ness joins the U.S. Department of Justice.

1957 Ness's autobiography is published posthumously.

Nevsky, Alexander

CA. 1220–1263 ● RUSSIAN PRINCE
& MILITARY HERO

lexander Nevsky was the son of Yaroslav II, grand
prince of Vladimir. In 1236, when only sixteen years
old, he was elected prince and military leader of the
republic of Novgorod. The many minor Russian states were
then subject to constant incursion by their neighbors to the
west. While Swedes and Germans attempted to assert their
control of the Baltic by barring Russian access to the sea,
smaller tribes such as the nomadic Finns and Lithuanians
were staking their own territorial claims in the region.

When the Swedish army invaded Novgorod in 1240,
Alexander met it at the juncture of the Neva and Izhora
rivers. In his first major encounter, he succeeded in repelling
the invaders, himself wounding the Swedish commander. He
commemorated his victory by adopting the title Nevsky ("of
the Neva") and came to consider himself the rightful heir to
Novgorod by merit of his success. When he began to meddle
in municipal matters, the citizens voted to have him expelled.
Soon, though, they were forced to ask him to return.

The Baltic region was then inhabited by a mixture of
Russian followers of the Orthodox church and nomadic
pagans. The Teutonic Knights, a zealous order of German
Catholics, eagerly responded to the call for a **crusade** issued
by Pope Gregory IX and invaded Novgorod. Nevsky, at the

pagan: not a Christian, Jew, or Muslim.

crusade: a religious war.

head of a small army, marched forward to meet them. The battlefield had been carefully chosen: the channel connecting Lakes Chud (Peipus) and Pskov. It was mid-April in the year 1242, and the ice-covered lakes were beginning to thaw. Nevsky hoped that if the Germans were kept on the thin ice their heavy armor would be their downfall. As the Germans marched across the frozen lake, Nevsky feigned retreat. German troops concentrated on the center of the Russian lines while Nevsky was moving his troops around the lake to the German flanks. Finally, he attacked. The Germans could not maneuver on the slippery surface and many fell through the ice to the freezing water below. The battle became known as the "Massacre on the Ice" and saved the Russian people from Teuton domination.

With his western boundary safe, Nevsky concentrated on securing himself from the Mongol Golden Horde in the east. Unlike many of his contemporaries, he realized that no military action could defeat the Mongols, and chose to follow his father's lead and to come to an accommodation with them. His father was poisoned in 1246 by a Russian nationalist. Nevsky and his younger brother Andrew journeyed to meet Khan Batu, prince of the western Mongols. Batu favored Nevsky to succeed his father as prince of Vladimir, but was unwilling to make the appointment without the consent of the Great Khan in Karakorum. The two brothers trekked to Mongolia, only to find that the Great Khan disapproved of Batu and rejected his advice. Vladimir was given to Andrew; Nevsky received Novgorod and Kiev in compensation. Andrew, however, attempted to organize a revolt against the Mongols. He was denounced to Batu's son by Nevsky and deposed. Nevsky now ruled Vladimir, Novgorod, and Kiev, uniting three of the leading Russian principalities.

As prince, Nevsky had considerable autonomy. He reorganized the legal system, fortified the western frontier, and fostered the growth of the Orthodox church. He was criticized, however, for his commitment to the Mongols and faced several revolts, one led by his own son.

The Russian nobles revolted against the Khan in 1262. Nevsky had opposed the revolt, but fearing reprisals, he again made the long journey to Karakorum to appeal for mercy. The journey was a success. Not only was the tax burden reduced, but the Khan agreed to forego his plan to enlist Russian troops

Nevsky became a symbol of Russia's determination to assert its independence.

1236 Nevsky, at 16, is elected prince and military leader of Novgorod.

1240 Nevsky repels Swedish army invasion of Novgorod.

1242 Nevsky-led "Massacre on the Ice" saves Russians from Teuton rule.

1547 Nevsky is canonized a saint in Russian Orthodox Church.

for an excursion against Iran. Nevsky turned for home, but died at Gorodets along the way. At his funeral his friend the Metropolitan Cyril prophesied, "The sun of Russia has set. Now we shall perish." Nevsky's united Russia disintegrated shortly after.

Russians have long esteemed Nevsky for preserving his country and church from foreign intrusion. More than an historical figure, he has become a symbol of Russia's determination to assert its independence. The same year that Nevsky's great-great-grandson finally expelled the Tatar descendants of the Golden Horde, Nevsky's tomb was suddenly rediscovered. He was canonized in 1547 and reinterred in Saint Petersburg by Peter the Great in 1725. ◆

Nicolini, Giuseppe

RESCUER OF JEWS DURING WORLD WAR II

> *"In all, about two hundred Jews were entrusted to us by Divine Providence; with God's help, and through the intercession of Saint Francis, not one of them fell into the hands of their persecutors."*
>
> Aldo Brunacci

Soon after the German invasion of Italy in September 1943, Giuseppe Nicolini, bishop of Assisi, summoned Rufino Nicacci, father guardian of the San Damiano monastery in Assisi. He charged Nicacci with finding temporary shelter for a group of fleeing Jews, mostly from the Trieste area in northern Italy, who had unexpectedly appeared in town. Nicacci arranged for some two hundred Jews to be supplied with false identities and hidden in parishioners' homes, moved out of the area, or given sanctuary in monasteries and convents. To provide for the religious needs of the Jews staying in the convent, the sisters operated a kitchen where dietary kosher laws were observed.

Also involved in this extensive rescue operation (several thousand Jews passed through the town at one point or another) was Aldo Brunacci, a professor canon at the San Rufino Cathedral of Assisi. The person formally in charge of the operation, he insisted that Jews could be hidden in cloisters as well, such as the Convent of the Stigmata. Father Brunacci was also in charge of a clandestine school for Jewish children, in which they received instruction in Judaism from their own mentors. In May 1944, Brunacci was arrested and tried by a Perugia court. He was spared only through the Vatican's intercession, on condition that he be banished from Assisi for the duration of the war.

Not a single Jew was ever betrayed in Assisi, nor was there any attempt to induce the many fleeing Jews passing through the town to convert. Father Brunacci remarked after the war: "In all, about two hundred Jews were entrusted to us by Divine Providence; with God's help, and through the intercession of Saint Francis, not one of them fell into the hands of their persecutors."

After the war, Giuseppe Nicolini, Rufino Nicacci, and Aldo Brunacci were recognized by Yad Vashem as "Righteous Among the Nations." ◆

Nightingale, Florence

1820–1910 ● BRITISH NURSE & HEALTH CARE REFORMER

Florence Nightingale received her first name from the Italian city her wealthy parents were visiting when she was born. Nightingale's upbringing was privileged and comfortable, imbued with the earnest humanitarian, cultural, and Christian religious commitments of her family. Her parents could not find a tutor for their daughters who matched their exacting standards and consequently the father undertook the task of educating them. The range of subjects they were taught was broad, embracing the classics, French and Italian, history, and philosophy.

In 1837 Nightingale felt the first of four divine calls to dedicate herself to holy works but initially she did not know in what field. She was free meanwhile to continue a busy social life and made an excellent impression on Paris society

> *"It may seem a strange principle to enunciate as the very first requirement in a Hospital that it should do the sick no harm."*
>
> Florence Nightingale, *Notes on Hospitals*, 1859

Florence Nightingale.

as a cultured and well-bred young lady. The social round continued with her presentation at Queen Victoria's court in 1839 and participation in all the other events that a lady of marriageable age was expected to patronize. She even had two suitors during the early 1840s, but neither won her favor. She had decided her mission demanded total commitment and that she must forgo marriage for she was taking upon herself the devotion of the Roman Catholic nuns whose medical missions she studied and admired.

By 1844 Nightingale had decided that nursing was to be her vocation. She had some experience from looking after sick family, friends, and some of the local villagers and wanted to get training working at Salisbury Infirmary. Her parents thought this was no place for a young lady of her class; hospitals in their view were unhealthy places and nurses had a poor moral reputation. Frustrated by family opposition, she toured Europe, visiting a model hospital at Kaiserswerth,

Germany, where there she found an institution run on high moral principles, though staffed by nurses who were "only peasants—none of them gentlewomen." Eventually, persistence met with success and her father granted her an allowance of five hundred pounds a year and did not oppose proposals to make her superintendent of the Institution for the Care of Sick Gentlewomen in Distressed Circumstances in London. With typical enthusiasm she began to make improvements in hospital organization, saving a considerable sum of money.

In 1854 the Crimean War began and the British public was dismayed when it learned of the incompetence with which the war was being managed. Disease was a far greater danger to the troops than Russian bullets: a fifth of the expeditionary force went down with cholera. There was a national outcry and Nightingale was approached and volunteered to lead a party of nurses to the Crimea under War Office sponsorship. However, her arrival was unwelcome to the army medical establishment, which resented female interference in their traditional preserve. The nurses were housed in cramped and insanitary quarters without the most basic amenities. To complete the unpleasant reception there was a Russian general whose dead body nobody had bothered to remove from the nurses' living quarters!

Nightingale was deferential toward the authorities and made do with the appalling living conditions. The state of the hospital was even worse, and following the Battle of Inkerman (1854) an influx of wounded overwhelmed the primitive facilities and the army medical men were forced to turn to Nightingale and her nurses for help. She was not intimidated by the dreadful conditions but found herself moved by the character of the ordinary soldiers, who had long been considered the lowest of the low. She recorded how "these poor fellows bear pain and mutilation with unshrinking heroism and die without complaint. Not so the officers."

The task was daunting. Nightingale ensured that the patients had clean linen and were bathed regularly, not just once in eighty days as had been the norm. Other innovations including scrubbing the floors of the wards and the distribution of literature and lectures for the wounded soldiers, as well as facilities for sending money home. Where necessary equipment was not forthcoming from the government supplies, she

1839 Nightingale is presented at Queen Victoria's court.

1844 Nightingale persists in following nursing vocation despite parental opposition.

1854 Nightingale leads a party of nurses to aid Crimean War troops.

1856 Nightingale returns to England an advocate for medical services reforms.

1907 Nightingale becomes the first woman awarded the Order of Merit.

"No man, not even a doctor, ever gives any other definition of what a nurse should be than this—'devoted and obedient.' This definition would do just as well for a porter."
Florence Nightingale, *Notes on Nursing*, 1860

drew on a fund raised by the British public and used her own personal allowance toward these purchases. To the nurses working under her she could appear as a harsh, intimidating figure, convinced nobody had a right to oppose her will. For the soldiers, as she toured the hospital at night with her lantern, she became a comforting figure—the legend of "the Lady with the Lamp" was born.

When the war ended in 1856, Nightingale returned to Great Britain a national heroine. Physically and emotionally exhausted, she took to her bed as an invalid, which she remained for the rest of her long life. Incapacity did not prevent her from using her considerable influence to press for further reforms in the army medical services. She met Queen Victoria and Prince Albert and enlisted their support for a thorough investigation of military hospitals to prevent the "scene of '54" from ever being reenacted. Queen Victoria commented of her: "Such a head! I wish we had her at the War Office."

Nightingale also took a deep interest in improving sanitary and medical conditions for the troops in India and invested a vast amount of time in promoting the development of professional training for nurses and the betterment of treatment of the sick in the workhouse infirmaries of London. Some of her attitudes became outdated—she refused to accept the germ theory of the spread of disease—but in other ways her views were in advance of the time. She argued that the sick in the workhouses were not the indolent poor to be punished but merely "poor and in affliction" and that every step necessary to their recovery should be taken.

In 1907 this elderly blind lady became the first woman to be awarded the Order of Merit by the king. ◆

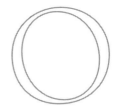

Otero-Warrren, Maria Adelina Emilia (Nina)

1881–1965 ● WOMEN'S RIGHTS ACTIVIST

Maria Adelina Emilia (Nina) Otero-Warren was the first Hispanic and the first woman to run for the U.S. House of Representatives. Born in Las Lunas, New Mexico, to an upper-class family, she was educated by tutors and attended an all-girls school and Maryville College of the Sacred Heart in St. Louis, Missouri. Leaving college before graduation, she married Lieutenant Rawson Warren in 1904. She lived in New York City from 1912 to 1914 and worked with the settlement-house movement in the inner-city.

After her mother's death in 1914, Otero-Warren returned to New Mexico to help care for her six half sisters and two brothers. She became involved with the suffrage movement in New Mexico and rose to lead the state chapter of the Congressional Union, the Women's Division of the Republican State Committee for New Mexico, and the Legislative Committee of the New Mexico Federation of Women's Clubs. Typical of Progressive-era women, Otero-Warren served and presided over many state committees on health and welfare reform. With her women's rights activism and her experience in social-welfare work, she gained the support of her politically powerful relatives for appointment as school superintendent in Santa Fe in 1917. She won election to the post in 1918 and remained in office until 1929.

Nominated as the Republican candidate for the U.S. House of Representatives in 1922, Otero-Warren ran a vig-

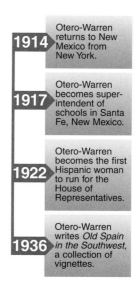

1914 Otero-Warren returns to New Mexico from New York.

1917 Otero-Warren becomes superintendent of schools in Santa Fe, New Mexico.

1922 Otero-Warren becomes the first Hispanic woman to run for the House of Representatives.

1936 Otero-Warren writes *Old Spain in the Southwest*, a collection of vignettes.

orous statewide campaign emphasizing her social activism and Hispanic bilingual heritage. Her candidacy received attention and publicity from many newspapers in the East and the Southwest. During the later days of the campaign, Otero-Warren was accused of misrepresenting her marital status to the public; she was not a widow but had been divorced from Rawson Warren before her political campaign. It seems hard to gauge whether this damaging information caused her to lose the election to Democrat John Morrow; no Republicans were elected in what turned out to be a Democratic sweep.

Otero-Warren decided not to seek higher office after 1922. Instead, she focused on educational and social-welfare issues. In 1936, she wrote *Old Spain in the Southwest*, a collection of romanticized **vignettes** of the lives and traditional customs of upper-class Hispanics in New Mexico. She worked as a state and federal government appointee and as a real-estate broker in Santa Fe until her death. ◆

vignette: a literary sketch.

Owens, James Cleveland (Jesse)

1913–1980 ● ATHLETE

Born in 1913, the tenth surviving child of sharecroppers Henry and Emma Owens, in Oakville, Alabama, Jesse Owens moved with his family to Cleveland, Ohio, for better economic and educational opportunities in the early 1920s. His athletic ability was first noticed by a junior high school teacher of physical education, Charles Riley, who coached him to break several interscholastic records and even to make a bold but futile attempt to win a place on the U.S. Olympic team. In 1933 Owens enrolled at Ohio State University on a work-study arrangement and immediately began setting Big Ten records. In Ann Arbor, Michigan, on May 25, 1935, he set new world records in the 220-yard

Jesse Owens at the
1936 Olympics.

sprint, the 220-yard hurdles, and the long jump and tied the
world record in the 100-yard dash.

In the racially segregated sports world of 1936, Owens and
Joe Louis were the most visible African-American athletes. In
late June, however, Louis lost to German boxer Max
Schmeling, making Owens's Olympic feats all the more dramatic. At Berlin in early August 1936, he stole the Olympic
show with gold-medal, record-making performances in the
100 meters, 200 meters, long jump, and relays. All this
occurred against a backdrop of Nazi pageantry and Adolf
Hitler's daily presence and in an international scene of tension and fear. Out of that dramatic moment came one of the
most enduring of all sports myths: Hitler's supposed "snub" in
refusing to shake Owens's hand after the victories. (Morally
satisfying but untrue, the yarn was largely created by
American sportswriters.)

Business and entertainment offers flooded Owens's way in the wake of the Berlin games, but he quickly found most of them were bogus. Republican presidential candidate Alf Landon paid him to stump for black votes in the autumn of 1936. After that futile effort, Owens bounced from one demeaning and low-paying job to another, including races against horses. He went bankrupt in a dry-cleaning business. By 1940, with a wife and three daughters to support (he had married Ruth Solomon in 1935), Owens returned to Ohio State to complete the degree he had abandoned in 1936. However, his grades were too low and his educational background too thin for him to graduate. For most of World War II, Owens supervised the black labor force at the Ford Motor Company in Detroit.

In the era of the cold war, Owens became a fervent American patriot, hailing the United States as the land of opportunity. Working out of Chicago, he frequently addressed interracial school and civic groups, linking patriotism and athletics. In 1955 the U.S. State Department sent him to conduct athletic clinics, make speeches, and grant interviews as means of winning friends for America in India, Malaya, and the Philippines.

In 1956 President Dwight D. Eisenhower sent him to the Melbourne Olympics as one of the president's personal goodwill ambassadors. Refusing to join the Civil Rights Movement, Owens became so politically conservative that angry young blacks denounced him as an "Uncle Tom" on the occasion of the famous black-power salutes by Olympic athletes Tommie Smith and John Carlos at Mexico City in 1968. Before he died of lung cancer in 1980, however, Owens received two of the nation's highest awards: the Medal of Freedom Award in 1976, for his "inspirational" life, and the Living Legends Award in 1979, for his "dedicated but modest" example of greatness. ◆

1933 Owens enters Ohio State University.

1935 Owens sets world track records in Michigan.

1936 Owens dazzles the world at the Berlin Olympics.

1954 Owens travels as goodwill ambassador to the Melbourne Olympics

1976 Owens is awarded the Medal of Freedom.

Pankhurst, Emmeline (née Goulden)

1858–1928 ● BRITISH SUFFRAGETTE

Emmeline Pankhurst's father, Robert Goulden, was a Manchester textile manufacturer and a friend of the political radical Dr. Richard Pankhurst, who had drafted the first women's suffrage bill in the late 1860s. Goulden and Dr. Pankhurst were campaigning together in 1875, when the doctor met Emmeline, recently returned from college in Paris. They were married the following year.

During her early married life, Mrs. Pankhurst was occupied with bringing up their four children. When she returned to public activities, she became increasingly involved with her husband's parliamentary work, and in 1889 they established the Women's **Franchise** League.

Beginning in 1895, Emmeline Pankhurst held several municipal posts in Manchester, but when Dr. Pankhurst died suddenly in 1898, she retreated from active politics. It was her eldest daughter, Christabel, who led her back into the suffrage campaign, and in 1903 she founded the Women's Social and Political Union. The WSPU gained widespread recognition

franchise: a privilege granted by the government.

in 1905 when two of its members were thrown out of a hall where the prime minister and several cabinet ministers were holding a meeting. These two demonstrators were arrested in the street for technical assault on the police, and after having refused to pay a fine, the Suffragettes—a name coined by the press—were imprisoned.

A year later, when Pankhurst moved to London, the campaign intensified. Neither the Liberal government nor the Labour opposition were taking the suffragettes' cause seriously. "Votes for women would do more harm than good," said Prime Minister Herbert Asquith. "Parliament is not elected on the basis of universal suffrage—children are not represented there." Reluctantly, the WSPU resorted to militant tactics. At first they were not violent, merely vociferous and obstructive. Nevertheless, in the year 1908–1909, Pankhurst was imprisoned three times.

In 1909 the WSPU began using hunger strikes as a political weapon. A truce was called a year later, but when the government blocked a franchise bill, the suffragettes launched a period of violent militancy. Arson attacks, directed from Paris by Christabel Pankhurst, were making the headlines. Under the notorious Cat and Mouse Act of 1913, Emmeline was arrested, released, and rearrested twelve times in one year.

It was a surprise to her colleagues when, at the outbreak of World War I, Emmeline Pankhurst immediately called off the campaign and urged the suffragettes to stand loyally with the government and England. She traveled around the country advocating national service for women, and wrote her autobiography, *My Own Story*, in 1914.

By 1915, there were severe problems keeping the factories open and producing and David Lloyd George, the minister of munitions, asked Mrs. Pankhurst to organize a march that would demonstrate women's readiness to fill men's places at work. Thousands marched under the slogan "We Demand the Right to Serve," and consequently a national register of women was compiled.

The war years gave women the chance to exercise their vital social power; finally, after the war, they were afforded the political power they had demanded for over five decades. An act in 1918, allowing women over thirty to vote, gave the franchise to women for the first time.

During the postwar years, Mrs. Pankhurst lived in the

1876 Emmeline marries Richard Pankhurst, who drafted first women's suffrage bill.

1889 The Pankhursts establish the Women's Franchise League.

1898 Pankhurst withdraws from active politics.

1903 Pankhurst founds Women's Social and Political Union.

1905 Arrest of two "suffragettes" draws widespread attention to the cause.

1908 Pankhurst is imprisoned.

1914 Pankhurst suspends campaign, urging loyalty to government during World War I.

1918 Women over 30 are given the right to vote.

1928 Pankhurst dies just weeks before women achieve voting rights.

United States, Canada, and Bermuda. She returned to England in 1926 and was immediately chosen as a Conservative candidate for a London constituency. Her declining health prevented her from being elected. She died in 1928, only a few weeks after the Representation of the People Act extended the vote to women on terms equal to male suffrage.

Her two daughters were also leaders of the women's suffrage movement. The fiery Christabel Pankhurst (1880–1958) was a militant suffragette who won an adoring following. Thrown out of the House of Commons, she screamed at a policeman, "I shall assault you, I shall spit at you!" For a time beginning in 1912, she was responsible for an arson campaign for which she was imprisoned. She became an evangelist and eventually was recognized by the establishment when created a dame of the British Empire in 1936.

Sylvia Pankhurst (1882–1960) opposed the institution of marriage and defended the right to be an unmarried mother (she was one herself). In the 1930s she was active in behalf of Ethiopian independence. ◆

> *"Remember the dignity of womanhood. Do not appeal, do not beg, do not grovel. Take courage, join hands, stand beside us, fight with us."*
>
> Christabel Pankhurst

Parks, Rosa Louise McCauley

1913–PRESENT ● CIVIL RIGHTS ACTIVIST

Rosa McCauley was born in Tuskegee, Alabama. She lived with relatives in Montgomery, where she finished high school in 1933 and attended Alabama State College. She met her husband, Raymond Parks, a barber, and they married in 1932. Rosa Parks worked as a clerk, an insurance salesperson, and a tailor's assistant at a department store. She was also employed at the time as a part-time seamstress by Virginia and Clifford Durr, two white residents of Montgomery who were staunch supporters of the black freedom struggle.

> *"I had felt for a long time, that if I was ever told to get up so a white person could sit, that I would refuse to do so."*
>
> Rosa Parks, 1955

Rosa Parks, at the front
of a bus, 1956.

1943 ▸ Parks joins the
NAACP.

1955 ▸ Parks refuses
to give up her
bus seat to a
white man.

1956 ▸ Parks helps
coordinate the
Montgomery bus
boycott.

1979 ▸ The NAACP
awards Parks the
Spingarn Medal.

Parks had been active in civil rights work since the 1930s.
She and her husband supported the Scottsboro defendants, a
notorious case in which nine young black men were convicted in 1931 on questionable evidence for raping two white
women. In 1943, Parks became one of the first women to join
the Montgomery NAACP. She worked as a youth adviser,
served as secretary for the local group from 1943 to 1956, and
helped operate the joint office of the NAACP and the
Brotherhood of Sleeping Car Porters. In addition, she worked
with the Montgomery Voters League to increase black voter
registration. During the summer of 1955, with the encouragement of the Durrs, Parks accepted a scholarship for a work-
shop for community leaders on school integration at the
Highlander Folk School in Tennessee. It was an important
experience for Parks, not only for the practical skills of organizing and mobilizing she learned, but because the racial har-
mony she experienced there nurtured and sustained her
activism.

Popularly known as the Mother of the Civil Rights
Movement, Parks is best known for her refusal to give up her
seat for a white man on a segregated bus in Montgomery on
December 1, 1955, an incident that sparked the Montgomery
Bus Boycott.

Contrary to popular belief, Parks was not simply a tired woman who wanted to rest her feet, unaware of the chain of events she was about to trigger. As she wrote in *Rosa Parks: My Story*, "The only tired I was, was tired of giving in." Parks was a veteran of civil rights activity and was aware of efforts by the Women's Political Council and the local NAACP to find an incident with which they could address segregation in Montgomery.

Parks was actively involved in sustaining the boycott and for a time served on the executive committee of the Montgomery Improvement Association, an organization created to direct the boycott. The **intransigence** of the city council was met by conviction and fortitude on the part of African Americans. For over a year, black people in Montgomery car-pooled, took taxis, and walked to work. The result was a ruling by the United States Supreme Court that segregation on city buses was unconstitutional.

intransigence: unwillingness to agree or compromise.

As a result of her involvement in the bus boycott, Parks lost her job at the department store in Montgomery. In 1957, she and her husband moved to Detroit, where she worked as a seamstress for eight years before becoming administrative assistant for Congressman John Conyers, a position she held until 1988. After she moved to Detroit, Parks continued to be active in the Civil Rights Movement and joined the Southern Christian Leadership Conference (SCLC). She participated in numerous marches and rallies, including the 1965 march from Selma to Montgomery.

In the mid-1980s she was a supporter of the free South Africa movement and walked the picket lines in Washington, D.C., with other antiapartheid activists. She has made countless public appearances, speaking out on political issues as well as giving oral history lessons about the civil rights movement. In 1987, ten years after the death of her husband, she founded the Rosa and Raymond Parks Institute for Self-Development in Detroit, a center committed to career training for black youth. The institute, a dream of hers, was created to address the dropout rate of black youth.

Parks, an international symbol of African-American strength, has been given numerous awards and distinctions, including ten honorary degrees. In 1979, she was awarded the NAACP's prestigious Spingarn Medal. In 1980, she was chosen by *Ebony* readers as the living black woman who had done the

Contrary to popular belief, Parks was not simply a tired woman who wanted to rest her feet, unaware of the events she was about to trigger.

most to advance the cause of black America. In the same year she was awarded the Martin Luther King, Jr., Nonviolent Peace Prize by the Martin Luther King, Jr., Center for Nonviolent Social Change. In addition, the SCLC has honored her by sponsoring the annual Rosa Parks Freedom award. ◆

Patton, George Smith

1885–1945 ● AMERICAN MILITARY LEADER

"Wars may be fought with weapons, but they are won by men."

George Patton, 1933

Born in San Gabriel, California, to a family steeped in military tradition, George Patton from a very early age showed a keen interest in history; papers that he wrote in grade school clearly express his desire to gain recognition, fame, and glory through heroic acts. Academic learning did not come easily to him, but he had a good sense of humor and a great love of the military. He worked conscientiously to improve himself in order to be accepted to military school.

To prepare himself for a military career, Patton first attended the Virginia Military Academy, where he proved himself an outstanding athlete. He set the school record in the 220-yard hurdles, won the 120-yard hurdles, and placed second in the 220-yard dash. He expressed his philosophy:

"By perseverance, study, and eternal desire, any man can be great." When he left the military academy, he went on to West Point, graduating in 1909, forty-sixth in a class of one hundred and three. Commissioned a second lieutenant in the cavalry, he remained deeply interested in the battles and history of the American Civil War.

Patton's first assignment was at Fort Sheridan in Illinois. In 1911 he was transferred to Fort Meyer, Washington, D.C., and was selected to compete in the fifth Olympic Games, which were held in Sweden. He was entered in the modern pentathlon, which involved shooting, swimming, fencing, cross-country steeplechase, and cross-country running, and finished fifth. This was a remarkable achievement, as he had not participated in sports competitions for over two years prior to beginning his training for the pentathlon.

In 1913 Patton was assigned to Fort Riley, Kansas, where he remained for two years. He was then transferred to Fort Bliss, Texas, and while he was there, Pancho Villa raided Columbus, New Mexico. Under General John J. Pershing, Patton became involved and remained in Mexico until February 1917. In appraising Patton, Pershing said, "Lieutenant Patton is a capable, energetic officer, and would perform the duties of a field officer of volunteers with credit to himself and the government."

With the onset of World War I, General Pershing brought Patton to France, where he served with distinction and was promoted several times. Returning to the United States in 1919, he served at Camp Meade, Maryland, and in 1920 was transferred back to Fort Meyer but this time as the commander of the cavalry. In a letter to his father, Patton wrote, "Some day I will show them. I fear that I will never be a general."

Between World War I and World War II Patton served at forts Riley and Leavenworth, both in Kansas, in Boston, and in Hawaii. His field of expertise changed from cavalry training to tanks, and he went on to prove his genius in tank warfare.

With the threat of war imminent, Patton was assigned to the Second Armored Division at Fort Benning, Georgia, promoted to divisional commander, and commanded what became the army's toughest outfit. He then took command of the First Armored Corps, a much larger unit; he and his

1911 Patton finishes fifth in pentathlon at fifth Olympic Games in Sweden.

1919 Patton returns to United States after serving under General Pershing in France.

1843 Patton commands Seventh Army during invasion of Sicily.

1944 Patton prepares for invasion of Normandy and launches brilliant offenses against German front.

1945 Patton, demoted in controversy over denazification policies, dies in fatal car crash.

*"By persever-
ance, study, and
eternal desire,
any man can be
great."*

George Patton

malingering: pretend-
ing to be sick to avoid
work.

troops were sent to fight in the North African Campaign, and he was promoted to lieutenant general. Under General Dwight Eisenhower, Patton was placed in charge of the Tank Force Troops and commanded the Seventh Army during the invasion of Sicily in 1943, capturing Palermo the following year.

Known for his quick temper and impetuosity, Patton created an incident that was to mark a reversal in his career. While visiting wounded soldiers in a military hospital, Patton struck a soldier who was suffering from battle fatigue because he felt that the man was **malingering**. Reprimanded by General Eisenhower, Patton was forced to make a public apology. This action delayed his promotion, and he lost his command; it was not until August 1944 that he was promoted to major general.

In March 1944 Patton assumed command of the Third Army and prepared it for the invasion of Normandy, where his brilliant sweep across the base of the Breton peninsula led to the liberation of Metz. The Germans then launched their Ardennes counteroffensive, and Patton turned his forces quickly northward against the German southern flank and helped contain the enemy. General Omar N. Bradley said later, "Patton accomplished one of the most astonishing feats of generalship of our campaign in the West."

Patton, together with his troops, caused the breakthrough in the Battle of the Bulge and went on to speed across Germany, cutting the country in half. "Old Blood and Guts," as Patton was known, proved himself to be one of the great tactical commanders of all times. However, he got himself into trouble once more, this time as military governor of Bavaria, when he made statements criticizing the "denazification" policies; it was felt he was too lenient with Nazis and was removed from his command. Patton was then assigned a lesser post and toward the end of 1945, was involved in a fatal automobile accident. ◆

Peary, Robert Edwin

1856–1920 ● AMERICAN EXPLORER

"The Eskimo, Ootah, had his own explanation. Said he: 'The devil is asleep or having trouble with his wife, or we should never have come back so easily.' "
Robert Edwin Peary, *The North Pole*, 1910

Robert Edwin Peary was the leader of the expedition that is generally credited with being the first to reach the North Pole. Robert Peary was born in Cresson, Pennsylvania. His father, a barrel maker, died when he was only three, after which his family moved to Maine. He attended the local schools and in 1877 earned a civil engineering degree from Bowdoin College. He was a competitive athlete, which undoubtedly stood him in good stead for the rigors he would endure later in his life.

His first job was as a county surveyor in Fryeburg. In 1881 he enlisted in the naval civil engineering corps with the rank of lieutenant. A few years later he was posted as assistant engineer on the team sent to survey the proposed Nicaraguan shipping canal, returning to the United States in 1885.

About this time, Peary came across a magazine article on Greenland and the Arctic wastes. He began to read voraciously on the subject, becoming increasingly consumed by the idea of being the first man to cross the polar ice cap. To this end, he secured a brief leave of absence from the navy in 1886, and set off on a whaler for Greenland. Along with him went Matthew Henson, his African American servant, who would accompany him on all his subsequent expeditions. Peary found this small taste of the northern reaches beyond his wildest expectations. He was unabashed in stating that his desire was for glory and fame, not for scientific achievement for the betterment of humanity.

Peary was once again posted by the navy to Nicaragua in 1887, this time as chief engineer. The following year, upon his return to the United States, he married, and devoted most of his spare time researching the Arctic and lobbying extensively among various scientific and geographical societies for support for his planned adventures. In 1891 he once again took a leave of absence from the navy, and with a team of six, which included his wife, Henson, and Dr. Frederick Cook, headed for Greenland on a small **sealer**, the *Kite*. His wife's presence was intended as a publicity exercise, as she was the first white woman to withstand the Arctic winter. The mission began badly when Peary broke his leg as the *Kite* was smashing its way through the pack ice, but Cook, the team's surgeon, set the break so well that Peary was back on his feet within a few weeks.

sealer: a ship used for hunting seals.

After the long winter night, the team moved inland, assisted by Eskimos, who proved invaluable in teaching Peary about Arctic survival. Peary now began studies of the Eskimo culture, which he continued on later visits. He also fathered a number of children by Eskimo women and took part in the local custom of wife sharing. He crossed Greenland and proved for the first time that it was an island.

modicum: a small portion.

Peary's success brought him a **modicum** of fame and renewed offers of support. His next expedition set off in 1893 with a larger team, and his first legitimate child was born in Greenland late that year. This time, however, he was plagued by bad weather and returned home in 1895 without much more to show for his years of effort than three large meteorite specimens he had discovered, including one that weighed over ninety tons.

Peary realized that he required a new approach and decided he would push as far north as possible in a ship and then strike out with sleds to reach the Pole in the summer. His plan received the support of the British, who presented him with the *Windward*, a ship that had previously served their own Arctic expedition. By 1897 public interest in the Arctic was at its peak, each "farthest north" making the headlines. Peary judged the time was right for a fresh attempt, but the navy was not inclined to grant him further leave despite the appeals of his backers and many prominent scientists. Only the personal intercession of President William McKinley made the navy yield. Yet despite all his preparations, this expedition, beginning in 1898, also failed to reach the North Pole. Peary returned to the United States in 1902 minus eight toes, which he had lost in 1899 to frostbite. He still believed his strategy for reaching the North Pole was correct, but now concluded that he needed a custom-built ship that could break much farther north than the *Windward*.

In 1905 he returned to Greenland with his new vessel, the *Roosevelt*. This time his expedition reached a new farthest north record of 174 miles from the Pole. He returned to New York the following year, by now over fifty years of age, feeling that his next expedition would likely be his last. By 1908 he was ready once again. The *Roosevelt* reached within four hundred miles of the Pole, a record in its own right for a ship under its own power. The winter was spent gathering scientific data and making preparations for the summer dash for the Pole, building igloos, and storing supplies along the intended route. Early in 1909 the party set off from the base camp with twenty-three men (seventeen of them Eskimos), nineteen sleds, and one hundred and thirty-one dogs. As they proceeded, groups peeled off, leaving more supplies for the lead party's return journey. The final leg to the Pole was to be attempted by Peary, Henson, and four Eskimos pulled by forty dogs on five sleds. By early April a desperately weary Peary reckoned he was within three miles of the Pole, after traversing treacherous pack ice flows for many miles. To be sure they did not miss the Pole, the party deliberately pulled out in several directions. Peary broke through the ice where he believed the Pole to be and confirmed that it was in fact in the midst of a vast ocean. He planted five flags—the United States, the U.S. Navy, the Daughters of the American Revolution, the Red Cross, and his college fraternity. Assisted by favorable weather, he made it back safely to base by late April, cabling his wife, "I have the old Pole."

The jubilant Peary, however, was shocked by the news that his erstwhile team surgeon, Cook, had claimed to have reached the North Pole in 1908. Whereas Peary had undertaken a well-planned, well-financed expedition, Cook claimed to have achieved the same goal almost singlehanded. Cook's bravado immediately captured popular attention, and

1877 Peary graduates from Bowdoin College in civil engineering.

1886 Peary takes leave from navy to serve aboard Greenland-bound whaler.

1891 Peary's team braves Greenland winter.

1893 Peary undertakes second Greenland expedition.

1898 Peary fails in first attempt to reach North Pole.

1905 Peary reaches new farthest north record of 174 miles from Pole.

1909 Peary, accompanied by Henson and four Eskimos, reaches the Pole.

official doubts as to the veracity of Cook's claim were dismissed by the press as attempts to discredit an independent explorer. Indeed, the press turned on Peary, accusing him of sinister motives and deceit in his own claims. Nevertheless, Peary was awarded the rank of rear admiral by Congress and received numerous awards from learned societies worldwide. He retired from the navy in 1910, although he served as chairman of the National Committee on Coast Defence by Air in World War I.

Cook's priority claim looked even more suspect when his supposed ascent of Mount McKinley in 1906 was alleged to have been an outrageous fraud. Today it is generally accepted that Peary and Henson were the first to reach the North Pole. ◆

Pérez Esquivel, Adolfo

1931–PRESENT ● ARGENTINE SCULPTOR & PEACE ACTIVIST

1970s Perez abandons his careers as a sculptor to promote nonviolence.

1974 Perez Esquivel helps form Serpaj.

1977 Perez is jailed by the Argentine government.

Born in Buenos Aires, Adolfo Pérez Esquivel was educated in Catholic schools and was deeply influenced by the writings of St. Augustine and Thomas Merton, as well as by the pacifist example of Mohandas Gandhi. Trained in sculpture at the National School of Fine Arts, he later taught there for fifteen years. He abandoned his successful career as a sculptor in the early 1970s to promote nonviolence as the most appropriate response to the violence that was afflicting Latin America as a result of increasing pressures for change.

In 1974 Pérez Esquivel joined with other Catholic activists to form Serpaj, an agency for the dissemination of knowledge of nonviolent strategies and for the promotion of greater observance of human rights, participatory models of economic development, greater political participation especially among the poor, disarmament, and demilitarization. That year Pérez Esquivel became the general coordinator of Serpaj, traveling throughout Latin America and elsewhere to promote nonviolence. As a result of his work, he was jailed for fourteen months in 1977–1978 by the Argentine military government. Upon his release, he resumed his work promoting nonviolence as the most effective way of creating a democratic and liberating social order. ◆

Pinkerton, Allan

1819–1884 ● PRIVATE DETECTIVE

"The Eye That Never Sleeps."
Motto for the Pinkerton National
Detective Agency

Allen Pinkerton was born in Glasgow, Scotland, in 1819. He was the son of a weaver, who sometimes served as a Glasgow policeman. His father died when he was only eight years old and young Allen had to quit school and begin working as a weaver for pennies. He later worked as a barrel maker. As a young adult, Pinkerton became active in a movement to reform the British Parliament. Pinkerton vocally advocated civil disobedience and his views were considered so radical that a warrant was issued for his arrest. To escape arrest, Pinkerton and his wife immigrated to the United States in 1842.

Allan Pinkerton and his wife settled in Dundee, Illinois, where Pinkerton started his detective work. They moved to Chicago, and in 1855, he founded the North West Police Agency, with a contract to check the honesty of railroad employees. In 1860, he added another large client, the Adams Express Company, and renamed his business Pinkerton's National Detective Agency.

The Pinkerton National Detective Agency grew into America's largest private police force, working on contract with businesses that needed detection and security services. The Pinkerton "operatives" pursued labor anarchists, murderers, Confederate spies, and bank and train robbers and investigated employees suspected of dishonesty. Watchmen from the Pinkerton Protective Patrol guarded businesses. These agency emphases have gradually changed; today, 98 percent of Pinkerton business is providing plant protection.

The Pinkertons later gained wide publicity by pursuing notorious train and bank robbers, but the foundation of the business lay in the need of railroads and other rapidly expanding companies to control their workers. The Pinkertons spied on employees and chased professional criminals as well; their detectives could work anywhere, whereas city police and county sheriffs had limited jurisdictions. Not until the twentieth century did public police agencies enjoy regional and national authority.

Allan Pinkerton began by investigating many cases personally and developing his own techniques. He had a talent for selecting good people. George H. Bangs, his first employee, became the general manager. Timothy Webster spied on the Confederates and was captured and hanged. Kate Warne became the first female detective. Charles Angelo Siringo wrote about his twenty-two years as a Pinkerton agent. Tom Horn, a cowboy detective subsequently hanged for murder, and Dashiell Hammett, an author of detective stories, worked as operatives.

Allan Pinkerton headed the agency until his death in 1884, although sons William and Robert were effectively in charge after their father suffered a severe stroke. The main office stayed in Chicago; new ones opened in New York and Philadelphia in 1865 and 1866 and in Denver in 1886. Boston, Kansas City, Portland, St. Paul, and St. Louis were added by 1893. A typical office consisted of the superinten-

1842 Pinkerton immigrates to USA from Scotland.

1855 Pinkerton founds the North West Police Agency.

1861 Pinkerton breaks up a Confederate spy ring.

1888 The Pinkerton agency provides strikebreakers in the Burlington Railroad Strike.

1896 The Pinkerton agency pursues Butch Cassidy's gang after a bank heist.

1907 The agency changes its emphasis to security and property protection.

dents, the clerical staff, the criminal department with its rogues' gallery, and the detectives. General operatives did undercover work and tracked criminals while secret operatives served as labor spies. Occasional special operatives dealt with minor cases. All training was informal.

Pinkerton techniques included shadowing or spying on employees, infiltrating organizations, gaining the confidence of criminal suspects, and paying informants. The rogues' gallery of photographs and descriptions of lawbreakers was continually expanded and updated, its contents shared with law enforcement agencies elsewhere. The Pinkerton motto became "The Eye That Never Sleeps."

Allan Pinkerton thwarted a plot to assassinate Abraham Lincoln before his inauguration. From 1861 to 1862, he broke up a Confederate spy ring that centered around Washington socialite Rose Greenhow. Pinkerton's agents gathered information from behind Confederate lines. After the Civil War, he chased the Renos, train and bank robbers, until vigilantes lynched them. When Jesse and Frank James held up the bank in Richmond, Missouri, the Pinkertons followed their trail. One detective died while trying to infiltrate the James brothers gang, and another died in a shootout with the Younger brothers. During an attack on a cabin thought to be a hideout of the James boys, Pinkerton agents killed the outlaws' younger half brother and badly injured their mother. After their disastrous Northfield, Minnesota, bank robbery, the James brothers vanished, but the Pinkertons kept after them. Jesse was murdered in 1882; Frank James surrendered later that year.

The Pinkertons trailed outlaw Sam Bass until a gun battle with the Texas Rangers ended his career. When night riders in New Mexico tried assassination, operative Charles Siringo infiltrated a lawless Hispanic organization, Las Gorras Blancas, or the White Caps, until he determined that they were not responsible. Governor Thornton employed the Pinkertons for two months when another prominent New Mexican, Albert Jennings Fountain, disappeared. That case remained unsolved. The Pinkertons pursued Butch Cassidy's Wild Bunch after the Montpelier, Idaho, bank heist in 1896. In 1901, Cassidy, the Sundance Kid, and their lady friend Etta Place sailed to Argentina, where operative Frank Dimaio chased them for a couple of months.

The Pinkertons earned a good reputation for recovering stolen loot from train and bank robberies.

When Jesse and Frank James held up a bank in Richmond, Missouri, the Pinkertons followed their trail.

The Pinkertons were probably at their best in gathering undercover information. They also earned a good reputation for recovering stolen loot from train and bank robberies. Detective James McParlan joined the Molly Maguires in the Pennsylvania coal mines and helped to send thirteen terrorists to the gallows. The company gained the hatred of organized labor after the Burlington Railroad Strike in 1888, when the Pinkerton agency provided scabs, or strikebreakers. At Homestead, Pennsylvania, Pinkerton guards were met with gunfire by striking steelworkers. Three guards and ten of the strikers died. This virtually ended the Pinkertons' involvement with strikebreaking.

At Coeur d'Alene in northern Idaho, the local miners' union made undercover agent Charles Siringo their recording secretary. Rioting broke out after the mine owners imported scab laborers, and National Guard and federal troops were then called in to restore order. Siringo helped convict eighteen union rioters. Labor troubles in Idaho and Colorado became something of a speciality for the Denver office, especially after the Industrial Workers of the World, or Wobblies, gained prominence.

Following Robert Pinkerton's death in 1907, his son Allan Pinkerton II took over the New York office and changed the emphasis to security and property protection. In the 1930s, Allan's son Robert Allan Pinkerton became the last descendant of Allan Pinkerton to head the business. Labor spying had disappeared by 1940, and detective work gave way to the guarding of property. In January 1988, California Plant Protection paid $95 million to American Brands for Pinkerton's, Inc., and renamed the firm Pinkerton's. By the 1990s, Pinkerton's was headquartered in Van Nuys, California, and the company had forty-three thousand employees and annual revenues of more than $700 million. ◆

Polo, Marco

1254–1324 ● VENETIAN EXPLORER

Marco Polo, whose detailed account of his journeys through Asia fired the medieval imagination, was born in Venice. His father and uncle, Nicolo and Maffeo Polo, successful merchants in the trade in Asian goods that had made Venice one of the West's richest cities, were attracted to Constantinople, where they opened a branch of their business shortly before Marco was born. In 1260 they moved their business eastward to Central Asia. When warring Tartar tribes blocked their return, they continued moving eastward. Accepting an invitation to accompany an envoy en route to the Mongol chieftain Kublai Khan, they eventually arrived at the Great Khan's court in Cathay, China, around 1265.

Distrusting the newly conquered Chinese, Kublai preferred employing foreigners. He made the Polos his emissaries, sending them back to Europe with gifts and letters asking the pope for one hundred learned missionaries. They arrived back in Venice to find Nicolo's wife dead and the election of a new pope delayed. After waiting in vain for two years for a new pope to be elected, the Polo brothers, fearing the consequences of keeping Kublai waiting, decided to return to China and take fifteen-year-old Marco with them. However, they were soon summoned back by the new pope, Gregory X, who supplied them with credentials and sent two friars to accompany them. The friars turned back at the first hint of danger, but the Polos pressed onward, trusting that the gold tablet that they carried, which was inscribed by Kublai himself, would ensure their safe passage.

They took three years to reach the Mongol court, having remained a year in Afghanistan while Marco recovered from an illness. Soon after their arrival, Kublai utilized Marco's gift for languages, keenly accurate observation, and vivid description by sending him on fact-finding missions to various parts of the Mongol Empire. Marco discharged his responsibilities so well that he was rewarded by being granted the governorship of Yangchow for three years, while his family was honored and protected from jealous courtiers.

> *"I shall tell you of the great and wonderful magnificence of the Great Kaan now reigning, by name Cublay Kaan . . . all men know for a certain truth that he is the most potent man, as regards forces and lands and treasures that existeth in the world."*
>
> Marco Polo, 1298

"I did not write half the things I saw."

Marco Polo, 1324

After seventeen years in China, the Polos, knowing that their position there would be precarious after Kublai's death, sought to overcome the eighty-year-old khan's resistance to letting them return to Venice. He was loath to see them go but finally, when they offered to guide a princess to her Persian bridegroom through the southern seas with which Marco was familiar (he had just returned from a mission there), Kublai reluctantly consented, supplying them with fourteen ships and a golden tablet to ensuring their safe passage. Their voyage to Persia was extremely rough (only eighteen of their six hundred passengers survived) but they delivered the princess and continued on to Venice, arriving home after being gone twenty-five years.

The written account of Marco Polo's journeys came into existence by chance. He was captured while participating in a naval battle with Genoa soon after returning to Venice. Imprisoned in Genoa, his tales of the fabulous East fascinated prisoners, jailers, and visitors alike and were written down by a fellow prisoner, a writer of romances named Rustichello. The completed manuscript described lands Polo had visited (or heard about in the East), their produce and trade, people, customs, curiosities, religions, and interesting historical incidents. Peace was declared soon after Rustichello completed his task and Polo was released from prison. He returned to Vienna, became involved in the daily life of a prosperous merchant, married, and had several children; on his death, his Tartar slave was freed according to the provisions of his will.

His manuscript's fate was more exotic. Considered fiction since it seemed too fantastic to be real, it was an immediate success throughout Italy. Translated and retranslated, it spread throughout Europe. Widely considered no more than an inventive storyteller, Polo, when asked to confess the truth on his deathbed, responded: "I did not write half the things I saw." Some suspected that there might be some truth in his tales: Columbus set sail in search of the riches of the East whose location and extent Polo had so carefully chronicled. Later explorers and researchers discovered that Polo was indeed an accurate and serious geographer. ◆

Powell, Colin Luther

1937–PRESENT ● ARMY OFFICER & CHAIR OF THE JOINT CHIEFS OF STAFF

"We accomplished the mission our political leaders gave us to do and that was to go to the Persian Gulf and kick Iraq out of Kuwait and put the legitimate government back in power." Colin Powell

Born and raised in New York City, Colin Powell grew up in a close-knit family of Jamaican immigrants in the Hunts Point section of the Bronx. After attending public schools, Powell graduated from the City College of New York (CCNY) in 1958. Although his grades were mediocre, he discovered an affinity for the military. Participating in CCNY's Reserve Officer Training Corps (ROTC) program, he finished as a cadet colonel, the highest rank attainable. Like all ROTC graduates, Powell was commissioned as a second lieutenant after completing college.

Powell served for two years in West Germany and two years in Massachusetts, where he met his wife, Alma. In 1962, already a captain, Powell received orders to report to Vietnam. He was one of the second wave of more than 15,000 military advisers sent by the United States to Vietnam and was posted with a South Vietnamese army unit for most of his tenure. During his first tour of duty, from 1962 to 1963, he was decorated with the Purple Heart after being wounded by a Viet Cong booby trap near the Laotian border.

After returning to the United States, Powell spent almost four years at Fort Benning in Georgia, serving as, among other things, an instructor at Fort Benning's Army Infantry School. In 1967, now a major, he attended an officers' training course

During his first tour of duty in Vietnam, Powell was wounded by a Viet Cong booby trap.

at the United States Army Command and General Staff College at Fort Leavenworth, Kansas, finishing second in a class of more than twelve hundred. In the summer of 1968, Powell was ordered back to Vietnam. On his second tour, Powell primarily served as a liaison to General Charles Gettys of the American Division and received the Soldier's Medal for his role in rescuing injured soldiers, including General Gettys, from a downed helicopter.

Powell returned to the United States in mid-1969 and began moving between military field postings and political appointments, a process that would become characteristic of his career. In 1971, after working in the Pentagon for the assistant vice chief of the army, he earned an M.B.A. from George Washington University in Washington, D.C. Shortly thereafter, Powell was accepted as a White House Fellow during the Nixon administration and was attached to the Office of Management and Budget (OMB), headed by Caspar Weinberger. In 1973, after a year at OMB, Powell received command of an infantry battalion in South Korea; his mission was to raise morale and restore order in a unit plagued by drug abuse and racial problems. He then attended a nine-month course at the National War College and was promoted to full colonel in February 1976, taking command of the 2nd Brigade, 101st Airborne Division, located at Fort Campbell, Kentucky.

In 1979 Powell was an aide to Secretary of Energy Charles Duncan during the crisis of the nuclear accident at Three Mile Island in Pennsylvania and the oil shortage caused by the overthrow of the shah of Iran. In June of that year, while working at the Department of Energy (DOE), he became a brigadier general. Powell returned to the field from 1981 until 1983, serving as assistant division commander of the Fourth Infantry (mechanized) in Colorado and then as the deputy commanding general of an Army research facility at Fort Leavenworth. In mid-1983, he became military assistant to Secretary of Defense Caspar Weinberger. In 1986, Powell, by then a lieutenant general, returned to the field as the commander of V Corps, a unit of 75,000 troops in West Germany. The following year, in the wake of the Iran-Contra scandal, he returned to serve as President Ronald Reagan's national security adviser. During the Intermediate Nuclear Forces (INF) arms-control negotiations with the Soviet

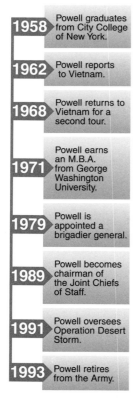

1958 Powell graduates from City College of New York.

1962 Powell reports to Vietnam.

1968 Powell returns to Vietnam for a second tour.

1971 Powell earns an M.B.A. from George Washington University.

1979 Powell is appointed a brigadier general.

1989 Powell becomes chairman of the Joint Chiefs of Staff.

1991 Powell oversees Operation Desert Storm.

1993 Powell retires from the Army.

General Benjamin O. Davis

Benjamin O. Davis Sr. was the first African American to reach to rank of Brigadier General in the U. S. Army. Davis was born in Washington, D.C. in 1880. After graduating from high school, he volunteered for service in the Spanish American War. The army appointed him a second lieutenant in the Eighth U. S. Volunteer Infantry. After the unit was deactivated at the end of the war in 1899, Davis decided to continue his military career. Two years later, he successfully passed a competitive examination and became an officer. In October 1940, President Franklin D. Roosevelt appointed Davis a brigadier general. During World War II, Davis carried out a variety of assignments in Washington and Europe, all generally connected with racial issues. He conducted investigations of racial incidents, tried to encourage the advancement of African-American soldiers and officers, and made efforts to convince the Army to face the consequences of its policies of segregation and discrimination. One of his most notable contributions occurred as a result of the manpower shortage created by the German attack in the Ardennes in December 1944. Davis advanced a proposal for retraining black troops as combat soldiers and inserting them into white units. Though General Dwight Eisenhower found this unacceptable, he was forced to accept integration of African-American platoons into white units. It was a significant breakthrough in the wall of segregation. Following the war, Davis served in a variety of positions before his retirement in 1948. He died in 1970.

Union, Powell was heralded as being a major factor in their success.

In July 1989, Powell, a newly promoted four-star general, was nominated by President George Bush to become the first black chairman of the joint Chiefs of Staff, the highest military position in the armed forces. As chairman, Powell was responsible for overseeing Operation Desert Storm, the 1991 international response to the 1990 Iraqi invasion of Kuwait. Through his commanding and reassuring television presence during the successful Persian Gulf War, Powell became one of the most popular figures in the Bush administration. Reappointed chairman in 1991, he was the recipient of various military decorations as well as a Presidential Medal of Freedom from Bush.

When Bill Clinton was elected president in 1992, he and Powell had differences over Clinton's plan to substantially reduce the defense budget. Powell also disagreed with Clinton's proposal to end the ban on homosexuals in the military and was instrumental in limiting the scope of the change. Powell retired from the army in September 1993 at the end of his second term as Chairman of the Joint Chiefs. ◆

Quezon y Molina, Manuel Luis

1878–1944 ● PRESIDENT OF THE PHILIPPINES

Born in Baler, Tayabas province, Manuel Luis Quezon y Molina quit school to participate in Emilio Aguinaldo's failed uprising against American colonial rule. Aguinaldo was defeated in 1901; after six months in jail for his role in the rebellion, Quezon returned to law school, convinced that the cause of independence was best served by negotiating with the American authorities.

After completing his degree in 1903, Quezon was appointed prosecuting attorney for the provinces of Mindaro and his native Tayabas. In 1905 he was elected governor of Tayabas, and in 1909 one of the two resident commissioners for the Philippines in Washington. There, the "Patrick Henry of the Philippines" became a vociferous champion of independence. As a nonvoting member of Congress, he questioned whether the Jones Act (1916), enabling the formation of a local legislature for the Philippines, went far enough in ensuring self-rule. The act depicted a continued American military presence on the islands even if independence were, at some

Called the "Patrick Henry of the Philippines," Quezon was a vociferous champion of independence.

future date, achieved. He, nonetheless, returned to the islands and was elected speaker of the newly formed Senate, the most prestigious post open to native Filipinos.

Similar reservations led Quezon to oppose deferred independence as proposed in the Heres-Hawes-Cutting bill of 1933. In 1934, however, he accepted the Tydings-McDuffie Act assuring complete independence by July 4, 1946. In view of Japanese expansionism in the Pacific, he recognized that only the American military was capable of defending the islands, while the proposed transitional Commonwealth of the Philippines would allow him to formulate an independent policy to tackle the pressing problems of the islands. The following year, Quezon was elected president of the new commonwealth.

The Americans were shocked to discover that Quezon's grand design for the islands exhibited totalitarian tendencies. He described the country as a "distributive state," in which the state allocated accumulated wealth so that "all citizens receive the means to live." Although essentially democratic, Quezon spoke of a "dictatorship of persuasion," and eventually of banning political parties. Essential to his doctrine of attaining total self-reliance was the establishment of a national defense force, for which he employed his old friend, American general Douglas MacArthur, a former governor and outspoken proponent of independence. Other problems he confronted included the settlement of the large southern island of Mindanao to quell a local Muslim revolt and corruption at all levels of government. At one point, Quezon studied the option of closer cooperation with the Japanese, and even made a state visit there in 1938 but concluded that the Japanese were already intent on occupying the country.

In 1941, with a Japanese invasion well underway, Quezon was elected to a second term as president by a seven to one margin. A heavy air raid shook Manila during the inauguration ceremonies, forcing the president and his entourage to flee to the U.S. garrison of Corregidor. After seventy-seven days and an impassioned plea from President Franklin D. Roosevelt, Quezon finally agreed to leave the Philippines. MacArthur received $500,000 to take Quezon and his immediate family to Australia, and in 1942, Quezon reached the United States to organize his government in exile.

Although Quezon had earlier decided to retire from poli-

1901 Quezon is jailed for his role in failed rebellion against American rule.

1909 Quezon champions Philippine independence in Washington.

1934 Tydings-McDuffie Act assures complete independence by July 4, 1946.

1935 Quezon is elected first president of the Philippines commonwealth.

1941 Quezon starts second term during Japanese invasion of islands.

1942 Quezon flees to the United States and organizes government in exile.

1944 Quezon dies of tuberculosis, six months before Americans liberate Manila.

tics in 1943, Roosevelt urged him to postpone his resignation until the Philippines were liberated in return for a promise of immediate independence. Quezon, however, died of tuberculosis in August 1944; the American invasion began in October of that year and only succeeded in liberating Manila in February 1945. Although Quezon never lived to see the Philippines liberated, he is considered the father and first president of his country. A new city built near Manila was named Quezon City in his honor. ◆

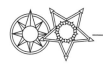

Revere, Paul

1735–1818 ● REVOLUTIONARY WAR HERO

> *"If the British went out by water, to show two lanterns in the North Church steeple; and if by land, one as a signal, for we were apprehensive it would be difficult to cross the Charles River or get over Boston Neck."*
> Paul Revere, 1775

An expert silversmith and engraver, Paul Revere was also a leader among the craftsmen and mechanics of Boston. He was active in the North End Caucus, a patriotic club, and in the early opposition to British government policy. He served as an official messenger on several occasions between the Boston patriots and the Sons of Liberty in New York and Philadelphia, and as official courier of the Massachusetts Provincial Assembly.

Revere engraved several cartoons that dealt with contemporary politics; he also issued an engraving of the Boston Massacre that helped arouse resentment against British policies. He is best known as one of three patriots who rode out to alarm the countryside when the British in Boston attempted a secret raid on Concord (April 19, 1775). His beautifully shaped and crafted silverware and other work in metal are today the proud possessions of American art museums. ◆

Richard I (Richard the Lionhearted)

1157–1199 ● KING OF ENGLAND

> *"Dear Lord, I pray thee to suffer me not to see thy holy city, since I cannot deliver it from the hands of thy enemies."*
>
> Richard I, attributed,
> upon seeing Jerusalem in 1192

The third son of Henry II and Eleanor of Aquitaine, Richard was born in Oxford. While still a child, he was granted the dukedom of Aquitaine, land Henry II had acquired on marriage. Richard ruled over his lands with a severity that brought him respect yet also aroused the resentment of the powerful barons he subjugated.

In 1173 Richard joined in a rebellion against his father instigated by his mother and elder brother Henry. Richard supposedly said of his family origins: "We came from the Devil, and to the Devil we will return." Not long after peace was restored with his father, Richard was fighting his brother Henry. Denied any estate of his own, Henry was envious of his brothers and when the barons of Aquitaine rebelled against Richard's harsh rule, he supported them. Henry died suddenly and the rebellion ended, leaving Richard with the claim to his father's kingdom.

Henry II refused to concede the power Richard believed he had the right to demand and when they met in 1188, with King Philip Augustus of France, Henry II declined to recognize Richard as the rightful heir. Richard then switched allegiance to his father's enemy, the king of France, and during the war that followed, Henry died in 1189 and Richard became king of England and Normandy. His coronation was marred by a massacre of Jews who wished to attend the ceremony, and the violence spread to York. Richard took steps to stop the attacks, for the Jews were a valuable source of funds and regarded as the king's private property.

Richard was tall and well proportioned, with blond hair and blue eyes. He proved himself a fearless soldier and possessed a keen understanding of issues and a gift of conversation. At the same time he was arrogant, devoid of compassion, and sunk in a **debauched** lifestyle sharply in contrast with the heroic image of "Lionheart." He was as tyrannical to his own family as he was **rapacious** to his subjects. His marriage to Berengaria of Navarre in 1191 was solely for its political expediency, for Richard was a homosexual.

Richard's interest in his new kingdom was largely financial, to obtain the funds he needed for an Anglo-French crusade to capture Jerusalem. Richard made victorious progress eastward, capturing Messina and Cyprus despite continual disputes with his French ally. The day after the capture of Acre in 1191, the two kings again quarreled as the French ruler, King Philip, accused Richard of trying to keep Cyprus for himself despite an agreement they had made to share their conquests. Richard replied: "The victory over the infidels in the Holy Land was indeed a joint endeavor but the conquest of Cyprus is no business of yours as I carried it off alone." After they captured Acre, Philip fell ill and returned to France, leaving Richard in charge. He was responsible for the massacre of twenty-seven hundred Muslim survivors of the garrison at Acre by having their throats cut. He moved his army down the coast and defeated Saladin's armies at the Battle of Arsuf. Richard was then able to enter Jaffa, which he fortified to give himself a strong base on the coast. His reputation was now at its highest and, as a result of his behavior on the battlefield, he was seen as the incarnation of the demon of war. However, by delaying in Jaffa, he gave Saladin the opportunity to reorganize and when he moved on his real goal, Jerusalem, his attacks were beaten off. Richard was only able to see the city from a distance but never entered it.

In 1192 Richard concluded a peace treaty with Saladin whereby the coastal cities were left in the hands of the Christians and the interior of the country remained with the Muslims; pilgrims were permitted to visit the holy sites. Richard set off to return to England. Bad weather forced his

debauched: morally corrupt.

rapacious: greedy; predatory.

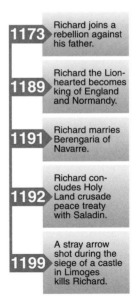

1173 Richard joins a rebellion against his father.

1189 Richard the Lionhearted becomes king of England and Normandy.

1191 Richard marries Berengaria of Navarre.

1192 Richard concludes Holy Land crusade peace treaty with Saladin.

1199 A stray arrow shot during the siege of a castle in Limoges kills Richard.

boat to call at Corfu. Fearing that he might be taken prisoner by the hostile Byzantines, he disguised himself as a Templar knight and traveled on a pirate boat headed for the north Adriatic. The boat was wrecked and, maintaining his disguise, he journeyed through the territories of his bitter enemy, Leopold, duke of Austria. Resting at an inn near Vienna, he was recognized and led before the duke, who imprisoned him. Three months later he was handed over to another enemy, the emperor Henry VI. He languished in prison for a year and was only released when his loyal subjects raised the huge ransom demanded after he gave the emperor an oath of vassaldom.

On his return, he found that his lands in England had been exposed to the intrigue of his brother John Lackland (the future King John). Richard's return to take over from John forms the background to the Robin Hood legend. Before long, Richard went to France where he spent the rest of his life at war with King Philip, defending his inheritance. A stray arrow shot by an archer during the siege of a castle in Limoges killed him. ◆

Riis, Jacob August

1849–1914 ● Journalist & Reformer

Jacob Riis was born on May 3, 1849, in Ribe, Denmark. He emigrated to New York City at the age of 21. He became famous as a reporter of conditions in American cities. Trained as a carpenter in Denmark, he had also helped his father turn out a small weekly newspaper. In New York, that experience landed him a newspaper job. In time, he secured work with the *New York Tribune* as a police reporter.

Riis reported on living conditions in New York slums and on the degrading lives that many poor people had to live in the big city. His work was so clear and so effective that he drew a great deal of local attention and helped bring about changes in the housing laws of New York City. This in turn gave him an audience in other cities in the country, and Riis was a spokesman for reforming urban conditions from the 1890s until his death. He was a great friend and supporter of Theodore Roosevelt, whose program for improving city life was in part a response to the conditions Riis exposed. Jacob Riis wrote several books that were important in his own day (*How the Other Half Lives*, published in 1890, and *Children of the Tenements*, published in 1903). His autobiography, *The Making of an American* (1901), was for many years a standard text used in many American high schools as an example of autobiography and of reform literature. ◆

Robinson, Jack Roosevelt (Jackie)

1919–1972 ● BASEBALL PLAYER & CIVIL RIGHTS ACTIVIST

Born in Georgia, the youngest of five children of share-crop farmers Jerry and Mallie Robinson, Jackie Robinson was raised in Pasadena, Calif., where the Robinson family confronted the West Coast variety of American racism. White neighbors tried to drive the family out of their home; segregation reigned in public and private facilities. Robinson became an outstanding athlete at Pasadena Junior College, before transferring to U.C.L.A. in 1940, where he won renown as the "Jim Thorpe of his race," the nation's finest all-around athlete. Robinson was an All-American football player, leading scorer in basketball, and record-setting broad jumper, in addition to his baseball exploits.

Drafted into the army in the spring of 1942 Robinson embarked on a stormy military career. Denied access to Officers' Candidate School, Robinson protested to heavy-

"I sit in my dining room and I look out through our picture window, and I look at the land that I have around and I think, had it not been for baseball, I couldn't have this."

Jackie Robinson,
1962

weight champion Joe Louis, who intervened with officials in Washington on Robinson's behalf. Once commissioned, Robinson fought for improved conditions for blacks at Camp Riley, Kansas, leading to his transfer to Fort Hood, Texas. At Fort Hood, Robinson was court-martialed and acquitted for refusing to move to the back of a bus. Robinson's army career demonstrated the proud, combative personality that would characterize his postwar life.

After his discharge from the army in 1944, Robinson signed to play with the Kansas City Monarchs of the Negro American League. After several months of discontent in the Jim Crow league, Robinson was approached by Branch Rickey of the Brooklyn Dodgers, who offered him the opportunity to become the first black player in major league baseball since the 1890s. Robinson gladly accepted the opportunity and responsibility of this pioneering role in "baseball's great experiment."

In 1946 Robinson joined the Montreal Royals of the International League, the top farm club in the Dodger system. Following a spectacular debut in which he stroked four hits including a three-run home run, Robinson proceeded to lead the league with a .349 batting average. An immediate fan favorite, Robinson enabled the Royals to set new attendance records while winning the International League and Little World Series championships. Robinson's imminent promotion to the Dodgers in 1947 triggered an unsuccessful petition drive on the part of southern players to keep him off the team. In the early months of the season, beanballs, death threats, and rumors of a strike by opposing players swirled about Robinson. Through it all, Robinson paraded his excellence. An electrifying fielder and baserunner as well as an outstanding hitter, Robinson's assault on baseball's color line captured the imagination of both black and white Americans. He batted .297 and won the Rookie of the Year Award en route to leading the Dodgers to the pennant.

Over the next decade Robinson emerged as one of the most dominant players and foremost gate attractions in the history of the major leagues. In 1949 he batted .342 and won the National League Most Valuable Player Award. During his ten years with the Dodgers the team won six pennants and one World Championship. Upon his retirement in 1956

Robinson had compiled a .311 lifetime batting average. He was elected to the Baseball Hall of Fame on the first ballot in 1961.

But Robinson's significance transcended his achievements on the baseball diamond. He became a leading symbol and spokesperson of the postwar integration crusade, both within baseball and in broader society. During his early years in Montreal and Brooklyn, Robinson had adhered to his promise to Branch Rickey to "turn the other cheek" and avoid controversies. After establishing himself in the major leagues, however, Robinson's more combative and outspoken personality reasserted itself. Robinson repeatedly pressed for baseball to desegregate more rapidly and to remove discriminatory barriers in Florida training camps and cities like St. Louis and Cincinnati. He also demanded opportunities for black players to become coaches, managers, and front office personnel. Baseball officials and many sportswriters branded Robinson an ingrate as controversies marked his career.

Upon retirement Robinson remained in the public eye. He continued to voice his opinions as speaker, newspaper columnist, and fundraiser for the NAACP. A believer in "black capitalism" through which blacks could "become producers, manufacturers, developers and creators of businesses, providers of jobs," Robinson engaged in many successful business ventures in the black community. He became an executive in the Chock Full O' Nuts restaurant chain and later helped develop Harlem's Freedom National Bank and the Jackie Robinson Construction Company. Robinson also became active in Republican Party politics, supporting Richard Nixon in 1960, and working closely with New York governor Nelson Rockefeller, who appointed him Special Assistant for Community Affairs in 1966. These activities brought criticism from young black militants in the late 1960s. Ironically, at this same time Robinson had also parted ways with the NAACP, criticizing its failure to include "younger, more progressive voices."

By the late 1960s Robinson had become "bitterly disillusioned" with both baseball and American society. He refused to attend baseball events in protest of the failure to hire blacks in nonplaying capacities. In his 1972 autobiography, *I Never Had It Made*, he attacked the nation's waning commitment to racial equality. Later that year the commemoration of

1940 Robinson enters UCLA.

1942 Robinson joins the military.

1944 Robinson begins play in the Negro American League.

1947 Robinson joins the Dodgers; becomes Rookie of the Year.

1949 Robinson is named the National League Most Valuable Player.

1956 Robinson retires from professional baseball.

1961 Robinson is elected to the Baseball Hall of Fame.

1972 Robinson publishes his autobiography *I Never Had It Made.*

his major league debut led him to lift his boycott of baseball games. "I'd like to live to see a black manager," he told a nationwide television audience at the World Series on October 15, 1972. Nine days later he died of a heart attack. ◆

Romero, Oscar Arnulfo

1917–1980 ● EL SALVADOR HUMAN RIGHTS ACTIVIST

Born in Ciudad Barrios and originally apprenticed as a carpenter, Oscar Arnulfo Romero's early religious inclinations won him over and in 1931 he enrolled in San Miguel seminary. In 1937 he progressed to the National Seminary, then proceeded to Rome to study at the Gregorian University. He was ordained in 1942 and began a doctorate in ascetic theology, but World War II curtailed his studies. He returned to El Salvador and served his home parish until he was elevated to monsignor in 1967. Shortly thereafter, Romero was appointed to the National Bishops' Conference and quickly earned additional responsibilities, including auxiliary bishop (1970), editor of the archdiocesan newspaper *Orientación* (1971), bishop of Santiago de María (1974), and membership on the Pontifical Commission for Latin America

(1975). Even at this late date, Romero still clung to a moderate, traditional interpretation of Catholic doctrines. He warned against the dangers of a politicized priesthood and instead advocated the higher ideals of brotherhood, faith, and charity. Although he frequently quoted the teachings of the Second Vatican Council, he refrained from mentioning those of the more radical conference of Catholic bishops at Medellín in 1968.

To the surprise of many, Romero was chosen over the equally qualified Arturo Rivera y Damas as archbishop of El Salvador in February 1977. The shy, retiring new archbishop faced growing tensions between church and state, and within the church itself. Shortly after his installation, Romero's close friend Father Rutilio Grande was murdered on his way to visit parishioners. When the government failed to investigate and instead stepped up its attacks on the church by expelling several priests, Archbishop Romero withdrew his support for the government and refused to attend the presidential inauguration of Carlos Humberto Romero (no relation) in 1977. Despite the rising tide of violence, Romero still tried to distance the church from the new liberation theology and denied the priests permission to participate in political organizations. As the situation deteriorated, Romero's position became untenable and the moderate archbishop metamorphosed into an impassioned crusader against the violation of human rights in El Salvador. He used his sermons to preach the equality and dignity of all peoples and set up a commission to monitor and document the abuses of power by governmental authorities.

For Romero's efforts the British Parliament nominated him for the Nobel Peace Prize. In February 1980 Romero angered the Vatican by speaking out against U.S. military aid to El Salvador, which he claimed would lead to further human rights abuses. On 24 March he was assassinated while saying evening mass. His death removed a powerful voice for peace in El Salvador and contributed to the bitterness of the struggle. Archbishop Romero remains a powerful symbol of the new direction of the Catholic Church in Latin America. ◆

1942 Romero is ordained a priest.

1967 Romero is promoted to monsignor.

1971 Romero becomes editor of the *Orientacion*.

1977 Romero is chosen archbishop of El Salvador.

1980 Romero is assassinated while saying evening mass.

Roosevelt, Eleanor

1884–1962 ● WOMEN'S RIGHTS ACTIVIST

> *"No one can make you feel inferior without your consent."*
>
> Eleanor Roosevelt, 1960

1905 Eleanor marries Franklin Delano Roosevelt.

1918 Mrs. Roosevelt discovers her husband's affair with Lucy Mercer.

1921 Franklin D. Roosevelt becomes paralyzed from polio.

1928 Eleanor Roosevelt heads the women's division of the national Democratic committee.

1936 Eleanor Roosevelt begins writing a syndicated newspaper column.

Born into a branch of the prominent Roosevelt family (she was Theodore Roosevelt's niece), Anna Eleanor Roosevelt experienced an unhappy childhood, a formative education abroad, and a brief stint teaching in a social settlement in New York City before marrying her third cousin Franklin D. Roosevelt in 1905. She devoted the following years to domesticity, bearing six children (five of whom lived), and supporting her husband's career. Her discovery in 1918 of his affair with her social secretary, Lucy Mercer, altered her domestic priorities. Thereafter, her marriage became a "business partnership," and she sought emotional sustenance primarily among a circle of women political friends.

In 1921, Franklin became paralyzed from poliomyelitis. At the urging of Louis Howe, Franklin's mentor and campaign manager, Eleanor Roosevelt joined New York women's political and advocacy groups, ostensibly to keep Franklin's name before the public. The leadership positions she attained in these groups not only brought her new friends but enabled her to pursue important reform issues such as unionization and protective legislation for women. In 1928, during Alfred E. Smith's presidential campaign, she headed the women's division of the national Democratic committee. These experiences influenced the evolution of her political views and honed her speaking, writing, and organizational skills.

As the president's wife, Eleanor Roosevelt represented the views of reformers to White House administrators, influenced federal appointments of women, and made certain that New Deal programs included women. In 1936 she began a syndicated newspaper column, "My Day," that reported on her travels to gather support for New Deal programs and collect information for the president. She also went on paid lecture tours.

Some of her activities drew criticism. Called a "busybody," she was told that a proper First Lady should confine herself to White House ceremonial functions. Criticism mounted when she invested her earnings in "Arthurdale," a subsistence homestead scheme for West Virginia miners, and when she took unpopular stands for free speech or against racial discrimination. During World War II, she served as codirector of the Office of Civilian Defense but resigned when the social-service programs she devised were ridiculed. Her travels on the president's behalf to bring comfort to troops were more appreciated although still censured for being costly. Criticism upset her, but it did not deter her public activities. Within the limits imposed bv her marital status, she was the most independent, activist of all First Ladies.

The Widow's Mandate

When Kansas Republican Nancy Landon Kassebaum was elected to the United States Senate in 1978, she became the first woman elected to a full term in the United States Senate who did not succeed her husband in either the Senate or House of Representatives. Originally, women were often appointed to fill Senate and House vacancies created by the death of their husbands, a practice known as "widow's mandate." In some cases, these widows led illustrious political careers of their own, at times outshining the husbands who had preceded them. Edith Nourse Rogers, a Republican from Massachusetts, became a representative as a result of her husband's death in 1925, and she remained a distinguished member of Congress until her death in 1960. Margaret Chase Smith, who also succeeded her husband in the House, rose to win election to the Senate, where she became one of the country's most influential senators. As these woman gained greater political clout, more women were elected on the basis of their own credentials and policy platforms.

After Franklin Roosevelt's death, President Harry S. Truman appointed her a delegate to the United Nations. She helped defeat Soviet delegate Andrei Vishinsky's position on refugee **repatriation** and later led the struggle to hammer out the Universal Declaration of Human Rights. When Dwight D. Eisenhower became president, she resigned but remained politically active: she helped form Americans for Democratic Action, opposed Senator Joseph McCarthy's anticommunist witch-hunts, supported presidential candidate Adlai E. Stevenson, and represented the American Association for the United Nations. President John F. Kennedy appointed her chair of his Commission on the Status of Women. Although she died before it completed its work, her role as chair provided fitting closure to a life that had been committed so fully to women's and other social concerns. ◆

repatriation: the act of restoring citizenship or returning to country of origin.

Roosevelt, Franklin Delano

1882–1945 ● PRESIDENT OF THE UNITED STATES

"*I pledge you, I pledge myself, to a new deal for the American people.*"

Franklin Delano Roosevelt, accepting Democratic nomination for president, 1922

Franklin D. Roosevelt—whose presidency saw America through the Great Depression and almost to the end of World War II—formed, with his wife Eleanor, an effective husband-wife team. Third cousins from the well-to-do, patrician Roosevelt family, they were both extremely energetic, educated in schools that stressed the idea of public service, and strongly influenced by the political career and exhortations of Eleanor's uncle President Theodore Roosevelt. However, Franklin Roosevelt's secure and indulged upbringing left him self-confident, frivolous, and convinced that his charm could overcome any opposition. Eleanor's grim childhood, separated from the weak, alcoholic father she adored and neglected by her guardian maternal grandmother, left her feeling shy, awkward, and unloved. At Harvard

University, Roosevelt neglected his studies for socializing and work on the college newspaper.

Roosevelt went to Columbia Law School and afterwards worked for years in a New York law firm, but his real interest lay in politics. The Democratic party nominated him for state senator because it believed that the Roosevelt name would make him a creditable and prestigious candidate; however, they were so sure he would lose the 1910 election that they refused to help with his campaign expenses, a disadvantage he turned into an asset in his campaign speeches: "I accept nomination with absolute independence. I am pledged to no man. If elected, I will give my entire time to serving the people of this district." He was elected.

Roosevelt's successful rebellion against the notoriously corrupt New York State Democratic party machinery (Tammany Hall) made his name known throughout the United States. Tammany Hall opposition was not able to prevent his reelection in 1912, but it did succeed in blocking his nomination for the U.S. Senate in 1914. His efforts in Woodrow Wilson's 1912 campaign for the presidency of the United States, however, were rewarded by an appointment as assistant secretary of the navy—a position he held throughout World War I.

In their personal life, Eleanor and Franklin moved apart, especially when she discovered his relationship with her social secretary. He rejected Eleanor's offer of a divorce and they rebuilt their marriage. Eleanor spent the next few years in a state of depression and deep unhappiness, about which she later wrote: "There are times in everyone's life when the wish to be done with the burdens and even the decisions of this life seem overwhelming." Roosevelt gained a reputation as one of the most promising young politicians in Washington. He was nominated for vice president in 1920 and regarded his defeat in the elections as just a temporary setback to his career. He accepted a position in a New York bank while awaiting the 1924 elections.

In 1921 Roosevelt contracted polio and spent the next seven years fighting spiritedly to regain his health ("I spent two years lying in bed trying to move my big toe"). His mother wanted to coddle him into invalidism, but his wife was sure that the only way he could overcome his illness was to live as normal and full a life as possible, and for Roosevelt this meant

1910 Roosevelt takes on New York's corrupt Tammany Hall Democrats.

1912 President Wilson appoints Roosevelt assistant secretary of the navy.

1921 Roosevelt contracts polio and loses use of his legs.

1928 Roosevelt wins governorship of New York.

1932 Elected the 32nd president, Roosevelt immediately launches New Deal reforms.

1940 Roosevelt is re-elected to an unprecedented third term.

1941 United States enters World War II after Japan's attack on Pearl Harbor.

1944 Roosevelt re-elected to fourth term.

1945 Roosevelt dies one month before German surrender.

maintaining an interest in politics. He never regained the use of his legs and spent much of his life in a wheelchair. Convinced that his welfare depended on it, Eleanor finally threw off his mother's domination. She became her husband's political representative, bringing him information, attending meetings, and preventing him from sinking into political obscurity. Her involvement in promoting the role of women in politics had been growing steadily since 1918, but it was only after Roosevelt became ill that she really began to emerge as a political figure.

By the time he won the governorship of New York in 1928, his battle against polio had matured Roosevelt, broadening his vision and deepening his understanding and compassion. Roosevelt's efforts to alleviate the Depression in New York—aiding the state economy and creating the first state relief agency—helped him win the Democratic presidential nomination in 1932. He accepted the nomination with words that named his plan for ending the Depression: "I pledge you, I pledge myself, to a new deal for the American people." Roosevelt expressed his confidence that the Depression could be beaten in his inaugural speech: "All we have to fear is fear itself."

Franklin Delano Roosevelt Memorial

After some forty years of delays over its financing and design, the Franklin Delano Roosevelt Memorial, a tribute to the thirty-second president of the United States, was dedicated on May 2, 1997. Built at a cost of $48 million, it lies in Washington, D.C.'s West Potomac Park, beside the Tidal Basin. Unlike the soaring Washington Monument and the massive Jefferson and Lincoln Memorials—the other three presidential structures on the National Mall—the FDR Memorial is a dispersed, 7.5-acre landscape of sculptures, granite walls, bronze bas-relief, inscriptions, waterfalls, and plants. Visitors walking through the grounds find an artistically rendered history of the Roosevelt presidency over its four terms, from 1933 to 1945. The Memorial's designer was Lawrence Halprin. It has been surrounded by political controversy: antismoking activists blocked the depiction of Roosevelt with his trademark cigarette holder; animal rights activists managed to veto the addition of a fox fur to a statue of Roosevelt's wife, Eleanor, although she customarily wore one; and both before and after the Memorial's dedication, controversy swirled over the demand of some disabled persons that a statue of Roosevelt in a wheelchair be added, although Roosevelt had gone to great lengths to hide his polio-induced infirmity.

Roosevelt started his New Deal reforms immediately. Both Democrats and Republicans were shaken by the country's condition and willing to follow his lead. A special session of Congress passed most of his bills into law as fast as they were presented, forging most of the legal basis for the New Deal reforms in the first hundred days of his presidency. The New Deal's goal was first to end the Depression and then to reform the economic system so that another depression could not occur. Roosevelt first closed all banks, then allowed only sound banks to reopen, and finally reformed the banking system itself with the Federal Reserve Act. The New Deal's attempt to reform every aspect of the American economy had mixed results. It did, however, bring about an immediate rise in prices, increase in business, and lessening of unemployment.

The first part of Roosevelt's second term was spent countering opposition to the New Deal. After Japan's 1937 invasion of China, his attention was increasingly diverted to international affairs. He could not openly oppose the strong isolationist sentiment prevalent in America, but he tried to prepare the country for the war he considered inevitable

Reelected for an unprecedented third term in 1940, Roosevelt convinced Congress to approve the Lend-Lease Act providing Great Britain with equipment on a "buy now, pay later" basis and issued the Atlantic Charter jointly with Winston Churchill. The Japanese attack on Pearl Harbor in December 1941 ended opposition to American involvement in the war.

Roosevelt was involved in planning strategy, developing and maintaining relations with the Allies, and trying to shape the postwar world. He appointed of Dwight D. Eisenhower as supreme commander of the Allied forces, favored the Allied policy of demanding unconditional surrender from the Axis, and participated in conferences with Churchill and Stalin to plan the war and the postwar world.

Eleanor's contribution was considerable. Her image as a genuinely caring mother figure involved in day-to-day matters, extending a helping hand to anyone in need was the perfect counterbalance to Roosevelt's amiable, fatherly, but more distant image. She provided an unofficial channel through which his attention could be drawn to any subject (if she considered it necessary), preventing his staff from sealing him off

"Human kindness has never weakened the stamina or softened the fiber of a free people. A nation does not have to be cruel to be tough."

Franklin Delano Roosevelt, 1940

from the world. She went on tours of inspection and good will missions and tried to keep New Deal reforms from being totally disregarded because of wartime exigencies. Although she trusted his political judgment and leadership, she did not hesitate to criticize him in private if she felt his actions were ethically wrong or that he was making concessions on important principles because of tiredness, impatience, or expediency. Despite their public partnership, however, they tended to lead separate lives.

Eleanor's sense of duty shaped her reaction to Roosevelt's running for president a fourth time in 1944. Once she was convinced that the Republican candidate could not cope with the demands of the presidency she supported her husband's decision to accept the nomination, well aware of what it might cost him; he was reelected. Hindsight blames exhaustion and ill-health for the many concessions he made to Stalin at their last conference, in Yalta, in 1945. However, at the time he was sure that Stalin's agreement to fight against Japan made it worthwhile. His health was failing, and he died two months after Yalta—and one month before Germany surrendered.

After Roosevelt's death Eleanor continued and even intensified her public career. She was a delegate to the United Nations and, as chairman of the UN Commission on Human Rights, tirelessly traveled the world. She wrote three autobiographical works, *This Is My Story* (1937), *This I Remember* (1949), and *On My Own* (1958). ◆

Roosevelt, Theodore

1858–1919 ● PRESIDENT OF THE UNITED STATES

Theodore Roosevelt was popularly known as "Teddy," a name he disliked and forbade his intimates to use. He was the only president to have been born in New York City. As a youngster, Theodore Roosevelt suffered from asthma and had poor eyesight. Through sheer determination, he

"There is a homely adage which runs, 'Speak softly and carry a big stick; you will go far.' "
Theodore Roosevelt, 1900

Theodore Roosevelt.

worked to improve his physical condition, exercising and teaching himself to box, ride, and shoot.

Born into an affluent family, Roosevelt was educated by private tutors and traveled extensively, broadening his experiences and expanding his knowledge. He entered Harvard and graduated in 1880. In his senior year he began work on a book entitled *The Naval War in 1812*, which was published in 1882 and enthusiastically received.

After graduation, he enrolled in Columbia University Law School but quickly discovered that he was more interested in history and politics than in law and dropped the idea of a legal career. He ran for and was elected to the New York state assembly where he served from 1882 to 1884. During those two years he demonstrated admirable leadership ability, which won him a place as delegate-at-large to the Republican national convention held in Chicago. In 1886 he ran for mayor of New York City but finished third.

In 1888 Roosevelt supported the winning presidential ticket and as a result was appointed in 1889 to the U.S. Civil Service Commission, which he headed for the next six years. During his tenure, he uncovered corruption, fraud, and discrimination against women, and instituted reforms. He also wrote several books on his philosophies of good government.

After the election of William McKinley in 1896, Roosevelt was appointed assistant secretary of the navy. With the outbreak of the Spanish-American War in 1898, he resigned from the cabinet and together with Leonard Wood, organized the first volunteer cavalry regiment, later known as the Rough Riders. Roosevelt led his cavalry up Kettle Hill in the battle of San Juan, winning promotion to the rank of colonel. He was popular with his troops and concerned for their welfare. The men, in turn, helped him in his political endeavors and when Roosevelt ran for governor of New York, his men escorted him up and down the state campaigning on his behalf; he won, albeit by a narrow margin.

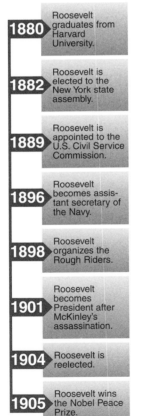

Roosevelt and Thomas Collier Platt, the Republican party boss, did not see eye to eye on many political issues. Despite strong opposition from Platt, Roosevelt did well as governor. He was able to tax corporation franchises and put through much practical reform, including a bill to outlaw racial prejudice in public schools. After two years in office, Platt wanted Roosevelt out of state government and talked him into running for vice president under McKinley.

Roosevelt was a hard campaigner, and he and McKinley won handily. On September 14, 1901, six months into his second term, McKinley was assassinated and Roosevelt became president. At the age of forty-two, he was the youngest man to serve in that position.

Upon assuming office, Roosevelt pledged to continue McKinley's policies. He soon discovered that there were newer philosophies being generated from abroad. Younger men like Robert M. La Follette were leading the crusade for reform in government. Even though Roosevelt kept the McKinley cabinet intact during his first term, he brought a new vitality to the office and changed many of the methods practiced in the White House.

Roosevelt turned over much of the official paper work to his subordinates while he concentrated on bringing dignity and formality to life in the White House. With his so-called tennis cabinet, he took part in games, rides, and hikes. Through these contacts, Roosevelt learned the inner workings of government and how to speed up the legislative process. He was the first president to use his office to fight the abuses of big business. He established the Bureau of Corporations, which had the power to inspect the books of businessmen engaged in interstate commerce. Using a revived Sherman Antitrust Act, he and his administration were able to sue forty-three major corporations in antitrust actions. He also intervened in the coal miners' strike, supporting the unions and infuriating their bosses. He referred to the above actions against industry and indirectly for labor as a "square deal."

Roosevelt reversed his hawkish approach to foreign affairs but maintained his support of a strong America and turned the country into a world naval power. In 1904, with Charles W. Fairbanks as his running mate, he was reelected by over two and a half million votes and by a margin of 336 to 140 in the Electoral College. His popularity with the people did not carry over to Congress, with whom he was constantly at odds. He said, "Congress does from one-third to a half of what I think is the minimum it ought to do."

Roosevelt's foreign-affairs philosophy as articulated in his statement, "Speak softly and carry a big stick," and "Don't hit at all if it is honorably possible to avoid hitting, but never hit softly," resulted in the acquisition of the Panama Canal Zone. His intervention in the Russo-Japanese War in 1905 won him the Nobel Peace Prize. His internal affairs policy was carried out through a series of quick administrative changes. He was a pioneer conservationist, concerned with soil and water, the preservation of wildernesses, and the establishment of national parks. He was consistently opposed by Congress and criticized by the press. The scope and depth of his interests and involvement, however, were recognized and it was said that no president since Thomas Jefferson had ranged his mind over so broad a field. Roosevelt coined such phrases as "lunatic fringe," "muckrakers," and "my hat is in the ring." Roosevelt supported William Howard Taft as his successor in 1908 and received a positive reaction from the public.

When Roosevelt left the presidency he was only fifty. He spent time big-game hunting and touring Europe. In 1912 he challenged Taft's presidential renomination but the party

> *"Power undirected by high purpose spells calamity; and high purpose by itself is utterly useless if the power to put it into effect is lacking."*
>
> Theodore Roosevelt, 1911

"No man is above the law and no man is below it; nor do we ask any man's permission when we require him to obey it."

Theodore
Roosevelt, 1904

bosses supported Taft, and so Roosevelt founded the Progressive party, which split the Republican vote and ensured the election of the Democrat candidate, Woodrow Wilson. Shortly before the election Roosevelt survived an assassination attempt—the bullet lodged in his chest—by an assailant who was declared insane. After the election he went exploring in the Brazilian jungle and won a libel suit against an article accusing him of excessive drinking. From the outbreak of World War I, he advocated the immediate entry of the United States into the war on the side of the Allies. His request to lead a volunteer division was refused and his son was killed on the battlefield. ◆

San Martin, José de

1778–1850 ● ARGENTINIAN SOLDIER & LIBERATOR

Born in Yapeyu in northern Argentina, where his father was a prominent official in the Spanish colonial administration, José de San Martin received a military education in Madrid, Spain, to where his family returned when he was six years old. In 1793 he was commissioned as a second lieutenant, rising to the rank of lieutenant colonel by 1808. During this period he saw action on the Portuguese frontier, against the British (by whom he was held captive for over a year from 1798), and in the Peninsular War, in which he served the British-backed Spanish guerilla forces opposing Napoleon Bonaparte's rule in Spain.

In 1812 San Martin resigned his commission and, after getting permission to travel to the Peruvian city of Lima—which was the center of Spanish power in South America—went instead to Buenos Aires, where he offered his services to the revolutionary government in Argentina, then threatened by Spanish royalist forces. His sudden switch to opposition to Spain, which he had served loyally for nearly twenty years, may in part be attributed to the persistent prejudice he experienced from peninsular Spaniards, who looked down on anyone who had been born in the colonies. It has been suggested that he was recruited by British sympathizers to the cause of Latin American independence; his own explanation was that he could no longer be indifferent to the call of his native land.

San Martin decided that the only way to liberate Argentina from the Spanish threat was in the context of a continental liberation plan that involved attacking Spain in

> Widely revered in the land of his birth, San Martin is hailed as the "Liberator of the South."

José de San Martin.

her Peruvian stronghold. To this end, he took his forces north, defeating the Spanish at San Lorenzo on the Parana River in 1813. The following year he was promoted to the rank of general and appointed commander of the army of Upper Peru, which had suffered a series of defeats at the hands of the Spanish on the Bolivian plateau.

In order to lay the foundations for his bid to conquer Peru, San Martin now feigned ill-health in order to justify ceasing the abortive campaign in which he was engaged, and had himself elected military governor of Cuyo, a district of northern Argentina. There, he spent three years developing his audacious and original plan to invade Chile and advance north towards Lima by sea, and drilled his soldiers into a force capable of such an ambitious venture. His task was made harder by the rout of the nationalist forces in Chile, with whom he had hoped to link up, and his army had to fight their way across the Andes. Their victory at the Maipo River in 1817 signaled the end of Spanish power in Chile.

Declining the Chilean presidency in favor of his lieutenant, Bernardo O'Higgins, San Martín set about creating the navy he needed to approach close enough to Lima for the final land-based attack. In 1820 his motley fleet of armed merchant ships set sail from Valparaiso with 4,500 soldiers on board. Disembarking at Parasian, his forces soon occupied the coast to within 150 miles south of Lima and roundly defeated the royalists at the Battle of Pisco, capturing the Spanish general and most of his artillery. San Martín rejected any terms that did not concede absolute independence and, when the royalists in Lima finally despaired of assistance from the Spanish king, was able to occupy the city virtually unopposed. Peruvian independence was declared on July 22, 1821, and San Martín was installed as "protector." In this capacity, he expelled the majority of Spaniards and introduced a number of liberal reforms, which included ending the exploitation of native Indian labor, abolishing slavery, and creating a system of annual redemptions of quotas of living slaves.

San Martín's political career ended abruptly after his secret meeting with Simón Bolívar, the liberator of northern Latin America, in 1822. They met at Guayaquil, which Bolívar had annexed despite San Martín's hope that it would opt for incorporation into Peru. The substance of their discussion remains the subject of speculation, but shortly thereafter San Martín resigned his protectorship and military command and returned to Argentina. First and foremost a military man, he had been unprepared for handling such problems as his own officers' suspicions that he had dictatorial or even monarchical ambitions, or his uncertainty that the Peruvian people would remain loyal to the new order. In 1824 he sailed for Europe, thereby distancing himself from the chaos that followed Latin American independence; he remained in self-imposed exile until his death in Boulogne, France. In 1880 his remains were removed and reinterred in the cathedral in Buenos Aires.

Widely revered in the land of his birth, where he is hailed as the "Liberator of the South," San Martín evinced a dedication to continent-wide independence, and was in favor of a centralized constitutional monarchy for Latin America. As a military leader, he exhibited outstanding ability in training and motivating his forces, while his feat in leading his men across the Andes has led to comparisons with Hannibal and Napoleon. ◆

1793 San Martín is commissioned as a second lieutenant.

1798 San Martín is captured by the British.

1812 San Martín resigns his commission.

1813 San Martín defeats the Spanish at San Lorenzo.

1821 San Martín becomes protector of Peru.

1822 San Martín resigns his protectorship after meeting with Simón Bolívar.

1824 San Martín leaves South America for Europe.

Schindler, Oskar

1908–1974 ● PROTECTOR OF JEWS
DURING WORLD WAR II

Schindler was born in Svitavy (Ger., Zwittau), in the Sudetenland, and came to Kraków in late 1939, in the wake of the German invasion of Poland. There he took over two previously Jewish-owned firms dealing with the manufacture and wholesale distribution of enamel kitchenware products, one of which he operated as a trustee (*Treuhänder*) for the German occupation administration.

Schindler then established his own enamel works in Zablocie, outside Kraków, in which he employed mainly Jewish workers, thereby protecting them from deportations. When the liquidation of the Kraków ghetto began in early 1943, many Jews were sent to the Plaszów labor camp, noted for the brutality of its commandant, Amon Goeth. Schindler used his good connections with high German officials in the Armaments Administration to set up a branch of the Plaszów camp in his factory compound for some nine hundred Jewish workers, including persons unfit and unqualified for the labor production needs. In this way he spared them from the horrors of the Plaszów camp.

In October 1944, with the approach of the Russian army, Schindler was granted permission to reestablish his now-defunct firm as an armaments production company in Brünnlitz (Brnenc, Sudetenland) and take with him the Jewish workers from Zablocie. In an operation unique in the annals of Nazi-occupied Europe, he succeeded in transferring to Brünnlitz some seven hundred to eight hundred Jewish men from the Grossrosen camp, and some three hundred Jewish women from Auschwitz. In Brünnlitz, the eleven hundred Jews were given the most humane treatment possible under the circumstances: food, medical care, and religious needs. Informed that a train with evacuated Jewish detainees from the Goleszow camp was stranded at nearby Svitavy, Schindler received permission to take workers to the Svitavy railway station. There, they forced the ice-sealed train doors open and removed some one hundred Jewish men and women, nearly frozen and resembling corpses, who were then

1939 — After German invasion of Poland, Schindler takes over two Jewish-owned firms.

1943 — Schindler employs Jewish workers, protecting them from death camps.

1944 — Schindler engineers transfer of 1,100 Jews to his armaments company.

1962 — Schindler plants a tree in the Garden of the Righteous in Jerusalem.

swiftly taken to the Brünnlitz factory and nourished back to life, an undertaking to which Schindler's wife, Emilie, particularly devoted herself. Those whom it was too late to save were buried with proper Jewish rites.

Schindler was devoted to the humane treatment of his Jewish workers and to their physical and psychological needs. He used his good connections with the Abwehr and with friends in high government positions, as well as his jovial and good-humored disposition, to befriend and ingratiate himself with high-ranking SS commanders in Poland. This stood him in good stead when he needed their assistance in extracting valuable and crucial favors from them, such as **ameliorating** conditions and **mitigating** punishments of Jews under his care. He was imprisoned on several occasions when the Gestapo accused him of corruption, only to be released on the intervention of his connections in Berlin ministries.

In 1962, Oskar Schindler planted a tree bearing his name in the Garden of the Righteous at Yad Vashem, Jerusalem. ◆

Oskar Schindler speaks about saving lives during the Holocaust of Germany's Third Reich at an interview, 1963.

ameliorate: to improve.

mitigate: to make less severe.

Schmid, Anton

1900–1942 ● GERMAN SOLDIER WHO
RESCUED JEWS DURING WORLD WAR II

Shocked by the brutalities of the mass killings at Ponary, Schmid decided in late 1941 to do whatever he could to help Jews survive.

A sergeant in the Wehrmacht, stationed in Vilna, Anton Schmid was responsible for collecting straggling German soldiers near the railway station and reassigning them to new units. A large group of Jews from the Vilna ghetto were assigned to different labor duties in Schmid's outfit: upholstering, tailoring, locksmithing, and shoe mending. He gained their affection and confidence. Shocked by the brutalities of the mass killings at Ponary, Schmid decided in late 1941 to do whatever he could to help Jews survive. He managed to release Jews incarcerated in the notorious Lakishki jail, rescued Jews in various ways, and surreptitiously supplied food and provisions to Jews inside the ghetto. In three houses in Vilna under his supervision, Jews were hidden in the cellars during Nazi-staged *Aktionen*. Schmid also became personally involved with leading figures in the Jewish underground, such as Mordecai Tenenbaum (Tamaroff), and cooperated with them. He helped some of them reach Warsaw and Bialystok (to report on the mass killings at Ponary) by transporting them over long distances in his truck. Some of these underground operatives met, planned activities, and slept in his home. He sent other Jews to ghettos that were relatively more secure at that time, those of Voronovo, Lida, and Grodno.

The circumstances of Schmid's arrest are still shrouded in mystery. It was later learned that he was arrested in January 1942 and was sentenced to death by a military tribunal. He was executed on April 13 of that year and was buried in a Vilna cemetery. In 1964, Schmid was posthumously recognized by Yad Vashem as a "Righteous Among the Nations." ◆

Schwarzkopf, Norman

1934–PRESENT ● MILITARY LEADER

> *"It doesn't take a hero to order men into battle. It takes a hero to be one of those men who go into battle."*
>
> Norman Schwarzkopf,
> *It Doesn't Take a Hero*, 1992

Schwarzkopf led the coalition of international military forces that liberated Kuwait from Iraqi occupation in the Gulf War of 1991. As a result of his success in this war, Schwarzkopf, nicknamed "Stormin' Norman," became one of the most popular American military leaders since Dwight D. Eisenhower.

Schwarzkopf was born on August 22, 1934, in Trenton, New Jersey. His father was General Herbert Norman Schwarzkopf, who had attended West Point and served during World Wars I and II. The elder Schwartzkopf gained national prominence in the 1930s when, as head of the New Jersey State Police, he led the investigation of the kidnapping of Charles Lindbergh's baby.

When Norman Schwarzkopf was a child, his family lived briefly in Iran, where his father had been sent to train Iran's police force. The family also lived in Switzerland, Germany, and Italy, where young Norman learned to speak French and German. Back in the United States, ten-year-old Norman enrolled in the Bordentown Military Institute. He later attended Valley Forge Military Academy. In 1952, Schwarzkopf began studies at the United States Military Academy at West Point. He graduated in 1956 with a bachelor of science degree in mechanical engineering. Upon gradu-

Schwarzkopf was shocked at the degree of public hostility to the Vietnam War.

ation, he was commissioned a 2nd Lieutenant in the United States Army and was assigned as platoon leader and executive officer to the 2nd Airborne Battle Group at Fort Benning, Georgia. His next assignments were with the 101st Airborne in Kentucky and the 6th Infantry in West Germany.

In 1964 Schwartzkopf earned a master's degree in guided missile engineering from the University of Southern California. He returned to West Point the next year to teach engineering, but soon left for Vietnam on the first of two tours during the Vietnam War. In Vietnam, Schwarzkopf served as Task Force Advisor to a South Vietnamese Airborne Division. At the end of this tour, he returned to his teaching post at West Point. In 1968, Schwarzkopf was promoted to Lieutenant Colonel. That same year, he married Brenda Holsinger, with whom he later had three children.

Colonel Schwarzkopf left for a second tour in Vietnam in 1969, this time serving as a battalion commander. Before this tour ended, he had been wounded twice and had earned three Silver Stars. He returned to the United State in 1971, wearing a cast from his hip to his shoulder. Following his recovery, the army directed Schwarzkopf to address civilian groups about the war in Vietnam. During these speaking engagements, Schwarzkopf was shocked at the degree of public hostility he encountered to the Vietnam War and toward the

The Purple Heart

The Purple Heart is the oldest military decoration in the United States and has a history as varied as the country itself. In 1782, George Washington instituted the Badge of Military Merit for "whenever any singularly meritorious action is performed." This Badge was the first available to enlisted personnel. Only three such awards were given, however, and the medal quickly fell into oblivion. The award was revived in 1932, through the efforts of then-Army Chief of Staff Douglas MacArthur. This new medal, designed by Elizabeth Will and widely regarded as one of the world's most beautiful government medals, was intended for army personnel wounded or killed in enemy action, including officers. In 1942, Franklin D. Roosevelt expanded the medal beyond the Army to apply to all branches of military service. Under later presidents, the medal was retroactively awarded to armed forces personnel or civilians killed or wounded in WWI or WWII. More recently, in 1984, Ronald Reagan, responding to the Beirut Marine bombing of October 1983, expanded the medal to include those wounded or killed in international terrorist attacks.

United States military. He was forced to reevaluate United States military strategy in Vietnam and he came to believe that public support and a clear strategy were essential to victory in any military operation.

During the 1970s and 1980s, Schwarzkopf rose steadily through the military ranks. During this period he served in administrative posts in Washington D.C., and various command assignments with mechanized infantry divisions in the United States and in Germany. In 1982, he was awarded his first star and became a brigadier general. The following year, a coup occurred in the tiny island nation of Grenada. Neighboring Caribbean countries voted to intervene militarily and appealed to the United States, Jamaica, and Barbados for support. Fearing that Grenadan revolutionaries would help supply rebels in Central America and that Americans living on the island would be taken hostage, President Ronald Reagan authorized the commitment of 6,000 troops from the United States and an invasion was planned. Although the Grenada invasion was largely an amphibious naval operation, General Schwartzkopf was placed in command of ground forces. Troops landed on the island on October 15, and quickly rescued the Americans and restored order.

Schwartzkopf became a full four-star general in 1988 and was appointed Commander in Chief of the United States Army Central Command based in Tampa, Florida. In this post, he was responsible for military operations in the Horn of Africa, South Asia, and the Middle East, including the Persian Gulf region. Early in 1990, Schwarzkopf and his staff had begun preparing a detailed plan for the defense of the Perisan Gulf oil fields in the event of attack by Iraq. When 140,000 Iraqi troops and 1,800 tanks invaded the small Gulf country of Kuwait on August 2, 1990, Schwartzkopf was ready.

Between August 1990 and January 1991, General Schwarzkopf lead an operation called Desert Shield, which aimed at forcing Iraqi forces out of Kuwait and protecting Saudi Arabia from Iraqi invasion. Schwarzkopf directed the mobilization of 765,000 troops from 28 countries, including 541,000 American troops, hundreds of ships, and thousands of planes and tanks. During this buildup period, prolonged negotiations and economic sanctions failed to dislodge Iraqi forces from Kuwait. As a result, Schwarzkopf was directed to implement Operation Desert Storm.

1956 Schwarzkopf graduates from West Point Military Academy.

1971 Schwarzkopf returns to the United States from the Vietnam War.

1983 Schwarzkopf is put in charge of ground troops during the Grenada invasion.

1988 Schwarzkopf becomes a full four-star general.

1991 Schwarzkopf leads Operation Desert Storm.

> "A very great man once said you should love you enemies, and that's not a bad piece of advice. We can love them, but, by God, that doesn't mean we're not going to fight them."
>
> Norman Schwarzkopf, 1991

Beginning on January 17, 1991, Allied forces carried out a devastating six-week aerial bombardment of Iraq to destroy Iraqi communications, supply lines, and infrastructure. Using high-tech weaponry that seriously outmatched the Iraqi military hardware, the air war quickly grounded the Iraqi air force. Schwarzkopf then began a massive land war on February 24. Allied troops advanced rapidly through Kuwait and into Iraq, moving to within 150 miles of Baghdad. The demoralized Iraqi soldiers put up little resistance and began to surrender in massive numbers. After only 100 hours of fighting on the ground, Iraq accepted a United Nations cease-fire, and the war was over. Total casualties of the U.S. forces were 148 killed in action (35 by friendly fire) and 467 wounded, out of a coalition total of 240 dead and 776 wounded. Iraq's military casualties were estimated to number more than 25,000 dead and 300,000 wounded.

After the war, Schwarzkopf and his troops returned to the United States national heroes. A jubilant public welcomed them with numerous victory parades. Schwarzkopf retired from the army in August 1991, and found himself in great demand as a public speaker. His autobiography, *It Doesn't Take a Hero*, was published in 1992. ◆

Schweitzer, Albert

1875–1965 ● HUMANITARIAN & MEDICAL DOCTOR

> "You don't live in a world all alone. Your brothers are here too."
>
> Albert Schweitzer, 1952

Albert Schweitzer was born in Kaysensberg, Alsace, into the family of an Evangelical Lutheran pastor whose views and sense of mission were a strong and lasting influence. He was an able student, while his obvious musical talents were nurtured through his lessons with the master organist Eugene Munch. In 1893 he entered the University of Strasbourg, with which he was to remain associated until his departure for Africa.

While in Strasbourg studying theology and philosophy (on which he also lectured after being awarded, in 1899, his doctorate for a thesis on Immanuel Kant), Schweitzer was also a preacher at St. Nicholas's church; meanwhile his reputation grew as one of the foremost organists in Europe. As well as playing the instrument superbly, he also came to be a master of organ design and building. He was especially recognized as an unparalleled interpreter of J. S. Bach's music; in 1905, he produced a biography of the composer that became a standard work on its subject. Schweitzer portrayed Bach as a religious mystic, likening his music to the impersonal and cosmic forces of the natural world.

Schweitzer's next literary effort, his *Quest of the Historical Jesus*, published in 1906, had an epochal impact on biblical scholarship. He demonstrated the contradictory nature of much of the available evidence on the life and character of Christ, and pointed out that previous biblical scholars had been less rigorous than they should; rather than having the courage to follow the evidence wherever it led, they were content to stop their researches as soon as they had unearthed a picture of Jesus that could act as a focus for their own liberal projections. The Jesus whom Schweitzer revealed was an apocalyptic zealot who believed that the end of days was imminent and presented his teachings with appropriate prophetic and messianic vigor. Despite the tenor of these findings, the author himself remained firmly rooted in the Christian spiritual tradition and was greatly influenced by the nature of Christ's ministry among the poor and oppressed.

By the age of thirty Schweitzer was respected and renowned, with the promise of even more successes ahead. Then, to the shock and dismay of many of his colleagues and friends, he chose to make good an earlier resolve that at that age he would turn to devoting his energies to helping mankind. Moved to missionary work in the Congo as the vehicle for this service, he enrolled in the Strasbourg medical faculty to train as a doctor that he might be of more use to his African congregation.

Shouldering an enormous workload, Schweitzer financed his arduous medical studies by organ recitals and teaching, and with the aid of the royalties from his book on Bach. In 1912 he married Helen Bresslau, an accomplished scholar who trained as a nurse that she might be of more use in the Congo venture. On Schweitzer's qualification as a doctor in 1913, the couple journeyed to French Equatorial Africa (tak-

1893 Schweitzer enters the University of Strasbourg to study theology and philosophy.

1899 Schweitzer is awarded his Ph.D.

1906 Schweitzer publishes *Quest for Historical Jesus*.

1913 Schweitzer qualifies as a medical doctor and travels to Africa.

1915 Schweitzer undergoes a life-affirming mystical experience.

1952 Schweitzer is awarded the Nobel Peace Prize.

ing with them a zinc-lined organ), where they established a hospital on the Ogooue river "at the edge of the primeval forest."

As the hospital mission grew, it became a place of pilgrimage. Nevertheless, some observers were disturbed by what they saw as Schweitzer's arbitrary, paternalistic, and dictatorial administrative techniques, but none could doubt his devotion to what he perceived as the well-being of his growing native Christian flock, even if they might object to his condescension toward them.

In 1915 a mystical experience he underwent while on a boat on the Ogooue converted Schweitzer to the philosophy of "reverence for life," which he outlined in the second volume of his magnum opus, *Philosophy of Civilization.* This boundless humanitarianism necessitated absolute nonviolence toward all sentient beings, and Schweitzer practiced what he preached with such vigor that he attempted to avoid harming the smallest insect; even such potential disease vectors as mosquitoes and flies were left unmolested.

With the exception of a period during World War I when he was interned by the French administration as an enemy alien, Schweitzer remained on the banks of the Ogooue until his death. In 1924 he relocated the hospital two miles upriver from its original site, where it grew until it accommodated 350 patients and their relatives, while the leper colony that was also established cared for some 150 people. Schweitzer's charisma and persuasive powers encouraged many people to come and work for him, so the project staff expanded until, at any given time, there were thirty-six white physicians and nurses and a varying number of native personnel in a complex of seventy buildings and 500 beds.

In order to maintain funding for the project Schweitzer occasionally returned to Europe, where he would give organ recitals and lectures on his work to raise money. He maintained a keen and intelligent interest in world affairs, and was quick to protest the terrible destructive capability of atomic power. In 1952 he was awarded the Nobel Peace Prize for his work. He wrote several works of autobiography, notably *Out of My Life and Thought.* ◆

Seton, Elizabeth Ann

1774–1821 ● AMERICAN RELIGIOUS LEADER

lizabeth Seton was born in New York City to a wealthy and distinguished family. As a young woman, her concern for the sick and poor earned her the title of Protestant sister of charity. Her father was a well-known area physician who brought his children up in an Episcopal home.

In 1794 she married William M. Seton, a merchant, and in the ensuing years the couple had five children. In 1803 the family traveled to Italy to care for William's ailing health, but he failed to recuperate and died. Seton was left to mourn her husband in a foreign country, and was taken in by the Filicchi family, who were old acquaintances. The Filicchis were Roman Catholics, and it was their devotion that eventually led Seton to the Roman Catholic church. She returned to the United States and after an inner, spiritual struggle, she joined the Catholic church in 1805, becoming a member of Saint Peter's congregation in New York City. Her choice was not popular among her friends, most of whom were influenced by the anti-Catholic sentiment of that era.

In 1808 she moved to Baltimore, where she opened a grade school for girls. Several young women were placed under her care, and they soon took vows to be the Sisters of Charity of Saint Joseph. She moved the school to Ermmitsburg, Maryland, in 1810 and opened the first free

1803 Seton's husband dies in Italy.

1805 Seton joins the Roman Catholic Church.

1808 Seton opens a school for girls in Baltimore.

1810 Seton opens the first free parochial school in the United States.

1975 Pope Paul VI declares Seton a saint.

parochial: part of a
church parish.

parochial school in the United States for both boys and girls, laying the foundation for the American parochial school system. In her work for the Sisters of Charity, as the organization was now called, Seton brought many black children into the school. She was now called Mother Seton, although she was allowed to keep legal guardianship over her natural children. Through her work with the Sisters of Charity, Seton became known as the mother of American Catholic sister-school nuns, as well as the mother of the parochial school system in the United States.

Her legacy outlived her. In 1852 the Sisters of Charity founded an orphanage, and in 1907 the case for her beatification was opened. In 1963 she was **canonized** by Cardinal Francis Spellman. In 1975, Pope Paul VI waived the usual requirement of four miracles for sainthood, and declared that in the case of Seton, three miracles were enough. Thus, she became the first native-born American saint of the Roman Catholic church. Her feast day is January 4. ◆

canonize: to formally
recognize as a saint.

Sitting Bull (Tatanka Iyotake)

CA. 1831–1890 ● NATIVE AMERICAN LEADER

> *"What treaty have the white man ever made with us have they kept? Not one."*
>
> Sitting Bull

Sitting Bull, the son of a Hunkpapa Sioux chieftain, was born near Grand River, South Dakota. At an early age he participated in pitched battles with rival Indian tribes (he fought the Crow Indians when only fourteen years old), and with American troops. During the 1860s and 1870s he participated in the Plains Wars against the American government. Despite occasional successes the Indians were no match for the better armed American forces.

A local gold rush and the expansion of the Northern Railroad in 1876 prompted the federal government to offer the Sioux a reservation. Sitting Bull considered the proposal an affront and refused the offer. Other chiefs followed Sitting

Sitting Bull.

Bull's example by refusing similar offers and the Indians and Americans prepared for war. Before the battle Sitting Bull had a recurring vision in which American troops fell into his encampment. This dream, interpreted as a good omen by the Indians, encouraged them to believe that they would soon defeat the white man. The U.S. 7th Cavalry (266 troops), led by General George A. Custer, faced 3,500 Sioux and Cheyenne warriors at Little Bighorn, Montana, on June 25, 1876. The Indian warriors were led by Crazy Horse; Sitting Bull remained in his camp to perform religious rites to assure victory. A three-hour battle ensued, in which the federal troops were massacred. Only one cavalry horse, suffering from seven bullet wounds, survived the battle.

"When I was a boy the Sioux owned the world; the sun rose and set on their land; they sent ten thousand men to battle. Where are the warriors today? Who slew them? Where are our lands? Who owns them?"

Sitting Bull

1876 Sitting Bull refuses the U.S. government offers of a reservation.

1876 Sioux defeat Custer's troops at Little Bighorn, flees to Canada.

1882 Sitting Bull returns to the United States.

1885 Sitting Bull tours with Buffalo Bill's Wild West Show.

1890 Sitting Bull is killed when Indian police attempt to arrest him.

Although Sitting Bull was not an active participant in the Battle of Little Bighorn he was blamed by the government for the massacre. American troops chased Sitting Bull and Crazy Horse through the Plains until finally defeating them on October 31 of that year. Sitting Bull escaped with his tribe and crossed the border into Canada but the Canadian government was unsympathetic to the Indian refugees and prevented them from settling in Canada, supposedly because they were not British subjects. Nevertheless, the Sioux ignored the Canadian government and remained in Canada until 1881, when Sitting Bull and his people were granted an amnesty and allowed to return to the United States.

His notoriety for the Battle of Little Big Horn earned Sitting Bull a certain degree of respect and recognition. He toured with Buffalo Bill's Wild West Show in 1885 and was often asked to speak at public functions, generally from prepared texts which would then be translated into English. On one occasion he ignored the prepared speech and said, "I hate all the white men. You are thieves and liars and have made us outcasts." The translator replaced Sitting Bull's statement with a text of his own and Sitting Bull received a standing ovation.

Further American expansion threatened to displace the Indians from what little land remained to them. Sitting Bull, when asked about the Indian response to the danger, declared, "Indians! There are no Indians left but me."

The distraught Indians of the Plains began participating in a mystical ritual, the Ghost Dance, upon the advice of a prophet who claimed that the ceremony would assure the impending disappearance of the white man from their land, the resurrection of Indian dead, and the restoration of their indigenous culture. Among the Indians encouraged by the Ghost Dance was Sitting Bull. The government regarded Sitting Bull's participation in the ceremony as a threat to the fragile peace they had enforced and in December 1890 forty-three Indian police came to arrest Sitting Bull. They were met by a large group of Ghost Dancers who attempted to interfere with them. One Indian, Catch a Bear, shot the arresting officer, and in the ensuing scuffle, Sitting Bull and his son Crow Foot were killed. No revenge was taken for the death of Sitting Bull. It was believed that the Ghost Dance would soon put an end to the white threat to the Indians. ◆

Smith, John

1580–1631 ● SOLDIER
& EXPLORER

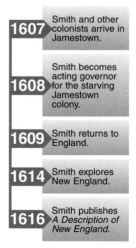

C aptain John Smith had been a soldier of fortune, serving in Hungary and Turkey, before he became involved in the colonial settlement of Virginia. He was one of the original colonists who arrived in Jamestown in 1607, and was one of the original Council named for the little colony.

He served the colony chiefly as the leader of exploring trips up the James, Potomac, and Rappahannock rivers. On one of these trips, seeking to gather food, Smith and his party were captured by Indians. Apparently Smith was threatened with death but (according to his own account of the affair) the Indian princess Pocahontas saved his life by interceding with her father. At any event, Smith survived, got back to Jamestown, and during the winter of 1608–1609 was acting as governor of the starving colony. There was a great deal of dispute among the colonists, and Smith sailed home to England in 1609.

He made a very important exploring voyage in 1614 to New England, of which he published a description and a valu-

1607 Smith and other colonists arrive in Jamestown.

1608 Smith becomes acting governor for the starving Jamestown colony.

1609 Smith returns to England.

1614 Smith explores New England.

1616 Smith publishes *A Description of New England*.

able map in a book entitled *A Description of New England* (1616). This was the first work in which the name "New England" is used as separate from Virginia. Smith wrote extensively in later years, describing his life and his travels, and giving a historical treatment of Virginia's foundation. Although some historians suspect that Smith was too fond of a good story, others regard his work as important, reliable source materials on the early history of New England and Virginia. ◆

Stanton, Elizabeth Cady

1815–1902 ● WOMEN'S RIGHTS ACTIVIST

"Woman's degradation is in man's idea of his sexual rights. Our religion, laws, customs, are all founded on the belief that woman was made for man."
Elizabeth Cady Stanton, 1860

Elizabeth Cady Stanton was a militant leader in social reforms and in the drive to improve the legal status of women in the nineteenth century. Stanton was born Elizabeth Cady in 1815 in Johnstown, New York. She studied under Emma Willard, an earlier reformer, at Troy Female Seminary. For a time, she studied law with her own father, Daniel Cady, who was one of New York State's leading authorities on property law cases. She was convinced that

Nineteenth Amendment

The Nineteenth Amendment to the U.S. Constitution, ratified in 1920, states that "The right of citizens of the United States to vote shall not be denied or abridged by the United States or by any State on account of sex." The women's suffrage movement began when a women's rights convention, meeting in Seneca Falls, New York, in 1848, urged women to fight for the franchise. The struggle became ongoing in 1869, when Elizabeth Cady Stanton and Susan B. Anthony formed a suffrage association, and Lucy Stone and Julia Ward formed another. In 1890 the groups merged to form the National American Woman Suffrage Association, which secured passage of woman's suffrage amendments in many states and in 1914 presented to Congress a suffrage petition signed by almost 500,000 people. Inspired by the militant tactics of British "suffragettes," as they were called, Lucy Burns and Alice Paul formed the National Woman's Party in 1916. In 1917 the party launched a campaign of parades, picketing, and hunger strikes. In 1918 the House of Representatives passed what would become the Nineteenth Amendment, and the Senate followed suit the next year. Thirty-six states having ratified the amendment, it became part of the Constitution on August 26, 1920.

women were not treated properly under the existing laws of the country. When she married Henry Brewster Stanton in 1840, she insisted that the ceremony must exclude "and obey" from the usual marriage vow to "love, honor, and obey" a husband.

Stanton was influenced by her husband to take up the cause of abolition. In London, she and other female abolitionists were denied seats at an abolition convention because of their sex. This led her to begin her long campaign to secure equal rights for women. Lucretia Mott, another of the Americans barred from the London convention, joined Stanton in the work. On July 19–20, 1848, the first women's rights convention in the United States was held at Seneca Falls, New York. It was guided by Stanton. As the leader in the drive to win votes for American women, she served as president of the National Woman Suffrage Association (1869–1890) and of the National American Woman Suffrage Association (1890–1902).

Elizabeth Cady Stanton was active in other social reform campaigns. She opposed slavery, and she was an active supporter of temperance movements to prohibit the manufacture and sale of alcoholic beverages. ◆

1848 Stanton heads the first women's rights convention in New York.

1869 Stanton becomes president of the National Woman Suffrage Association.

1890 Stanton becomes president of the National American Woman Suffrage Association.

Tecumseh

1768–1813 ● SHAWNEE WARRIOR
& LEADER

*"These lands are ours. No one has a right
to remove us, because we were the first
owners. The Great Spirit above has
appointed this place for us, on which to
light our fires, and here we will remain."*
Tecumseh, 1810

B orn into one of the twelve Algonquian-speaking tribes
called "Shawnee," Tecumseh became the best-known
Indian leader of his day to the American public and,
aside from the Sioux chief Sitting Bull, arguably the
best-known in history. Born in Ohio, perhaps around
Springfield, Tecumseh was the older brother of a Shawnee
shaman named Tenskwatawa, frequently called by whites "the
Prophet." As a young man, Tecumseh fought with distinction
in the forty-year Algonquian resistance against Euro-American
incursions in the Ohio Valley and the Old Northwest—a conflict that began with the French and Indian War, included
Pontiac's Rebellion, and ended with the victory of "Mad"
Anthony Wayne at the Battle of Fallen Timbers in 1794. Both
Tecumseh's father and his two older brothers were killed during
the long struggle, and following Fallen Timbers, an embittered
Tecumseh moved west to present-day Indiana, although he
returned regularly to the Ohio Valley to hunt. During the last
five years of the eighteenth century and into the first few years

of the nineteenth, he earned the admiration, respect, even affection of not only the Indians but also whites, for his veracity and for his opposition to the traditional Algonquian practices of captive torture and ritual cannibalism. Among the tribes of the Old Northwest, he quickly became a one-man political power who consciously modeled himself on Pontiac.

After the defeat of the Old Northwest tribes was finalized in the Treaty of Greenville in 1795, the trans-Appalachian frontier remained relatively peaceful, and an encouraged President Thomas Jefferson directed the governor of the Indiana Territory, William Henry Harrison, to obtain "legal" title to as much Indian land as possible in preparation for further white expansion into the West. Harrison, who made no effort to ensure that he dealt with legitimate tribal representatives, acquired seventy million acres in less than three years by a series of questionable treaties, resulting in growing dissension among the tribes. Tecumseh, a persuasive and charismatic leader of remarkable strategic acumen, realized that, while his tribe could not survive a prolonged peace that ushered in thousands of new settlers, his people were not powerful enough alone to endure a prolonged war.

Tecumseh and Tenskwatawa worked closely together. Tenskwatawa claimed inspiration from the Great Spirit, preached a mixture of Shaker-influenced doctrine and traditional beliefs, and called on Indians to cleanse themselves of the unclean white race. His visions attracted recruits to the transtribal alliance that Tecumseh had begun to put together in 1805. In 1807, Tecumseh established headquarters for the alliance at the abandoned site of Fort Greenville on Indiana's Tippecanoe River, which quickly became known to the whites—who considered Tenskwatawa, not Tecumseh, the leader of the new "religious" movement—as Prophet's Town. Using the threat of war to intimidate Governor Harrison and to buy time while he traveled in 1811 throughout the Ohio country and beyond—west to the Sioux and south to the land of the Chickasaws, Choctaws, and Creeks—Tecumseh preached the need for an Indian confederation stretching from the Great Lakes to the Gulf of Mexico. Only as a unified, sovereign state, Tecumseh reasoned, could the Native Americans resist displacement or absorption and death as a people.

While Tecumseh was gone, Tenskwatawa managed to embroil the Ohio Valley tribes that had already joined the

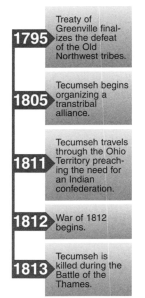

1795 Treaty of Greenville finalizes the defeat of the Old Northwest tribes.

1805 Tecumseh begins organizing a transtribal alliance.

1811 Tecumseh travels through the Ohio Territory preaching the need for an Indian confederation.

1812 War of 1812 begins.

1813 Tecumseh is killed during the Battle of the Thames.

alliance into a disastrous battle at Tippecanoe. The Shawnees, Delawares, Miamis, Potawatomis, Ottawas, Winnebagos, Ojibwas (Chippewas), and Wyandots, angry at Harrison's treaties and defiantly ensconced at the old fort where Tecumseh had placed them, were joined by Black Hawk's Sac (Sauk) and Fox (Mesquakie) before Harrison mustered his troops, attacked, and soundly defeated them. The Prophet was discredited. When Tecumseh returned from his largely unsuccessful recruiting expedition in the South, he joined in the public rebuke of his brother. After the Battle of Tippecanoe, the Potawatomi, Winnebago, and Sac and Fox Indians, though shaken, remained loyal to Tecumseh's confederacy. Wyandot followers of the militant Chief Roundhead likewise adhered to the cause. But among the Delaware, Miami, and even Shawnee tribes, there were wholesale defections. The alliance began to crumble.

At this crisis point, however, the United States and Great Britain commenced the War of 1812. Tecumseh, who had sought the support of the British in Canada in 1810, only to be rebuffed, now eagerly embraced an alliance with England against the Americans. Initially, the alliance went well for the Indians. In the course of the war's first year, some four thousand Americans were either killed or captured, while combined British and Indian casualties numbered around five hundred. Yet even the Indian victories were pyrrhic, and their losses—homes burned, crops destroyed, populations displaced—were grim. By the second year, the British in the West had experienced a number of reverses, and the Indians' alliance with them began to disintegrate. As the British evacuated the territory, Tecumseh grew desperate. He persuaded the British to take a stand against the American army at Moravian Town on the north bank of the Thames River.

In a battle especially distinguished by the brilliant performance of a Kentucky mounted regiment under Colonel Richard Mentor Johnson, William Henry Harrison defeated the combined British and Indian forces at the Battle of the Thames on October 5, 1813. The Americans never found Tecumseh's body. Some say grieving warriors bore him off the field and gave him a secret burial, so even the site of his grave is a mystery. No one knows who killed him. But he was dead, and there would be no confederate Indian state in the American West. In fact, by the time Richard Johnson became

"Sell a country! Why not sell the air, the clouds, and the great sea, as well as the earth? Did not the Great Spirit make them all for the use of his children?"
Tecumseh, 1810

Tecumseh was the last credible hope the Native Americans had of containing land-hungry Americans east of the Mississippi.

vice-president of the United States under Martin Van Buren, Kentucky, Ohio, Indiana, Illinois, and Michigan were no longer even be considered the real American West. Those running his political campaign in the election of 1836 claimed Johnson had felled the great warrior, but he would never confirm it. On the day Tecumseh died, vengeful frontiersmen jumped on the body of a fallen warrior they thought to be the great Shawnee sachem, stripped the skin from his body, and cut it into strips. Later, in some of the fashionable shops in Washington, D.C., Americans could buy imitations of these "Tecumseh Razor Strops."

Dying with Tecumseh was the last credible hope the Native Americans had of containing land-hungry Americans east of the Mississippi. All barriers to migration into the trans-Mississippi had, in effect, been removed. It was only a matter of years before the tribes themselves would also be removed across the river. ◆

Tubman, Harriet

CA. 1820–1913 ● ABOLITIONIST

"I started with this idea in my head, 'There's two things I've got a right to . . . death or liberty.'"

Harriet Tubman, 1868

Harriet Tubman was born a slave in Dorchester, Maryland; her given name was Araminta Ross. Separated from her mother when only ten years old, she received no education and remained illiterate throughout her life. She was to learn weaving but instead spent her time watching rat traps. A later attempt to teach her a trade was a similar failure, so Tubman was sent to work in the fields with the men. Once asked to help tie down a fellow slave for a thrashing, she refused; incensed by her impudence, her master threw a heavy iron weight at her head. The injury was permanent; even in her most active period she suffered from losses of consciousness, sometimes in midsentence.

In 1844 Harriet's master married her to John Tubman, whose name she assumed. Although it was stated in her master's will that his slaves would receive their freedom upon the

Harriet Tubman.

deaths of himself and his immediate heirs, his death and that of his only son prompted the family to sell his slaves. Harriet Tubman refused to be put on auction. In 1849 she ran away, making her way to Auburn, New York, where she worked as a cook and a laundress. She also became active in the abolitionist movement. Her piercing eyes, deep voice, love of singing and oft-repeated motto, "Mah people mus' go free," endeared her to crowds in New York and Boston. Despite her illiteracy she contributed to the *National Anti-Slavery Standard*, and befriended such important abolitionists as John Brown, the essayist Ralph Waldo Emerson, and the novelist Louisa May Alcott.

Tubman's greatest role was as a conductor of the Underground Railroad, an abolitionist network helping slaves to escape to the North and Canada. After earning enough money for the fare, Tubman would travel south to guide slaves to their freedom. She took only the weakest who could no longer endure the hardships of their bondage. In nineteen trips she succeeded in helping over three hundred slaves—including her aged parents—to escape. Tubman became known as Moses and her followers were "the black wool she had come to gather." The trips were carried out with considerable danger; there was a sizable reward, at one point reaching $40,000, for her arrest, yet neither she nor any of her followers was ever caught. Tubman was a large woman who was able to lift a heavy man and run with him. She always carried a pistol and frequently reminded her anxious followers that, "Dead Negroes tell no tales." Messages with obscure hints, such as "The good ship Zion will arrive shortly," were sent to elderly slaves prior to her appearance. She generally planned escapes for Saturday nights since no announcements of escaped slaves could be prepared until Monday. Routes were never planned in advance, Tubman would often knock on the doors of unsuspecting Quakers and other sympathizers late at night, asking them to harbor the fugitives.

Tubman was aware of the dangers she faced and was often saved by her own ingenuity. Traveling north on a train she heard her name mentioned. Turning around, she saw a placard advertising a 5,000-dollar reward for her capture. Tubman covered her face with her bonnet, remaining that way until the next station, where she got off and took a train back south to avoid suspicion by crossing state lines. Getting off near her hometown, she bought chickens and limped, pretending to be an elderly slave. She even passed her old master, who failed to recognize her.

During the Civil War Tubman served in the Union army as a nurse; her cure for dysentery, made from local roots, saved countless lives. Because of her intimate knowledge of the countryside she frequently served as a scout and spy, often infiltrating enemy lines to collect information on troop movements and numbers. Although her reputation in the Underground Railroad won her considerable fame, common soldiers often failed to recognize Tubman. On her final voyage north, accompanying a group of wounded Union soldiers, she was told by a conductor that she would not be allowed to travel with the soldiers in the first class coach. A scuffle ensued in

1844 Harriet's master marries her to John Tubman.

1849 Tubman runs away from her slave master.

1850 Tubman befriends John Brown, Ralph Waldo Emerson, and Louisa May Alcott.

1869 Sarah H. Bradford publishes *Scenes in the Life of Harriet Tubman.*

1908 Tubman establishes a home in Auburn for elderly and needy blacks.

which Tubman's arm was broken and she was thrown into a baggage compartment.

After the war Tubman returned to Auburn, where she founded a shelter for needy blacks. A biography, written by Sarah Bradford in 1869, made her something of a celebrity, yet, at the time of her death in 1913 Tubman was still struggling with the federal government to obtain a military pension. ◆

Tutu, Desmond Mpilo

1931–PRESENT ● SOUTH AFRICAN RELIGIOUS LEADER & CIVIL RIGHTS ACTIVIST

> *"In the land of my birth I cannot vote, whereas a young person of eighteen can vote. And why? Because he or she possesses that wonderful biological attribute—a white skin."* Desmond Tutu, 1984

Born in Klerksdorp in the Transvaal, Desmond Mpilo Tutu became a high school teacher in 1955 after having graduated from the Pretoria Bantu College in 1953. He obtained a bachelor of arts degree from the University of South Africa in 1958. After a serious illness, and under the influence of Father Trevor Huddleston of the Community of the Resurrection, Tutu studied for the priesthood at Saint Peter's College, Johannesburg. He was ordained deacon in 1960 and priest the following year. From 1962 to 1965 he studied at King's College, University of London, obtaining a bachelor's degree in divinity and a master's degree

1958 Tutu graduates from the University of South Africa.

1960 Tutu is ordained a deacon.

1961 Tutu is ordained a priest.

1976 Tutu becomes bishop of Lesotho.

1984 Tutu is awarded the Nobel Peace Prize.

1986 Tutu becomes archbishop of Cape Town.

1996 Nelson Mandela appoints Tutu chair of the Commission on Truth and Reconciliation.

in theology. From 1967 to 1969 he lectured at the Federal Theological Seminary in Alice, Cape, and from 1970 to 1972, at the universities of Botswana, Lesotho, and Swaziland (in Roma, Lesotho). From 1972 to 1975 he was associate director of the Theological Education Fund of the World Council of Churches, based in England.

Having been elected dean of Johannesburg in 1975, he returned to South Africa. In 1976 he was consecrated bishop of Lesotho, but two years later he accepted appointment as the general secretary of the South African Council of Churches. During his tenure in this office he became an international spokesperson in the struggle against apartheid and was awarded the Nobel Peace Prize in 1984. The same year he was elected bishop of Johannesburg, and in 1986 he became archbishop of Cape Town. He retired from this office in June 1996. In January 1996 he was appointed the chairperson of the Commission on Truth and Reconciliation by President Nelson Mandela. Recipient of many honorary doctorates and other awards, Tutu was elected president of the All Africa Conference of Churches in 1987, and reelected to that office in 1993. After the unbanning of the liberation movements in South Africa in February 1990, Tutu played a major role in facilitating peace, reconciliation, and national reconstruction in South Africa. Tutu is married to Leah Nomalizo Shenxane; the couple has four children. ◆

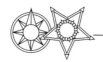

Walesa, Lech

1943–PRESENT ● WORKERS RIGHTS
ACTIVIST & PRESIDENT OF POLAND

*"They wanted us not to believe in God and
our churches are full . . . to be materialis-
tic and incapable of sacrifices but we are
anti-materialistic, capable of sacrifice . . .
to be afraid of the tanks, of the guns, and
instead we don't fear them at all."*

Lech Walesa, describing the failure of
communism in Poland, 1981

Lech Walesa is a Polish labor activist who helped played a pivotal role in leading Poland out of communism. Walesa helped form and lead Solidarity, the first independent trade union of communist Poland. He served as president of Poland between 1990 and 1995, and he won the Nobel Peace Prize in 1983.

Walesa was born on September 29, 1943, in Popow, Poland, to Boleslaw and Fela (Kaminska) Walesa. Boleslaw was a carpenter. After imprisonment at a labor camp during World War II, Boleslaw's health failed and he died when Lech was only eighteen months old. Lech's mother married her brother-in-law, Stanislaw Walesa, a year later.

Walesa trained to be an electrician at a state vocational school in Lipno near Popow and in 1967 he went to Gdansk to work at the Lenin Shipyard. In 1970 strikes against the communist government broke out in Poland after the government raised food prices, and Gdansk became the center of the protest movement. Riots spread through the streets and the police killed a number of demonstrators. The government ended the protest by making concessions to the people. But Poland was faced with food shortages and price increases again in the mid-1970s, and protests erupted once more. During these protests, Walesa became an antigovernment union activist, losing his job as a result. Walesa then held a number of temporary jobs and was occasionally thrown in jail for his labor activity.

On August 14, 1980, strikes began again at the Gdansk Shipyard. Workers at the shipyard were protesting dramatic meat shortages at a time when meat was being exported and food prices were rising. Walesa had been banned from the yard, but he jumped over the shipyard walls to join the protesting workers and was elected head of a strike committee to negotiate with the management. The workers made a number of demands, including a pay raise, a reinstatement of dismissed persons, a commemoration of the victims of the strike of 1970, and the right to form trade unions free from party control. After three days, the management conceded on the pay raise and a reinstatement of dismissed persons. In the meantime, however, the protest movement had spread to other cities, and thousands of workers were on strike. At the urging of these workers, the strike continued.

On August 17 and 18 the Interfactory Strike Committee (MKS) was created to represent the demands of workers from different industries, and Walesa became its leader. The committee had a list of demands that were both political and economic. Fearing a revolution, the government yielded to the main demands of the MKS, and on August 31, Walesa and Deputy Prime Minister Mieczyslaw Jagielski signed an accord that became known as the Gdansk Agreements. Among its provisions were the right to form free trade unions and the right to strike. It was the first time such rights had ever been given in a Soviet bloc country.

Soon after the Gdansk Agreements, the Interfactory Strike Committee formed a national organization of unions called Solidarity with Walesa at its helm. In November, the Polish government recognized Solidarity, marking the first time in history that a communist country recognized a labor organization that was independent of the Communist Party. Under Walesa's guidance, the group worked for economic improvements and greater political freedom while carefully

1967 Walesa begins working as an electrician in Gdansk shipyards.

1970 Strikes against the Communist government break out in Poland.

1980 Strikes begin again at the Gdansk Shipyard.

1981 The government imposes marshall law and imprisons Walesa.

1982 Walesa is released from prison.

1983 Poland's government ends marshall law; Walesa is awarded the Nobel Peace Prize.

1990 Walesa is elected president in Poland's first direct presidential election.

avoiding confrontations that might lead to Soviet military intervention in Poland.

In 1981 Wojciech Jaruzelski, an army general, became head of the Communist Party and the relationship between Solidarity and the communist authorities deteriorated. In December Jaruzelski imposed martial law, suspended Solidarity's activities, and imprisoned Walesa and hundreds of other union leaders. The government then officially outlawed Solidarity in October 1982, but the organization continued its activities as an underground movement. Walesa was imprisoned for almost a year. He was released in November 1982. The government ended martial law in mid-1983 but continued many restrictions on personal freedom.

In 1983, Walesa was awarded the Nobel Peace Prize for his efforts to prevent violence while trying to gain workers' rights. However, he was afraid that if he left Poland, he would not be allowed to return. As a result, his wife, Danuta, flew to Oslo, Norway, to accept the award for him.

More labor unrest forced the government to meet with Walesa and other Solidarity leaders in 1988. This meeting led to the lifting of the ban on Solidarity in 1989. It also led to free elections on a limited number of parliamentary seats in 1989. In that election, almost every candidate who was endorsed by Solidarity won a seat. The political reforms of Poland led to a cascade of reforms around Central Europe.

In 1990 Walesa was elected president in Poland's first direct presidential election. After the election he resigned as chairman of Solidarity. As president, Walesa helped guide the country through a series of economic reforms intended to lead Poland to a free-market system. He also led the country through its first free parliamentary elections since the imposition of communist rule in 1945. Many people were discouraged by the economic hardships that accompanied the transition to the free market economy, and in the elections of 1993 many former Communist Party members returned to parliament. The Polish people also became disenchanted with Walesa. As leader of Solidarity he displayed a genius for politics, but his skills as head of state were questioned. Some people liked his plain speech and confrontational style. Others found him too undignified to serve as head of state. His authoritarianism and his rigid support of the Roman Catholic position on prohibiting abortion also eroded his support. In

1995, Walesa lost the presidency to former communist Aleksander Kwasniewski, head of the Democratic Left Alliance. Walesa went back to Gdansk, to his villa, his wife, Danuta and their eight children. ◆

Wallenberg, Raoul

1912–? ● RESCUER OF JEWS DURING WORLD WAR II

In the days preceding Budapest's liberation, Wallenberg saved some 100,000 Jews by foiling a German plan to blow up the city's ghettos.

Raoul Wallenberg was born into a distinguished family of bankers, diplomats, and officers; his father, who died before he was born, was an officer in the Swedish navy. Wallenberg grew up in the house of his stepfather, Frederik von Dardell. He studied architecture in the United States, but then took up banking and international trade, which brought him to Haifa in 1936 for a six months' stay. On the recommendation of the Swedish branch of the World Jewish Congress and with the support of the American War Refugee Board, the Swedish Foreign Ministry, in July 1944, sent Wallenberg to Budapest, in order to help protect over 200,000 Jews who were left in the Hungarian capital after the deportation of 437,000 Hungarian Jews to Auschwitz.

The Swedish legation in Budapest initiated its operation on behalf of the persecuted Jews a short while after the German occupation of Hungary, on March 19, 1944. At that time, Adolf Eichmann and a special detachment under him, together with the Hungarian authorities, began organizing the deportation of the Jews to their death. The Swedish foreign minister, Ivar Danielsson, had proposed giving provisional Swedish passports to Hungarian Jews who had family ties or commercial connections with Swedish citizens. By the time Wallenberg arrived in Budapest, several hundred such "protective passports" had been issued. His arrival, on July 9, 1944, coincided with the stoppage of the deportations, a decision taken by the Hungarian government as a result of international pressure, including intervention by King Gustav V of Sweden.

The protective operation carried out by the Swedish legation, in conjunction with other diplomatic missions, was nevertheless maintained, and Wallenberg, the new legation
attaché was put in charge of a section created expressly for
this purpose. Before taking up his post he had been given special authority, at his request, for certain arrangements to be
left in his hands, such as the transmission of funds by means
of the War Refugee Board (which in turn received the money
from Jewish organizations in the United States).

The summer of 1944 was relatively quiet but this quiet
came to an end when the coup d'état of October 15 took
place and the **anti-Semitic fascist** Arrow Cross Party, headed by Ferenc Szálasi, seized power in the country. The Jews of
Budapest now faced mortal danger, both from the Arrow
Cross murder actions and from Eichmann's deportations.
From that moment on, Wallenberg displayed his courage and
heroism in the rescue actions he undertook. Over the course
of three months he issued thousands of "protective passports."
Most of the time, both the Hungarian authorities and the
Germans honored the signature of the Swedish legation, and
the protective documents afforded protection for many Jews.

When Eichmann organized the Death Marches of thousands of Jews to the Austrian border, Wallenberg pursued the
convoy in his car and managed to secure the release of hundreds of bearers of such passports and take them back to
Budapest. His impressive and self-assured manner enabled
him even to remove persons from the trains in which they
were about to be sent to Auschwitz, or to release them from
the Munkaszolgálat (Labor Service System), into which they
had been drafted.

The Jews were also in danger of being killed by Arrow
Cross men, and to prevent this, Wallenberg set up special hostels accommodating fifteen thousand persons—an operation
in which other diplomatic missions were also involved by issuing protective documents of their own. There were thirty-one
protected houses, which together formed the "international
ghetto," a separate entity, quite apart from Budapest's main
ghetto. The management of these houses posed many complicated problems, since it involved the provision of food as well
as sanitation and health services, all requiring much money; as
many as six hundred Jewish employees were engaged in the
administration and maintenance of the houses.

anti-Semetic: preju-
diced against Jews.

fascist: strongly
nationalistic.

Both the "international ghetto" and the main ghetto were situated in Pest, which was the first part of Budapest to be occupied by the Soviets. Wallenberg made efforts to negotiate with the Soviets and to ensure proper care for the liberated Jews. The Soviets were highly suspicious of the Swedish mission and charged its staff with spying for the Germans. The large number of Swedish documents in circulation also raised doubt in their minds. When the Soviets requested him to report to their army headquarters in Debrecen, Wallenberg must have believed that he would be protected by his diplomatic immunity, especially since the Swedish legation had represented Soviet interests vis-à-vis the Germans, and he made his way to the Soviet headquarters. He returned to Budapest on January 17, 1945, escorted by two Soviet soldiers, and was overheard saying that he did not know whether he was a guest of the Soviets or their prisoner. Thereafter, all trace of him, and of his driver, Vilmos Langfelder, was lost. The other staff members of the Swedish legation were also held by the Soviets, but within a few months they all returned to Stockholm, via Bucharest and Moscow.

In the first few years following Wallenberg's disappearance, the Soviets claimed that they had no knowledge of a person named Wallenberg and were not aware that a person of that name was being held in any of their prisons. German prisoners of war, however, coming back from Soviet imprisonment, testified that they had met Wallenberg in prisons and camps in various parts of the Soviet Union. In the mid-1950s, on the basis of these accounts, Sweden submitted a strong demand to the Soviets for information on Wallenberg, to which the Soviets replied, in 1956, that they had discovered a report of Wallenberg's death in 1947 in a Soviet prison. Wallenberg's family, and especially his mother, did not accept this claim, which conflicted with testimonies from other sources.

As the years went by, public opinion, in Sweden and all over the world, became increasingly critical of the manner in which the Swedish government had handled the issue. The subject of Wallenberg came up time and again, and with even greater force after the death of his mother in 1979. Books were published about Wallenberg and public committees were set up to deal with the case, especially in Britain, the United States, and Israel. The reports that were published revealed that in the final days preceding Budapest's liberation,

1936 Banking and trade interests keep Wallenberg in Haifa for six months.

1944 Wallenberg begins heroic protection of 200,000 Jews remaining in Budapest.

1945 Wallenberg disappears while in Soviet custody after Soviet occupation of Budapest.

1956 After years of denials, Soviets claim Wallenberg died in Soviet prison in 1947.

Wallenberg, with the help of Hungarians and the Zsidó Tandács (Jewish Council), was able to foil a joint SS and Arrow Cross plan to blow up the ghettos before the city's impending liberation. Through this act—the only one of its kind in the Holocaust—some 100,000 Jews were saved in the two ghettos. In recognition of this rescue action on Wallenberg's part, the United States Congress awarded Wallenberg honorary American citizenship. Memorial institutions were created in his honor, streets were named after him, and films were produced about his work in Budapest. Wallenberg's name and reputation as a "Righteous Among the Nations" have become a legend. ◆

Washington, Booker Taliaferro

C. 1856–1915 ● EDUCATOR

> *"No race can prosper till it learns there is as much dignity in tilling a field as in writing a poem."*
>
> Booker T. Washington

Founder of Tuskegee Institute in Alabama and prominent race leader of the late nineteenth and early twentieth centuries, Booker T. Washington was born a slave on the plantation of James Burroughs near Hale's Ford, Virginia. He spent his childhood as a houseboy and servant. His mother was a cook on the Burroughs plantation, and he never knew his white father. With Emancipation in 1865, he moved with his family—consisting of his mother, Jane; his stepfather, Washington Ferguson; a half-brother, John; and a half-sister, Amanda—to West Virginia, where he worked briefly in the salt furnaces and coal mines near Malden. Quickly, however, he obtained work as a houseboy in the mansion of the wealthiest white man in Malden, General Lewis Ruffner. There, under the tutelage of the general's wife, Viola Ruffner, a former New England schoolteacher, he learned to read. He also attended a local school for African Americans in Malden.

From 1872 to 1875 Washington attended Hampton Institute, in Hampton, Virginia, where he came under the influence of the school's founder, General Samuel Chapman Armstrong, who inculcated in Washington the work ethic that would stay with him his entire life and that became a hallmark of his educational philosophy. Washington was an outstanding pupil during his tenure at Hampton and was placed in charge of the Native American students there. After graduation he returned to Malden, where he taught school for several years and became active as a public speaker on local matters, including the issue of the removal of the capital of West Virginia to Charleston.

In 1881, Washington founded a school of his own in Tuskegee, Alabama. Beginning with a few ramshackle buildings and a small sum from the state of Alabama, he built Tuskegee Institute into the best-known African-American school in the nation. While not neglecting academic training entirely, the school's curriculum stressed industrial education, training in specific skills and crafts that would prepare students for jobs. Washington built his school and his influence by tapping the generosity of northern philanthropists receiving donations from wealthy New Englanders and some of the leading industrialists and businessmen of his time, such as Andrew Carnegie, William H. Baldwin Jr., Julius Rosenwald, and Robert C. Ogden.

In 1882 Washington married his childhood sweetheart from Malden, Fanny Norton Smith, a graduate of Hampton Institute, who died two years later as a result of injuries suffered in a fall from a wagon. Subsequently Washington married Olivia A. Davidson, a graduate of Hampton and the Framingham State Normal School in Massachusetts, who

1881 ▶ Washington founds the Tuskegee Institute.

1895 ▶ Washington delivers his "Atlanta Compromise" speech.

1900 ▶ Washington founds the National Negro Business League.

1901 ▶ Washington publishes *Up from Slavery*.

held the title of lady principal of Tuskegee. She was a tireless worker for the school and an effective fund-raiser in her own right. Always in rather frail health, Davidson died in 1889. Washington's third wife, Margaret James Murray, a graduate of Fisk University, also held the title of lady principal and was a leader of the National Association of Colored Women's Clubs and the Southern Federation of Colored Women's Clubs.

Washington's reputation as the principal of Tuskegee Institute grew through the late 1880s and the 1890s; his school was considered the **exemplar** of industrial education, viewed as the best method of training the generations of African Americans who were either born in slavery or were the sons and daughters of freed slaves. His control of the purse strings of many of the northern donors to his school increased his influence with other African-American schools in the South. His fame and recognition as a national race leader, however, resulted from the impact of a single speech he delivered before the Cotton States and International Exposition in Atlanta, in 1895. This important speech, often called the Atlanta Compromise, is the best single statement of Washington's philosophy of racial advancement and his polit-

exemplar: something worth imitating.

Tuskegee University

Tuskegee University is an historically black institution of higher learning located in Tuskegee, Alabama, with students from most states, the District of Columbia, and a number of foreign nations. Its roots go back to 1881, when the Alabama legislature appropriated $2,000 for the establishment of the Tuskegee Normal School for training black teachers. Booker T. Washington served as its head from 1881 until his death in 1915. The school was renamed the Tuskegee Normal and Industrial Institute in 1893, and it taught industrial arts, farming, and homemaking skills. At Washington's death it had some 1,500 students, compared to 40 in 1881. The school continued to grow rapidly under Washington's successors, including Robert Russa Morton, Frederick D. Patterson, and Luther H. Foster. It became Tuskegee Institute in 1937 and Tuskegee University in 1985. In the late 1990s it has over 3,700 students and features programs in engineering, nursing, veterinary medicine, and biotechnology. It produces over 70 percent of African-American veterinarians and more African-American aerospace science engineers than any other institution. It is home to the National Center for Bioethics in Research and Health Care and an International Center of Excellence for Biotechnology Research.

Washington's private papers document an elaborate secret life that contradicted many of his public utterances.

ical accommodation with the predominant racial ideology of his time. For the next twenty years, until the end of his life, Washington seldom deviated publicly from the positions taken in the Atlanta address.

In his speech, Washington urged African Americans to "cast down your bucket where you are"—that is, in the South—and to accommodate to the segregation and discrimination imposed upon them by custom and by state and local laws. He said the races could exist separately from the standpoint of social relationships but should work together for mutual economic advancement. He advocated a gradualist advancement of the race, through hard work, economic improvement, and self-help. This message found instant acceptance from white Americans, north and south, and almost universal approval among African Americans. Even W. E. B. Du Bois, later one of Washington's harshest critics, wrote to him immediately after the Atlanta address that the speech was "a word fitly spoken."

While Washington's public stance on racial matters seldom varied from the Atlanta Compromise, privately he was a more complicated individual. His voluminous private papers, housed at the Library of Congress, document an elaborate secret life that contradicted many of his public utterances. He secretly financed test cases to challenge Jim Crow laws. He held great power over the African-American press, both north and south, and secretly owned stock in several newspapers. While Washington himself never held political office of any kind, he became the most powerful African-American politician of his time as an adviser to presidents Theodore Roosevelt and William Howard Taft and as a dispenser of Republican party patronage.

Washington's biographer, Louis R. Harlan, called the Tuskegean's extensive political network "the Tuskegee Machine" for its resemblance to the machines established by big-city political bosses of the era. With his network of informants and access to both northern philanthropy and political patronage, Washington could make or break careers, and he was the central figure in African-American public life during his heyday. Arguably no other black leader, before or since, has exerted similar dominance. He founded the National Negro Business League in 1900, to foster African-American business and create a loyal corps of supporters throughout the country. Indirectly he influenced the National Afro American Council, the leading African-American civil rights group of his day. The publication of his autobiography, *Up from Slavery*, in 1901 spread his fame even more in the United States and abroad. In this classic American tale, Washington portrayed his life in terms of a Horatio Alger success story. Its great popularity in the first decade of the twentieth century won many new financial supporters for Tuskegee Institute and for Washington personally.

Washington remained the dominant African-American leader in the country until the time of his death from exhaustion and overwork in 1915. But other voices rose to challenge his conservative, accommodationist leadership. William Monroe Trotter, the editor of the *Boston Guardian*, was a persistent gadfly. Beginning in 1903 with the publication of Du Bois's *The Souls of Black Folk*, and continuing for the rest of his life, Washington was criticized for his failure to be more publicly aggressive in fighting the deterioration of race relations in the United States, for his avoidance of direct public support for civil rights legislation, and for his single-minded emphasis on industrial education as opposed to academic training for a "talented tenth" of the race. Washington, however, was adept at outmaneuvering his critics, even resorting to the use of spies to infiltrate organizations critical of his leadership, such as the Niagara Movement, led by Du Bois. His intimate friends called Washington "the Wizard" for his mastery of political intrigue and his exercise of power.

Washington's leadership ultimately gave way to new forces in the twentieth century, which placed less emphasis on individual leadership and more on organizational power. The founding of the National Association for the Advancement of Colored People (NAACP) in 1909 and of the National Urban League in 1911 challenged Washington in the areas of civil rights and for his failure to address problems related to the growth of an urban black population. The defeat of the Republican party in the presidential election of 1912 also spelled the end of Washington's power as a dispenser of political patronage. Nevertheless, he remained active as a speaker and public figure until his death, in 1915, at Tuskegee.

Washington's place in the **pantheon** of African-American leaders is unclear. He was the first African American to

"You can't hold a man down without staying down with him."

Booker T. Washington, attributed

pantheon: all the deities of a country or culture.

appear on a United States postage stamp (1940) and commemorative coin (1946). While he was eulogized by friend and foe alike at the time of his death, his outmoded philosophy of accommodation to segregation and racism in American society caused his historical reputation to suffer. New generations of Americans, who took their inspiration from those who were more outspoken critics of segregation and the second-class status endured by African Americans, rejected Washington's leadership role. While much recent scholarship has explored his racial philosophy and political activity in considerable depth, he remains a largely forgotten man in the consciousness of the general public, both black and white. In recent years, however, there has been some revival of interest in his economic thought by those who seek to develop African-American businesses and entrepreneurial skills. Indeed, no serious student of the African-American experience in the United States can afford to ignore the lessons that can be gleaned from Washington's life and from the manner in which he exercised power. ◆

Washington, George

1732–1799 ● FOUNDING FATHER &
FIRST PRESIDENT OF THE UNITED STATES

> *"I can answer but for three things, a firm belief in the justice of our cause, close attention to the prosecution of it, and the strictest integrity."*
>
> George
> Washington, 1775

Of British ancestry, the eldest of five children of his father's second wife, George Washington was born in a modest farmhouse (destroyed by fire in 1799) near Fredericksburg, Virginia. His education was limited—he was the only one of the first six presidents who did not go to college. The marriage of his beloved elder half-brother Lawrence into an aristocratic English family, the Fairfaxes, provided the young Washington with his first experience as a land surveyor.

In the early 1750s Britain and France both laid claim to the upper Ohio Valley. The Fairfax family recommended Washington to head a small expedition representing English interests, but tragedy resulted when Washington attacked a small French encampment, thinking they were spies. Ten men, including the diplomatic commander, were killed; the French claimed they were on a peace mission. The event exacerbated tensions that led to the French and Indian War. In 1755, although war had not been declared, Washington served as an aide to British general Edward Braddock in his campaign to capture Fort Duquesne at the Forks of the Ohio. The campaign ended in catastrophic defeat for the British, although Washington drew praise from the British commanders for his "courage and resolution."

At twenty-two, Washington was elected commander of all Virginia forces, his main task that of protecting the Virginia border from Indian attacks. After the retreat of the French from Fort Duquesne the war ended, having engaged Washington from 1753 to 1759. Resigning from military life, he turned his energies to Mount Vernon, the plantation home he had rented from the widow of his half-brother, which would later become his permanent estate in Virginia. In 1759 he married Martha Dandridge Custis, a wealthy widow with two small children. The Washingtons were charitable landowners, believing that no needy person should be turned away from Mount Vernon "lest the deserving suffer." Though he employed slaves, Washington was greatly troubled by the institution of slavery all his life. In his will he granted all his slaves their freedom, the only Virginia founding father to do so.

In the mid-1760s Britain's policy of taxing its colonies precipitated the American Revolution. At first Washington hoped that armed rebellion could be avoided. As a member of Virginia's House of Burgesses he protested the Stamp Act, which imposed taxes on the colonies to support the British army, and the Townshend Revenue Act, a tax on tea and other staples. In 1774 Washington was a delegate to the First Continental Congress in Philadelphia, which agreed to ban all British goods. Not until after the battles of Lexington and Concord and the convening of the Second Continental Congress in May 1775 did it become clear that the colonies would have to take up arms.

In the year preceding the signing of the Declaration of Independence (July 4, 1776), Washington created a navy of six ships that were ordered to capture British vessels; initiated a campaign to arrest and detain British Tories; and encouraged leaders of the colonies to adopt independence.

1755 Washington serves as an aide to British General Braddock.

1774 Washington serves as a delegate to the first Continental Congress.

1775 Washington creates a navy of six ships.

1781 Washington's army defeat the British at Yorktown.

1789 Washington becomes the first president of the United States.

1793 Washington is reelected to a second term.

"It is clear to my conception that no government before introduced among mankind ever contained so many checks and such efficacious restraints to prevent it from . . . oppression."

George Washington

With the exception of Washington's stunning success at Trenton on December 25–26, 1776, when he recrossed the Delaware and surprised the Hessian mercenaries, his army had suffered several defeats in New York, culminating in the misery of the hard winter at Valley Forge. The battle of Monmouth (June 28, 1778), when Washington took the initiative boldly and drove the the British back to their strongholds in New York, was the critical breakthrough for the Continental Army. In September 1781 Washington's army, assisted by able French troops, defeated the British garrison at Yorktown, Virginia, thereby inducing Britain's war-weary withdrawal. Washington was lauded for his outstanding conduct of the war, personal courage, and his concern for the underfed and ill-equipped men of his army. His suffering with them in their harshest trials, and his leadership and organizational ability, were later recognized by Congress as indisputably qualifying him for the presidency. He was already being called "the father of his country."

A period of longed-for retirement from 1783 to 1787 ended when Washington was called on to attend the Philadelphia Convention in May 1787. Lack of foreign markets for American goods and Britain's prohibition of trade with the British West Indies had led to a shortage of money and mounting debts. Following a mass insurgency in Massachusetts in 1786 called Shays' Rebellion, in which farmers demanded liquidation of their debts, fears of anarchy led to the growing conviction that a strong federal government was necessary. Washington used his influence with all the delegates to draft the Constitution. Signed first by Washington, the proposed Constitution established a national government consisting of "a supreme legislative, executive, and judiciary." Washington wrote: "It is clear to my conception that no government before introduced among mankind ever contained so many checks and such efficacious restraints to prevent it from . . . oppression." By June 1788 ten of the thirteen states had ratified the Constitution and on April 30, 1789, after unanimous election by the Electoral College, Washington took the oath in New York City as first president of the United States.

The judicial system and executive departments (the latter later known as the cabinet) established by Washington during his presidency have remained American institutions to the

George Washington.

present time. Describing Washington's selection of executive heads for the five departments established by Congress, John Adams, the vice president, wrote, "He seeks information from all quarters and judges more independently than any man I ever knew." Perhaps no two appointments had more repercussions for Washington's administration than the appointment of Alexander Hamilton as secretary of the treasury and Thomas Jefferson as secretary of state. Beginning in Washington's first term, Jefferson's opposition to Hamilton's economic and political philosophy eventually gave rise to two distinct parties: the Republican party (later to become the Democratic party) represented by Jefferson of Virginia, advocating an agrarian-based economy, and the Federalists, represented by Hamilton, whose proposal for the Bank of the United States and for increased industrialization anticipated the business interests of modern America.

Washington's foreign policy emphasized avoiding involvement in a European war, seeking treaties with Britain and Spain to open up the Ohio Valley to American settlement, and promoting the nation's import trade. On April 22, 1793, two days after his reelection, again unanimous, to a second term, and ten days after hearing of war between Britain and France, Washington voted for the Proclamation of Neutrality prohibiting Americans from sending war materials to either country.

Despite Washington's efforts to resolve the Indian problem on the western front peacefully, it proved necessary to send an army against the Northwestern Indians. General Wayne's victory at the battle of Fallen Timbers in 1794 led to the Treaty of Greenville in 1795. The Indians gave up nearly all their land in Ohio, enabling pioneers to establish a new state. The Treaty of San Lorenzo in 1795 with Spain granted Americans the right to trade on the Mississippi.

In his farewell address of September 17, 1796, Washington set forth his principles for the future well-being of the nation. He stressed the need for religion to guide public morality, warned against foreign entanglements and partisan politics, and enjoined Americans to respect the Constitution and cherish the Union. He retired to his Mount Vernon plantation and, three days before his death, drafted a long document planning the rotation of crops on his farm. ◆

Weill, Joseph

1902–1988 ● RESCUER OF JEWS DURING WORLD WAR II

Born in Bouxwiller, Alsace, Weill was the son of Rabbi Ernest Weill, a leading French scholar. Weill was a physician, and before the war he directed a private hospital in Strasbourg. At the outbreak of World War II he was recruited into the army and was responsible for health services for the inhabitants of the French region bordering on

Germany, who had been dispersed throughout central France. The temporary resettlement had been carried out by the French authorities in order to protect these civilians.

When France fell, in June 1940, Weill was the medical adviser of the Jewish organization Oeuvre de Secours Aux Enfants (Children's Aid Society; OSE). Thanks to his extensive connections in government circles, he was allowed access to the detention camps in the south of France, where the Vichy government had assembled tens of thousands of Jews with their families in degrading conditions of distress and malnutrition. The detailed and exact reports that Weill circulated on the condition of these detainees alerted Swiss and American humanitarian organizations to the need for assistance. As a direct consequence, the French authorities released from the camps hundreds of old people and thousands of children, a process involving many months of negotiations and not completed until the spring of 1941. Most of those released were taken into OSE institutions.

When deportations from France to eastern Europe began, Weill and his helpers rescued hundreds of Jewish children from the hands of the police. Weill showed his aides how to prepare forged identity cards for these children in order to hide their Jewish identity. He created an underground organization, the Reseau Garel (Garel Network), which placed the children with Christian and nonreligious families and institutions involved in saving Jews.

Activists in the Reseau Garel kept in constant touch with each child and paid his or her monthly maintenance. They worked to bolster the children's spirits and helped them to maintain their attachment to Judaism. In all, the Reseau Garel cared for four thousand children, and smuggled over one thousand of them into Switzerland. Not one of the children entrusted to this organization was lost.

In May 1943, with the Gestapo on his trail, Weill was compelled to flee to Switzerland. There, he dealt with the absorption of the Jewish children smuggled out of France and, with the aid of the smuggling network, was responsible for transferring Joint Distribution Committee funds to Jewish underground workers in France. On Weill's initiative, extension courses in local medical schools were authorized in the first half of 1944 for about two hundred Jewish doctors interned in refugee camps in Switzerland. Weill also brought

1940 France falls to Germany during World War II.

1943 Weill flees to Switzerland to escape the Gestapo.

1944 Weill initiates courses in medicine and social work for Jewish refugees in Switzerland.

1983 Weill publishes his autobiography *Deja . . . Essai autobiographique.*

about sixty young people from these camps into an abridged social-work course taught by Dr. Paul Baerwald, in an effort to prepare a professional labor force to care for survivors of the Nazi camps.

After the war, Weill served as president of the Consistoire Israelite, the umbrella organization of the Jewish communities of Alsace.

His autobiography, titled *Déjà' . . . Essai autobiographique,* was published in 1983. ◆

Wiesel, Elie (Eliezer)

1928–PRESENT ● WRITER & PEACE ACTIVIST

> *"I was the accuser, God the accused. My eyes were open and I was alone—terribly alone in a world without God and without man."*
>
> Elie Wiesel, *Night,* 1958

Raised in a religious home in Sighet Marmatiel, Transylvania, Elie Wiesel tenuously held on to his faith in God after being deported to Auschwitz with his family in 1944. Liberated from Buchenwald, he later took up studies at the Sorbonne in Paris, and became a foreign correspondent for the Israeli daily newspaper *Yediot Aharonot.* In his memoir *Un di Velt Hot Geshvigen* (1956), written in Yiddish and adapted and translated into eighteen languages (Fr., *La Nuit*; Eng., *Night*), Wiesel epitomizes the experience of a concentration camp inmate in a unique style and syntactic structure that have provided a verbal resource for discourse about the Holocaust. He has written twenty-five novels whose underlying artistic *modus operandi* is to bring to life pictures drawn from the Jewish annals, transforming them into vibrant human experiences.

While his novels and discursive prose deal with the fragility of the human condition, the anguished memories of his ordeals, woven into the text of the story, express the collective loss of a scared generation. Always mindful of the suffering of the other victims, Wiesel has nevertheless continuously pointed out the uniqueness of the Jewish experience,

Nobel Peace Prize

The Nobel Peace Prize was established by the will of Alfred Nobel, the Swedish inventor of dynamite, who died in 1896. Winners of the endowed award were to be persons "who shall have done the most . . . work for fraternity between nations, for the abolition or reduction of standing armies, and for the holding and promotion of peace conferences." After Nobel's death, provisions were modified to permit awarding of the Peace Prize to organizations. Recipients are chosen by the Nobel Committee, which is selected by the Norwegian parliament. Those eligible to nominate candidates include members of national assemblies and governments; university professors of law, political science, history, and philosophy; members and former members of the Nobel Committee; and Peace Prize holders. The prize is awarded annually on December 10, in Oslo, Norway, except when the Nobel Committee cannot agree on a winner. The first Nobel Peace Prize, granted in 1901, was shared by Herni Dunant and Frederic Passy. More recent recipients include Martin Luther King Jr. (1964), Amnesty International (1977), Lech Walesa (1983), and Nelson Mandela and Frederick W. de Klerk (1993). By the late 1990s the value of the prize had risen to over $1 million.

stated in a memorable formulation: "While not all victims were Jews, all Jews were victims."

On accepting the Congressional Medal from President Ronald Reagan in 1985, Wiesel appealed to the president not to visit the cemetery in Bitburg, Germany, in which forty-seven SS men are buried. "Your place, Mr. President, is with the victims," he declared. This impulse to boldly jolt the conscience of society earned Wiesel the Nobel Peace Prize. In his presentation address, Egil Aarvik, the chairman of the Norwegian Nobel Committee, summed up Wiesel's message to humanity: "Do not forget, do not sink into a new blind indifference, but involve yourselves in truth and justice, in human dignity, freedom, and atonement."

In his tenure as chairman of the U.S. Holocaust Memorial Council between 1980 and 1986, Wiesel instituted a national Days of Remembrance in the United States, and his leadership inspired the introduction of Holocaust curricula in numerous states, cities, and counties. In his words and deeds, Wiesel has helped to bring the Holocaust to the frontiers of American consciousness. He is a professor in the humanities at Boston University. ◆

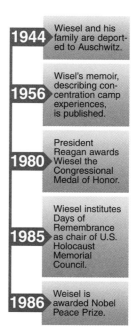

1944 Wiesel and his family are deported to Auschwitz.

1956 Wisel's memoir, describing concentration camp experiences, is published.

1980 President Reagan awards Wiesel the Congressional Medal of Honor.

1985 Wiesel institutes Days of Remembrance as chair of U.S. Holocaust Memorial Council.

1986 Weisel is awarded Nobel Peace Prize.

Wiesenthal, Simon

1908–PRESENT ● INVESTIGATOR OF
NAZI WAR CRIMINALS

1945 Wiesenthal is liberated from Nazi war camp.

1947 Wiesenthal establishes Jewish Historical Documentation Center in Linz.

1961 Eichmann trial generates new interest in prosecution of ex-Nazis.

1977 Yeshiva University opens Simon Wiesenthal Center for Holocaust Studies.

Born in Buchach (Pol., Buczacz), Galicia, Simon Wiesenthal studied architecture at the Prague Technical University and was living in Lvov, Poland, when World War II began. He was arrested by Ukrainian police and spent most of the war in concentration and forced-labor camps, among them Janówska (Lvov), Plaszów, Gross-Rosen, and Buchenwald. He was liberated in Mauthausen on May 5, 1945, by the United States Army.

After the war Wiesenthal devoted himself to the investigation of Nazi war criminals. He worked initially for the War Crimes section of the United States Army in Austria, and in 1947 established the Jewish Historical Documentation Center in Linz. Public interest in Nazi war criminals waned, and Wiesenthal therefore closed his Linz center in 1954. He resumed his work in Vienna in 1961 in the wake of the Eichmann Trial, which generated renewed interest in the prosecution of Nazi war criminals.

Among the most prominent Nazis whom Wiesenthal helped discover and/or bring to justice were Franz Stangl, commandant of the Treblinka and Sobibór extermination camps; Gustav Wagner, deputy commandant of Sobibór; Franz Mürer, commandant of the Vilna ghetto; and Karl Silberbauer, the policeman who arrested Anne Frank. In 1977 the Simon Wiesenthal Center for Holocaust Studies was established at the Yeshiva University of Los Angeles in honor of Wiesenthal's life's work. Besides his efforts to prosecute Nazi war criminals, Wiesenthal has played an important role in commemorating the victims of the Holocaust. His works on the Holocaust include *The Murderers Among Us*; *Sunflower*; *Max and Helen*; and *Every Day Remembrance Day: A Chronicle of Jewish Martyrdom.* ◆

Winnemucca, Sarah

1844–1891 ● NATIVE AMERICAN RIGHTS ACTIVIST

Born in western Nevada into a band of Paiutes led by her father, Chief Winnemucca, and centered around Humboldt and Pyramid lakes, Sarah Winnemucca (Tocmetone, or Shell Flower) became a champion of Indian rights and the author of the influential *Life among the Paiutes: Their Wrongs and Claims* (1883). When her mother and sister were killed in 1865 during disturbances that followed the Paiutes' confinement to a reservation around Pyramid Lake, Winnemucca blamed Indian agents for causing the troubles. She served as an interpreter and messenger for General Oliver Otis Howard during the Paiute and Bannock hostilities of 1877 and 1878 when the general could find no man willing to negotiate with the Indians. Instrumental in persuading Chief Winnemucca to lead his band out of the war camp, she traveled with her father to Washington, D.C., in 1879 and 1880 to seek permission for the Paiutes to leave the Washington Territory and return to the Malheur Reservation in Nevada. Although the secretary of the interior granted the request, the Yakima Indian agent thwarted the move, which only hardened Winnemucca's dislike of such men. Back East in 1881 and 1882, she lectured in Boston and other cities.

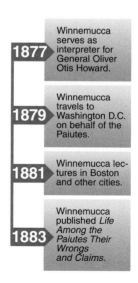

1877 Winnemucca serves as interpreter for General Oliver Otis Howard.

1879 Winnemucca travels to Washington D.C. on behalf of the Paiutes.

1881 Winnemucca lectures in Boston and other cities.

1883 Winnemucca published *Life Among the Paiutes Their Wrongs and Claims.*

Condemning the practices of Indian agents, she won sympathy for her people and the indignations visited upon them and converted many to the new Indian reform movement just then coming into full swing.

Winnemucca was married three times. The first marriage, to Lieutenant Edward Bartlett, lasted scarcely a year. When her second marriage to a Paiute also failed, she married Lieutenant Lambert H. Hopkins, probably an officer in the volunteers, who assisted her in the writing of her book. Her attacks on Indian agents led to savage countercharges that she was a liar and a "drunken prostitute," but these were refuted by General Howard and other distinguished officers, who praised her for the brave work she bad done with them in the field. Money from her speaking tours allowed her to buy land in Nevada and to establish, near Lovelock, an Indian school, which she ran for three years. But in 1886, her husband died of tuberculosis, and Winnemucca—afflicted with psychological and emotional problems, her physical health failing—retired to Monida, Montana, to live with her sister. Hailed as "the most famous Indian woman on the Pacific Coast" by the whites, called "Mother" by her Paiute tribe, Sarah Winnemucca died in Montana of tuberculosis on October 16, 1891. ◆

Winnemucca's attacks on Indian agents led to savage countercharges that she was a liar and a "drunken prostitute."

Xuan Zang
(Hsuian-tsang;
Hsuan-chuang;
Huien-tsiang)

602–664 ● EXPLORER

Xuan Jang undertook a sixteen-year trip from China to India and back. Xuan Zang did not endure the rigors of his long, seventh-century journey to India in order to write his Records of the Western Regions of the Great T'ang Dynasty. He went because, as a student of Buddhist philosophy, he was troubled by the contradictory teachings he found in Buddhist holy books. He thought that if he could locate original Buddhist texts, and perhaps even visit some holy places, he could resolve the discrepancies. So the twenty-eight-year-old monk set out for India, the birthplace of Buddhism. By the time he returned sixteen years later with 520 cases of Buddhist scriptures, Xuan Zang had traveled through much of central Asia. The T'ang emperor then called him to the Chinese capital to give a detailed report on the climate, resources, agriculture, and culture of the places he had visited. Xuan Zang's written narrative of his journey of more than 40,000 miles—the Records—proved an important resource for later scholars interested in the geography and history of early China and India.

Xuan Zang was introduced to the teachings of Buddha by one of his older brothers, who was a Buddhist monk. It quickly became apparent that Xuan Zang was a young man with exceptional promise. Shortly after he also became a monk, he

629 Xuan Zang begins his sixteen-year journey through central Asia.

633 Xuan Zang reaches India, the birthplace of Buddhism.

645 Xuan Zang returns to China with 520 cases of Buddhist scriptures.

*His coloring
was delicate, his
eyes brilliant.
His bearing was
grave and
majestic, and his
features seemed
to radiate charm
and brightness.*

and thirteen other monks were selected by royal mandate from among several hundred candidates to be fully supported while they pursued their studies. Xuan Zang worked diligently, traveling throughout China to study under the most celebrated Buddhist scholars.

Although he mastered even the most difficult texts with apparent ease, he became increasingly troubled. Every scholar interpreted the holy texts in a different way, and Xuan Zang was at a loss to determine which interpretation was correct. The only way to resolve his dilemma, he decided, was to travel to the birthplace of Buddhism—India.

Xuan Zang departed for India from the Chinese city of Liang-zhou, an important center for merchants and traders. At the start, he was accompanied by two companions, but one soon deserted and the other proved too frail for the difficult journey. So Xuan Zang continued alone, intent on reaching his distant goal. A biography written by a disciple, Hui-li, includes this description of the young wayfarer:

> *His coloring was delicate, his eyes brilliant. His bearing was grave and majestic, and his features seemed to radiate charm and brightness. . . . His voice was pure and penetrating in quality and his words were brilliant in their nobility, elegance, and harmony, so that his hearers never grew weary of listening to him.*

Xuan Zang's resources were put to the test on more than one occasion. When seized by river pirates who wanted to sacrifice him to the goddess they worshiped, he protested that he was on a holy pilgrimage, but to no avail. As he was preparing for his death, a fierce storm arose, and the terrified pirates, seeing it as an omen, begged Xuan Zang's forgiveness and sent him on his way. Another time, as he passed through Turpan (now in Xinjiang Province), the **khan** was so impressed with the young monk that he asked Xuan Zang to stay to become leader of the Buddhist church in Turpan. Xuan Zang declined, but the khan insisted, so Xuan Zang resorted to a hunger strike to emphasize his will to continue his journey. The khan not only relented, but he subsequently became Xuan Zang's greatest benefactor. He gave the monk enough gold and silver to support him for twenty years, and provided him with letters and gifts to help ensure safe passage to his destination.

khan: the former title of a ruler in parts of Central Asia.

Not all the obstacles Xuan Zang met were human: he also crossed the vast deserts of central Asia and the rugged mountains of northwest India. But in 633, four years after he left China, he finally reached Buddhism's homeland. While there, he visited all the sites in India made holy by their association with the Buddha. He traveled up and down the east and west coasts of the subcontinent. True to his mission, however, Xuan Zang spent most of his time at Nalanda, where he studied **Sanskrit** and Buddhist philosophy. In all his wanderings, Xuan Zang was a relentless collector of Buddhist images and holy books and of descriptions of people he met and places through which he traveled.

Sanskrit: an ancient language of India.

Though Xuan Zang's fame spread throughout India, he resisted the effort by Indian monks to convince him to remain in the birthplace of the Buddha. He rejected their contention that China was a land of barbarians, pointing to China's effective laws, virtuous rulers, loyal subjects, and advances in astronomy, music, and engineering. Xuan Zang, at first acting as a sort of ambassador for his native land to the people of India, effectively became an ambassador for India upon his return to China in 645. There he began to translate the Sanskrit texts he brought from India and to enlighten the people of China about their neighbors to the west. He also composed his Records, the account of his travels. Some scholars believe that his crosscultural efforts caused the beginning of political relations between India and China. Whatever his role in that development, the Buddhist texts and the invaluable geographical information he gathered on his hazardous journey ensured his standing as one of the most famous Buddhist monks in history, as well as one of the most accomplished Asian travelers of the Middle Ages. ◆

York, Alvin C.

1887–1964 ● WORLD WAR I HERO

"Well, seeing the boys all shot up, gassed, blown to pieces, and killed lying about us, there is no tongue or human being who can ever tell the feeling of a man during this time. But I never doubted in the thickest of the battle but what God would bring me through safe."

Alvin C. York, from his diary

Alvin C. York, better know as Sergeant York, was born at Pall Mall, Tennessee, on December 13, 1887. He was the son of William and Mary (Brooks) York. Alvin York was raised on his father's farm amid the mountains of Tennessee, and after leaving school engaged in his father's trade of blacksmith.

When the United States entered World War I, York enlisted in the United States Army despite an active membership in the Church of Christ and Christian Union, a strict religious sect opposed to war. After a period of training at Camp Gordon, Georgia, where he displayed unusual skill in marksmanship acquired by long practice among his native hills, York went to France with his company (the 328th infantry regiment in the 82nd division) and was made a corporal.

On October 8, 1918, during the battle of the Argonne, York was one of sixteen men ordered to charge and silence a nest of German machines guns on the other side of a slope. It

1918 In World War I, York defeats a German machine-gun battalion.

1919 York marries Grace Williams.

1964 York dies in a Veterans Administration hospital.

was hazardous work, but the detachment climbed the hill without loss. The descent on the other side was a series of surprises. The soldiers came suddenly upon two Germans, one of whom surrendered, while the other disappeared. Anticipating a fight, the detachment went into skirmish order while continuing to advance. At a small stream they surprised twenty or thirty Germans, whom they captured. The little party of Americans were now exposed to the enemy, and soon dozens of machine guns, hidden on the slope of the hill, opened fire on them and their German prisoners. All dropped to the ground, but not before six of the American had been killed and several wounded, including three noncommissioned officers. One had taken refuge behind a tree, ranked on both sides by enemy fire; the others were guarding the German prisoners, and Corporal York was left to fight the entire machine-gun battalion alone. Unperturbed by the heavy odds against him and with no thought of surrender, he lay on the ground on the outer edge of the huddle of German prisoners just below the firing line, and with his rifle picked off the Germans in the machine-gun nests one at a time. After disposing of some twenty of the enemy in this way, he saw a German lieutenant and seven men rise only twenty yards away and charge at him. He killed them all with his automatic, and then resumed his sharpshooting work. Finally a German major among the prisoners called out to York in English: "Don't shoot any more and I will make them surrender." He was as good as his word, and a little later York and his seven privates marched into the American lines with 132 prisoners, including four German officers.

This remarkable display of American valor was soon afterwards reported in the press, and upon Corporal York's return to American with his regiment a rousing reception was given him in many quarters. At a dinner and reception in New York city by the Tennessee Society, his division commander, Major General Duncan, said: "It is a unique distinction for me to have on one side of me the admiral who safely conducted all of our troops overseas, and on the other side one of the most distinguished soldiers the world has ever produced." For the intrepidity and gallantry displayed on this occasion he was awarded the congressional medal of honor and was offered a colonelcy by the governor of Tennessee, but preferred to return to his native village. Public appreciation of his bravery

> The little party of Americans were exposed to the enemy, and soon dozens of machine guns, hidden on the slope of the hill, opened fire on them.

found practical expression in the presentation to him of a $50,000 farm, well stocked, near his home.

York was married June 7, 1919, to Grace, daughter of S. A. Williams, a farmer of Pall Mall, Tennessee. He died at the veteran's hospital in Nashville in 1964. ◆

Sources

The biographies in *Macmillan Profiles: Heroes and Pioneers* were extracted from the following sources:

Encyclopedia of Africa South of the Sahara, Charles Scribner's Sons, 1997.
Encyclopedia of African-American Culture and History, Macmillan Reference USA, 1996.
Encyclopedia of Asian History, Charles Scribner's Sons, 1988.
Encyclopedia of Latin American History and Culture, Charles Scribner's Sons, 1996.
Encyclopedia of the American Presidency, Simon & Schuster, 1994.
Encyclopedia of the American West, Macmillan Reference USA, 1996.
Encyclopedia of the Holocaust, Macmillan Library Reference USA, 1990.
Record of America: A Reference History of the United States, Charles Scribner's Sons, 1996.
Scribner Encyclopedia of American Lives, Charles Scribner's Sons, 1998.
They Made History: A Biographical Dictionary, Simon & Schuster, 1993.
Who's Who in Space, Macmillan Publishing Company, 1998.
World Explorers and Discoverers, Macmillan Publishing Company, 1992.

The following authors contributed articles to the publications listed above:

Axelrod, Alan: Chief Joseph
Baker, William J.: James Cleveland (Jesse) Owens
Bell, John Patrick: Oscar Arias Sánchez
Bodo, Peter: Arthur Robert Ashe Jr.
Bushnell, David: Simón Bolívar
Carson, Clayborne/Garrow, David J.: Martin Luther King Jr.
Cassutt, Michael: Neil Alden Armstrong, Yuri Alexeyevich Gagarin
Claussenius, David R.: Corazon Cojuangco Aquino
Cone, James H.: Malcolm X
Crahan, Margaret E.: Adolfo Pérez Esquivel
Crutchfield, James A.: David (Davey) Crockett
De Gruchy, John W.: Desmond Mpilo Tutu
Early, Gerald: Muhammed Ali
Hayden, Robert C.: Charles Richard Drew
Hogan, Patricia: Sarah Winnemucca
Jones, John N.: Steve Biko
Jostock, Carolyn: Francisco Alves (Chico) Mendes Filho
Kampwirth, Karen: Violeta Barrios de Chamorro
Kaufman, Burton: Jimmy Carter
Kennedy, Randall: Thurgood Marshall
Lazare, Lucien: Joseph Weill
Martin, Waldo E., Jr.: Frederick Douglass
McKinley, Edward H.: William Booth
McNeill, Lydia: Mae Carol Jemison
Meer, Fatima: Nelson Mandela

Moors, Marilyn M.: Rigoberta Menchú Tum
Moulton, Gary: Meriwether Lewis
Nadasen, Pam: Rosa Louise McCauley Parks
Paldiel, Mordecai: Elisabeth Abegg, Arnold Douwes, Giuseppe Nicolini, Oskar Schindler, Anton Schmid
Paldiel, Mordecai/Rozeit, Robert: Carl (Charles) Lutz
Perry, Elisabeth Israels: Eleanor Roosevelt
Pfefferkorn, Eli: Elie (Eliezer) Wiesel
Phillips, Charles: Tecumseh
Porter, Joseph C.: Crazy Horse
Racine, Karen: Oscar Arnulfo Romero
Rampersad, Arnold: William Edward Burghardt Du Bois
Reeve, W. Paul/Gowans, Fred R.: Daniel Boone
Ronda, James P.: William Clark
Salas, Elizabeth: Maria Adelina Emilia (Nina) Otero-Warren
Smock, Raymond W.: Booker Taliaferro Washington
Stoner, John C.: Colin Luther Powell
Tygiel, Jules: Jack Roosevelt (Jackie) Robinson
Venter, Denis: Frederik Willem de Klerk
Wilson, John P.: Allan Pinkerton
Wilson, Raymond: Charles Alexander (Ohiyesa) Eastman
Yahil, Leni: Raoul Wallenberg
Zuroff, Efraim: Simon Wiesenthal

The following articles were reprinted with permission of American Reference Publishing Company from *National Cyclopedia of American Biography*:

Name	Copyright Date	Copyright Holder	Vol/Page Number(s)
Thomas Hopkins Gallaudet	1907	James T. White & Company	v9:138-140
Alvin C. York	1930	James T. White & Company	A:393

The following articles were newly written for *Macmillan Profiles: Heroes & Pioneers*:

Name	Author
Aung San Suu Kyi	Patricia Ohlenroth
César Chávez	Patricia Ohlenroth
Dalai Lama	Patricia Ohlenroth
Václav Havel	Patricia Ohlenroth
Mother Teresa	Patricia Ohlenroth
Eliot Ness	Patricia Ohlenroth
Lech Welesa	Patricia Ohlenroth

Photographs and images used in this volume were obtained from the following sources:

Suggested Reading

ELISABETH ABEGG

Block, Gay, and Malka Drucker. *Rescuers: Portraits of Moral Courage in the Holocaust.* TV Books Inc., 1998.

Fogelman, Eva. *Conscience & Courage: Rescuers of Jews During the Holocaust.* Anchor, 1995.

Leuner, H. D. *When Compassion Was a Crime.* 1966.

Michalczyk, John J. *Resisters, Rescuers, and Refugees: Historical and Ethical Issues.* Theological Book Service, 1997.

Oliner, Samuel P., and Pearl M. Oliner. *The Altruistic Personality: Rescuers of Jews in Nazi Europe.* Free Press, 1992.

Paldiel, Mordecai. *Sheltering the Jews: Stories of Holocaust Rescuers.* Fortress Press, 1997.

JOHN WILLIAM ALCOCK

Sloan, Carolyn, and Simon Smith. *The Story of Allock and Brown.* Silver Burdett Press, 1998.

MUHAMMAD ALI

Conklin, Thomas. *Muhammad Ali: The Fight for Respect.* Millbrook, 1991.

Early, Gerald Lyn (editor). *The Muhammad Ali Reader.* Ecco Press, 1998.

Freedman, Suzanne. *Clay v. United States: Muhammad Ali Objects to War* (Landmark Supreme Court Cases). Enslow Publishing, Inc., 1997.

Hauser, Thomas. *Muhammad Ali: His Life and Times.* Touchstone Books, 1992.

Mailer, Norman. *The Fight.* Vintage Books, 1997.

ETHAN ALLEN

Bellesiles, Michael A. *Revolutionary Outlaws: Ethan Allen and the Struggle for Independence on the Early American Frontier.* University Press of Virginia, 1993.

Clinton, Susan. *The Story of the Green Mountain Boys.* Children's Press, 1987.

Hahn, Michael T. *Ethan Allen: A Life of Adventure.* New England Press, 1994.

Jellison, Charles Albert. *Ethan Allen: Frontier Rebel.* Syracuse University Press, 1983.

SUSAN B. ANTHONY

Barry, Kathleen L. *Susan B. Anthony: Biography of a Singular Feminist.* New York University Press, 1988.

Clinton, Susan. *The Story of Susan B. Anthony.* Children's Press, 1986.

Dubois, Ellen Carol. *The Elizabeth Cady Stanton—Susan B. Anthony Reader: Correspondence, Writings, Speeches.* Northeastern University Press, 1992.

Mosher, Kiki. *Learning About Fairness from the Life of Susan B. Anthony.* Powerkids Press, 1997.

Weisberg, Barbara. *Susan B. Anthony.* Chelsea House, 1988.

CORAZON AQUINO

Crisostomo, Isabelo T., and Heherson T. Alvarez. *Cory: Profile of a President.* Branden Publishing Company, 1990.

Gullas, Cecilia. *Corazon Aquino: The Miracle of a President: A Biography.* Cultural House, 1987.

Haskins, James. *Corazon Aquino: Leader of the Philippines.* Enslow Publishers, 1988.

Nadel, Laurie. *Corazon Aquino: Journey to Power.* Julian Messner, 1987.

Reid, Robert H., and Eileen Guerrero. *Corazon Aquino and the Brushfire Revolution.* Lousiana State University Press, 1995.

OSCAR ARIAS SANCHEZ

Peduzzi, Kelli. *Oscar Arias: Peacemaker and Leader Among Nations.* 1991.

NEIL ARMSTRONG

Armstrong, Neil, and Milton O. Thompson. *At the Edge of Space: The X-15 Flight Program.* Smithsonian Institution Press, 1992.

Bredeson, Carmen. *Neil Armstrong: A Space Biography.* Enslow Publishers, Inc., 1998.

Kramer, Barbara. *Neil Armstrong: The First Man on the Moon.* Enslow Publishers, Inc., 1997.

Langley, Andrew, and Alex Pang. *Journey into Space: The Missions of Neil Armstrong.* Chelsea Juniors, 1993.

ARTHUR ASHE

Ashe, Arthur, and Alexander McNab. *Arthur Ashe on Tennis: Strokes, Strategies, Traditions, Players, Psychology, and Wisdom.* Avon Books, 1996.

Weissberg, Ted, and Coretta Scott King. *Arthur Ashe.* Chelsea House Publishers Paperbacks, 1992.

Wright, David L. *Arthur Ashe: Breaking the Color Barrier in Tennis.* Enslow Publishers, Inc., 1996.

ASOKA

Kanitkar, Helen. *Asoka and Indian Civilization*. Greenhaven Press, 1980.

Nikam, N. A. (editor). *The Edicts of Asoka*. University of Chicago Press, 1978.

AUNG SAN SUU KYI

Aung San Suu Kyi. *Freedom From Fear And Other Writings*. Penguin Books, 1995.

Aung San Suu Kyi and Alan Clements. *The Voice of Hope*. Seven Stories Press, 1997.

Aung San Suu Kyi and Heinn Htet (illustrator). *Letters from Burma*. Penguin USA, 1998.

Lintner, Bertil. *Aung San Suu Kyi and Burma's Unfinished Renaissance*. White Lotus Company, 1991.

Parenteau, John. *Prisoner for Peace: Aung San Suu Kyi and Burma's Struggle for Democracy*. Morgan Reynolds, 1994.

Victor, Barbara. *The Lady: Aung San Suu Kyi: Nobel Laureate and Burma's Prisoner*. Faber & Faber, 1998.

VIOLETA BARRIOS DE CHAMORRO

Arnson, Cynthia, and David Holiday. *Fitful Peace: Human Rights and Reconciliation in Nicaragua Under the Chamorro Government*. Human Rights Watch, 1991.

Barrios de Chamorro, Violeta, Guido Fernandez, and Sonia Cruz de Baltodano. *Dreams of the Heart: The Autobiography of Violeta Barrios de Chamorro, President of Nicaragua*. 1996.

STEVE BIKO

Biko, Steve, and Aelred Stubbs (editor). *I Write What I Like: A Selection of His Writings*. Bowerdean Publishing Company, 1996.

Woods, Donald. *Biko*. Henry Holt, 1991.

SIMÓN BOLÍVAR

De Madariaga, Salvador. *Bolívar*. Greenwood Publishing Group, 1979.

De Varona, Frank. *Simón Bolívar*. Millbrook, 1993.

Garcia Marquez, Gabriel. *The General in His Labyrinth*. Penguin USA, 1991.

Goodnough, David. *Simón Bolívar: South American Liberator*. Enslow Publishers, Inc., 1998.

Greene, Carol. *Simón Bolívar*. Children's Press, 1989.

Martinez, Nelson. Simón Bolívar. Aims International Books, 1996.

Masur, Gerhard. *Simón Bolívar*. University of New Mexico Press, 1969.

DANIEL BOONE

Bakeless, John E. *Daniel Boone: Master of the Wilderness*. University of Nebraska Press, 1989. First published in 1939.

Draper, Lyman C., and Ted Franklin Belue (editor). *The Life of Daniel Boone*. Stackpole Books, 1998.

Faragher, John Mack. *Daniel Boone: The Life and Legend of an American Pioneer*. Owlet, 1993.

Lofaro, Michael A. *The Life and Adventures of Daniel Boone*. University Press of Kentucky, 1986.

WILLIAM BOOTH

Bennett, David. *William Booth*. Bethany House, 1994.

Green, Roger Joseph, and Kay F. Rader (introduction). *Catherine Booth: A Biography of the Cofounder of the Salvation Army*. Baker Book House, 1996.

McKinley, Edward. *Marching to Glory: The History of the Salvation Army in the United States, 1880-1992*. Wm B. Eerdmans Publishing Company, 1995.

Murdoch, Norman H. *Origins of the Salvation Army*. University of Tennessee Press, 1996.

OMAR BRADLEY

Bradley, Omar. *A General's Life*. Buccaneer Books, 1993.

LOUIS BRAILLE

Bryant, Jennifer Fisher, John Callahan, and Jerry Lewis. *Louis Braille: Inventor*. Chelsea House Publishing, 1994.

Davidson, Margaret. *Louis Braille: The Boy Who Invented Books for the Blind*. Scholastic Trade, 1991.

ROBERT BRUCE

McNair Scott, Ronald. *Robert Bruce: King of Scots*. Carroll & Graf, 1996.

JIMMY CARTER

Brinkley, Douglas. *The Unfinished Presidency: Jimmy Carter's Journey Beyond the White House.* Viking Press, 1998.

Carter, Jimmy, and Sarah Elizabeth Chuldenko (illustrator). *Always a Reckoning and Other Poems.* Times Books, 1995.

Dumbrell, John. *The Carter Presidency: A Re-Evaluation.* Manchester University Press, 1995.

Kaufman, Burton. *The Presidency of James Earl Carter, Jr.* University Press of Kansas, 1993.

Richman, Daniel A. *James E. Carter.* Garrett Educational, 1989.

Sandak, Cass R. *The Carters.* Crestwood, 1993.

Thornton, Richard C. *The Carter Years.* Paragon House, 1991.

CÉSAR CHÁVEZ

Ferriss, Susan, Ricardo Sandoval, and Diana Hembree (editor). *The Fight in the Fields: César Chávez and the Farmworkers Movement.* Harcourt Brace, 1998.

Griswold del Castillo, Richard, and Richard A. Garcia. *César Chávez: A Triumph of Spirit.* University of Oklahoma Press, 1997.

Holmes, Burnham. *César Chávez* (American Troublemakers). Raintree/Steck Vaughn, 1993.

WINSTON CHURCHILL

Callahan, Raymond A. *Churchill: Retreat from Empire.* Scholarly, 1984.

Charmley, John. *Churchill: The End of Glory: A Political Biography.* Harcourt Brace, 1994.

Churchill, Winston S. *Memoirs of the Second World War: An Abridgement of the Six Volumes of the Second World War with an Epiloque by the Author on the Postwar Years.* Houghton Mifflin, reprint edition 1991.

Edmonds, Robin. *The Big Three: Churchill, Roosevelt, and Stalin in Peace & War.* Norton, 1991.

Gilbert, Martin. *Churchill: A Life.* Henry Holt, 1992.

Rose, Norman. *Churchill: The Unruly Giant.* Free Press, 1995.

Sainsbury, Keith. *Churchill and Roosevelt at War: The War They Fought and the Peace They Hoped to Make.* New York University Press, 1994.

EL CID

Fletcher, Richard. *The Quest for El Cid.* Oxford Univeristy Press, 1991.

McCaughrean, Geraldine, and Victor G. Ambrus (illustrator). *El Cid.* Oxford University Press, 1997.

WILLIAM CLARK

Ambrose, Stephen E. *Undaunted Courage: Meriwether Lewis, Thomas Jefferson, and the Opening of the American West.* Touchstone Books, 1997.

Blumberg, Rhoda. *The Incredible Journey of Lewis & Clark.* Beech Tree Books, 1995.

Moulton, Gary E. *Lewis and Clark and the Route to the Pacific.* Chelsea House, 1991.

CLOVIS

Currier, John W. *Clovis, King of the Franks.* Marquette University Press, 1997.

CHRISTOPHER COLUMBUS

Bedini, Silvio A. (editor). *The Christopher Columbus Encyclopedia.* 2 vols. Simon & Schuster, 1991.

Gleiter, Jan, Kathleen Thompson, and Rick Whipple. *Christopher Columbus.* Raintree/Steck Vaughn, 1987.

Lunenfeld, Marvin (editor). *1492: Discovery, Invasion, Encounter.* Heath, 1991.

Meltzer, Milton. *Columbus and the World Around Him.* Watts, 1990.

Pelta, Kathy. *Discovering Christopher Columbus.* Lerner, 1991.

Stannard, David E. *American Holocaust: Columbus and the Conquest of the New World.* Oxford University Press, 1992.

Yue, Charlotte, and David. *Christopher Columbus.* Houghton, 1992.

CRAZY HORSE

Ambrose, Stephen E. *Crazy Horse and Custer: The Parallel Lives of Two American Warriors.* Anchor, 1996.

Guttmacher, Peter. *Crazy Horse: Sioux War Chief.* Chelsea House Publishing, 1994.

DAVEY CROCKETT

Crockett, Davis. *Davey Crockett: His Own story—A Narrative of the Life of David Crockett of the State of Tennessee.* Applewood Books, reprint edition 1993.

Davis, William C. *Three Roads to the Alamo: The Lives and Fortunes of David Crockett, James Bowie, and William Barret Travis.* HarperCollins, 1998.

Derr, Mark. *The Frontiersman: The Real Life and the Many Legends of Davey Crockett.* William Morrow & Company, 1993.

Lofaro, Michael A. *Davey Crockett: The Man, The Myth, The Legacy, 1786-1836.* University of Tennessee Press, 1989.

Lord, Walter, *A Time to Stand: An Epic of the Alamo.* University of Nebraska Press, 1978.

DALAI LAMA

Dalai Lama, Bstan-Dzin-Rgya-Mtsho. *The Buddha Nature: Death and Eternal Soul in Buddhism*. Bluestar Communication Corp., 1997.

Dalai Lama. *The Four Noble Truths: Fundamentals of the Buddhist Teachings of His Holiness the XIV Dalai Lama*. Thorsons Publishing, 1998.

Dalai Lama. *Freedom in Exile: The Autobiography of the Dalai Lama*. Harper San Francisco, 1991.

Stewart, Whitney. *The 14th Dalai Lama: Spiritual Leader of Tibet*. Lerner Publications Company, 1996.

STEPHEN DECATUR

Blassingame, W. *Stephen Decatur Fighting Sailor*. 1964.

Brady, Cyrus T. *Stephen Decatur*, 1978.

WILLEM DE KLERK

Ottaway, David. *Chained Together: Mandela, De Klerk, and the Struggle to Remake South Africa*. 1993.

DOROTHEA DIX

Gollaher, David L. *Voice for the Mad: The Life of Dorothea Dix*. Free Press, 1995.

ARNOLD DOUWES

Block, Gay, and Malka Drucker. *Rescuers: Portraits of Moral Courage in the Holocaust*. TV Books Inc., 1998

De Jong, L. *Het Koninkrijk der Nderlandern in de Tweede Wereldoorlog*. Vols. 6 and 7. The Hague, 1975-1976.

Fogelman, Eva. *Conscience & Courage: Rescuers of Jews During the Holocaust*. Anchor, 1995.

Leuner, H. D. *When Compassion Was a Crime*. 1966.

Michalczyk, John J. *Resisters, Rescuers, and Refugees: Historical and Ethical Issues*. Theological Book Service, 1997.

Oliner, Samuel P., and Pearl M. Oliner. *The Altruistic Personality: Rescuers of Jews in Nazi Europe*. Free Press, 1992.

Paldiel, Mordecai. *Sheltering the Jews: Stories of Holocaust Rescuers*. Fortress Press, 1997.

FREDERICK DOUGLASS

Douglass, Frederick, and Peter J. Grimes (editor). *Narrative of the Life of Frederick Douglass: An American Slave*. Signet, 1977.

Miller, Douglas T. *Frederick Douglass and the Fight for Freedom*. Facts on File, 1988.

CHARLES DREW

Love, Spencie and John Hope Franklin. *One Blood: The Death and Resurrection of Charles R. Drew*. University of North Carolina Press, 1996.

W. E. B. DU BOIS

Byerman, Keith E. *Seizing the Word: History, Art and Self in the Work of W. E. B. Du Bois*. University of Georgia Press, 1994.

Cavan, Seamus. *W. E. B. Du Bois and Racial Relations*. Millbrook, 1993.

Du Bois, W. E. B. *W. E. B. Du Bois: A Reader*. Henry Holt, 1994.

Du Bois, W. E. B., and Eric J. Sundquist (editor). *The Oxford W. E. B. Du Bois Reader*. Oxford University Press, 1996.

Du Bois, W. E. B., and Herbert Aptheker (editor). *Autobiography of W. E. B. Du Bois: A Soliloquy on Viewing My Life from the Last Decade of Its First Century*. International Publishers Company, 1968.

Lewis, David L. *W. E. B. Du Bois*. Henry Holt, 1993.

Zamir, Shamoon. *Dark Voices: W. E. B. Du Bois and American Thought, 1888–1903*. University of Chicago Press, 1995.

JEAN-HENRI DUNANT

Hutchinson, John F. *Champions of Charity: War and the Rise of the Red Cross*. Westview Press, 1996.

Pollard, Michael. *The Red Cross and the Red Crescent*. New Discovery, 1995.

AMELIA EARHART

Earhart, Amelia. *Last Flight*. 1937. Reprint, Crown, 1988.

Goldstein, Donald M. and Katherine V. Dillon. *Amelia: The Centennial Biography of an Aviator Pioneer*. Brasseys Inc., 1997.

Lovell, Mary S. *The Sound of Wings: The Life of Amelia Earhart*. St. Martin's, 1989.

Morrissey, Muriel Earhart. *Amelia Earhart*. Bellerophon Books, 1977.

Rich, Doris L. *Amelia Earhart*. Smithsonian Institution, 1989.

CHARLES ALEXANDER EASTMAN

Eastman, Charles Alexander. *From the Deep Wood to Civilization: Chapters in the Autobiography of an Indian*. 1916.

Eastman, Charles Alexander. *Indian Boyhood*. 1902

Eastman, Charles Alexander. *The Indian Today: The Past and Future of the First American*. 1915

Eastman, Charles Alexander. *The Soul of the Indian: An Interpretation*. 1911.

Wilson, Raymond. *Ohiyesa: Charles Eastman, Santee Sioux*. 1983.

DWIGHT D. EISENHOWER

Ambrose, Stephen E. *Eisenhower*. 2 vols. Simon & Schuster, 1983–1984.

Beschloss, Michael R. *Eisenhower*. Harper, 1990.

Cannon, Marian G. *Dwight David Eisenhower*. Watts, 1990.

Ellis, Rafaela. *Dwight D. Eisenhower*. Garrett Educational, 1989.

Pach, Chester J., Jr., and Elmo Richardson. *The Presidency of Dwight D. Eisenhower*. Rev. ed., University Press of Kansas, 1991.

Sandak, Cass R. *The Eisenhowers*. Crestwood, 1993.

YURI GARGARIN

Cole, Michael D. *Vostok 1: First Human in Space*. Enslow Publishers, Inc., 1995.

Sharpe, Michell R. *Yuri Gagarin: First Man in Space*. 1969.

MAHATMA GANDHI

Bondurant, Joan Valerie. *Conquest of Violence: The Gandhian Philosophy of Conflict*. Princeton University Press, 1988.

Brown, Judith M. *Gandhi: Prisoner of Hope*. Yale, 1989.

Fischer, Louis. *The Life of Mahatma Gandhi*. Easton Press, 1988. First published in 1950.

Mohandas Gandhi and Mahandez Desai (translator). *An Autobiography: The Story of My Experiments with Truth*. Beacon Press, 1993.

Settel, Trudy S. *The Book of Gandhi Wisdom*. Citidel Press, 1995.

ULLYSSES S. GRANT

Arnold, Matthew, and James Y. Simon (editor). *General Grant*. Kent State University Press, 1995.

Bentley, Bill. *Ulysses S. Grant*. Watts, 1993.

Marrin, Albert. *Unconditional Surrender: U. S. Grant and the Civil War*. Atheneum, 1994.

Simpson, Brooks D. *Let Us Have Peace: Ulysses S. Grant and the Politics of War and Reconstruction*. University of North Carolina Press, 1991.

NATHAN HALE

Darrow, Jane. *Nathan Hale: A Story of Loyalties*. Century Company, 1932.

Hagman, Harlan. *Nathan Hale and John Andre*. Heart of the Lakes Publishing, 1992.

Johnston, Henry P. *Nathan Hale, 1776: Biography and Memorials*. Revised edition. Yale, 1914.

ALEXANDER HAMILTON

Flaumenhaft, Harvey. *The Effective Republic*. Duke, 1992.

Hamilton, Alexander, James Madison, and John Jay. *The Federalist*. Everyman Paperback Classics, reissue edition, 1990.

O'Brien, Steve. *Alexander Hamilton*. Chelsea House, 1989.

Rogow, Arnold A. *A Fatal Friendship: Alexander Hamilton and Aaron Burr*. Hill & Want Publishing, 1998.

JOHN HANCOCK

Allan, Herbert S. *John Hancock, Patriot in Purple*. 1948. Reprint, Reprint Services, 1993.

Fradin, Dennis B. *John Hancock: First Signer of the Declaration of Independence*. Enslow, 1989.

VÁCLAV HAVEL

Havel, Václav, Josef Skvorecky, and Ivan Klima. *Literature and Tolerance: Views from Praque*. Readers International, 1995.

Havel, Václav, and Paul Wilson (translator). *The Art of the Impossible: Politics As Morality in Practice—Speeches and Writings, 1990-1996*. Knopf, 1997.

Symynkywicz, Jeffrey B. *Václav Havel and the Velvet Revolution*. Dillon Press, 1995.

MIGUEL HILDALGO Y COSTILLA

De Varona, Frank. *Miguel Hidalgo y Costilla: Father of Mexican Independence*. Millbrook Press, 1993.

Gleiter, Jan, and Kathleen Thompson. *Miguel Hidalgo y Costilla*. Raintree, 1989.

Hamill, Hugh M. *The Hidalgo Revolt: Prelude to Mexican Independence*. 1966. Reprint, Greenwood, 1981.

ANDREW JACKSON

Cole, Donald B. *The Presidency of Andrew Jackson*. University Press of Kansas, 1993.

Meltzer, Milton. *Andrew Jackson and His America*. Watts, 1993.

Schlesinger, Arthur M., Jr. *The Age of Jackson*. 1945. Reprint. Little, Brown, 1988.

Stefoff, Rebecca. *Andrew Jackson*. Garrett Educational, 1988.

Wallace, Anthony F. C. *The Long, Bitter Trail: Andrew Jackson and the Indians*. Hill & Wang, 1993.

Watson, Harry L. *Liberty and Power: The Politics of Jacksonian America*. Hill & Wang, 1990.

THOMAS JEFFERSON

Bedini, Silvio A. *Thomas Jefferson: Statesman of Science*. Macmillan, 1990.

Ellis, Joseph J. *American Sphinx: The Character of Thomas Jefferson*. Knopf, 1997.

Giblin, James C. *Thomas Jefferson*. Scholastic, 1994.

McLaughlin, Jack. *Jefferson and Monticello*. Henry Holt, 1988.

Randall, Willard S. *Thomas Jefferson*. Henry Holt, 1993.

Randolph, Sarah Nicholas. *The Domestic Life of Thomas Jefferson*. University Press of Virginia, 1979.

MAE JEMISON

Ceasor, Ebraska D. *Mae C. Jemison: 1st Black Female Astronaut*. New Day Press, 1992.

Yannuzzi, Della A. *Mae Jemison: A Space Biography*. Enslow Publishers, Inc., 1998.

JOAN OF ARC

Brooks, Polly S. *Beyond the Myth: The Story of Joan of Arc*. Lippincott, 1990.

Christopher, Tracy. *Joan of Arc*. Chelsea House., 1993.

Duby, Georges and Juliet Vale (translater). *France in the Middle Ages 987-1460 : From Hugh Capet to Joan of Arc (A History of France)*. Blackwell Publishing, 1992.

Pernoud, Regine. *Joan of Arc: By Herself and Her Witnesses*. Scarborough House, 1994.

JOHN PAUL JONES

Morrison, Samuel Eliot. *John Paul Jones: A Sailor's Biography*. Northeastern University Press, 1985. First published in 1959.

Walsh, John E. *Night on Fire: The First Complete Account of John Paul Jones's Greatest Battle*. McGraw, 1978.

HELEN ADAMS KELLER

Hermann, Dorothy. *Helen Keller: A Life*. Knopf, 1998.

Keller, Helen. *Story of My Life*. Doubleday, reprint edition 1991.

Lash, Joseph P. *Helen and Teacher: The Story of Helen Keller and Anne Sullivan Macy*. Dell, 1980.

JOMO KENYATTA

Aseka, Eric M. *Jomo Kenyatta: A Biography*. Nairobi, Kenya, 1992.

Kenyatta, Jomo. *Facing Mount Kenya: The Tribal Life of the Gikuyu*. AMS Press, 1972.

Kenyatta, Jomo. *Suffering Without Bitterness: The Founding of the Kenyan Nation*. 1968.

MARTIN LUTHER KING JR.

Branch, Taylor. *Parting the Waters: America in the King Years, 1954–63*. Simon & Schuster, 1988.

Garrow, David J. *Bearing the Cross: Martin Luther King, Jr., and the Southern Christian Leadership Conference*. Morrow, 1986.

Jakoubek, Robert E. *Martin Luther King, Jr*. Chelsea House., 1989.

King, Martin Luther Jr., Coretta Scott King, and James Melvin Washington (editor). *I Have a Dream : Writings and Speeches That Changed the World*. Harper San Francisco, 1992.

Lewis, David L. *King: A Biography*. University of Illinois Press, 1978.

Naveh, Eyal. *Crown of Thorns : Political Martrydom in American from Abraham Lincoln to Martin Luther King, Jr*. New York University Press, 1992.

T. E. LAWRENCE.

Mack, John E. *A Prince of Our Disorder: The Life of T. E. Lawrence*. 1976. Reprint. Little, Brown, 1978.

Wilson, Jeremy. *Lawrence of Arabia*. Atheneum, 1989.

ROBERT E. LEE

Connelly, Thomas L. *The Marble Man: Robert E. Lee and His Image in American Society*. 1977

Dowdey, Clifford, and Louis H. Manarin (editors). *The Wartime Papers of R. E. Lee*. 1961.

Marrin, Albert. *Virginia's General: Robert E. Lee and the Civil War*. Atheneum, 1994.

Smith, Gene. *Lee and Grant*. 1984. Reprint. NAL, 1985.

MERIWETHER LEWIS

Dillon, Richard. Meriwether Lewis: A Biography. 1965. Reprint 1988.

Moulton, Gary E. *Lewis and Clark and the Route to the Pacific*. Chelsea House, 1991.

Moulton, Gary E. (editor). *Journals of the Lewis and Clark Expedition*. 12 vols. 1983– .

Ronda, James P. *Lewis and Clark Among the Indians*. 1984.

ABRAHAM LINCOLN

Boritt, Gabor S. (editor). *The Historian's Lincoln*. University of Illinois Press, 1988.

Donald, David Herbert. *Lincoln*. Touchstone Books, 1996.

Holzer, Harold, Gabor S. Boritt, and M. E. Neely. *The Lincoln Image: Abraham Lincoln and the Popular Press*. Scribner, 1984.

Jacobs, William J. *Lincoln*. Scribner, 1991.

Kunhardt, Philip B. Jr. *Lincoln: An Illustrated Biography*. Knopf, 1992.

Lincoln, Abraham. *Speeches and Writings*. 2 vols. Library of America, 1989.

McPherson, James M. *Abraham Lincoln and the Second American Revolution*. Oxford, 1991.

Vidal, Gore. *Lincoln*. Ballantine Books, reissue 1985.

CHARLES AUGUSTUS LINDBERGH

Denenberg, Barry. *An American Hero: The True Story of Charles A. Lindbergh*. Scholastic Trade, 1998.

Lindbergh, Charles A. *Autobiography of Values*. Ed. William Jovanovich. Harcourt, 1978.

Randolph, Blythe. *Charles Lindbergh*. Watts, 1990.

Ross, Walter S. *The Last Hero: Charles A. Lindbergh*. Rev. ed. Harper, 1976.

ALBERT JOHN MVUMBI LUTHULI

Callan, E. *Albert John Luthuli and the South African Race Conflict*. 1965.

Gordimer, Nadine. "Chief Luthuli." *Atlantic Monthly* 203, no. 4 (1959): 34-39.

Luthuli, Albert. *Let My People Go*. 1962.

CARL LUTZ

Block, Gay, and Malka Drucker. *Rescuers: Portraits of Moral Courage in the Holocaust*. TV Books Inc., 1998

Fogelman, Eva. *Conscience & Courage: Rescuers of Jews During the Holocaust*. Anchor, 1995.

Grossman, A. *Nur das Gewissen: Carl Lutz und seine Budapester Aktion; Geschichte und Portrat*. N.P., Switzerland, 1986.

Leuner, H. D. *When Compassion Was a Crime*. 1966.

Michalczyk, John J. *Resisters, Rescuers, and Refugees: Historical and Ethical Issues*. Theological Book Service, 1997.

Oliner, Samuel P., and Pearl M. Oliner. *The Altruistic Personality: Rescuers of Jews in Nazi Europe*. Free Press, 1992.

Paldiel, Mordecai. *Sheltering the Jews: Stories of Holocaust Rescuers*. Fortress Press, 1997.

DOUGLAS MACARTHUR

Darby, Jean. *Douglas MacArthur*. Lerner, 1989.

Finkelstein, Norman H. *The Emperor General: A Biography of Douglas MacArthur*. Dillon Press, 1989.

James, D. Clayton. *The Years of MacArthur*. 3 vols. Houghton, 1970-1985.

Manchester, William Raymond. *American Caesar, Douglas MacArthur, 1880-1964*. Little Brown & Company, 1978.

Rovere, Richard H., and Arthur M. Schlesinger. *General MacArthur and President Truman*. 2nd ed. Transaction Pubs., 1992.

JAMES MADISON

Brant, Irving. *James Madison*. 6 vols. Bobbs, 1941-1961.

Fritz, Jean. *The Great Little Madison*. Putnam, 1989.

Ketcham, Ralph L. *James Madison: A Biography*. University Press of Virginia, 1990. First published in 1971.

Malone, Mary. *James Madison*. Enslow Publishers, Inc., 1997.

Rutland, Robert A. *James Madison: The Founding Father*. Macmillan, 1987.

Rutland, Robert A. *The Presidency of James Madison*. University Press of Kansas, 1990.

MALCOLM X

Barr, Roger. *Malcolm X*. Lucent Books., 1994.

Haley, Alex, and Malcolm X. *The Autobiography of Malcolm X*. African American Images, 1989.

Malcolm X. *By Any Means Necessary*. Pathfinder Press, 1992.

Myers, Walter D. *Malcolm X: By Any Means Necessary*. Scholastic, 1993.

Perry, Bruce. *Malcolm: The Life of a Man Who Changed Black America*. Station Hill, 1990.

NELSON MANDELA

Hoobler, Dorothy and Thomas. *Mandela*. Watts, 1992.

Hughes, Libby. *Nelson Mandela*. Dillon Press, 1992.

Mandela, Nelson. *Long Walk to Freedom: The Autobiography of Nelson Mandela*. Little, Brown, 1994.

Mandela, Nelson. *Nelson Mandela Speaks*. Pathfinder Press, 1993.

Mandela, Nelson. *Nelson Mandela: The Struggle Is My Life*. Rev. ed., 1990.

GEORGE CATLETT MARSHALL

Barber, James B., and Larry I. Bland. *George C. Marshall, Soldier of Peace*. Johns Hopkins University Press, 1997.

Cray, Ed. *General of the Army: George C. Marshall, Soldier and Statesman*. Norton, 1990.

Pogue, Forrest C. *George C. Marshall*. 3 vols. Viking, 1963-1987.

THURGOOD MARSHALL

David, Michael D., and Hunter R. Clark. *Thurgood Marshall : Warrior at the Bar, Rebel on the Bench*. Citadel Press, 1994.

Rowan, Carl T. *Dream Makers, Dream Breakers: The World of Justice Thurgood Marshall*. Little Brown & Co, 1994.

Williams, Juan. *Thurgood Marshall: American Revolutionary*. Times Books, 1998.

RIGOBERTA MENCHÚ TUM

Burgos-Debray, and Ann Wright (translator). *Rigoberta Menchú: An Indian Woman in Guatemala*. 1983.

CHICO MENDES

Mendes, Chico. *Fight for the Forest: Chico Mendes in His Own Words*. Inland Book Company, 1990.

Reykin, Andrew C. *The Burning Season: The Murder of Chico Mendes and the Fight for the Amazon Rain Forest*. Plume, 1994.

JAMES MONROE

Ammon, Harry. *James Monroe: The Quest for National Identity*. University Press of Virginia, 1990.

Ammon, Harry. *James Monroe*. 1971. Reprint. University Press of Virginia, 1990.

Stefoff, Rebecca. *James Monroe*. Garrett Educational, 1988.

MOTHER TERESA

Mother Teresa, Becky Benenate, Marianne Williamson. *In the Heart of the World: Thoughts, Stories, & Prayers*. New World Library, 1997.

Mother Teresa and Lucinda Vardey. *Meditations from a Simple Path*. Ballantine Books, 1996.

Mother Teresa. *Heart of Joy: The Transforming Power of Self Giving*. Servant Publications, 1987.

Rai, Raghu, and Navin Chawla. *Faith and Compassion: The Life and Work of Mother Teresa*. Element, 1997.

HORATIO NELSON

Howarth, David A. and Stephen. *Lord Nelson: The Immortal Memory*. Viking, 1988.

Tracy, Nicholas. *Nelson's Battles: The Art of Victory in the Age of Sail*. United States Naval Institute, 1996.

ELIOT NESS

Heimel, Paul, and Piet Sawvel. *Eliot Ness: The Real Story*. Knox Books, 1997.

Nickel, Steven. *Torso: The Story of Eliot Ness and the Search for a Psychopathic Killer*. John F. Blair Publishing, 1989.

FLORENCE NIGHTINGALE

Bullough, Vern L. and others (editors). *Florence Nightingale and Her Era*. Garland, 1990.

Hobbs, Colleen A. *Florence Nightingale*. Twayne, 1997.

Selanders, Louise C. *Florence Nightingale*. Sage, 1993.

Shor, Donnali. *Florence Nightingale*. Silver Burdett, 1990.

Vicinus, Martha, Bea Nergaard (editors), and Florence Nightingale. *Ever Yours, Florence Nightingale: Selected Letters*. Harvard University Press, 1990.

JESSE OWENS

Adler, David A., and Robert Casilla (illustrator). *A Picture Book of Jesse Owens*. Holiday House, 1992.

Baker, William J. *Jesse Owens: An American Life*. 1986.

EMMELINE PANKHURST

Pankhurst, Emmeline. *My Own Story*. Greenwood Publishing Group, 1985.

ROSA PARKS

Brown, Roxanne. "Mother of the Movement." *Ebony* (February 1988): 68-72.

Garrow, David (editor). *The Montgomery Bus Boycott and the Women Who Started It: The Memoir of Jo Ann Gibson Robinson*. 1987.

Parks, Rosa. *Rosa Parks: My Story*. 1992.

GEORGE S. PATTON

Blumenson, Martin *Patton: The Man Behind the Legend*. Morrow, 1985.

D'Este, Carlo. *Patton: A Genius for War*. Harperperennial Library, 1996.

Nye, Roger H. *The Patton Mind: The Professional Development of an Extraordinary Leader*. Avery Pub., 1993.

Patton, George S. *War as I Knew It*. Houghton Mifflin Company, reissue edition 1995.

ROBERT EDWIN PEARY

Rozakis, Laurie E. *Matthew Henson and Robert Peary: The Race for the North Pole (Partners)*. Blackbirch, 1994.

ALLAN PINKERTON

MacKay, James A. *Allan Pinkerton: The First Private Eye*. John Wiley & Sons, 1997.

Wormser, Richard. *Pinkerton: America's First Private Eye*. Walker & Company, 1990.

MARCO POLO

Hart, Henry H. *Marco Polo: Venetian Adventurer*. Rev. ed. University of Oklahoma Press, 1967.

Humble, Richard. *The Travels of Marco Polo*. Watts, 1990.

Wood, Francis. *Did Marco Polo Go to China?* Westview Press, 1998.

COLIN LUTHER POWELL

Means, Howard. *Colin Powell: Soldier/Statesman—Statesman/Soldier*. 1992.

Powell, Colin, and Joseph E. Persico. *My American Journey*. 1995.

Rowan, Carl. "Called to Service: The Colin Powell Story." *Reader's Digest* (December 1989): 121–26.

PAUL REVERE

Fischer, David H. *Paul Revere's Ride*. Oxford, 1994.

Fritz, Jean, and Margot Tomes. *And Then What Happened, Paul Revere?* Coward McCann, 1998.

Forbes, Esther. *Paul Revere and the World He Lived In*. 1942. Reprint, Peter Smith, 1992.

RICHARD I (the LIONHEARTED)

Storr, Chatherine, and Peter Gregory. *Richard the Lion-Hearted*. Raintree/Steck Vaughn, 1989.

JACOB AUGUST RIIS

Riis, Jacob A., and Luc Sante (introduction). *How the Other Half Lives: Studies Among the Tenements of New York*. Penguin USA, reprint edition, 1997.

Riis, Jacob A. *The Battle With the Slum*. Dover Publications, 1998.

JACKIE ROBINSON

Alvarez, Mark. *The Official Baseball Hall of Fame Story of Jackie Robinson*. Crestwood House, 1992. Younger readers.

Robinson, Jackie and Alfred Duckett. *I Never Had It Made*. Putnam, 1972.

Rowan, Carl. *Wait Till Next Year*. 1960.

Tygiel, Jules. *Baseball's Great Experiment: Jackie Robinson and His Legacy*. 1983. Reprint, Oxford, 1993.

Weidhorn, Manfred. *Jackie Robinson*. Atheneum, 1993.

OSCAR ROMERO

Brockman, James R. *The World Remains: A Life of Oscar Romero*, 1982.

Erdozain, Placido. *Archbishop Romero: Martyr of Salvador*, 1981.

Sobrino, Jon. *Archbishop Romero: Memories and Reflections*, 1960.

ELEANOR ROOSEVELT

Beasley, Maurine H. *Eleanor Roosevelt and the Media: A Public Quest for Self-Fulfillment*. University of Illinois Press, 1987.

Goodwin, Doris Kearns. *No Ordinary Time: Franklin and Eleanor Roosevelt: The Home Front in World War II*. Touchstone Books, 1995.

Lash, Joseph P. *Eleanor and Franklin: The Story of Their Relationship*. Norton, 1971.

FRANKLIN DELANO ROOSEVELT

Davis, Kenneth S. *FDR*. Random House. 1972.

Ferrel, Robert H. *The Dying President: Franklin D. Roosevelt 1944–1945*. University of Missouri Press, 1998.

Freedman, Russell. *Franklin Delano Roosevelt*. Clarion, 1990.

Freidel, Frank B. *Franklin D. Roosevelt*. 4 vols. Little, Brown, 1952–1973.

Goodwin, Doris K. *No Ordinary Time: Franklin and Eleanor Roosevelt: The Home Front in World War II*. Simon & Schuster, 1994.

Graham, Otis L., Jr., and M. R. Wander (editors). *Franklin D. Roosevelt: His Life and Times*. 1985. Reprint, Da Capo, 1990.

Morris, Jeffrey. *The FDR Way*. Lerner, 1996.

THEODORE ROOSEVELT

Brands, H. W. *T.R.: The Last Romantic*. Basic Books, 1997.

Fritz, Jean. *Bully for You, Teddy Roosevelt!* Putnam, 1991.

Gould, Lewis L. *The Presidency of Theodore Roosevelt*. University Press of Kansas, 1991.

McCullough, David G. *Mornings on Horseback: The Story of an Extraordinary Family, a Vanished Way of Life, and the Unique Child Who Became Theodore Roosevelt*. Simon & Schuster, 1981.

Meltzer, Milton. *Theodore Roosevelt and His America*. Watts, 1994.

Morris, Edmund. *The Rise of Theodore Roosevelt*. Ballantine Books, 1988.

Whitelaw, Nancy. *Theodore Roosevelt Takes Charge*. Whitman, 1992.

JOSE DE SAN MARTIN

Godoy, Cristian Garcia. *The San Martin Papers*. San Martin Society, 1988.

OSKAR SCHINDLER

Block, Gay, and Malka Drucker. *Rescuers: Portraits of Moral Courage in the Holocaust*. TV Books Inc., 1998

Fogelman, Eva. *Conscience & Courage: Rescuers of Jews During the Holocaust*. Anchor, 1995.

Keneally, T. *Schindler's List*. 1982.

Leuner, H. D. *When Compassion Was a Crime*. 1966.

Michalczyk, John J. *Resisters, Rescuers, and Refugees: Historical and Ethical Issues*. Theological Book Service, 1997.

Oliner, Samuel P., and Pearl M. Oliner. *The Altruistic Personality: Rescuers of Jews in Nazi Europe*. Free Press, 1992.

Paldiel, Mordecai. *Sheltering the Jews: Stories of Holocaust Rescuers*. Fortress Press, 1997.

ANTON SCHMID

Arad, Y. *Ghetto in Flames*, Jerusalem, 1980.

Michalczyk, John J. *Resisters, Rescuers, and Refugees: Historical and Ethical Issues*. Theological Book Service, 1997.

Oliner, Samuel P., and Pearl M. Oliner. *The Altruistic Personality: Rescuers of Jews in Nazi Europe*. Free Press, 1992.

Paldiel, Mordecai. *Sheltering the Jews: Stories of Holocaust Rescuers*. Fortress Press, 1997.

NORMAN SCHWARZKOPF

Italia, Robert, and Rosemary Wallner (editor). *General H. Norman Schwarzkopf (War in the Gulf)*. Abdo & Daughters, 1992.

Schwarzkopf, Norman. *It Doesn't Take a Hero*. Bantam Books, 1993.

Stefoff, Rebecca, and Vito Perrone. *Norman Schwarzkopf*. Chelsea House Publishing, 1992.

ALBERT SCHWEITZER

Cousins, Norman. *The Words of Albert Schweitzer: Selected by Norman Cousins*. Newmarket Press, 1990.

Schweitzer, Albert. *Reverence for Life*. Irvington Publishing, 1993.

ELIZABETH ANNE SETON

Dirvin, Joseph. *The Soul of Elizabeth Seton*. Ignatius Press, 1990.

Sister Marie Celeste. *Elizabeth Anne Seton, a Self Portrait 1774–1821: A Study of Her Spirituality in Her Own Words*. Prow Book, 1986.

SITTING BULL

Black, Sheila. *Sitting Bull and the Battle of the Little Bighorn*. Silver Burdett, 1989.

Bodow, Steven. *Sitting Bull*. Steck-Vaughn, 1994.

Vestal, Stanley. *Sitting Bull, Champion of the Sioux*. 1957.

Utley, Robert M. *The Lance and the Shield: The Life and Times of Sitting Bull*. Holt, 1993.

JOHN SMITH

Barbour, Philip L. *The Three Worlds of Captain John Smith*. Houghton Mifflin, 1964.

Emerson, Everett. *Captain John Smith*. Twayne, 1993.

Leo Lemay, J. A. *The American Dream of Captain John Smith*. University Press of Virginia, 1991.

Gerson, Noel B. *The Glorious Scoundrel: A Biography of Captain John Smith*. Dodd, 1978.

ELIZABETH CADY STANTON

Gleiter, Jan, and Kathleen Thompson. *Elizabeth Cady Stanton*. Raintree, 1988.

Griffith, Elisabeth. *In Her Own Right: The Life of Elizabeth Cady Stanton*. Oxford, 1985.

Stanton, Elizabeth Cady, and Ellen Carol DuBois. *Eighty Years and More : Reminiscences 1815-1897*. Northeastern University Press, 1992.

TECUMSEH

Edmunds, R. David. *Tecumseh and the Quest for Indian Leadership*. 1984.

Gilbert Bill. *God Gave Us This Country: Tekamthi and the First American Civil War*. 1989.

Tucker, Glenn. *Tecumseh: Vision of Glory*. 1955.

HARRIET TUBMAN

Bentley, Judith. *Harriet Tubman*. Watts, 1990.

Bradford, Sara. *Harriet Tubman: The Moses of Her People*. 1886. Reprint 1961.

Conrad, Earl. *Harriet Tubman*. 1943. Reprint, Eriksson, 1970.

DESMOND TUTU

Du Boulay, Shirley. *Tutu: Voice of the Voiceless*. 1988.

Tlhagale, Buti, and Itumuleng Mosala. *Hammering Swords into Ploughshares: Essays in Honor of Archbiship Mpilo Desmond Tutu*. 1986.

Tutu, Desmond M. *Hope and Suffering: Sermons and Speeches*. 1984.

LECH WALESA

Lazo, Caroline Evensen. *Lech Walesa*. Dillon Press, 1993.

Vnenchak, Dennis. *Lech Walesa and Poland*. Franklin Watts, 1994.

Walesa, Lech. *The Struggle and the Triumph : An Autobiography*. Arcade Publishing, 1992.

RAOUL WALLENBERG

Anger, P. *With Raoul Wallenberg in Budapest: Memories of the War Years in Hungary*. 1981.

Werbell, F. E., and T. Clark. *Lost Hero: The Mystery of Raoul Wallenberg*. 1982.

Yahil, L. "Raoul Wallenberg: His Mission and His Activities in Hungary." *Yad Vashem Studies* 15 (1983): 7–54.

BOOKER T. WASHINGTON

Harlan, Louis R. *Booker T. Washington. The Making of a Black Leader, 1856–1901*. 1972.

Harlan, Louis R. *Booker T. Washington. The Wizard of Tuskegee, 1901–1915*. 1983.

Neyland, James. *Booker T. Washington, Educator*. Holloway House, 1993.

Washington, Booker T. *Up from Slavery: An Autobiography*. 1901.

GEORGE WASHINGTON

Brookhiser, Richard. *Founding Father : Rediscovering George Washington*. Free Press, 1997.

Jacobs, William J. *Washington*. Scribner, 1991.

Phelps, Glenn A. *George Washington and American Constitutionalism*. University Press of Kansas, 1993.

Randall, Willard S. *George Washington: A Life*. Henry Holt & Company, Inc., 1997.

JOSEPH WEILL

Block, Gay, and Malka Drucker. *Rescuers: Portraits of Moral Courage in the Holocaust*. TV Books Inc., 1998

Fogelman, Eva. *Conscience & Courage: Rescuers of Jews During the Holocaust*. Anchor, 1995.

Keren-Patkin, N. "Jewish Children: Salvation Projects in France." *Yalkut Moreshet* 36 (1983): 101–150.

Kieval, H. J. "Legality and Resistance in Vichy France: The Rescue of Jewish Children." *Proceedings of the American Philosophical Society* 124 (1980): 339–366.

Michalczyk, John J. *Resisters, Rescuers, and Refugees: Historical and Ethical Issues*. Theological Book Service, 1997.

Oliner, Samuel P., and Pearl M. Oliner. *The Altruistic Personality: Rescuers of Jews in Nazi Europe*. Free Press, 1992.

Paldiel, Mordecai. *Sheltering the Jews: Stories of Holocaust Rescuers*. Fortress Press, 1997.

Weill, J. *Contributions a l'histoire des camps d'internement dans l'anti-France*. Paris 1946.

ELIE WIESEL

Abramson, I. (editor). *Against Silence: The Voice and Vision of Elie Wiesel*. 3 vols. 1985.

Fine, E. S. *Legacy of Night: The Literary Universe of Elie Wiesel*. 1982.

Rosenfeld, A. H., and I. Greenberg (editors). *Confronting the Holocaust: The Impact of Elie Wiesel*. 1978.

Wiesel, Elie. *Night*. Bantam Books, Reissue edition 1982.

Wiesel, Elie, Lacey B. Smith, and Dorothy Rabinowitz. *Dimensions of the Holocaust*. Northwestern University Press, 1990.

SIMON WIESENTHAL

Cooper, A. "Simon Wiesenthal: The Man, the Mission, His Message." In *Genocide: Critical Issues of the Holocaust*, edited by A. Grobman and D. Landes, pp. 384–388. 1983.

Pick, Hella. *Simon Wiesenthal: A Life in Search of Justice*. Northeastern University Press, 1996.

Wiesenthal, Simon, Harry James Cargas (editor). *The Sunflower: On the Possibilities and Limits of Forgiveness*. Schocken Books, 1998.

WINNEMUCCA, SARAH

Gaye, Canfield. *Sarah Winnemucca of the Northern Paiutes*. 1983.

Morrison, Dorothy N. *Chief Sarah; Sarah Winnemucca's Fight for Indian Rights*. Oregon Historical Society Press, 1996.

XUAN ZANG

Waley, Arthur. *The Real Tripitaka*. Macmillan, 1952.

ALVIN C. YORK

Lee, David D. *Sergeant York: An American Hero*. University Press of Kentucky, 1985.

Perry, John. *Sgt. York: His Life, Legend & Legacy: The Remarkable Untold Story of Sergeant Alvin C. York*. Broadman & Holman Publishers, 1997.

Glossary

abolitionist A person who supports the abolishment, or ending, of slavery.

acculturation The changes brought to the culture of a group or individual as the result of contact with a different culture.

activist A person who is involved in the support or practice of a social or political end, often in the form of militant action.

acumen A term for the accuracy or keenness of a person's judgment or insight.

ad hoc A Latin phrase meaning only for the specific case or situation at hand. It is also used to mean impromptu, or improvised.

affirmative action The collective term for government policies in the United States intended to promote opportunities for minorities by setting specific goals or quotas. Affirmative action favors minorities in hiring, promotion, college admissions, and government contracts to offset the effects of past discrimination against a group. The term was first used by President Lyndon B. Johnson in 1965, and the first federal policies designed to guarantee minority hiring were implemented by President Richard Nixon in 1969.

African National Congress (ANC) A South African political organization founded in 1912 as a nonviolent civil rights organization intended to promote and protect the interests and rights of black Africans. Initially committed to bringing about change through constitutional reform and other peaceful means, membership greatly increased after the South African government implemented the policy of apartheid in 1948, and in 1959 a rival party, the Pan-African Congress (PAC) was formed, espousing more radical views. In 1960 the government banned all black political organizations, including the ANC, and in 1961 a military wing called Unkhonto we Sizwe, meaning "Spear of the Nation," was formed, and began a campaign of sabotage. Nelson Mandela, a leader of the ANC, was sentenced to life imprisonment shortly thereafter, and for the next three decades the ANC was essentially an underground organization. In the 1990s, in the face of increased political and economic pressure from the world community, the government of South Africa ended apartheid, lifted its ban on the ANC, and freed Mandela from prison. The ANC then became a political organization, and in 1994, in South Africa's first democratic elections, Mandela was elected to the presidency, and the ANC became South Africa's ruling party.

agrarian A sociological term used to refer to cultures or economies that are based on or derive their primary economic means from uses of the land, such as farming.

ambassador From the Latin *ambactus*, meaning servant, an ambassador is the highest-ranking diplomat residing in a foreign country, accredited as a representative of the government of one nation toward another. In the United States, an ambassador is a member of the Foreign Service Officer Corps, and is charged with maintaining peaceful, cordial relations between the United States and the country to which he or she is assigned, seeing to the implementation of U.S. foreign policy, and protecting the rights and interests of America and American citizens abroad.

Americans with Disabilities Act (ADA) Landmark civil rights legislation, passed in 1990, that significantly reduced physical and legal obstacles for citizens with physical or mental disabilities, and prohibiting discrimination against the disabled in business, public accommodations, transportation, and telecommunications. Under the provisions of the ADA, disabled people are afforded the legal protection to insure that they are judged solely according to individual merit, without regard to their disability; and certain changes, such as wheelchair access to public places, were required to enable disabled people to participate more easily in business and social activities.

amnesty In its most common usage, amnesty refers to a type of pardon granted by the government to a person who has been found guilty of a crime, often political in nature. Unlike a legal pardon, which exempts the criminal from further punishment, amnesty causes the crime to be forgotten. It is most often used in cases of crimes against the government, when "forgetting" a crime in order to restore peace is politically or socially desirable.

anglicized To make something or someone English. The term is often used to refer to colonial cultures, in which native culture and customs came to resemble more closely those of the ruling British.

antitrust A general term for the principles or laws opposing or regulating business monopolies.

apartheid A policy of racial segregation formerly followed in the Republic of South Africa, meaning "separation" in the Afrikaans language. Introduced in 1948 and maintained until the early 1990s, the intensely controversial system maintained strict politic, social, and economic divisions between the governing white minority population and the nonwhite majority. Under apartheid, people were classified according to their ethnic or racial group, and the laws determined where members of each group could live, what type of jobs they could hold, and what education they could receive. Perhaps most significantly, nonwhites were denied representation in the national government, and opposition to apartheid was considered "communism" and was subject to strict security legislation. In the face of increasing opposition, the South African government began to implement a series of reforms beginning in the mid-1970s, but internal revolts and international political pressure continued to intensify, and in 1990 President F. W. de Klerk announced the formal end of apartheid.

apologist A person who writes or speaks in defense of someone or something. The term is often used to refer to a person who seeks to justify the actions of another, or to reconcile behavior or beliefs with established principles.

aristocracy From the Greek words *aristos*, meaning "best," and *kratos*, meaning "power," a term used either for a form of government ruled by a elite class or group, or to refer to the members of such a group. In principle, aristocrats were considered, usually by virtue of their birth into an acknowledged noble family, as the best fit to rule, and they governed in the best interests of all the people. An aristocracy that comes to serve the interests of the few is known as an oligarchy. True aristocracies are rare in history, and the term is often used to refer to the group of nobles and noble families that surrounds the king or queen in a monarchy.

assimilation In sociological terms, assimilation is the process by which individuals or groups are brought and absorbed into a new and dominant culture. It is most often used to refer to the integration of immigrants, who acquire new customs and attitudes, and contribute some of their own, in order to succeed in a new land.

atomic power Also called atomic energy, nuclear energy, or nuclear power, the theory or process by which energy is released during the splitting or fusing of atomic nuclei. Most commonly used to refer to electrical power generated by nuclear reactors, the term is also used to refer to atomic weapons.

attache A person assigned, or "attached," to a diplomatic mission to serve in a specific capacity or area of expertise.

autonomy From the Greek word *autonomos*, meaning self-ruling, autonomy is a lack of control by others, or self-governing.

avant-garde A term used to describe the leaders in a given field, those noticeably ahead of most of the rest in the application and invention of new techniques. The term is often used in the arts, where those in the avant-garde are seen as the primary innovators and the first to try or introduce new ideas.

Axis The coalition of countries that opposed the United States and its allies in World War II. It originated as the Rome-Berlin axis, a result of the 1936 accord between Hitler and Mussolini and their military alliance in 1939. It was extended to include Japan with the Berlin Pact in 1940, and ultimately encompassed many eastern European nations. The alliance came to an end when the Allies ratified the unconditional surrender of Germany on May 8, 1945.

baron A title of low-ranking nobility. Most commonly used in Europe, it also refers to a Japanese nobleman of the lowest rank

battalion An Army unit consisting of a headquarters and two or more companies, organized as one of a number of separate, specialized units within a division.

bootlegger Most often used to refer to a person who illegally transported or sold liquor during the Prohibition era. It may also refer to anyone who makes illegal copies of copyrighted works, such as music albums or videotaped music, for unauthorized distribution or sale.

Boston Massacre An early encounter between Americans and British forces, more than five years before the beginning of the American Revolution. On March 5, 1770, during a demonstration against the Townshend Acts, which imposed duties on imports to the colonies, a squad of British soldiers was struck by objects thrown by the colonists. The soldiers fired into the crowd, killing five men. The soldiers were tried for murder; two were found guilty of manslaughter and were branded on the thumb after claiming the benefit of clergy; the rest, including the commanding officer, were acquitted. The incident was later exploited to help build anti-British sentiment in the colonies.

boycott A form of protest in which a person or group refuses to buy products from or support companies, individuals, nations, or other groups with which they disagree. The intent of a boycott is to bring about or force change. It is used as a tool or weapon in labor disputes, by consumers, and in international affairs.

braille Also known as Standard English Braille, the code or alphabet used to create books readable by blind people. Based on a system of "point type" developed by a French army captain named Charles Barbier in 1921, it was adapted by Louis Braille and adopted, with a few modifications, in 1932. It is now used in all English-speaking countries, and has been adapted to most other languages.

brigade An army unit made up of a varying number of battalions, along with their supporting units and services.

Buddhism One of the world's major religions, Buddhism began in northeastern India and is based on the teachings of Siddhartha Gautama, known as the Buddha, or Enlightened One. Originally a monastic movement within the Brahman tradition, it developed in a distinctive direction, as the Buddha rejected significant aspects of the Hindu philosophy and structure. It its present form, it consists of two major branches known as Theraveda, the Way of the Elders, and Mahayana, the Great Vehicle. Buddhism has great force and significance not only in India, but throughout much of southeast Asia.

bulwark A term often used to refer to something or someone serving as a source of strength, or a safeguard.

bureaucracy A general term for the employees and administrative structure of a company or organization. A bureaucracy is characterized by a specific hierarchy of authority or responsibility, and each member carries out specialized or assigned tasks based on a consistent set of internal rules and procedures. Although sometimes used to refer in a negative sense to government rules and regulations, no modern government can function without a bureaucracy.

cabinet In political terms, the name used to refer to a formal group of advisors, or council, to the executive head of a parliamentary government. In the United States, the Cabinet consists of fourteen different "secretaries," each responsible for a specific aspect of national policy. In addition, the vice president is considered part of the Cabinet, and the president may give Cabinet rank or status to other executive-branch officials.

cadre The core personnel in an organization or military unit, around which the larger group can be built.

capital punishment The legal infliction of death as the penalty for the commission of a crime. Capital punishment has its roots in the oldest recorded human history, including the Code of Hammurabi, dating from 1750 B.C., and the Bible. Since the end of the eighteenth century, reform movements, originally led by Quakers, have sought to limit its use or end it outright. Currently legal in much of the United States and the world, it remains a hotly contested issue on both moral and legal grounds.

capitalism The overall term for the economic system in which individuals and companies produce and exchange goods and services through a network of prices and markets. The essential principles of what we perceive as modern capitalism were first set forth by the Scottish philosopher Adam Smith in his book *An Inquiry into the Nature and Causes of the Wealth of Nations*, published in 1776, and the term "capitalism" was introduced by Karl Marx in the mid-19th century.

cartographer A person who makes maps.

cavalry In its most common usage, cavalry refers to soldiers who are trained to fight on horseback. In contemporary warfare, it also refers to troops who make use of lightly armored vehicles.

centrist A person whose political views are for the most part at equal extremes from the right (conservatism) and the left (liberalism), as in "in the center."

charter In legal terms, a document issued or granted by a government, creating a business or political entity such as a corporation or colony, and defining its privileges and purposes.

citizenship The legal recognition of a person as a member of a national body, and the duties, rights, and privileges that accompany such status.

coalition An alliance or union of two or more parties, usually temporary, established for the purpose of attaining goals favorable to those involved. The term is most often used to refer to political alliances.

collective bargaining The process by which an individual or group may negotiate on behalf of a larger body of members who have selected them to do so. Most often used to refer to the process of labor negotiations between companies and unions, in which a team of elected leaders presents the positions voted on by union members.

colonialism The theory and practice of extending the authority, the political and economic control, of one nation over another, alien nation that has been conquered or settled.

colonist The term used to refer to an inhabitant or one of the original settlers of a colony. The core of what became the United States began as a colony of Great Britain, and the term colonist or "colonial" is often used to refer to the Americans who fought the British in the Revolutionary War.

commission A group or body, similar to a committee, assembled for the purpose of dealing with specific duties, tasks, or issues. Also used to refer to the legal document that confers the rank of military officer.

committee A group authorized to perform certain duties or tasks. In government, committees are often appointed to prepare specific legislation, or to review or advise in matters that require in-depth study or expertise.

communism A political theory and model for a government system in which all resources, businesses, and means of production are jointly owned by all members of the community. Communism provides for equal sharing of work, according to ability, and benefits, according to need. While primarily a theoretical concept only, communist principles have been widely applied to governmental systems, with mixed results, as in the former Soviet Union and the People's Republic of China.

concentration camp A concentration camp is a place where groups of people are confined, usually for political reasons, and often under inhumane conditions. Prisoners are held without regard to legal rights, or have been deprived of their right of due process. While used often and by many nations, the most comprehensive and horrifying use of concentration camps was during the Nazi reign in Germany from 1933 to 1945. During this time religious, national, and cultural groups were deprived of their constitutional protection against arbitrary arrest, and many, most notably Jews, were sent to concentration camps, where millions were worked to death or killed outright by shooting, gassing, or fatal injections.

Confederate States of America (Confederacy, CSA) The name adopted by the eleven Southern states that seceded from the United States, beginning with South Carolina in 1860, precipitating the American Civil War and bringing about the end of slavery in this country. Modeled on the governmental systems of the United States, the Confederacy attempted to recreate the organization and structure that resulted when the American colonies had won their freedom from Great Britain nearly a century before, but were hampered by the lack of resources and infrastructure, and infighting among government members and factions. U.S. president Abraham Lincoln rejected the right of the states to secede, and after attempts to conciliate the South, the Civil War began. Overmatched by U.S. forces and resources, the Confederacy was defeated and the states restored to the Union in the process known as Reconstruction. In 1869, the U.S. Supreme Court declared secession unconstitutional.

Congress The inclusive term for the United States House of Representatives and Senate. The "legislative" branch of the government of the United States, together with the presidency (the "executive" branch) and the court system (the "judicial" branch), the Congress has certain powers and authority established in the U.S. Constitution, including authority to collect taxes, declare war, and pass laws. The Senate, called the upper house, is comprised of two representatives from each state, who are elected for a six-year term, with one-third of the members eligible for reelection every two years. Originally, as provided in the Constitution, senators were selected by the legislatures of each state; since 1913, and the passage of the 17th Amendment, senators have been elected by popular vote. The House of Representatives, often called the lower house, is made up of at least one representative per state and one representative for "not fewer than" 30,000 inhabitants of each state—currently, membership in the House is fixed at 435, meaning that each member represents about 500,000 inhabitants. Representatives are elected by popular vote for a two-year term, with all elections falling in the same year.

constitutional amendment The process by which changes are made, or new legislation is added, to the Constitution of the United States. Because the U.S. Congress does not have the authority to alter the Constitution itself, provision was made in Article V, which states that an amendment passes after a two-thirds vote of both houses of Congress or after the petition of two-thirds of the state legislatures. An amendment must then be ratified by the legislatures of three-fourths of the states or by "constitutional conventions" in three-fourths of the states. There are currently 27 amendments to the Constitution, of which the first ten, added immediately after the ratification of the Constitution itself, are referred to as the Bill of Rights.

Continental Congress The assembly of about 50 representatives from the American colonies, which became the revolutionary government that initiated the Declaration of Independence and the American Revolution. The First Continental Congress met in Philadelphia on September 5, 1774, in response to the "Intolerable Acts" legislation passed by the British Parliament in retaliation for the Boston Tea Party. The Second Congress, which assembled in Philadelphia on May 10, 1775, shortly after the battles of Lexington and Concord, began the process of preparing for separation from Great Britain, which culminated with the adoption of the Declaration of Independence on July 4, 1776. On November 15, 1777, the delegates agreed on the Articles of Confederation, which codified their procedures and determined their powers and authority; the Articles were passed by the last of the original thirteen states, Maryland, on March 1, 1781, and the Continental Congress was replaced by the Congress of the Confederation.

coronation The ceremony, or act itself, of crowning a sovereign such as a king or queen.

cosmonaut The term used to refer to a Soviet or Russian astronaut.

coup d'etat The quick and sometimes unexpected overthrow of a government by an often small group of people in or formerly in authority.

courtier A member of a group of attendants at a monarch's court. A study based on observations of courtly life, *The Book of the Courtier* by Conte Baldassare Castiglione, published in 1528, outlined the accomplishments and code of behavior required of a proper courtier. The book came to be seen as the definitive treatise on aristocratic manners, and was highly influential among Renaissance nobility and writers throughout Europe.

crusade In historical terms, used to refer to any of the several Christian military expeditions of the 11th, 12th, and 13th centuries, whose intent was to free the Holy Land from the rule of Muslims. The word may also be used to describe any spirited and dedicated movement for a cause.

dauphin A term used from 1349 to 1830 to refer to the eldest son of the king of France.

Declaration of Independence The document, written by Thomas Jefferson and adopted by the Second Continental Congress on July 4, 1776, that outlined the complaints of the American colonies against the king of England, and declared them in revolt from Great Britain, as a free and independent nation to be called the United States of America.

delegate A person authorized to act as a representative for another person or group. The term is most often used to refer to a political representative who represents the opinions and interests of his constituency at a political convention.

Democrat A member of a political party of the United States, or a general term used to describe someone who is an advocate of the political system of democracy.

demonstration An organized form of protest, often political in nature, in which a public display of opposition is made.

deportation The legal expulsion of a person from a country.

desegregation The opposite of segregation, which separates one group from another, desegregation refers to the end of the separation. Most often used in reference to the civil rights struggles of the 1960s, which sought to end the forced segregation of blacks and whites.

dictator Originally the title of a magistrate in ancient Rome, appointed by the Senate in times of emergency, in modern times the term has come to refer to an individual who assumes sole and often absolute power over a country. The original Roman concept granted only limited power, and only for six months; contemporary dictators, while some may retain the trappings or appearance of a delegation of authority, are for the most part the only political power, and often remain in power for life, or until overthrown.

disenfranchise In general, meaning to deprive of any of the rights and privileges of citizenship, but used most often to refer specifically to taking away the right to vote.

dissident In a political sense, one who opposes governmental policies.

dogfight An aerial battle between two or more fighter planes.

egalitarian The affirmation of one who affirms political, economic, and social equality for all people.

emancipation Literally meaning to free from bondage, oppression, or restraint, most often used to refer to freedom from slavery, as in the Emancipation Proclamation.

Emancipation Proclamation Proclamation issued by U.S. President Abraham Lincoln on January 1, 1863, effectively ending slavery in the United States. Although excluding some slaves in areas of the Confederacy held by Union armies, the Emancipation Proclamation was a radical change in governmental policy, and was instrumental in leading to the enactment of the 13th Amendment to the Constitution in 1865, by which slavery was wholly abolished.

embargo The government prohibition of certain or all trade with another nation.

evangelism The preaching or spreading of a religion, as with missionary work. The term was first used in the New Testament to designate workers of the church who traveled to distant places to announce the gospel, and prepare the way for the coming of the apostles. Later, the designation of "evangelist" was applied to the writers of the gospels that appear in the New Testament. In modern times, the term is often used to refer to a type of minister who attempts to bring conversion to large masses of people, and carries connotations of showmanship and personality.

expatriates A term used to refer to citizens of one country who leave permanently to reside in another country.

fealty A legal term used to refer to the loyalty owed by a vassal to his feudal lord.

Federalist A member of a United States political party of the 1790s that advocated a strong central government, the dominant force in national politics from 1789 until 1801. Led by men who were instrumental in drafting the Constitution, the Federalists' power waned after the election of Thomas Jefferson to the presidency in 1800, and eventually, after years of virtually no political success, they were no longer an effective political force.

Founding Fathers The name given to the group of men, including George Washington, Thomas Jefferson, and Benjamin Franklin, who were instrumental in the creation of the United States. As a group, the Founding Fathers wrote and ratified most of the important documents of the United States, including the Declaration of Independence, the Constitution, and the Bill of Rights. Many, including Washington, Jefferson, and James Madison, went on to serve as presidents, and their work formed the basis of most of the American governmental policies that remain to this day.

frigate Most often used to refer to a fast, mid-sized sailing warship used during the 17th, 18th, and 19th centuries.

frontier A term often used to describe the end of civilized land, or the area just beyond it. In American mythology, the frontier represented the boundary of western expansion.

General Assembly One of the six principal organizations of the United Nations, comprised of all member nations, each having one vote.

Gestapo The name given to the German political police who operated during the Nazi reign from 1933 to 1945.

ghetto An Italian term used originally to refer to a specific area of a city where Jews were required by law to reside, it has come to mean any section of a city, often depressed, occupied primarily by one or more minority groups, who live there because of social, economic, or legal pressure.

guerrilla From the Spanish word *guerra*, meaning war, a term used to refer to a soldier who is a member of a small, irregular military force that operates in small bands in hostile or occupied territory, harassing and working to undermine and disrupt the enemy. "Guerrilla warfare" refers to an organized campaign along these lines.

Hinduism One of the world's most followed and enduring religions, which originated in India and is still practiced by most of its inhabitants. The basic principles of Hinduism are defined more by the way people behave than what they think or believe; there are very few common practices and beliefs shared by all. Some practices observed by mostly all Hindus include reverence for Brahmans, the highest caste or class, and for cows; the abstention from eating meat; and worship of the gods Shiva, who personifies both the destructive and creative forces in the universe, and Vishnu, considered the preserver of the universe.

Holocaust Derived from the Greek words *holo*, meaning "whole," and *causto*, meaning "burned," the term originally referred to a religious rite in which the offering was consumed by fire, but has come to be identified with the widespread persecution and murder of the Jews in Europe by Nazi Germany in the 1930s and 1940s. Hermann Goring, second only to Adolf Hitler in the German hierarchy, was ordered to organize "a final solution to the Jewish question" in all of German-dominated Europe. By 1941, German Jews were forced to wear badges or armbands marked with a yellow star; in the following months, thousands were deported to ghettos in Poland and elsewhere; and camps equipped with facilities for gassing people were set up in occupied Poland. Over the course of the next four years, more than six million Jews were gassed, shot, or died from starvation and disease.

humanism A philosophy or belief that emphasizes the dignity and worth of individual human beings.

ideology The collective term for the body of ideas and principles reflecting the social needs and aspirations of an individual, group, or culture.

imperialism The policy and practice by which a powerful nation extends and maintains economic and political control over weaker countries. Imperialism is similar in some respects to colonialism, and the terms are sometimes used interchangeably, but while colonialism implies a more formal type of political control, imperialism may refer to influence or control, exercised formally or informally, directly or indirectly, politically or economically.

inauguration The formal ceremony by which a person is inducted into political office.

incumbent A term used to refer to the person currently holding a political office.

indigenous A person or object originating and living in an area or environment.

industrialization An economic condition in which the importance of industry in the overall economy of a nation increases substantially. The term is used to describe the process by which a nation makes the transition from an economy based on agriculture to one based on industry.

infantry Combat troops trained to fight on foot.

insurgent Most often used in a political sense to refer to a person who revolts against civil authority, or a member of a political party who rebels against or challenges its leadership.

integration The incorporation of diverse ethnic or social groups into a unified society. The term is most often used to refer to the process of racial integration, by which black Americans and other ethnic minorities are afforded the same rights, status, and opportunities as whites. True integration implies that an individuals ability to enjoy any benefits of society are not denied or restricted by reason of race, religion, or national origin.

isolationism A political policy or philosophy that advocates the belief that a nation's interests are best served by avoiding alliance or excessive contact with other nations.

jurist A lawyer, or anyone who is recognized as skilled in the law, such as a judge or legal scholar.

khan The term used to refer to a ruler, official, or otherwise important person in India and certain central Asian countries.

knighthood In modern times, an honor by a nation or ruler that confers nobility on a person who has performed great service. There are three distinct orders of knighthood: royal orders, generally limited to men and women of royal blood or the highest ranks of nobility; noble or family orders, open to members of the nobility in general; and orders of merit, which may be bestowed on persons from any class as reward for distinguished service.

legislation The act or process of making laws, or the laws themselves.

levy A term generally used to refer to the imposing or collection of taxes, or to the confiscation of property in default of an unpaid debt.

libel The legal term for a written, published, or pictorial statement that maliciously damages another person's reputation.

litigation Legal proceedings, such as the bring of charges, or a trial.

Louis and Clark Expedition The first overland exploration of the American West and Pacific Northwest conducted by the United States. It was commissioned in 1804 by President Thomas Jefferson, and led by army officers Meriwether Lewis and William Clark. The principal goal of the expedition was to locate the presumed "Northwest Passage," a water route from the Atlantic to the Pacific Ocean. Although no such route existed, the expedition was successful in making peaceful contact with many Native American people and contributing a wealth of knowledge about the people, plants, animals, and geography of the largely unknown western United States.

Louisiana Purchase The term used to refer to a huge region, more than 800,000 square miles, of the United States purchased from France in 1803 for $15 million. The territory includes all or part of 13 present-day states, and represents the largest area ever added to the United States at one time.

loyalist One who maintains political loyalty to the government during a time of revolt.

luminary A term used to refer to a notable or famous person in a specific field.

lunar module The spacecraft used for landing on the moon during the Apollo spaceflight missions. After launch, the lunar module (LM) and Command and Service Module (CSM) traveled to the moon together and went into orbit; the LM then detached and landed on the moon. It was made up of two parts: the descent stage, for landing and delivery of equipment; and the ascent stage, which included the crew compartment, which returned the astronauts to the CSM.

lunatic fringe Members of a movement, usually political or social, espousing extreme or fanatical views.

martial law The state of government in which the military assumes control of governmental systems, replacing some or all civil agencies. Martial law is often used when the civil authorities prove inadequate at suppressing riots or political uprisings. In the United States, martial law is not specifically mentioned in the Constitution, but has been invoked by state governments in specific areas on specific occasions, such as the Pullman and railroad strikes in Illinois in 1895, and in Little Rock, Arkansas, to enforce a federal court order that blacks be admitted to a high school formerly reserved for white students.

martyr   Generally used to refer to a person who dies rather than renounce his religious principles, or one who makes great sacrifices for a cause.

medieval   A term used to describe someone or something as belonging to, or a part of, the Middle Ages.

menial   A kind of work regarded as servile, or the person who performs such work.

metaphysical   Referring to a branch of philosophy concerned with the ultimate nature of reality and the relationship between mind and matter. The term metaphysics is believed to have been first used by the Greek philosopher Andronicus of Rhodes in about 70 B.C. In his arrangement of Aristotle's works, the treatise called *First Philosophy* followed the treatise *Physics*, so the *First Philosophy* came to be known as *meta (ta) physica*, meaning literally "following (the) *Physics*." Because of the nature of the work, the term in popular usage came to refer to matters transcending material reality.

migration   The movement of people from one country to another.

militant   A term used to refer to a person who is combative or aggressive in defense or pursuit of a cause.

militia   The term used to describe an army made up of ordinary citizens rather than professional or career soldiers. A militia would be intended to function as reserve or contingent forces, available to be called on in case of emergency.

missionary   A member of a particular religious organization whose tradition is to "witness" by word and deed to the beliefs of his or her religion, so that others may come to know and understand it. The primary missionary religions of the world are Christianity, Buddhism, and Islam. The term is most often used to refer to Christian emissaries, sent to foreign countries, to bring the gospel to non-Christian populations.

monarchy   A form of government in which the leader rules by hereditary right, or the nation that is governed. Monarchs include such rulers as kings, emperors, and czars. The power of the monarch has varied over history, from men and women who wielded absolute power to the most common present-day form, known as a constitutional monarchy, in which the monarch shares power with a parliamentary body.

Mongol Golden Horde   The Golden Horde is the name that refers to a great army or Tatars, or people of Turkic origin, who overran eastern Europe in the 13th century, and to the empire, also known as Kipchak, they established. Led by Batu Khan, the grandson of Genghis Khan, the Golden Horde was one of three armies dispatched in 1235, which crossed the Ural River in 1237 and penetrated to the center of Russia. Moscow was among the cities taken. They then passed into Poland, Silesia, and Hungary before being stopped by the unsuccessful siege of Neustadt. The Horde turned eastward and settled on the banks of the Volga River, where Batu's empire maintained power over the Russians until the late 15th century.

monk   A member of a religious community who lives in a monastery.

Monroe Doctrine   A statement of United States policy in regard to the activities and rights of the European powers in the western hemisphere. Made by President James Monroe in his address to Congress on December 2, 1823, it became one of the foundations of American foreign policy, especially in Latin America. Because it was not a law, it remained only a declaration of policy, but increased popularity and use made it more of a principle, and it was termed the Monroe Doctrine after the mid-1840s. Although considered an argument for a policy of isolationism, the Monroe Doctrine was actually intended to warn the European powers against further colonization in the Americas and the establishment of monarchies in the newly independent Spanish American republics. It also stated that the United States would not interfere with already establish colonies or in Europe itself. In later years, the Doctrine was used to justify western expansion, and U.S. involvement in other American nations, which continues to this day.

muckraker   One who searches for and exposes the misconduct of those in public or political life.

NAACP   An acronym for the National Association for the Advancement of Colored People, an organization founded in 1909 to protect the rights and improve the living and working conditions of black Americans. Over the years, the NAACP has been an effective force in promoting and protecting the civil rights of African Americans, leading the efforts that resulted in the enacting of the Civil Rights Acts of 1957 and 1964, along with other important regulation aimed at overcoming discrimination and abuse in business as well as social affairs.

NASA An acronym for the Nation Aeronautics and Space Administration, the organization that oversees all noncommercial, nonmilitary spaceflight in the United States. NASA was established by the National Aeronautics and Space Act of 1958, in order to involve the scientific community in the planning and aims of the space program, to participate in the development of international cooperation in joint activities, and to spread the knowledge gained by the space program.

nationalist A person devoted to the interests or culture of a particular nation.

Nazism Also called National Socialism, Nazism is a political movement that began in Germany in 1920 with the organization of the National Socialist Workers' Party, which was also called the Nazi Party. It culminated in the establishment of the Third Reich, the totalitarian state led by Adolf Hitler, which came to an end with Germany's unconditional surrender in 1945. Similar in some respects to fascism, Nazism was heavily influenced by various aspects of German culture, including a tradition of military authoritarianism, expansion, and racism.

New Deal The collective name given to a large-scale program of domestic government policies enacted under President Franklin D. Roosevelt, especially those intended to counteract the effects of the Great Depression between 1933 and 1938. Programs ranged from the creation of new organizations such as the Federal Deposit Insurance Corporation (FDIC) to regulate banking and provide protection for depositors, to government subsidies and public relief efforts such as the Work Projects Administration, which put unemployed people to work on public projects. A controversial and hugely influential program, the New Deal continues to have considerable effect on domestic government policy.

Nobel Peace Prize An annual award granted to the person or persons, not more than three, who "shall have done the most or the best work for fraternity between nations, for the abolition or reduction of standing armies and for the holding and promoting of peace congresses." Established in the will of Swedish chemist, inventor, and philanthropist Alfred Bernhard Nobel, the winner(s) receives a cash

award and a diploma bearing his or her name and field of achievement. The first Nobel Prizes were awarded in 1901.

North Atlantic Treaty Organization (NATO) A regional defense alliance, formed by the signing of the North Atlantic Treaty on April 4, 1949, in response to the perceived threat of Soviet expansion and aggression after World War II. It was originally comprised of twelve nations, including the United States and Great Britain, with four additional countries added during the 1950s.

notary Also called a notary public, a person legally authorized to witness and certify the validity of documents, and to take affidavits and depositions.

orator One who practices or is known for the art of speech or speechmaking, especially speeches designed to influence the judgments or feelings of those listening.

ordination The formal process a candidate undergoes to become a recognized and accredited member of a religion's clergy.

pacifism An ideology or belief that opposes war and other violence as a means of political gain. The goals of pacifism are to maintain a state of peace, eliminate the potential causes of conflict, the settlement of disagreements through an outside party, and to ensure that the conflict resolutions are followed by those involved.

pamphlet A small, informal publication, often political in nature, used to express a specific viewpoint or opinion.

Pan-African Congress A splinter or rival organization formed in 1959 by members of the African National Congress who were opposed to the ANC's policy of nonviolent practices as a means of protecting the rights of black Africans.

papal nuncio A papal electorate of the highest rank permanently accredited to civil government.

Parkinson's Disease A slowly progressive neurological illness that disables its sufferers by stiffening the muscles of the body to the point of losing function. Tremors, excessive salivation, and poor coordination also accompany the disease. In victims, a degeneration of the part of the brain that produces a chemical called "dopamine" is deficient, and nerve signals are thus interrupted. Synthetic forms of the drug do alleviate some of the symptoms, but a transplantation of the dopamine-producing cells is required in those who are severely afflicted.

parliament A branch of government, similar to the U.S. Congress, that is responsible for enacting laws, levying taxes, and serving as the highest court of appeal.

patronage The support of a cause by means of financial assistance.

pedagogy The art or profession of teaching.

petition A formal written request made by an official person or group. A petition often requires that a certain number of people agree with the request before it is considered.

philanthropy In business, a term used to describe the ongoing practice or philosophy, usually of an individual, of giving to or establishing charitable or humanistic causes or foundations. Many wealthy persons who express a desire to "give something back" to their communities or to the general public support or create such public-serving organizations as charities, scholarships, libraries and museums, either during the course of their lifetimes, or in the form of behests made in wills and estates.

philosophy In general terms, a speculative inquiry into the source and nature of human knowledge, or the system and ideas based on such thinking.

pilgrim Literally, a person who travels to or visits a place of spiritual or political importance to seek refuge or insight, the term is also commonly used to refer to the English Puritans who migrated to America in 1620.

pilgrimage The voyage taken by a pilgrim to a site of spiritual or political importance. Most often used to refer to a religious journey.

pioneer The first to discover, found, or settle a particular land or scientific discovery. Widely used to refer to the early settlers of the American West.

plantation A term originating in colonial times, a plantation is a settlement or piece of land used to grow crops and house the workers who tend the crops. The land was independently owned and self-contained, often housing the owner of the land as well.

political asylum Protection granted by a specific person or country to someone who is a fugitive from his own country for reasons of political turmoil or crimes.

poll A survey of people used to determine their thoughts and views with regard to a specific person or topic. Polls are widely used by politicians and news organizations to determine public opinion regarding specific issues, such as elections.

posterity The offspring of one original ancestor to the furthest generation.

pragmatism The belief that the purpose of thoughts is to guide action, and that the effect of an idea is more important than its origin.

premillennialist One who believes that Christ's return will usher in a future millennium of Messianic rule referred to in the New Testament's Book of Revelation.

promissory note A written promise to repay a debt by a specific time, much like a loan.

prophecy A religious phenomenon in which a message is sent by a god predicting future events. Also often used to refer to a warning, encouragement, or a piece of information.

prosecutor One who seeks to prove guilt by another individual.

prospector A person who seeks a specific item. Most often associated with the search for gold or other valuable ores.

Protestant In religious terms, an individual or church organization that follows a religious belief denying the universal authority of the Pope, and ascribes to the beliefs of the Reformation. In the United States, Lutherans, Methodists, and Baptists are among the most widely followed Protestant faiths.

heterodoxy The practice of believing something that is different from the mainstream belief.

Puritan A follower of the Puritan sect of the Church of England, established in the latter part of the 16th century, and active through the 1660s. Similar to Calvinism, Puritan beliefs assert the basic sinfulness of humankind, but also that God had determined that some would be saved through the righteousness of Christ despite their sins. The religion stressed a life of self-discipline and introspection. The exact definition of Puritanism is uncertain, and later groups such as the Society of Friends, also known as Quakers, are sometimes referred to by the same name. Puritans are notable in American history as the passengers who came to this country aboard the *Mayflower* in 1620, known today as the Pilgrims.

Quaker Also known as the Society of Friends, a branch of Christianity believing that divine revelation is immediate and individual and that Christ is within all people. The Quakers believe in basic human goodness, but recognize the fact of human evil and work to eliminate it as much as possible. Quakerism is also a way of life that emphasizes living in accord with basic Christian principles such as truth and sincerity, avoiding luxury, and exercising simplicity in manners, dress, and speech.

racism The belief by one group of people that another group is inferior due to the color of their skin.

radicalism A belief to an extreme degree in a specific social institution.

ratify To formally amend or approve, most often used to refer to a treaty, act, or law such as a Constitutional amendment.

Reconstruction The term used for the rebuilding plan established for the southern, formerly Confederate states following the American Civil War.

rector A clergyman in charge of a parish.

refugee camps A place in which people who have fled, or been expelled, from their country due to natural catastrophe, war, or political or racial prosecution are set up to live.

regiment A military unit made up of ground troops, consisting of at least two battalions.

Republican A member of a political party of the United States, or one who advocates a republican form of government.

reservation Land set aside by a government that provides a place for a specific group of people to live. This land is "reserved" for them to use. Most often used to refer to the areas used for the forced relocation of Native Americans during the settlement of the American West.

sabotage A destructive action taken by an enemy intended to force its opponent to surrender.

sanction Penalties placed by one country or state onto another to persuade or compel those living in that area to follow the rules being enforced or to make up for the wrongdoing they caused.

Sandinistas A leftist Nicaraguan rebel force that opposed and ultimately defeated the Somoza regime. Formed in the early 1960s and named after the guerrilla leader Augusto Sandino, the Sandinistas were nearly wiped out by the end of the decade, but revived in the early 1970s, staging a series of raids that netted them the money needed for their operations and won the release of many captured comrades. When U.S. support of the Somoza government was withdrawn in 1979, it quickly collapsed, and the Sandinistas came to power.

Sanskrit The classical sacred and literary language of the Hindus of India.

scab A derogatory term used to refer to workers who cross picket lines to take the place of striking workers.

scion A descendant or heir, usually from a noble or royal house.

secede To withdraw from a union or branch.

segregation To be separated, usually through force, from the mainstream for reasons of race or creed. The term is most often used to refer to the forced separation of blacks and whites, most notably in the South.

sharecropper A person who is placed in a position of servitude by which he or she provides labor for the landowner in return for a share of the profits of the merchandise, usually an agricultural crop. The landowner not only provides the land to be tended, but also the equipment, animals and seed, and housing to the sharecropper.

siege A military blockade of an area intended to bring about surrender.

sit-in A nonviolent protest during which the protesters literally sit as a means of reaching their goal. By the protesters physically being in place, the normal process of events is interrupted, therefore creating the obstacle that in turn gets results.

slavery A social institution that is considered to be the most involuntary form of human servitude. The people, or slaves, are obtained by force, are property of an owner, and are subject to perform whatever work the owner demands.

socialist A person who believes that state ownership and control is the fundamental means of production and distribution of wealth, and that all aspects of life should be run and controlled by the government.

sociology The scientific study of human social relations or group life. Socialists examine the ways in which social structures and institutions influence society.

Solidarity The independent trade union federation founded in Poland in 1980, which under the leadership of Lech Walesa and the support of the Polish Roman Catholic Church, quickly became a political power that menaced and ultimately brought about the fall of the Polish communist government. By 1981, Solidarity claimed 10 million members, and had shown the ability to impede and harass the government by backing strikes and protests. In December 1981, supported by the Soviet government, Communist Party leader General Wojciech Witold Jaruzelski declared martial law, suspended Solidarity, and imprisoned many of its leaders, including Walesa. After Walesa's release in 1982, Solidarity remained an underground movement for the most part, effectively blocking the governments attempts at reform, and forcing Jaruzelski to negotiate with them in 1988. On April 5, 1989, the two sides signed an agreement legalizing Solidarity, and by the end of August a coalition government had been formed under the leadership of Solidarity. Walesa was elected president of Poland in December 1990, and Solidarity remains a potent political force in Poland.

Soviet bloc A group of nations united under the influence of the Soviet Union.

Stamp Act An act, originated by the British, that required all legal documents, licenses, commercial contracts, newspapers, pamphlets, and playing cards, to carry a tax stamp.

statesman A person who is knowledgeable in the principles of government.

stereotype To place an absolute belief on a specific classification of person, based on proof of only a few examples.

strike An organized work stoppage carried out by a group of employees, usually as a tactic to enforce demands or protest unfair labor conditions. Strikes are most frequently conducted by workers organized into trade unions, and are often used as a bargaining tool during contract negotiations.

subjugate The process of bringing a nation or group of people under control and governing rule as a subject.

succession The line by which a rank or position is replaced after the death or resignation of the previous holder. Usually it is the first-born son, but in the event that there is no direct heir by relation, a plan of who will follow is devised.

suffrage The right or privilege of voting.

suffragette A woman who advocates the right of women to vote.

superannuated To be made, declared, or proved out of date or obsolete.

suzerainty A dominant state controlling the foreign relations of a state, but not allowing it sovereign authority in its internal affairs.

temperance The organized efforts to temper or abstain from the use of alcoholic beverages. In order to achieve their aims, most temperance organizations advocated the enactment of legislation prohibiting both the sale and consumption of alcohol.

territory A name given in the United States to a partially self-governing region that has not been granted statehood. The District of Columbia , the Samoan Islands, and Guam are the only remaining U.S. territories.

theology A discipline that attempts to express the content of a religious expression in words that are contained in faith.

treaty A written agreement between two nations stating that each must adhere to a set of laws in good faith.

truce An agreement made by conflicting parties or nations to put an end to the disagreement through certain conditions.

Underground Railroad A network of antislavery northerners that illegally helped black southern slaves escape slavery and reach safety in free states and Canada. The refugees traveled from "station" to "station" (usually farms), aided by a "conductor" who helped them find safe places to hide during their journey.

Union The term used to refer to the United States and the U.S. forces during the Civil War.

universal man Also called "renaissance man," a term that refers to a person who is skilled in a wide range of disciplines or studies.

urban A classification for an area that refers to its characteristics of a city.

urbanization The process of building up and area and applying the attributes of a city.

Vatican The city located within Rome, where the Pope resides.

veteran A survivor of a war.

viceroy The governor of a country or province who rules as the representative of a king or sovereign.

vocation The summons or strong inclination to a particular state or course of action. Often used to refer to a religious calling.

war criminals People charged with having been in violation of the laws and customs of war.

welfare A public assistance program providing at least a minimum amount of economic aid to individuals who earn less money than is needed to maintain an adequate standard of living.

Whig One of the two dominant political parties in power in the U.S. from the mid-1830s to the mid-1850s. The Whig party was opposed to the Jacksonian Democrats, associated mainly with manufacturing, commercial, and financial interests. The Whigs were replaced by the Republicans in 1854.

white supremacist One who believes that those of the Caucasian race are superior to all other races, especially blacks, and are opposed to interracial relations of any kind.

Zionist One who is involved in an international movement originally established to set up a Jewish nation in Palestine.

Index